Eat Well, Lose Weight

Library of Congress Cataloging-in-Publication Data is available upon request.
ISBN: 978-0-470-54031-2 (comb)
ISBN: 978-0-470-58764-5 (special edition, comb)

Printed in China

10 9 8 7 6 5 4 3 2 1

Meredith Corporation
Editor: Jeanne Ambrose; Sheena Chihak, R.D.
Associate Design Director: Chad Jewell
Copy Chief: Doug Kouma
Copy Editor: Kevin Cox
Contributing Editor: Stephanie Karpinske, M.S., R.D.
Contributing Graphic Designer: Doug Samuelson,
   Diana Van Winkle
Publishing Operations Manager: Karen Schirm
Edit and Design Production Coordinator: Mary Lee
   Gavin
Editorial Assistant: Marlene Todd
Book Production Managers: Marjorie J. Schenkelberg,
   Mark Weaver
Contributing Photographers: Marty Baldwin, Jason
   Donnelly, Scott Little, Blaine Moats, Jay Wilde
Contributing Copy Editor: Peg Smith
Contributing Proofreaders: Emmy Clausing, Judy
   Friedman, Gretchen Kauffman, Candy Meier,
   Stephanie Petersen, Lynn Stratton
Contributing Indexer: Elizabeth Parson
Test Kitchen Director: Lynn Blanchard
Test Kitchen Product Supervisor: Laura Marzen, R.D., L.D.
Test Kitchen Culinary Specialists: Marilyn Cornelius,
   Juliana Hale, Maryellyn Krantz, Jill Moberly,
   Colleen Weeden, Lori Wilson
Test Kitchen Nutrition Specialists: Elizabeth Burt, R.D.,L.D.;
   Laura Marzen, R.D., L.D.

Cover photo: Lime-Marinated Flank Steak, page 201

John Wiley & Sons, Inc.
Publisher: Natalie Chapman
Associate Publisher: Jessica Goodman
Executive Editor: Anne Ficklen
Production Director: Diana Cisek
Manufacturing Manager: Tom Hyland

Better Homes and Gardens®

Test Kitchen

Our seal assures you that every recipe in *Eat Well, Lose Weight* has been tested in the Better Homes and Gardens® Test Kitchen. This means that each recipe is practical and reliable, and meets our high standards of taste appeal. We guarantee your satisfaction with this book for as long as you own it.

CONTENTS

Grain Pancakes with
Strawberry Sauce, Page 26

Lime-Marinated Flank Steak,
Page 201

Chocolate Cream Cheese Pie,
Page 420

THIS IS "DIET" FOOD?

People always want to know which foods will help them drop weight quickly. Since there are no magic foods, the answer to all the dieters out there is to eat foods that offer the most nutrients and are the least processed. Do that and you'll automatically be eating fewer calories than if you ate high-calorie processed foods that fill you out but don't fill you up.

That simple guideline was used to create the more than 500 delicious recipes in *Eat Well, Lose Weight*. The goal was to develop recipes that include wholesome, basic ingredients, including whole grains, lean protein, nutrient-rich fruits and vegetables, and healthy fats. All of the recipes were developed and tested by registered dietitians in the Better Homes and Gardens® Test Kitchen to ensure that each one is delicious and satisfying. The finished dishes were so good that many of the taste testers couldn't believe these were "diet" foods.

As an added bonus, you'll find a shortcut dinner chapter for those times when you need a superfast meal. Although those recipes contain convenience foods, they use the best of the bunch, including frozen vegetable blends, vegetarian products, and spice blends.

And since many of you eat out and wish you could enjoy those same flavors at home, this book contains a chapter featuring restaurant entrées. Now you can re-create your favorite foods from some of the most popular chain restaurants in a version that's lower in calories, fat, and sodium. (Yes, the healthier versions still taste great!)

Why live on grapefruit and celery sticks while dieting when you could be eating BBQ Chicken Pizza and Blue Cheese Burgers? Welcome to *Eat Well, Lose Weight*—a dieter's best friend. Get cooking, lose weight, and feel great!

Chapter 1

Eat for Health

EAT WELL. LOSE WEIGHT.

Remember the grapefruit diet? How about the cabbage soup diet? These diets worked for a while because you were limited to eating only a few foods—which meant that your calories each day were extremely low. These diets also lacked important nutrients and left many people feeling tired and sick. Dieters did lose weight but quickly gained it back when they started eating regular food again.

As a dieter today, you don't want to live on grapefruit. You want to eat foods that are good for you but also lead to weight loss. You want to have energy and feel good even though you are dieting. In this book you'll find foods that let you lose weight and eat healthfully. When you've reached your goal and just want to maintain your weight, you'll find that this cookbook is perfect for everyday family meals. The recipes may be lower in calories and fat, but they aren't your typical diet foods. You'll find lots of pizzas, burgers, soups, pasta dishes, and desserts. A restaurant chapter even helps you re-create those favorite dishes at home—without all the calories and fat.

The Eat Well Food Groups

Thinking back to your elementary school days, you may remember the four food groups poster hanging on the wall. Now those four food groups have been placed into a food pyramid. In addition to the four food groups of grains, dairy, fruits, and vegetables, the pyramid includes a new category for oils.

Although the pyramid includes the original food groups, the foods within each group have changed. For instance, instead of a slice of white bread or a cup of regular pasta, guidelines now recommend that you choose a hearty, whole grain bread and a cup of whole grain, high-fiber pasta. In this cookbook, the basic, yet updated food groups are called the Eat Well Food Groups. Why? Because they remind you that not all foods are created equal. Some are better than others. When you are trying to lose or maintain your weight, choosing the best foods is even more important. If you only have a limited number of calories each day, you want to get the most nutrition you can out of those calories. The Eat Well Food Groups can help guide you to the best choices.

WHOLE GRAINS

Great for Dieters!

You may have heard a lot about whole grains recently. The media are talking about them. Nutrition professionals are promoting them. And food companies are adding them to as many products as they can. Whole grains are high in fiber to help you feel full, making them perfect for dieters. They also have iron and B vitamins, as well as other important nutrients. Whole grains help to control blood glucose levels and reduce your risk of heart disease, among many other health benefits.

What exactly are whole grains? Basically they are grains that haven't been stripped of their outer coat. Still confused? A grain, such as wheat, has several layers to it. The outer layers have fiber and various nutrients that are brown in color and rough in texture. Food manufacturers sometimes strip that layer off the grain, leaving only the inside layers, which are smooth in texture and lighter in color. You can see and taste the difference when you eat a slice of soft white bread versus a slice of 100% whole wheat bread. The whole wheat slice has a grainier texture and darker color. Examples of whole grains include whole wheat flour (and products made with it), oatmeal, brown rice, wild rice, quinoa (pronounced KEEN-wa), and popcorn.

Many people grew up on soft white bread and other refined grains, so they prefer those over whole grain varieties. As research continues to show the benefits of whole grains, manufacturers are working hard to include whole grains in products and also preserve some qualities of the original refined products, as you'll see in whole grain white breads.

If you're a fan of white bread and other refined grains, it's time to give whole grains a try. Start with products that aren't too far from what you're used to, such as a whole grain white bread or multigrain pasta. Then as you get used to the taste and texture of whole grains, add more of them to your diet.

DON'T FORGET FIBER!

Most people are far from meeting their fiber needs. You need 25–35 grams a day, but if your diet lacks whole grains and is low in fruits and vegetables, you probably don't come near that recommended range. Check labels and you'll quickly learn which foods are highest in fiber. Also eat plenty of fruits and vegetables, which are naturally high in fiber.

CHECK THE LABEL!

To search out whole grain products, don't just look at the front of the package. Go to the ingredient panel and make sure that the first or second ingredient says 100% whole wheat or 100% whole grain. Also check the Nutrition Facts panel. If the product has 0–1 gram fiber per serving, it contains no or very little whole grains.

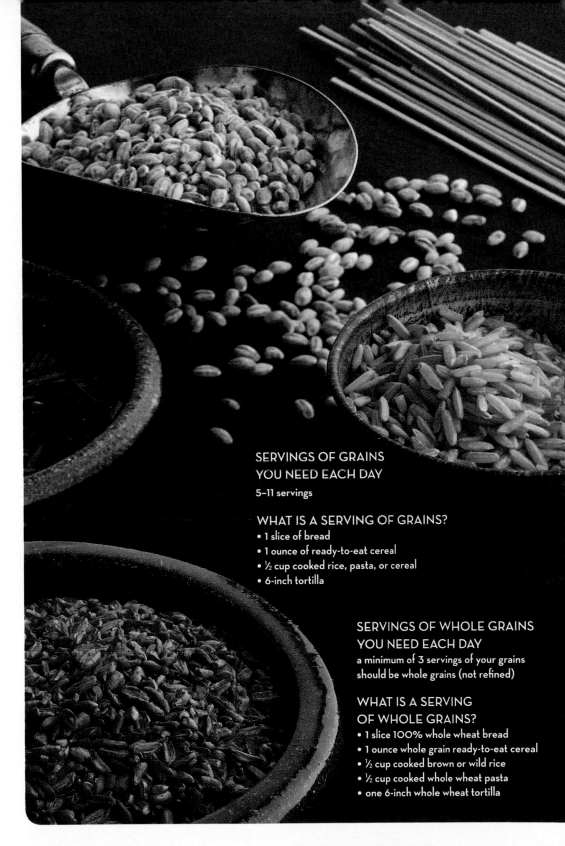

SERVINGS OF GRAINS YOU NEED EACH DAY
5–11 servings

WHAT IS A SERVING OF GRAINS?
- 1 slice of bread
- 1 ounce of ready-to-eat cereal
- ½ cup cooked rice, pasta, or cereal
- 6-inch tortilla

SERVINGS OF WHOLE GRAINS YOU NEED EACH DAY
a minimum of 3 servings of your grains should be whole grains (not refined)

WHAT IS A SERVING OF WHOLE GRAINS?
- 1 slice 100% whole wheat bread
- 1 ounce whole grain ready-to-eat cereal
- ½ cup cooked brown or wild rice
- ½ cup cooked whole wheat pasta
- one 6-inch whole wheat tortilla

Are You Getting Enough?

Although the protein and dairy groups are separated on the food pyramid, many dairy foods are also high in protein. Both groups are discussed together here.

Protein Confusion

Many people worry that they aren't getting enough protein, but the truth is they probably get more protein than they need even when you're dieting. Protein is found in bread, milk, and many other foods, not just meat or fish, so it's easy to meet your needs.

As a dieter, you just need to know which proteins to eat and when to eat them. For maximum weight loss results, choose the leanest cuts of meat or choose naturally lean white meat chicken or fish. Add a little protein to each meal and you will feel full for longer since the body needs time to digest the protein. Between meals eat snacks that are mainly protein, such as some deli turkey or a small piece of low-fat cheese. Foods with protein are more satisfying than just a piece of fruit or some crackers.

Dairy: Last on Most Diets

Foods in the dairy group are often left out of diets. It's probably due to the calories and fat found in these foods, but with low-fat versions available, there's really no reason to leave this group out. Despite low-fat options, most diets either cut out dairy completely or suggest only 1 or 2 servings a day. But your body requires at least 3 servings to meet vital calcium needs. Of course, a calcium supplement is always an option, but since dairy foods also have protein, B vitamins, and other nutrients, you should think twice before eliminating them.

THE IMPORTANCE OF THE SUNSHINE VITAMIN

Recent studies have shown that people aren't getting enough vitamin D, the vitamin that's crucial for strong bones. Why? Because this vitamin isn't that easy to get. Milk is fortified with vitamin D, and it's the main source of vitamin D in our diets. But what if you don't drink milk? You also can get your body to make vitamin D if you expose your skin to about 20 minutes of sun each day. People in northern climates don't get much sun in the winter, so they could be vitamin D deficient. If you don't drink milk or get much sun, you may need a supplement.

DO YOU MEET YOUR CALCIUM NEEDS?

With all the talk about calcium, you would think we all get enough. But the majority of us still don't meet our needs, especially women. Calcium is found in most dairy products, and small amounts are in broccoli and dark, leafy greens. But lots of people don't like dairy products or can't eat them due to an allergy. And dieters often don't want to spend their limited calories on milk or other dairy products.

If dairy isn't in your diet, make sure you take a calcium supplement. But don't take all of your calcium at once. The body can absorb only a small amount at a time—no more than 500 mg—so be sure to divide up your calcium intake, from food or supplements, throughout the day.

SERVINGS OF PROTEIN YOU NEED EACH DAY
5–6 ounces or equivalent

WHAT IS A SERVING?
- 1 ounce meat, poultry, or fish,
- 1 egg
- ½ ounce nuts or seeds
- 1 tablespoon peanut butter
- ¼ cup dried beans
- ¼ cup baked or refried beans
- ¼ cup tofu
- 1 ounce tempeh
- 2 tablespoons hummus

AMOUNT OF DAIRY YOU NEED EACH DAY
3 cups milk or equivalent

WHAT IS A CUP OR EQUIVALENT?
1 cup milk, 1 cup yogurt,
1½ ounces cheese (unprocessed)

COMMON MILK EQUIVALENTS
- ½ cup cottage cheese = ¼ cup milk
- 1 scoop ice cream = ⅓ cup milk
- ½ cup pudding made with milk = ½ cup milk
- 1 slice processed cheese = ½ cup milk

FRUITS AND VEGETABLES

Add Color to Your Plate

Your mom always said to eat your fruits and veggies, right? But did she say which ones were best to eat? Sure, they are all good and eating a variety is best, but some fruits and vegetables are better than others. Iceberg lettuce, for example, is basically just water and a little fiber. You would be much better off eating dark green romaine and purple radicchio, which have more fiber and a lot more vitamins than plain old iceberg.

It's All About Color

When searching for the best fruits and vegetables, go for color. The latest research shows that those color pigments in fruits and vegetables are actually types of phytochemicals, a fancy word for nutrients that are believed to do everything from slowing the aging process to preventing cancer. There are many different types of phytochemicals, so eating a variety of foods from each color is your best bet for better health.

As a dieter, you need to sneak veggies in whenever you can. They are very low in calories, so you can fill up your plate with them. Starchier veggies, such as sweet potatoes, are also very filling, but they are higher in calories than other vegetables. Go ahead and enjoy them, but watch your serving sizes on the starchy vegetables.

Fruits are a great diet food too, but you need to watch the amounts. Fruit is high in natural sugar, making it higher in calories. Tropical fruits, such as mango or pineapple, are very high in sugar. You still can eat them, but the calories will add up quickly. Since most fruits are very sweet, they make the perfect diet dessert or snack.

Quick Color Guide

Which colors should you look for? Follow this quick guide. Try to eat from as many color groups as you can each day.

Green: kiwifruit, broccoli, Brussels sprouts, cabbage, avocado, green peppers, zucchini, leafy greens (spinach, kale)

Orange/Yellow: oranges, mangoes, cantaloupe, peaches, carrots, sweet potatoes, acorn squash, lemons, pineapple

Red: strawberries, pink grapefruit, watermelon, cranberries, tomatoes, red sweet peppers

Purple/Blue: grapes, plums, cherries, blueberries, raisins, eggplant, purple cabbage, beets

White: bananas, white peaches, garlic, onions, leeks, mushrooms, jicama, white potatoes, cauliflower

PRODUCE IN A PILL

Health food stores and supplement companies now sell pills that claim to have the same nutrients as a serving of fruit or vegetable. Some even claim to have multiple servings in one pill! Can that be? The answer is no. Fruits and vegetables are naturally very complex plants that can't be replicated in a single pill made in a laboratory. A pill may contain the same vitamins and minerals, but there are other nutrients—some we probably don't even know about yet—that make the real fruit or vegetable better than a pill.

AMOUNT OF FRUIT YOU NEED EACH DAY
1½–2 cups or equivalent

WHAT IS A CUP OR EQUIVALENT?
- 1 cup fresh fruit
- 1 small banana
- 32 grapes
- 8 large strawberries
- 1 large orange or peach
- 1 cup fruit juice
- ½ cup dried fruit

AMOUNT OF VEGETABLES YOU NEED EACH DAY
2½–3 cups or equivalent

WHAT IS A CUP OR EQUIVALENT?
- 1 cup raw or cooked vegetables or fruit
- 2 cups raw spinach
- 1 large sweet potato
- 1 medium regular potato
- 1 large ear of sweet corn
- 12 baby carrots

When is the last time you measured your plates?

If your plates are 10 years old, they are probably about 10 inches in diameter. If they are older than that, they might be 9 inches. If they are new, chances are your plates have a diameter of 12 or more inches. It's no coincidence that plate size has increased along with our waistlines. Nobody wants to eat from a half-empty plate of food. You want a nicely filled plate, especially if you paid good money for that food at a restaurant. If you think your home plates are big, restaurant plates are even bigger—more like platters than plates.

It's human nature to eat everything on your plate, even if you are full after eating just half.

That's why many diet books tell you to fill just the inner rim of your plate or to downsize to a plate that's a few inches smaller than the typical dinner plate.

Those are good ideas if you're eating at home, but if you eat out, you have to make a point of not eating the whole platterlike plate, which is tough. Splitting a meal with a fellow diner is always an option. Or you could divide your plate in half as soon as you get it and eat only from one side. The trick is to make sure to stop as soon as you feel even a little bit full. Otherwise your natural habit to eat everything on your plate will take over.

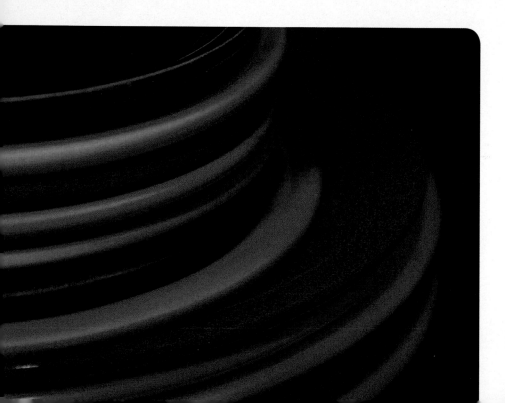

PLATE CHECK

Still not convinced that the plate size is a big deal? Check out this visual. Each plate has a normal serving of spaghetti—1 cup cooked pasta with ½ cup pasta sauce. Which serving looks most appealing?

8 ½ –INCH PLATE

9¾–INCH PLATE

11 ¼ –INCH PLATE

CHECK YOUR CUPS TOO!

Plates aren't the only serving pieces that have grown in size. Cups and glasses have too! Just look at the coffee cups below. The one on the left is a coffee cup today, which holds about 16 ounces. The one on the right is what was typical about 20 years ago. It holds 6 ounces. It's easy to see how calories add up fast with today's big cups and glasses. We may be drinking the same beverages as we did years ago, but now we're drinking twice the amount or more (and that means more calories!).

FOR MORE INFORMATION

Learn more about nutrition, portion sizes, and calorie control at these websites:

eatright.org
Find current nutrition news, advice on weight control, and other helpful tips at this website of the American Dietetic Association.

calorieking.com
Quickly look up calorie levels for thousands of foods at this site.

Think you're eating the right amount?

You could be eating three or four times what you really need. Check the difference in sizes of the following common foods. The first food in each photo shows a typical portion today. The second food shows what an actual serving should be. It's easy to see how your version of one serving actually could contain multiple portions. And with multiple portions, the calories add up quickly.

ORANGE JUICE

- 12 OUNCES (2 FRUIT SERVINGS)
  165 CALORIES
- 6 OUNCES (1 FRUIT SERVING)
  83 CALORIES

BAGEL

- 3.5 OUNCES (3 ½ GRAIN SERVINGS)
  250 CALORIES
- 2 OUNCES (2 GRAIN SERVINGS)
  140 CALORIES

CEREAL

- 2 ¼ CUPS (3 GRAIN SERVINGS)
  330 CALORIES
- 1 OUNCE OR ¾ CUP (1 GRAIN SERVING)
  110 CALORIES

APPLE

- 7 OUNCES (2 FRUIT SERVINGS)
  186 CALORIES
- 3 OUNCES (1 FRUIT SERVING)
  80 CALORIES

STEAK

- 12 OUNCES (3 MEAT SERVINGS)
  1,080 CALORIES
- 5 OUNCES (1½ MEAT SERVINGS)
  450 CALORIES

POTATO

- 9 OUNCES (2 VEGETABLE SERVINGS)
  350 CALORIES
- 4½ OUNCES (1 VEGETABLE SERVING)
  175 CALORIES

ICE CREAM

- 3 SCOOPS (1 MILK SERVING)
  450 CALORIES
- ONE ½-CUP SCOOP (⅓ MILK SERVING)
  150 CALORIES

CALORIE COUNT

Many dieters can roughly estimate the calories in food but don't know how many calories they should be eating in a day. Everyone is different, so it's easy to see why people get confused.

How can your friend, who seems to be the same size as you, eat more and not gain weight? It has to do with your activity level, your muscle mass, how much you fidget throughout the day, and your age, along with several other factors.

You can see how figuring this out can be complicated. At right is a basic calculation to help you ballpark your appropriate calorie level. Once you have that number, you can record what you eat for a few days and see how close your calorie intake is compared to what your body needs.

Eat less than what you need, you'll lose weight. Eat more and you'll gain weight. Or you can use up those extra calories by burning them off with exercise. It's a constant balancing act, but one that can be managed if you know your calorie needs and don't go over those limits.

Calculation

1. Take your weight in pounds and multiply by 10. This covers your basal metabolic needs—what you need to breathe and perform other basic bodily functions.
2. Add 10% for digestion. Eating and digesting food takes energy. The more often you eat, the harder your body has to work, which is why many diets suggest eating 5 mini meals a day rather than just 3 big meals.
3. Add 10% for light activity level. Add 20% for moderate activity level. Add 30% for high-intensity activity level. Activity level varies by person; larger people burn more calories than smaller people doing the same activity. So the add-on for activity calories is not precise, but it works for the purpose of an estimate. If you move a little during the day doing basic household tasks, use the light activity number. If you stay fairly active all day and include a little exercise as well, go for moderate. If you do an intense workout each day or have a very active job, go for the 30% add-on. See the sample below for an example.

Calculation Sample

_____150_____ (Your Weight) x 10 = __1,500__ (Base Metabolism)

__1,500__ + 10% (Digestion) = __1650__

__165__ + 10% light (Activity Level)

_____ + 20% moderate

_____ + 30% high

= __1,815__ **TOTAL Calorie Needs**

Your Estimate of Total Calorie Needs

The calories you need are complex to calculate because there are other factors—besides activity level—that impact the number. These include your age and how much muscle you have. Your metabolism slows with age, meaning you need fewer calories, especially after age 30. Muscular people burn more calories than people who have a lot of fat. Since men are naturally more muscular, they tend to burn more calories than women.

The Weight Loss Number

The number you calculated is the calorie amount you need to maintain your weight. To lose a pound of body weight, you need a deficit of 3,500 calories. So to lose a pound a week, you could either eat 500 fewer calories a day or burn off those 500 calories each day with exercise. To lose weight faster than that, you would need to shave off even more calories from your diet (or exercise more). But don't take your calories too low. Your body will think it's starving and will slow down your metabolism—something you don't want when trying to lose weight.

Your Estimate of Total Calorie Needs

_____ (Your Weight) x 10 = _____ (Base Metabolism)

_____ + 10% (Digestion) = _____

_____ + 10% light (Activity Level)

_____ + 20% moderate

_____ + 30% high

= _____ TOTAL Calorie Needs

My Weight Loss Plan of Action

Amount of weight I want to lose: _____

Calories I need each day to maintain my current weight: _____

Calories I need each day to lose one pound/week* (subtract 500 calories/day from the number above)_____

To meet that calorie goal, I will eat _____ fewer calories per day and/or burn _____ calories each day by exercising.

*Remember that a pound is equivalent to 3,500 calories. To lose two pounds each week you would need a

calorie deficit of 7,000 calories.

MEAL PLANS

Some people like to create their own meal plans using the nutrition information on each recipe. Others like a more structured plan to follow. Either way, here are some sample meal plans that show you how to combine foods for three common calorie levels. Use these as an example to plan your own diet based on the calorie goals you calculated on page 19.

Sample Menu Plan

DAY	BREAKFAST	LUNCH	DINNER	SNACK
For 1,200 calories:	Spiced Oatmeal, p. 49, 1 cup fat-free milk	Chicken Salad Sandwich, p. 109, one orange, 1 6-oz. container light yogurt	Classic French Dip, p. 466, New Potato Salad, p. 354, Fruit Pizza, p. 417	
1 **For 1,500 calories add:**	Mocha Scone, p. 62, one banana			
For 1,800 calories add:	Mocha Scone, p. 62, one banana			Sweet 'n' Salty Snack Mix (1 cup), p. 389, Cherry Citrus Cooler, p. 400
For 1,200 calories:	Fruit and Yogurt Parfait, p. 52, one slice Easy Oatmeal Bread, p. 76, with 1 Tbsp. low-sugar jelly	Dilled Tuna and Potato Salad, p. 145, five multigrain crackers with 1 oz. low-fat cheese	Penne with Chicken and Broccoli, p. 257, tossed green salad with 2 Tbsp. low-calorie dressing, one Nutty Carrot Cake Cheesecake Bar, p. 409	
2 **For 1,500 calories add:**				Afternoon snack: Mini Walking Taco, p. 381, one apple Evening snack: Creamy Fruit Morsels, p. 428
For 1,800 calories add:		three Chocolate-Drizzled Graham Cookies, p. 406, 1 cup fat-free milk		Afternoon snack: Mini Walking Taco, p. 381, one apple Evening snack: Creamy Fruit Morsels, p. 428
For 1,200 calories:	Berry-Banana Smoothie, p. 54, one Pear-Almond Muffin, p. 60	Zesty Gazpacho, p. 182, 1 oz. low-fat cheese with five multigrain crackers, one orange	Grilled Beef Salad with Cilantro Vinaigrette, p. 125, Southwestern Drop Biscuit, p. 71, ½ cup frozen yogurt	
3 **For 1,500 calories add:**				Mini Bagel Sandwich, p. 380, 1 cup fat-free milk, one apple
For 1,800 calories add:		three Almond Fudge Rounds, p. 405, 1 cup fat-free milk		Mini Bagel Sandwich, p. 380, 1 cup fat-free milk, one apple

DAY	BREAKFAST	LUNCH	DINNER	SNACK
For 1,200 calories:	Fruity Oatmeal, p. 48, 1 cup fat-free milk	Chicken Minestrone Soup, p. 161, one slice Easy Oatmeal Bread, p. 76, with 2 Tbsp. light margarine, one apple	Broiled BBQ-Spiced Rubbed Salmon, p. 283, Blue Cheese Coleslaw, p. 356, 1 cup steamed green beans, Fresh Fruit with Yogurt and Honey, p. 429	
4 **For 1,500 calories add:**				Mocha Scone, p. 62, 1 cup fat-free milk
For 1,800 calories add:	one slice Easy Oatmeal Bread, p. 76, with 1½ Tbsp. peanut butter			Mocha Scone, p. 62, 1 cup fat-free milk
For 1,200 calories:	Breakfast Tortilla Wrap, p. 36, ½ cup cantaloupe cubes	Greek Garbanzo Salad, p. 330, five multigrain crackers, one 6-oz. container light yogurt	Greek-Style Pizza, p. 473, tossed green salad with 2 Tbsp. low-calorie dressing, two Chocolate-Chunk Cookies, p. 403	
5 **For 1,500 calories add:**				Chicken Salad with Apple Slices, p. 375, one orange, 1 cup fat-free milk
For 1,800 calories add:		two Chocolate Chunk Cookies, p. 403, 1 cup fat-free milk		Chicken Salad with Apple Slices, p. 375, one orange, 1 cup fat-free milk
For 1,200 calories:	Apple Griddle Cakes, p. 25, 1 cup fat-free milk	Tomato-Barley Soup with Garden Vegetables, p. 181, one Italian-Style Dinner Roll, p. 81, ½ cup cubed cantaloupe	Blue Cheese-Topped Burger with Caramelized Onions, p. 463, Herbed Potato Wedges, p. 368	
6 **For 1,500 calories add:**				Caprese Bruschetta, p. 382, and add a dessert to dinner: Lemon Bars, p. 408
For 1,800 calories add:		two Chocolate Chunk Cookies, p. 403, 1 cup fat-free milk		Caprese Bruschetta, p. 382 and add a dessert to dinner: Lemon Bars, p. 408
For 1,200 calories:	Ham and Cheese Quesadilla, p. 44, one orange	Copycat Chili, p. 459, 1 oz. purchased baked tortilla chips	Pecan Cornmeal-Crusted Pork, p. 223, Roasted Garlic Mashed Potatoes, p. 367, 1 cup steamed broccoli	
7 **For 1,500 calories add:**			Coffee-Chocolate Marble Cake, p. 416, plus 1 cup fat-free milk	
For 1,800 calories add:		three Almond Fudge Rounds, p. 405, 1 cup fat-free milk	Coffee-Chocolate Marble Cake, p. 416, 1 cup fat-free milk	

MY MEAL PLAN

Create your own meal plans with this simple template. You can use it to plan ahead by filling in what you are going to eat. Or you can use it as a diet journal and record your actual eating. Then you can see how close you come to meeting your calorie target.

DAY	BREAKFAST	LUNCH	DINNER	SNACK
_____ calories:				
_____ calories:				
_____ calories:				

Chapter 2

Breakfast

On the divider: Fresh Tomato Omelet with Mozzarella Cheese *(see recipe, page 33)*

- 1   cooking apple (such as Jonathan or Granny Smith), cored and finely chopped (about ¾ cup)
- 1   teaspoon lemon juice
- ¾   cup whole wheat flour
- 1   tablespoon sugar
- 1   teaspoon baking powder
- ¼   teaspoon apple pie spice or ground cinnamon
- ⅛   teaspoon salt
- ¾   cup fat-free milk
- 1   egg white
- 2   tablespoons canola oil
-      Nonstick cooking spray
- 1   cup unsweetened applesauce
- ⅛   teaspoon apple pie spice or ground cinnamon
-      Apple pie spice or ground cinnamon (optional)
-      Fresh fruit (optional)

Apple Griddle Cakes

PREP: 25 minutes

COOK: 2 minutes per batch

NUTRITION FACTS per serving:

CALORIES 214
TOTAL FAT 7 g (1 g sat. fat)
CHOLESTEROL 1 mg
PROTEIN 6 g
CARBOHYDRATE 34 g
FIBER 4 g
SODIUM 169 mg

EXCHANGES 1.5 Starch, 0.5 Fruit, 1 Fat

1 In a small bowl combine apple and lemon juice; set aside. In a medium bowl combine whole wheat flour, sugar, baking powder, ¼ teaspoon apple pie spice, and salt. In another small bowl combine milk, egg white, and oil; beat with a rotary beater or wire whisk.

2 Add milk mixture all at once to flour mixture; stir just until moistened (batter should be lumpy). Gently fold in apple mixture.

3 Coat an unheated griddle or heavy nonstick skillet with nonstick cooking spray. Preheat over medium heat until a few drops of water dance across the surface. For each pancake, pour a scant ¼ cup batter onto the hot griddle; spread batter into a 3- to 4-inch circle.

4 Cook for 1 to 2 minutes on each side or until pancakes are golden brown, turning when pancake surfaces are bubbly and edges are slightly dry. In a small bowl stir together applesauce and ⅛ teaspoon apple pie spice; serve with pancakes.

5 If desired, sprinkle with additional apple pie spice. If desired, serve with fresh fruit. Makes 4 (2-pancake) servings.

Grain Pancakes with Strawberry Sauce

START TO FINISH: 25 minutes

NUTRITION FACTS per serving:
- -

CALORIES 242
TOTAL FAT 6 g (1 g sat. fat)
CHOLESTEROL 36 mg
PROTEIN 6 g
CARBOHYDRATE 40 g
FIBER 3 g
SODIUM 192 mg

EXCHANGES 2 Starch, 0.5 Fruit, 1 Fat

1	cup all-purpose flour
⅓	cup yellow cornmeal
⅓	cup quick-cooking rolled oats
2	tablespoons packed brown sugar
1½	teaspoons baking powder
¼	teaspoon salt
1	egg
1	cup fat-free milk
2	tablespoons canola oil
	Nonstick cooking spray
4	cups fresh strawberries, hulled
1	tablespoon granulated sugar
1	teaspoon vanilla

1 In a medium bowl combine flour, cornmeal, rolled oats, brown sugar, baking powder, and salt. Make a well in the center of the flour mixture; set aside.

2 In a small bowl combine egg, milk, and oil; beat with a fork or whisk until combined. Add the egg mixture all at once to the flour mixture. Stir just until moistened (batter should be lumpy).

3 Lightly coat an unheated griddle or large skillet with nonstick cooking spray. Preheat griddle over medium heat. For each pancake, pour a scant ¼ cup of the batter onto the hot griddle. Spread each to a 3- to 3½-inch circle. Cook over medium heat for 1 to 2 minutes on each side or until pancakes are golden brown, turning to second sides when pancakes have bubbly surfaces and slightly dry edges.

4 Meanwhile, for sauce, in a blender or food processor combine 2 cups strawberries, granulated sugar, and vanilla. Cover and blend or process until smooth. Transfer to a small saucepan; heat sauce until warm. Quarter remaining 2 cups strawberries. Serve pancakes with sauce and berries. Makes 6 servings (2 pancakes per serving).

1¼ cups regular rolled oats
¾ cup all-purpose flour
½ cup whole wheat flour
1 tablespoon baking powder
¼ teaspoon salt
3 egg whites
2¼ cups buttermilk
2 tablespoons canola oil
2 tablespoons honey (optional)
1 teaspoon vanilla
 Nonstick cooking spray
 Bottled light pancake syrup
  (optional)

1 In a large bowl combine oats, all-purpose flour, whole wheat flour, baking powder, and salt. Make a well in the center of flour mixture; set aside.

2 In a medium bowl beat egg whites with a fork; stir in buttermilk, oil, honey (if desired), and vanilla. Add egg white mixture all at once to flour mixture. Stir just until moistened (batter should be lumpy). If you prefer softened oats, cover batter and allow to stand at room temperature for 15 to 30 minutes.

3 Coat an unheated griddle or heavy skillet with nonstick cooking spray. Preheat over medium-high heat. For each pancake, pour about ¼ cup of the batter onto the hot griddle or skillet. Spread batter into a circle about 4 inches in diameter. Cook over medium heat for 4 to 6 minutes or until the pancakes are golden, turning to cook second sides when pancakes have bubbly surfaces and edges are slightly dry. If desired, serve with syrup. Makes 8 servings (2 pancakes per serving).

Oat Pancakes

PREP: 25 minutes

COOK: 4 minutes per batch

NUTRITION FACTS per serving:

CALORIES 229
TOTAL FAT 6 g (1 g sat. fat)
CHOLESTEROL 3 mg
PROTEIN 10 g
CARBOHYDRATE 34 g
FIBER 4 g
SODIUM 257 mg

EXCHANGES 2 Starch, 0.5 Very Lean Meat, 1 Fat

NUTRITION NOTE

Whole wheat flour is made from the entire wheat grain—bran, germ, and endosperm—and has many more nutrients than refined flours, plus more fiber.

2 eggs
½ cup fat-free milk
½ teaspoon finely shredded orange peel
¼ teaspoon vanilla
⅛ teaspoon ground cinnamon or nutmeg
8 slices whole grain bread
Nonstick cooking spray
Powdered sugar (optional)
¾ cup fresh blueberries
½ cup light pancake syrup
Sliced fresh strawberries (optional)

1 In a shallow bowl beat eggs with a fork or wire whisk. Beat in milk, orange peel, vanilla, and cinnamon. Dip bread into egg mixture, turning to coat both sides.

2 Coat an unheated large nonstick skillet or griddle with nonstick cooking spray. Preheat over medium heat. Place bread on hot skillet or griddle; cook for 4 to 6 minutes or until golden brown, turning once. Serve warm. If desired, dust with powdered sugar. Serve with blueberries and syrup. If desired, garnish with strawberries. Makes 4 (2-slice) servings.

Sun-Kissed French Toast

START TO FINISH: 25 minutes

NUTRITION FACTS per serving:

CALORIES 236
TOTAL FAT 5 g (1 g sat. fat)
CHOLESTEROL 106 mg
PROTEIN 9 g
CARBOHYDRATE 42 g
FIBER 4 g
SODIUM 372 mg

EXCHANGES 2 Starch, 1 Other Carbohydrates, 0.5 Very Lean Meat, 0.5 Fat

NUTRITION NOTE

Blueberries are antioxidant powerhouses! Anthocyanins and phenolics, the antioxidants in blueberries, protect the body against damaging free radicals and many chronic diseases associated with aging.

Nonstick cooking spray

3 eggs

1 cup evaporated fat-free milk

3 tablespoons sugar

2 teaspoons vanilla

½ teaspoon ground cinnamon

¼ teaspoon ground nutmeg

6 1-inch-thick slices crusty whole wheat country-style bread

2 tablespoons sugar

½ teaspoon ground cinnamon

⅔ cup crushed shredded wheat biscuits

1 tablespoon butter, melted

2 cups sliced fresh strawberries

1 Lightly coat a 3-quart rectangular baking dish with nonstick cooking spray; set aside. In a medium bowl lightly beat eggs with a rotary beater or wire whisk. Beat in evaporated milk, 3 tablespoons sugar, vanilla, ½ teaspoon cinnamon, and nutmeg. Arrange bread slices in a single layer in prepared baking dish. Pour egg mixture evenly over bread. Cover and chill for 2 to 24 hours, turning bread slices once with a wide spatula.

2 Preheat oven to 375°F. In a small bowl combine 2 tablespoons sugar and ½ teaspoon cinnamon; set aside. In another small bowl combine crushed biscuits, butter, and 2 teaspoons of the cinnamon-sugar mixture. Sprinkle evenly over bread slices in dish. Bake, uncovered, about 30 minutes or until lightly browned.

3 Meanwhile, in a small bowl combine strawberries and remaining cinnamon-sugar mixture. Serve with French toast. Makes 6 servings.

Streusel-Crunch French Toast

PREP: 20 minutes **CHILL:** 2 to 24 hours
BAKE: 30 minutes **OVEN:** 375°F

NUTRITION FACTS per serving:

CALORIES 248
TOTAL FAT 6 g (2 g sat. fat)
CHOLESTEROL 113 mg
PROTEIN 10 g
CARBOHYDRATE 40 g
FIBER 4 g
SODIUM 273 mg

EXCHANGES 2 Starch, 0.5 Fruit, 0.5 Medium-Fat Meat, 0.5 Fat

Walnut Waffles with Blueberry Sauce

PREP: 15 minutes
BAKE: per waffle baker directions

NUTRITION FACTS per serving:

CALORIES 229
TOTAL FAT 7 g (1 g sat. fat)
CHOLESTEROL 3 mg
PROTEIN 9 g
CARBOHYDRATE 34 g
FIBER 4 g
SODIUM 319 mg

EXCHANGES 2 Starch, 0.5 Very Lean Meat, 1 Fat

1 cup all-purpose flour
1 cup whole wheat flour
¼ cup coarsely ground toasted walnuts
2 teaspoons baking powder
1 teaspoon baking soda
4 egg whites
2¼ cups buttermilk
2 tablespoons canola oil
1 recipe Blueberry Sauce
Walnut halves (optional)

1 In a medium bowl stir together all-purpose flour, whole wheat flour, ground walnuts, baking powder, and baking soda. In a large bowl beat egg whites with an electric mixer on medium speed until very foamy. Stir in buttermilk and oil. Gradually add flour mixture, beating by hand until smooth.

2 Lightly grease a round or square waffle baker; preheat. Pour ⅔ cup of the batter (for round waffle baker) or 1 cup of the batter (for square waffle baker) onto grids of prepared waffle baker. Close lid quickly; do not open lid until waffle is done. Bake according to manufacturer's directions. When done, use a fork to lift waffle off grids. Repeat with remaining batter. Serve waffles warm with Blueberry Sauce. If desired, garnish with walnut halves. Makes 8 servings (¾ of a round waffle; ½ of a square waffle).

Blueberry Sauce: In a medium saucepan combine 1 cup fresh or frozen blueberries, ¼ cup white grape juice, and 1 tablespoon honey. Heat just until bubbles form around edge. Cool slightly. Transfer to a blender. Cover and blend until smooth. Transfer sauce to a serving bowl. Stir in 1 cup fresh or frozen blueberries. Makes about 1⅔ cups sauce.

1½ cups fat-free milk
1 cup all-purpose flour
1 **egg**
  Nonstick cooking spray
1 15-ounce carton light
    ricotta cheese
2 tablespoons low-sugar
    orange marmalade
⅛ teaspoon ground cinnamon
1 8-ounce carton light
    dairy sour cream
  Shredded orange peel (optional)
1½ cups fresh raspberries
    and/or blueberries

Brunch Blintzes

PREP: 30 minutes   **BAKE:** 15 minutes
OVEN: 350°F

NUTRITION FACTS per blintz:

CALORIES 101
TOTAL FAT 3 g (2 g sat. fat)
CHOLESTEROL 27 mg
PROTEIN 5 g
CARBOHYDRATE 12 g
FIBER 1 g
SODIUM 51 mg

EXCHANGES 1 Other Carbohydrates, 0.5 Fat

1 For crepes, in a medium bowl combine milk, flour, and egg; beat with a rotary beater or wire whisk until smooth. Lightly coat an unheated 6-inch skillet or crepe pan with nonstick cooking spray. Preheat over medium heat. Remove skillet or crepe pan from heat and pour in about 2 tablespoons of the batter. Lift and tilt skillet to spread batter evenly. Return skillet to heat; cook 30 to 60 seconds or until crepe is browned on bottom. Turn out onto paper towels. Repeat with remaining batter to make 15 crepes total. When necessary, coat skillet with additional nonstick cooking spray, removing skillet from heat before coating.

2 Preheat oven to 350°F. Lightly coat a 15×10×1-inch baking pan with nonstick cooking spray. Set aside.

3 For filling, in a medium bowl combine ricotta cheese, orange marmalade, and cinnamon. Spread about 2 tablespoons of the filling on the unbrowned side of a crepe. Fold in half. Fold in half again, forming a wedge. Place in prepared pan. Repeat with remaining filling and crepes, overlapping as necessary to fit in pan.

4 Bake for 15 to 20 minutes or until heated through. To serve, spoon sour cream onto blintzes. If desired, sprinkle with orange peel. Top with berries. Makes 15 blintzes.

COOK'S TIP

This crepe recipe is a more healthful option than most packaged crepes, but if you're pressed for time, substitute packaged crepes and make the fresh filling.

5 to 6 slices whole wheat cinnamon-swirl bread or cinnamon-raisin bread

Nonstick cooking spray

1½ cups fat-free milk

3 eggs

2 tablespoons sugar

1 teaspoon vanilla

¼ teaspoon ground nutmeg

1 5½-ounce can apricot nectar or peach nectar (⅔ cup)

2 teaspoons cornstarch

Breakfast Bread Pudding

PREP: 30 minutes **BAKE:** 30 minutes
STAND: 15 minutes **OVEN:** 325°F

NUTRITION FACTS per serving:

CALORIES 178
TOTAL FAT 4 g (1 g sat. fat)
CHOLESTEROL 107 mg
PROTEIN 9 g
CARBOHYDRATE 27 g
FIBER 3 g
SODIUM 179 mg

EXCHANGES 2 Starch, 0.5 Medium-Fat Meat

1 Preheat oven to 325°F. Cut enough of the bread into cubes to make 4 cups. Place bread cubes in a shallow baking pan. Bake about 10 minutes or until bread is dry, stirring once. Cool on a wire rack.

2 Lightly coat six 6-ounce soufflé dishes or custard cups with nonstick cooking spray. Divide bread cubes among the prepared dishes. In a medium bowl combine milk, eggs, sugar, vanilla, and nutmeg; beat with a rotary beater or wire whisk. Pour milk mixture evenly over bread cubes. Press lightly with the back of a spoon to thoroughly moisten bread.

3 Place soufflé dishes in a 13×9×2-inch baking pan. Place baking pan on oven rack. Carefully pour hot tap water into the baking pan around dishes to a depth of 1 inch.

4 Bake for 30 to 35 minutes or until a knife inserted near centers comes out clean. Transfer dishes to a wire rack. Let stand for 15 minutes.

5 Meanwhile, for sauce, in a small saucepan gradually stir apricot nectar into cornstarch until combined. Cook and stir over medium heat until thickened and bubbly. Reduce heat. Cook and stir for 2 minutes more.

6 If desired, remove puddings from soufflé dishes. Spoon sauce over warm puddings. Makes 6 servings.

Make-Ahead Directions: Prepare as above through step 2. Place soufflé dishes in a 13×9×2-inch baking pan. Cover with plastic wrap. Chill overnight in the refrigerator. Uncover; add hot tap water to pan. Continue with steps 4 through 6.

- 4 eggs
- ⅛ teaspoon salt
- ⅛ teaspoon black pepper
  Nonstick cooking spray
- 4 medium tomato slices
- ¼ cup shredded reduced-fat mozzarella cheese (1 ounce)
- 1 teaspoon snipped fresh oregano or ¼ teaspoon dried oregano, crushed

1 In a small bowl combine eggs, salt, and pepper; beat with a rotary beater or wire whisk. Coat an unheated 8-inch nonstick skillet with nonstick cooking spray. Preheat over medium heat. Pour half of the egg mixture into the hot skillet.

2 Using a wooden spoon or plastic spatula, immediately begin stirring egg mixture gently but continuously until mixture resembles small pieces of cooked egg surrounded by liquid egg. Stop stirring. Cook for 30 to 60 seconds more or until egg mixture is set but shiny.

3 Place two tomato slices on half of the egg mixture in skillet. Top with half of the mozzarella. Using a spatula, lift and fold opposite edge of the omelet over tomato slices. Sprinkle half of the oregano onto omelet. Transfer to a warm plate.

4 Repeat with remaining egg mixture, tomato, cheese, and oregano. Makes 2 servings.

COOK'S TIP

If you use fresh oregano in this recipe, select oregano that is bright green with no signs of wilting or yellowing. Oregano can be refrigerated in a plastic bag for up to three days.

Fresh Tomato Omelet with Mozzarella Cheese

START TO FINISH: 20 minutes

NUTRITION FACTS per serving:

CALORIES 228
TOTAL FAT 13 g (4 g sat. fat)
CHOLESTEROL 432 mg
PROTEIN 18 g
CARBOHYDRATE 11 g
FIBER 3 g
SODIUM 398 mg

EXCHANGES 2 Medium-Fat Meat, 2 Vegetable, 0.5 Fat

Nonstick cooking spray
2 cups sliced fresh mushrooms
3 tablespoons sliced green onion
1 clove garlic, minced
4 eggs
¼ teaspoon herbes de Provence or dried thyme or basil, crushed
⅛ teaspoon salt
Dash black pepper
1 teaspoon olive oil
¼ cup shredded part-skim mozzarella cheese (1 ounce)
1 medium plum tomato, chopped
1 tablespoon finely shredded Asiago or Parmesan cheese
Snipped fresh parsley (optional)

Omelet de Provence

START TO FINISH: 30 minutes

NUTRITION FACTS per serving:

CALORIES 255
TOTAL FAT 16 g (6 g sat. fat)
CHOLESTEROL 436 mg
PROTEIN 21 g
CARBOHYDRATE 8 g
FIBER 2 g
SODIUM 422 mg

EXCHANGES 2.5 Lean Meat, 1.5 Vegetable, 1.5 Fat

1 Lightly coat an unheated 6- to 7-inch nonstick skillet with flared sides with nonstick cooking spray. Preheat skillet over medium heat. Add mushrooms, green onion, and garlic; cook and stir until mushrooms are tender. Using a slotted spoon, remove mushroom mixture from skillet; set aside. If necessary, drain skillet; carefully wipe out skillet with paper towels.

2 In a medium bowl combine eggs, herbes de Provence, salt, and pepper; beat with a rotary beater or wire whisk.

3 Add half of the oil to the skillet; heat skillet over medium heat. Pour half of the egg mixture into skillet. Using a wooden spoon or plastic spatula, immediately begin stirring the eggs gently but continuously until mixture resembles small pieces of cooked egg surrounded by liquid egg. Stop stirring. Cook for 30 to 60 seconds more or until egg mixture is set and shiny.

4 Sprinkle with half of the mozzarella cheese. Top with half of the mushroom mixture. Continue cooking until cheese just begins to melt. Using the spatula, lift and fold an edge of the omelet partially over filling. Remove from skillet; cover and keep warm.

5 Repeat with remaining oil, egg mixture, mozzarella cheese, and mushroom mixture. Top omelets with tomato, Asiago cheese, and, if desired, parsley. Makes 2 servings.

4 eggs

1 tablespoon snipped fresh cilantro

Dash salt

Dash ground cumin

Nonstick cooking spray

¼ cup shredded Monterey Jack cheese with jalapeño chile peppers, reduced-fat cheddar cheese, or reduced-fat Swiss cheese (1 ounce)

¾ cup fresh baby spinach leaves

1 recipe Corn-Pepper Relish

1 In a medium bowl combine eggs, cilantro, salt, and cumin; beat with a rotary beater or wire whisk until frothy.

2 Coat an unheated 10-inch nonstick skillet with flared sides with nonstick cooking spray. Preheat skillet over medium-high heat.

3 Pour egg mixture into hot skillet; lower heat to medium. Using a wooden spoon or plastic spatula, immediately begin stirring the eggs gently but continuously until mixture resembles small pieces of cooked egg surrounded by liquid egg. Stop stirring. Cook for 30 to 60 seconds more or until egg mixture is set and shiny.

4 Sprinkle with cheese. Top with three-fourths of the spinach and half of the Corn-Pepper Relish. Using the spatula, lift and fold an edge of the omelet partially over filling. Top with remaining spinach and remaining Corn-Pepper Relish. Cut omelet in half; transfer omelet to warm plates. Makes 2 servings.

Corn-Pepper Relish: In a small bowl combine ¼ cup chopped red sweet pepper; ¼ cup loose-pack frozen whole kernel corn, thawed; 2 tablespoons chopped red onion; and 1 tablespoon snipped fresh cilantro.

Tex-Mex Spinach Omelet

START TO FINISH: 25 minutes

NUTRITION FACTS per serving:

CALORIES 232
TOTAL FAT 15 g (6 g sat. fat)
CHOLESTEROL 438 mg
PROTEIN 17 g
CARBOHYDRATE 8 g
FIBER 1 g
SODIUM 322 mg

EXCHANGES 0.5 Starch, 2.5 Lean Meat, 0.5 Vegetable, 1.5 Fat

Breakfast Tortilla Wrap

START TO FINISH: 15 minutes

NUTRITION FACTS per serving:

CALORIES 248
TOTAL FAT 11 g (4 g sat. fat)
CHOLESTEROL 227 mg
PROTEIN 17 g
CARBOHYDRATE 17 g
FIBER 11 g
SODIUM 573 mg
EXCHANGES 1 Starch, 2 Medium-Fat Meat

Nonstick cooking spray
2 slices turkey bacon, chopped
¼ cup chopped green sweet pepper
¼ teaspoon ground cumin
⅛ teaspoon crushed red pepper
2 eggs
¼ cup chopped tomato
2 8-inch whole wheat flour tortillas, warmed*
Bottled salsa (optional)

1 Coat an unheated large nonstick skillet with nonstick cooking spray. Preheat over medium heat. Add bacon; cook until browned. Add sweet pepper, cumin, and crushed red pepper. Cook for 3 minutes, stirring occasionally.

2 In a small bowl lightly beat eggs with a fork. Add eggs to skillet; cook without stirring until eggs begin to set on the bottom and around edges. Using a spatula or wooden spoon, lift and fold the partially cooked egg mixture so the uncooked portion flows underneath. Continue cooking for 1 to 2 minutes or until egg mixture is cooked through but is still glossy and moist. Remove from heat. Stir in tomato. Spoon onto tortillas and roll up. If desired, secure with wooden picks. If desired, serve with salsa. Makes 2 servings.

*To warm tortillas, preheat oven to 350°F. Wrap tortillas tightly in foil; bake for 5 to 8 minutes or until warm. (Or wrap tortillas in white microwave-safe paper towels; microwave on 100% power [high] for 20 to 30 seconds or until tortillas are softened.)

2   6-inch corn tortillas

½   cup canned black beans,
       rinsed and drained

2   eggs

1   tablespoon fat-free milk

⅛   teaspoon black pepper

       Dash salt

       Nonstick cooking spray

½   cup chopped tomato

2   tablespoons crumbled queso
       fresco or shredded Monterey
       Jack cheese

2   teaspoons snipped fresh cilantro

       Fresh cilantro sprigs (optional)

       Purchased chunky salsa (optional)

1 Warm tortillas according to package directions. Meanwhile, in a small bowl use a potato masher or fork to slightly mash beans; set aside. In another small bowl or 1-cup glass measure combine eggs, milk, pepper, and salt; beat with a rotary beater or wire whisk.

2 Lightly coat an unheated medium nonstick skillet with nonstick cooking spray. Preheat over medium heat. Pour egg mixture into hot skillet. Cook, without stirring, until egg mixture begins to set on the bottom and around edge. With a spatula or large spoon, lift and fold the partially cooked egg mixture so the uncooked portion flows underneath. Cook for 2 to 3 minutes more or until egg mixture is cooked through but is still glossy and moist. Immediately remove from heat.

3 Spread one tortilla with mashed beans. Top with remaining tortilla, cooked egg mixture, tomato, cheese, and snipped cilantro. If desired, garnish with cilantro sprigs. If desired, serve with salsa. Serve immediately. Makes 2 servings.

Southwestern Breakfast Tostadas

START TO FINISH: 20 minutes

NUTRITION FACTS per serving:
- - - - - - - - - - - - - - - - - - -

CALORIES 213
TOTAL FAT 7 g (2 g sat. fat)
CHOLESTEROL 217 mg
PROTEIN 12 g
CARBOHYDRATE 26 g
FIBER 5 g
SODIUM 446 mg

EXCHANGES 2 Starch, 1 Lean Meat, 0.5 Fat

COOK'S TIP

Queso fresco, also known as queso blanco, is a fresh white Mexican cheese with a slightly salty, mild flavor. If you can't find it at the supermarket, try a local Mexican market.

Asparagus and Zucchini Frittata

PREP: 30 minutes   **BAKE:** 40 minutes
STAND: 10 minutes   **OVEN:** 350°F

NUTRITION FACTS per serving:

CALORIES 176
TOTAL FAT 9 g (3 g sat. fat)
CHOLESTEROL 353 mg
PROTEIN 15 g
CARBOHYDRATE 11 g
FIBER 3 g
SODIUM 527 mg
EXCHANGES 1.5 Medium-Fat Meat,
2 Vegetable

NUTRITION NOTE

Asparagus, which is at its best from
February to June, is one vegetable choice
for health-conscious consumers. Low in
calories, without fat and cholesterol, it
boasts potassium, fiber, and folic acid.

Nonstick cooking spray
1½ pounds fresh asparagus, trimmed
   and cut into 1-inch-long pieces
1 medium yellow sweet pepper,
   cut into strips
⅓ cup chopped onion
¼ cup bottled roasted red sweet
   peppers, drained and chopped
1 small zucchini, halved lengthwise
   and cut into ¼-inch-thick slices
   (about 1 cup)
10 eggs
1 cup fat-free milk
2 tablespoons snipped fresh dill or
   ½ teaspoon dried dill
1 teaspoon salt
½ teaspoon black pepper
   Fresh dill sprigs (optional)

1 Preheat oven to 350°F. Coat a 3-quart oval
or rectangular baking dish with nonstick
cooking spray; set aside.

2 In a large saucepan bring about 1 inch water
to boiling. Add asparagus, sweet pepper
strips, and onion. Return to boiling; reduce heat.
Cover and simmer about 1 minute or until crisp-
tender. Drain well. Stir in roasted red peppers.
Evenly spread asparagus mixture in prepared
baking dish. Layer zucchini slices on top.

3 In a large bowl beat eggs with a rotary beater
or wire whisk until combined. Beat in milk,
snipped or dried dill, salt, and black pepper. Pour
over vegetables in baking dish. Bake, uncovered,
for 40 to 45 minutes or until a knife inserted near
center comes out clean. Let stand for 10 minutes
before serving. If desired, garnish with dill sprigs.
Makes 6 servings.

Nonstick cooking spray

1   cup chopped cooked ham
(5 ounces)

½   cup sliced green onion or chopped
onion

½   cup chopped green or red
sweet pepper

6   eggs

¾   cup low-fat cottage cheese

⅛   teaspoon black pepper

2   plum tomatoes, thinly sliced

¼   cup shredded reduced-fat
cheddar cheese (1 ounce)

Sliced green onions (optional)

Ham and Cheese Skillet

START TO FINISH: 25 minutes

NUTRITION FACTS per serving:

CALORIES 148
TOTAL FAT 7 g (3 g sat. fat)
CHOLESTEROL 228 mg
PROTEIN 16 g
CARBOHYDRATE 5 g
FIBER 1 g
SODIUM 581 mg

EXCHANGES 2.5 Lean Meat, 0.5 Vegetable

1 Preheat broiler. Lightly coat an unheated 10-inch ovenproof skillet with nonstick cooking spray. Preheat skillet over medium heat. Add ham, ½ cup green onion, and sweet pepper. Cook and stir about 4 minutes or until vegetables are tender and ham is lightly browned.

2 Meanwhile, in a medium bowl beat eggs with a rotary beater or wire whisk. Beat in cottage cheese and black pepper. Pour over ham mixture in skillet. Cook over medium-low heat. As egg mixture sets, run a spatula around the edge of the skillet, lifting egg mixture so the uncooked portion flows underneath. Continue cooking and lifting edge until egg mixture is almost set but still glossy and moist.

3 Broil 5 inches from heat for 1 to 2 minutes or until eggs are set. Arrange tomato slices on frittata. Sprinkle cheese over tomato. Broil for 1 minute more. If desired, garnish with additional green onions. Makes 6 servings.

4	ounces tiny new potatoes, cut into ¼-inch-thick slices (1 cup)
¼	cup chopped red onion or onion
¼	cup chopped red or green sweet pepper
	Nonstick cooking spray
4	eggs
½	teaspoon snipped fresh rosemary or ¼ teaspoon dried rosemary, crushed
⅛	teaspoon salt
¼	cup shredded reduced-fat Swiss cheese (1 ounce)
	Cracked black pepper

Rosemary-Potato Frittata

START TO FINISH: 25 minutes

NUTRITION FACTS per serving:

CALORIES 260
TOTAL FAT 13 g (5 g sat. fat)
CHOLESTEROL 433 mg
PROTEIN 19 g
CARBOHYDRATE 16 g
FIBER 2 g
SODIUM 350 mg

EXCHANGES 1 Starch, 2.5 Lean Meat, 1 Fat

1 In a covered 6- to 7-inch nonstick skillet with flared sides cook potatoes and onion in a small amount of boiling water for 7 minutes. Add sweet pepper. Cover and cook for 3 to 5 minutes more or until vegetables are tender. Drain vegetables. Cool skillet; dry with paper towels. Lightly coat the skillet with nonstick cooking spray. Return vegetables to the skillet.

2 In a small bowl combine eggs, rosemary, and salt; beat with a rotary beater or wire whisk. Pour egg mixture over vegetables in the skillet; do not stir. Cook over medium heat. As mixture sets, run a spatula around the edge of the skillet, lifting egg mixture so uncooked portion flows underneath. Continue cooking and lifting edge until egg mixture is almost set (surface will be moist).

3 Remove skillet from heat. Sprinkle with cheese. Cover and let stand for 3 to 4 minutes or until top is set and cheese is melted. Sprinkle with cracked black pepper. Makes 2 servings.

Nonstick cooking spray

4 slices whole wheat bread

½ cup diced cooked lean ham
    (about 2¼ ounces)

⅓ cup shredded reduced-fat
    cheddar cheese

4 eggs

⅔ cup fat-free milk

¼ teaspoon black pepper

1 Lightly coat two 16- to 20-ounce casseroles with nonstick cooking spray. Tear bread into bite-size pieces; divide half of the bread pieces between the prepared dishes. Sprinkle ham and cheese over bread. Top with remaining torn bread.

2 In a medium bowl combine eggs, milk, and pepper; beat with a rotary beater or wire whisk. Pour egg mixture evenly over bread; press lightly with the back of a spoon to thoroughly moisten bread. Cover and chill for 2 to 24 hours.

3 Preheat oven to 325°F. Bake casseroles for 30 to 35 minutes or until a knife inserted near centers comes out clean. Let stand for 10 minutes before serving. Makes 4 servings.

COOK'S TIP

For a touch of extra flavor, add ½ teaspoon dried thyme, dill, or oregano, crushed, or 1 tablespoon snipped fresh chives or sliced green onion to the egg mixture.

Breakfast Bake

PREP: 15 minutes **CHILL:** 2 to 24 hours

BAKE: 30 minutes **STAND:** 10 minutes

OVEN: 325°F

NUTRITION FACTS per serving:

CALORIES 198
TOTAL FAT 9 g (3 g sat. fat)
CHOLESTEROL 228 mg
PROTEIN 16 g
CARBOHYDRATE 15 g
FIBER 2 g
SODIUM 547 mg

EXCHANGES 1 Starch, 2 Lean Meat

Egg and Potato Casserole

PREP: 20 minute **BAKE:** 50 minutes
STAND: 5 minutes **OVEN:** 350°F

NUTRITION FACTS per serving:

CALORIES 216
TOTAL FAT 10 g (4 g sat. fat)
CHOLESTEROL 296 mg
PROTEIN 16 g
CARBOHYDRATE 16 g
FIBER 1 g
SODIUM 529 mg

EXCHANGES 1 Starch, 1.5 Medium-Fat
Meat, 0.5 Vegetable

Nonstick cooking spray
2   cups frozen diced hash brown
      potatoes with onion
      and peppers
1   cup loose-pack frozen cut broccoli
      or asparagus
⅓   cup finely chopped Canadian-style
      bacon or lean cooked ham
      (2 ounces)
⅓   cup evaporated fat-free milk
2   tablespoons all-purpose flour
8   eggs
½   cup shredded reduced-fat
      cheddar cheese (2 ounces)
1   tablespoon snipped fresh basil or
      1 teaspoon dried basil, crushed
¼   teaspoon salt
¼   teaspoon black pepper
      Cooked broccoli florets (optional)

1 Preheat oven to 350°F. Lightly coat a 2-quart square baking dish with nonstick cooking spray. Arrange hash brown potatoes and frozen broccoli in bottom of baking dish; top with Canadian-style bacon. Set aside.

2 In a medium bowl gradually add evaporated milk to flour, beating with a fork or wire whisk. In another medium bowl beat eggs with a rotary beater or wire whisk until combined. Stir milk mixture, half of the cheese, basil, salt, and pepper into the egg mixture. Pour mixture over vegetables.

3 Bake about 50 minutes or until a knife inserted near center comes out clean. Sprinkle with remaining cheese. Let stand for 5 minutes before serving. If desired, serve with cooked broccoli florets. Makes 6 servings.

Make-Ahead Directions: Prepare as directed through step 2. Cover and chill for at least 4 hours or for up to 24 hours. Uncover and bake as directed in step 3.

Nonstick cooking spray

4	eggs
⅓	cup whole wheat pastry flour or whole wheat flour
¼	teaspoon black pepper
⅛	teaspoon salt
1½	cups low-fat cottage cheese (12 ounces), drained
1	10-ounce package frozen chopped broccoli, cooked according to package directions and drained
1	cup shredded reduced-fat cheddar cheese (4 ounces)
¾	cup crumbled reduced-fat feta cheese (3 ounces)

1 Preheat oven to 350°F. Lightly coat a 9-inch pie pan or pie plate with nonstick cooking spray; set aside.

2 In a medium bowl lightly beat eggs with a rotary beater or wire whisk. Beat in whole wheat pastry flour, pepper, and salt. Stir in cottage cheese, broccoli, cheddar cheese, and feta cheese. Spoon into prepared pie pan.

3 Bake for 40 to 45 minutes or until a knife inserted near center comes out clean. Cool on a wire rack for 10 minutes before serving. Makes 6 servings.

Crustless Cheese Quiche

PREP: 20 minutes **BAKE:** 40 minutes
COOL: 10 minutes **OVEN:** 350°F

NUTRITION FACTS per serving:

CALORIES 207
TOTAL FAT 10 g (5 g sat. fat)
CHOLESTEROL 162 mg
PROTEIN 21 g
CARBOHYDRATE 9 g
FIBER 2 g
SODIUM 731 mg

EXCHANGES 2.5 Medium-Fat Meat, 1 Vegetable

NUTRITION NOTE

Broccoli is great for bone health. It's an excellent source of calcium and vitamin C, both of which help strengthen and maintain teeth and bones.

Ham and Cheese Quesadillas

START TO FINISH: 20 minutes

NUTRITION FACTS per serving:
- -

CALORIES 238
TOTAL FAT 8 g (3 g sat. fat)
CHOLESTEROL 25 mg
PROTEIN 14 g
CARBOHYDRATE 29 g
FIBER 2 g
SODIUM 704 mg

EXCHANGES 2 Starch, 1 Medium-Fat Meat

¾   cup shredded reduced-fat Swiss, Monterey Jack, or cheddar cheese (3 ounces)

4   7- to 8-inch spinach, tomato, whole wheat, or plain flour tortillas

3   ounces thinly sliced extra-lean cooked ham

⅔   cup chopped tomato

2   tablespoons sliced green onion

     Baby red sweet peppers, sliced (optional)

1 Sprinkle cheese over half of each tortilla. Top with ham, tomato, and green onion. Fold tortillas in half, pressing together gently.

2 In a 10-inch skillet cook quesadillas, 2 at a time, over medium heat for 3 to 4 minutes or until lightly browned, turning once. Cut into wedges. If desired, garnish with pepper slices. Serve immediately. Makes 4 servings.

4	light brown-and-serve sausage links
½	cup shredded reduced-fat Mexican blend cheese
4	8-inch whole wheat flour tortillas
2	tablespoons Pineapple Salsa or drained purchased pineapple or regular salsa
1	small red onion, thinly sliced and separated into rings
2	tablespoons snipped fresh cilantro
	Fresh cilantro sprigs (optional)
½	cup Pineapple Salsa or purchased pineapple or regular salsa

1 Preheat oven to 300°F. Cook sausage according to package directions; drain. Coarsely chop sausage; set aside.

2 Divide cheese among tortillas, sprinkling over half of each tortilla. Top with sausage, the 2 tablespoons Pineapple Salsa, some of the onion, and snipped cilantro. Fold tortillas in half, pressing gently.

3 Preheat a 10-inch nonstick skillet or griddle over medium heat. Add two quesadillas to skillet or griddle. Cook for 2 to 3 minutes or until golden brown on bottoms. Turn quesadillas; cook for 2 to 3 minutes more or until golden brown on bottoms. Remove quesadillas from skillet to a baking sheet; keep warm in oven while cooking remaining quesadillas in the same way.

4 Garnish quesadillas with remaining onion slices and, if desired, cilantro sprigs. Serve quesadillas with ½ cup Pineapple Salsa. Makes 4 servings.

Pineapple Salsa: In a small bowl stir together ½ cup chopped fresh pineapple; ¼ cup chopped red sweet pepper; 2 tablespoons chopped red onion; 1 tablespoon snipped fresh cilantro; ½ of a fresh serrano or jalapeño chile pepper (see handling note, page 103), seeded and finely chopped; ½ teaspoon finely shredded lime peel; and ⅛ teaspoon salt. Serve immediately or store in an airtight container in the refrigerator for up to 24 hours. Makes 1 cup.

Incredible Quesadillas

START TO FINISH: 30 minutes

OVEN: 300°F

NUTRITION FACTS per serving:

CALORIES 225
TOTAL FAT 9 g (4 g sat. fat)
CHOLESTEROL 16 mg
PROTEIN 15 g
CARBOHYDRATE 19 g
FIBER 11 g
SODIUM 631 mg

EXCHANGES 1 Starch, 2 Medium-Fat Meat

COOK'S TIP

If you don't have time to make salsa but want something fresher than canned salsa, look in the produce department for fresh salsa blends available for purchase.

Breakfast Taco Roll-Ups

START TO FINISH: 20 minutes

NUTRITION FACTS per serving:
- -

CALORIES 136
TOTAL FAT 6 g (2 g sat. fat)
CHOLESTEROL 18 mg
PROTEIN 12 g
CARBOHYDRATE 17 g
FIBER 9 g
SODIUM 507 mg

EXCHANGES 1 Starch, 1 Medium-Fat Meat

Nonstick cooking spray
⅓ cup chopped celery
⅓ cup chopped green sweet pepper
1 cup chopped cooked ham (5 ounces)
1 8-ounce can crushed pineapple (juice pack), well drained, or ¾ cup finely chopped apple
1 cup reduced-fat shredded cheddar cheese (4 ounces)
8 6-inch whole wheat or plain flour tortillas, warmed*

1 Lightly coat an unheated small nonstick skillet with nonstick cooking spray. Preheat skillet over medium heat. Add celery and sweet pepper; cook and stir until tender. Stir in ham and pineapple. Cook and stir until heated through. Remove from heat. Stir in cheese.

2 Spoon about ¼ cup of the ham-cheese mixture into the center of each warmed tortilla. Roll up tortillas. Makes 8 servings.

*To warm tortillas, preheat oven to 350°F. Wrap tortillas tightly in foil; bake about 10 minutes or until warm. (Or wrap tortillas in white microwave-safe paper towels; microwave on 100% power [high] about 30 seconds or until tortillas are softened.)

3 cups water
1 cup steel-cut oats
1 tablespoon packed brown sugar
¼ teaspoon ground cinnamon
⅛ teaspoon salt
⅛ teaspoon ground allspice
  Dash ground cloves or nutmeg
3 cups fat-free milk
  Ground cloves or nutmeg
    (optional)

1 In a 2-quart saucepan combine water, steel-cut oats, brown sugar, cinnamon, salt, allspice, and cloves.

2 Bring to boiling; reduce heat. Simmer, uncovered, for 10 to 15 minutes or until desired doneness and consistency, stirring occasionally. Serve with milk. If desired, sprinkle with additional cloves. Makes 6 (½-cup) servings.

COOK'S TIP

Steel-cut oats, which are larger than ordinary rolled oats, take longer to cook because they're cut into pieces rather than rolled.

Spiced Irish Oatmeal

PREP: 10 minutes
COOK: 10 minutes

NUTRITION FACTS per serving:

CALORIES 157
TOTAL FAT 2 g (0 g sat. fat)
CHOLESTEROL 2 mg
PROTEIN 9 g
CARBOHYDRATE 26 g
FIBER 3 g
SODIUM 103 mg

EXCHANGES 1.5 Starch, 0.5 Milk

2 cups water

¼ teaspoon salt

1 cup rolled oats

1 cup chopped apple or chopped peeled peach

¼ cup raisins or snipped whole pitted dates

1 teaspoon vanilla

¼ teaspoon ground cinnamon

Fat-free milk (optional)

1 In a medium saucepan bring water and salt to boiling. Stir in oats, apple, raisins, vanilla, and cinnamon. Reduce heat. Simmer, uncovered, for 3 minutes (for quick oats) or 5 minutes (for regular oats), stirring occasionally. Remove from heat. Cover and let stand for 2 minutes before serving. If desired, serve with fat-free milk. Makes 4 servings.

Fruity Oatmeal

START TO FINISH: 15 minutes

NUTRITION FACTS per serving:

- -

CALORIES 140
TOTAL FAT 2 g (0 g sat. fat)
CHOLESTEROL 0 mg
PROTEIN 4 g
CARBOHYDRATE 28 g
FIBER 4 g
SODIUM 151 mg

EXCHANGES 1.5 Starch, 0.5 Fat

NUTRITION NOTE

Rolled oats are highly nutritious. They contain plenty of thiamine, iron, and cholesterol-fighting soluble fiber.

2 cups fat-free milk

2 tablespoons sugar

⅓ cup quick-cooking wheat cereal (farina)

¼ cup raisins

1 teaspoon ground cinnamon

Ground cinnamon (optional)

1 In a medium saucepan combine milk and sugar. Bring just to boiling; reduce heat. Add cereal, stirring constantly. Stir in raisins and cinnamon.

2 Cook, uncovered, for 2 to 3 minutes or until thickened, stirring frequently. Serve warm. If desired, sprinkle with additional cinnamon. Makes 4 (½-cup) servings.

Spiced Oatmeal: Prepare as above, except substitute 1 cup quick-cooking rolled oats for quick-cooking wheat cereal.

Spiced Hot Cereal

START TO FINISH: 10 minutes

NUTRITION FACTS per serving:

CALORIES 120
TOTAL FAT 0 g (0 g sat. fat)
CHOLESTEROL 2 mg
PROTEIN 5 g
CARBOHYDRATE 25 g
FIBER 1 g
SODIUM 53 mg

EXCHANGES 0.5 Starch, 0.5 Fruit, 0.5 Milk

Nonstick cooking spray

2½ cups regular rolled oats

1 cup wheat cereal flakes

⅓ cup raw sunflower kernels

¼ cup flaxseeds

⅓ cup orange juice

2 tablespoons packed brown sugar

2 tablespoons honey

½ teaspoon apple pie spice

1 teaspoon vanilla

Fresh blueberries

Fat-free milk (optional)

Sweet and Crunchy Granola

PREP: 15 minutes   **BAKE:** 30 minutes
OVEN: 325°F

NUTRITION FACTS per serving:

CALORIES 242
TOTAL FAT 7 g (1 g sat. fat)
CHOLESTEROL 0 mg
PROTEIN 6 g
CARBOHYDRATE 43 g
FIBER 7 g
SODIUM 36 mg

EXCHANGES 2 Starch, 0.5 Fruit, 1 Fat

NUTRITION NOTE

Because the human body cannot make omega-3 fatty acids, it is essential to consume foods that contain them. Flaxseeds are loaded with this heart-healthy fatty acid.

1 Preheat oven to 325°F. Coat a 15×10×1-inch baking pan with nonstick cooking spray; set aside. In a large bowl stir together oats, wheat cereal flakes, sunflower kernels, and flaxseeds. In a small saucepan stir together orange juice, brown sugar, honey, and apple pie spice. Cook and stir just until boiling. Remove from heat. Stir in vanilla. Pour over oat mixture, tossing just until coated.

2 Spread oat mixture evenly in prepared pan. Bake, uncovered, for 30 to 35 minutes or until oats are lightly browned, stirring twice. Remove from oven. Immediately turn out onto a large piece of foil; cool completely. Refrigerate in an airtight container for up to 2 weeks or freeze for up to 3 months. Serve with blueberries. If desired, serve with milk. Makes 8 (about ½-cup) servings.

- 1 cup regular rolled oats
- 1 cup quick-cooking barley
- 1 cup bulgur or cracked wheat
- 1 cup dried cranberries, raisins, and/or snipped dried apricots
- ¾ cup sliced almonds, toasted
- ⅓ cup sugar
- 1 tablespoon ground cinnamon
- ¼ teaspoon salt
- Fat-free milk (optional)

1 In an airtight container stir together oats, barley, bulgur, cranberries, almonds, sugar, cinnamon, and salt. Cover; seal. Store at room temperature for up to 2 months or freeze for up to 6 months.

2 For two breakfast servings, in a small saucepan bring 1⅓ cups water to boiling. Stir cereal mix before measuring; add ⅔ cup of the cereal mix to the boiling water. Reduce heat. Cover and simmer for 12 to 15 minutes or until cereal reaches desired consistency. If desired, serve with milk. Makes 14 (about ⅓-cup) servings.

Microwave Directions: For one breakfast serving, in a microwave-safe 1-quart bowl combine ¾ cup water and ⅓ cup cereal mix. Microwave, uncovered, on 50% power (medium) for 8 to 11 minutes or until cereal reaches desired consistency, stirring once. Stir before serving. If desired, serve with milk.

COOK'S TIP

Bulgur, a staple in the Middle East, can sometimes be a challenge to find in American grocery stores. If it's not stocked with other grains at the store, check the health food section or a natural food store.

Cranberry-Almond Cereal Mix

PREP: 10 minutes
COOK: 12 minutes

NUTRITION FACTS per serving:

CALORIES 168
TOTAL FAT 3 g (0 g sat. fat)
CHOLESTEROL 0 mg
PROTEIN 4 g
CARBOHYDRATE 33 g
FIBER 5 g
SODIUM 44 mg

EXCHANGES 1.5 Starch, 0.5 Fruit, 0.5 Fat

1 medium fresh peach or nectarine

1 6-ounce carton plain fat-free yogurt

½ teaspoon vanilla

½ cup bite-size shredded wheat biscuits, coarsely crushed

⅛ teaspoon ground cinnamon

2 teaspoons sugar-free maple-flavor syrup or light maple-flavor syrup

1 tablespoon sliced almonds, toasted

Fresh peach or nectarine slices (optional)

1 If desired, peel peach, then pit and finely chop. Place fruit in a small bowl. Stir in yogurt and vanilla.

2 Spoon half of the yogurt mixture into two 8- to 10-ounce parfait glasses. Top with crushed shredded wheat biscuits; sprinkle with some cinnamon. Drizzle with maple-flavor syrup. Spoon remaining yogurt mixture over all. Top yogurt with almonds and remaining cinnamon. If desired, garnish with fruit slices. Makes 2 servings.

COOK'S TIP

Look for peaches or nectarines that give slightly to the pressure of your palm, are fragrant, and are free of soft spots or bruises.

Fruit and Yogurt Parfaits

START TO FINISH: 20 minutes

NUTRITION FACTS per serving:

CALORIES 118
TOTAL FAT 2 g (0 g sat. fat)
CHOLESTEROL 2 mg
PROTEIN 7 g
CARBOHYDRATE 19 g
FIBER 2 g
SODIUM 75 mg

EXCHANGES 0.5 Starch, 0.5 Fruit, 0.5 Milk

½ cup ground espresso coffee or French roast coffee

1 teaspoon finely shredded orange peel

4 cups water

3 cups fat-free milk

3 tablespoons sugar

Ice cubes

Orange wedges (optional)

1 teaspoon grated semisweet chocolate (optional)

1 In a small bowl combine coffee and shredded orange peel. In a drip coffee maker or percolator brew coffee according to manufacturer's directions, using the coffee mixture and the water. Pour coffee into a heatproof pitcher; cool slightly. Add milk and sugar, stirring until sugar dissolves. Cover and chill for at least 3 hours or until serving time.

2 To serve, fill six glasses with ice cubes; pour coffee mixture over ice. If desired, garnish with orange wedges and grated chocolate. Makes 6 (about 8-ounce) servings.

Iced Espresso

PREP: 20 minutes

CHILL: 3 hours

NUTRITION FACTS per serving:

CALORIES 69
TOTAL FAT 0 g (0 g sat. fat)
CHOLESTEROL 2 mg
PROTEIN 4 g
CARBOHYDRATE 12 g
FIBER 0 g
SODIUM 74 mg

EXCHANGES 5 Other Carbohydrates, 0.5 Milk

1 cup orange juice
1 cup loose-pack frozen
   strawberries, raspberries,
   and/or blackberries
1 medium banana, peeled and cut up
¼ cup plain low-fat yogurt
   Fresh strawberries, sliced (optional)

1 In a blender combine orange juice, frozen berries, banana, and yogurt. Cover and blend until smooth.

2 To serve, pour into two glasses. If desired, garnish with fresh strawberries.
Makes 2 (about 9-ounce) servings.

Berry-Banana Smoothie

START TO FINISH: 10 minutes

NUTRITION FACTS per serving:

CALORIES 151
TOTAL FAT 1 g (0 g sat. fat)
CHOLESTEROL 2 mg
PROTEIN 4 g
CARBOHYDRATE 34 g
FIBER 3 g
SODIUM 24 mg

EXCHANGES 2 Fruit, 0.5 Milk

Chapter 3

Breads

On the divider: Pear-Almond Muffins *(see recipe, page 60)*

Nonstick cooking spray

1   cup all-purpose flour

1   cup whole wheat flour or
     white whole wheat flour

⅓   cup packed brown sugar

2½   teaspoons baking powder

1   teaspoon apple pie spice

¼   teaspoon salt

2   eggs

1   cup buttermilk

2   tablespoons canola oil

¾   cup shredded, peeled apple
     (1 medium)

2   tablespoons finely
     chopped pecans

1   tablespoon flaxseed meal or
     toasted wheat germ

1   tablespoon packed brown sugar

1   tablespoon butter

Apple-Streusel Muffins

PREP: 25 minutes   **BAKE:** 18 minutes
COOL: 5 minutes   **OVEN:** 375°F

NUTRITION FACTS per muffin:

CALORIES 163
TOTAL FAT 6 g (1 g sat. fat)
CHOLESTEROL 39 mg
PROTEIN 4 g
CARBOHYDRATE 25 g
FIBER 2 g
SODIUM 167 mg

EXCHANGES 1.5 Starch, 1 Fat

1 Preheat oven to 375°F. Lightly coat twelve 2½-inch muffin cups with nonstick cooking spray or line with paper bake cups and coat insides of paper cups with nonstick cooking spray; set aside. In a large bowl stir together all-purpose flour, whole wheat flour, ⅓ cup brown sugar, baking powder, apple pie spice, and salt. Make a well in the center of the flour mixture; set aside.

2 In a medium bowl lightly beat eggs with a fork; stir in buttermilk and oil. Add egg mixture all at once to flour mixture; stir just until moistened (batter should be lumpy). Fold in shredded apple. Spoon batter into prepared muffin cups, filling each about three-fourths full.

3 In a small bowl combine pecans, flaxseed meal, and 1 tablespoon brown sugar. Using a pastry blender, cut in butter until mixture resembles coarse crumbs. Spoon pecan mixture on top of muffin batter.

4 Bake for 18 to 20 minutes or until a toothpick inserted in centers comes out clean. Cool in muffin cups on a wire rack for 5 minutes. Remove muffins from muffin cups. Serve warm. Makes 12 muffins.

Nonstick cooking spray

1 cup all-purpose flour

¾ cup white whole wheat flour or whole wheat flour

½ cup sugar

2 teaspoons baking powder

¾ teaspoon ground cinnamon

¼ teaspoon salt

1 egg

¾ cup fat-free milk

3 tablespoons canola oil

⅓ cup dried cranberries, coarsely snipped

⅓ cup chopped pecans, toasted

Cranberry-Pecan Muffins

PREP: 20 minutes **BAKE:** 12 minutes
COOL: 5 minutes **OVEN:** 400°F

NUTRITION FACTS per muffin:

CALORIES 176
TOTAL FAT 6 g (1 g sat. fat)
CHOLESTEROL 18 mg
PROTEIN 4 g
CARBOHYDRATE 27 g
FIBER 1 g
SODIUM 134 mg

EXCHANGES 2 Starch, 1 Fat

1 Preheat oven to 400°F. Coat twelve 2½-inch muffin cups with nonstick cooking spray or line with paper bake cups and coat insides of paper cups with nonstick cooking spray; set aside. In a large bowl stir together all-purpose flour, whole wheat flour, sugar, baking powder, cinnamon, and salt. Make a well in the center of the flour mixture; set aside.

2 In a medium bowl whisk together egg, milk, and oil. Add milk mixture all at once to flour mixture; stir just until moistened (batter should be lumpy). Gently stir in dried cranberries and pecans.

3 Spoon batter into prepared muffin cups, filling each about half full. Bake for 12 to 15 minutes or until a toothpick inserted in centers comes out clean. Cool in muffin cups on a wire rack for 5 minutes. Remove muffins from muffin cups. Serve warm. Makes 12 muffins.

COOK'S TIP

White whole wheat flour, lighter in color and milder tasting than traditional whole wheat flour, contains more vitamins, minerals, and fiber than all-purpose flour. To substitute it for whole wheat flour or to mix a little with all-purpose flour, begin with ⅓ white whole wheat flour combined with ⅔ all-purpose flour when the recipe calls for all-purpose flour. Gradually increase the ratio of white whole wheat flour to all-purpose flour.

Nonstick cooking spray

- 2 cups regular rolled oats
- ¾ cup whole wheat flour
- ⅓ cup sugar
- 1 teaspoon baking powder
- ¾ teaspoon apple pie spice or ground cinnamon
- ½ teaspoon baking soda
- ½ teaspoon salt
- 2 eggs
- 1 cup buttermilk
- 1 large ripe banana, mashed
- 2 tablespoons butter, melted
- 1 teaspoon vanilla
- ¼ cup regular rolled oats
- ½ teaspoon apple pie spice or ground cinnamon
- 1 tablespoon butter

1 Preheat oven to 350°F. Line twelve 2½-inch muffin cups with paper bake cups and coat insides of paper cups with nonstick cooking spray; set aside. Place 2 cups oats in a food processor or blender; cover and process or blend until finely ground. Transfer finely ground oats to a large bowl. Stir in whole wheat flour, sugar, baking powder, ¾ teaspoon apple pie spice, baking soda, and salt. Make a well in the center of the flour mixture; set aside.

2 In a medium bowl whisk together eggs and buttermilk; whisk in banana, 2 tablespoons melted butter, and vanilla. Add buttermilk mixture all at once to flour mixture; stir just until moistened (batter should be lumpy). Spoon batter into prepared muffin cups, filling each about two-thirds full.

3 For topping, in a small bowl stir together ¼ cup oats and ½ teaspoon apple pie spice. Using a pastry blender, cut in 1 tablespoon butter until mixture resembles coarse crumbs. Sprinkle the oat mixture on top of muffin batter.

4 Bake for 20 to 22 minutes or until a toothpick inserted in centers comes out clean. Cool in muffin cups on a wire rack for 5 minutes. Remove muffins from muffin cups. Serve warm. Makes 12 muffins.

Banana-Oat Muffins

PREP: 20 minutes **BAKE:** 20 minutes
COOL: 5 minutes **OVEN:** 350°F

NUTRITION FACTS per muffin:

CALORIES 174
TOTAL FAT 5 g (2 g sat. fat)
CHOLESTEROL 44 mg
PROTEIN 6 g
CARBOHYDRATE 27 g
FIBER 3 g
SODIUM 225 mg

EXCHANGES 1.5 Starch, 0.5 Other Carbohydrates, 0.5 Fat

Make-Ahead Directions: Place baked muffins in an airtight container. Cover; seal. Store at room temperature for up to 3 days or freeze for up to 1 month.

Nonstick cooking spray

1	cup all-purpose flour
½	cup packed brown sugar
2	teaspoons baking powder
½	teaspoon ground ginger
¼	teaspoon salt
¾	cup whole bran cereal
¾	cup fat-free milk
¾	cup chopped, peeled pear
2	egg whites, lightly beaten
3	tablespoons canola oil
2	tablespoons finely chopped almonds
1	recipe Ginger-Cream Spread

Pear-Almond Muffins

PREP: 20 minutes   **BAKE:** 15 minutes
COOL: 5 minutes   **OVEN:** 400°F

NUTRITION FACTS per muffin:

CALORIES 154
TOTAL FAT 5 g (1 g sat. fat)
CHOLESTEROL 5 mg
PROTEIN 4 g
CARBOHYDRATE 24 g
FIBER 2 g
SODIUM 163 mg

EXCHANGES 1.5 Other Carbohydrates, 1 Fat

1 Preheat oven to 400°F. Lightly coat twelve 2½-inch muffin cups with nonstick cooking spray or line with paper bake cups and coat insides of paper cups with nonstick cooking spray; set aside. In a large bowl stir together flour, brown sugar, baking powder, ginger, and salt. Make a well in the center of the flour mixture; set aside.

2 In a medium bowl stir together cereal and milk; let mixture stand for 5 minutes. Stir in pear, egg whites, and oil. Add cereal mixture all at once to flour mixture; stir just until moistened (batter should be lumpy).

3 Spoon batter into prepared muffin cups, filling each three-fourths full. Sprinkle with almonds. Bake for 15 to 18 minutes or until a toothpick inserted near centers comes out clean.

4 Cool in muffin cups on a wire rack for 5 minutes. Remove muffins from muffin cups. Serve warm with Ginger-Cream Spread. Makes 12 muffins.

Ginger-Cream Spread: In a small bowl stir together half of an 8-ounce tub light cream cheese, 2 teaspoons finely chopped crystallized ginger or ¼ teaspoon ground ginger, and 2 teaspoons honey.

Make-Ahead Directions: Store the batter in the refrigerator for up to 3 days and bake a few at a time, if you like.

Nonstick cooking spray

1¼ cups all-purpose flour

⅔ cup oat bran

½ cup packed brown sugar

2 teaspoons baking powder

⅛ teaspoon salt

1 egg or 2 egg whites

½ cup light dairy sour cream

¼ cup fat-free milk

2 tablespoons canola oil

1 cup chopped fresh mango or chopped thawed frozen unsweetened mango chunks, drained

⅓ cup pistachio nuts, chopped

Pistachio-Mango Muffins

PREP: 25 minutes   **BAKE:** 18 minutes
COOL: 5 minutes   **OVEN:** 400°F

NUTRITION FACTS per muffin:

CALORIES 162
TOTAL FAT 6 g (1 g sat. fat)
CHOLESTEROL 21 mg
PROTEIN 4 g
CARBOHYDRATE 27 g
FIBER 2 g
SODIUM 103 mg

EXCHANGES 2 Other Carbohydrates, 1 Fat

1 Preheat oven to 400°F. Coat twelve 2½-inch muffin cups with nonstick cooking spray or line with paper bake cups and coat insides of paper cups with nonstick cooking spray; set aside. In a large bowl combine flour, oat bran, brown sugar, baking powder, and salt. Make a well in the center of the flour mixture; set aside.

2 In a medium bowl whisk together egg, sour cream, milk, and oil. Add egg mixture all at once to flour mixture; stir just until moistened (batter should be lumpy). Fold in mango and pistachio nuts.

3 Spoon batter into prepared muffin cups, filling each about three-fourths full. Bake about 18 minutes or until golden brown and a toothpick inserted in centers comes out clean.

4 Cool in muffin cups on a wire rack for 5 minutes. Remove muffins from muffin cups. Serve warm. Makes 12 muffins.

NUTRITION NOTE

Nuts, which are high in calories and fat, should be eaten in moderate amounts. Fortunately the fat in nuts such as pistachios is mostly monounsaturated fat, which can help lower bad cholesterol and raise good cholesterol.

1½ cups all-purpose flour
½ cup rolled oats
½ cup sugar
3 tablespoons unsweetened cocoa powder
1 tablespoon instant espresso coffee powder or instant coffee crystals
2 teaspoons baking powder
¼ teaspoon salt
¼ cup butter, cut into pieces
1 6-ounce carton plain fat-free or low-fat yogurt
1 egg white, lightly beaten
⅓ cup semisweet chocolate pieces
Rolled oats (optional)

Mocha Scones

PREP: 15 minutes   **BAKE:** 13 minutes
COOL: 5 minutes   **OVEN:** 400°F

NUTRITION FACTS per scone:

CALORIES 185
TOTAL FAT 6 g (4 g sat. fat)
CHOLESTEROL 10 mg
PROTEIN 4 g
CARBOHYDRATE 30 g
FIBER 2 g
SODIUM 153 mg

EXCHANGES 2 Other Carbohydrates, 1 Fat

1 Preheat oven to 400°F. Lightly grease a large baking sheet or line with parchment paper; set aside.

2 In a medium bowl combine flour, ½ cup oats, sugar, cocoa powder, espresso powder, baking powder, and salt. Using a pastry blender, cut in butter until mixture resembles coarse crumbs. Make a well in the center of the flour mixture; set aside.

3 In a medium bowl combine yogurt and egg white. Stir in chocolate pieces. Add yogurt mixture all at once to flour mixture; stir just until moistened.

4 Turn out dough on a lightly floured surface. Knead by folding and gently pressing dough for 10 to 12 strokes or until nearly smooth. Pat or lightly roll dough into an 8×6-inch rectangle. Cut rectangle crosswise into 4 strips. Cut each strip into 3 rectangles to make 12 pieces.

5 Place dough pieces 1 inch apart on prepared baking sheet. If desired, sprinkle with additional rolled oats. Bake for 13 to 15 minutes or until tops are set. Remove scones from baking sheet. Cool on a wire rack for 5 minutes. Serve warm. Makes 12 scones.

Nonstick cooking spray

1½	cups all-purpose flour
½	cup white whole wheat flour or whole wheat flour
¼	cup sugar
1	tablespoon baking powder
1	tablespoon finely shredded orange peel
¼	teaspoon baking soda
¼	teaspoon salt
¼	cup butter
1	egg
½	cup buttermilk or sour fat-free milk*
1	teaspoon vanilla
1	cup fresh or frozen blueberries
1	recipe Orange Glaze (optional)

Blueberry Breakfast Scones

PREP: 30 minutes   **BAKE:** 15 minutes
OVEN: 400°F

NUTRITION FACTS per scone:

CALORIES 171
TOTAL FAT 5 g (3 g sat. fat)
CHOLESTEROL 34 mg
PROTEIN 4 g
CARBOHYDRATE 27 g
FIBER 1 g
SODIUM 215 mg

EXCHANGES 2 Other Carbohydrates, 1 Fat

1 Preheat oven to 400°F. Lightly coat a baking sheet with nonstick cooking spray; set aside. In a large bowl stir together all-purpose flour, whole wheat flour, sugar, baking powder, orange peel, baking soda, and salt. Using a pastry blender, cut in butter until mixture resembles coarse crumbs. Make a well in the center of the flour mixture.

2 In a small bowl whisk together egg, buttermilk, and vanilla. Add egg mixture all at once to flour mixture; stir just until moistened. Gently stir in blueberries. (Do not thaw frozen blueberries; thawed berries will discolor the dough.) (Mixture will not completely come together in a ball.)

3 Turn out dough on a lightly floured surface. Knead dough by folding and gently pressing dough for 10 to 12 strokes or until nearly smooth. Transfer dough to the prepared baking sheet; pat or lightly roll dough to a 7-inch circle. Cut circle into 10 wedges. Separate wedges so they are about 1 inch apart.

4 Bake about 15 minutes or until golden brown. Remove from baking sheet. Cool slightly on a wire rack. If desired, drizzle scones with Orange Glaze. Serve warm. Makes 10 scones.

*To make ½ cup sour fat-free milk, place 1½ teaspoons lemon juice or vinegar in a glass measuring cup. Add enough fat-free milk to make ½ cup total liquid; stir. Let stand for 5 minutes before using.

Orange Glaze: In a small bowl stir together ¾ cup powdered sugar and ¼ teaspoon finely shredded orange peel. Stir in enough orange juice or fat-free milk (3 to 4 teaspoons) to make drizzling consistency.

Nonstick cooking spray

1	cup all-purpose flour
⅓	cup yellow cornmeal
1½	teaspoons finely shredded lemon peel
1	teaspoon baking powder
½	teaspoon baking soda
¼	teaspoon salt
1	6-ounce carton plain low-fat yogurt
2	egg whites
¼	cup sugar
¼	cup honey
¼	cup canola oil
1	cup fresh or frozen blueberries
½	cup chopped fresh peach or chopped thawed frozen unsweetened peach slices, drained
1	tablespoon all-purpose flour

Blueberry-Peach Coffee Cake

PREP: 25 minutes **BAKE:** 40 minutes
COOL: 30 minutes **OVEN:** 350°F

NUTRITION FACTS per serving:

CALORIES 206
TOTAL FAT 7 g (1 g sat. fat)
CHOLESTEROL 1 mg
PROTEIN 4 g
CARBOHYDRATE 35 g
FIBER 1 g
SODIUM 201 mg

EXCHANGES 1.5 Starch, 1 Other Carbohydrates, 1 Fat

1 Preheat oven to 350°F. Lightly coat an 8×8×2-inch baking pan with nonstick cooking spray; set aside. In a large bowl stir together 1 cup flour, cornmeal, lemon peel, baking powder, baking soda, and salt. Make a well in the center of the flour mixture; set aside.

2 In a medium bowl combine yogurt, egg whites, sugar, honey, and oil. Add yogurt mixture all at once to flour mixture; stir just until combined. In a small bowl combine blueberries, peach, and the 1 tablespoon flour; toss gently to coat.

3 Spread about half of the batter in the prepared baking pan. Sprinkle with fruit mixture. Spoon mounds of remaining batter over the fruit mixture. Spread evenly over fruit (the batter may not completely cover the fruit).

4 Bake about 40 minutes or until coffee cake is golden brown and a toothpick inserted near the center comes out clean. Cool in pan on a wire rack for 30 minutes. Serve warm. Makes 9 servings.

Nonstick cooking spray

1	cup all-purpose flour
½	cup white whole wheat flour or whole wheat flour
1	teaspoon baking powder
¼	teaspoon salt
¼	teaspoon ground cinnamon
⅛	teaspoon ground ginger
1	egg
½	cup snipped dried apricots
½	cup fat-free milk
¼	cup sugar
¼	cup unsweetened applesauce
¼	cup canola oil
2	tablespoons reduced-sugar apricot preserves, melted
2	tablespoons sliced almonds, toasted

Apricot-Almond Coffee Cake

PREP: 20 minutes **BAKE:** 25 minutes
COOL: 10 minutes **OVEN:** 350°F

NUTRITION FACTS per serving:

CALORIES 182
TOTAL FAT 7 g (1 g sat. fat)
CHOLESTEROL 21 mg
PROTEIN 4 g
CARBOHYDRATE 28 g
FIBER 2 g
SODIUM 97 mg

EXCHANGES 2 Other Carbohydrates, 1 Fat

1 Preheat oven to 350°F. Lightly coat an 8×1½-inch round baking pan with nonstick cooking spray; set aside. In a medium bowl stir together all-purpose flour, whole wheat flour, baking powder, salt, cinnamon, and ginger.

2 In a medium bowl lightly beat egg with a fork; stir in dried apricots. Stir in milk, sugar, applesauce, and oil. Add apricot mixture all at once to flour mixture; stir until combined. Spread batter in the prepared baking pan.

3 Bake for 25 to 30 minutes or until a toothpick inserted near the center comes out clean. Cool in pan on a wire rack for 10 minutes. Cut up any large pieces of fruit in preserves; spoon over coffee cake. Sprinkle with toasted almonds. Serve warm. Makes 10 servings.

COOK'S TIP

Because whole wheat flour contains the whole grain, it has shorter shelf life than refined products. Refrigerate whole wheat flour in an air-tight container to keep it fresh.

Banana Bread

PREP: 20 minutes   **BAKE:** 45 minutes
COOL: 2 hours   **STAND:** overnight
OVEN: 350°F

NUTRITION FACTS per serving:

CALORIES 143
TOTAL FAT 2 g (0 g sat. fat)
CHOLESTEROL 0 mg
PROTEIN 3 g
CARBOHYDRATE 28 g
FIBER 1 g
SODIUM 152 mg

EXCHANGES 2 Other Carbohydrates

Nonstick cooking spray
1   cup all-purpose flour
½   cup white whole wheat flour or
       whole wheat flour
2   teaspoons baking powder
½   teaspoon pumpkin pie spice
¼   teaspoon baking soda
¼   teaspoon salt
1   cup mashed banana
       (2 to 3 medium)
¾   cup packed brown sugar
¼   cup fat-free milk
2   egg whites
2   tablespoons canola oil
¼   cup chopped walnuts, toasted
       (optional)

1 Preheat oven to 350°F. Lightly coat the bottom and about ½ inch up the sides of an 8×4×2-inch loaf pan with nonstick cooking spray; set aside.

2 In a large bowl stir together all-purpose flour, whole wheat flour, baking powder, pumpkin pie spice, baking soda, and salt. Make a well in the center of the flour mixture; set aside.

3 In a medium bowl combine mashed banana, brown sugar, milk, egg whites, and oil. Add banana mixture all at once to flour mixture; stir just until moistened (batter should be lumpy). If desired, fold in 2 tablespoons walnuts. Spoon batter into prepared loaf pan. If desired, sprinkle with remaining 2 tablespoons walnuts.

4 Bake for 45 to 50 minutes or until a toothpick inserted near the center comes out clean. Cool in pan on a wire rack for 10 minutes. Remove bread from pan. Cool on wire rack. Wrap and store overnight before slicing. Makes 1 loaf (12 servings).

¾ cup packed brown sugar

⅓ cup creamy peanut butter

1½ teaspoons baking powder

¼ teaspoon baking soda

¼ teaspoon salt

2 egg whites

2 tablespoons canola oil

1 cup all-purpose flour

½ cup white whole wheat flour or whole wheat flour

1 cup fat-free milk

2 tablespoons unsweetened cocoa powder

1 tablespoon fat-free milk

1 Preheat oven to 350°F. Grease the bottom(s) and ½ inch up the sides of one 8×4×2-inch loaf pan or four 4½×2½×1½-inch individual loaf pans; set aside.

2 In a large bowl combine brown sugar, peanut butter, baking powder, baking soda, and salt. Beat with an electric mixer until combined. Beat in egg whites and oil until combined. In a small bowl combine all-purpose flour and whole wheat flour. Alternately add flour mixture and 1 cup milk to peanut butter mixture, beating on low speed after each addition just until combined. Transfer ½ cup of the batter to a small bowl; stir in cocoa powder and 1 tablespoon milk.

3 Spoon half of the light-color batter evenly into prepared loaf pan(s). Drop all of the chocolate batter by small spoonfuls on top of batter in pans. Spoon remaining light-color batter evenly over chocolate batter. Using a narrow metal spatula, swirl batters to create a marbled effect.

4 Bake for 50 to 55 minutes for the 8-inch pan, 30 to 35 minutes for the 4½-inch pans, or until a toothpick inserted near center(s) comes out clean. Cool in pan(s) on a wire rack for 10 minutes. Remove bread from pan(s). Cool on wire rack. Wrap and store overnight before slicing. Makes 12 servings.

Peanut Butter and Chocolate Swirl Bread

PREP: 25 minutes   **BAKE:** 50 minutes
COOL: 2 hours   **STAND:** overnight
OVEN: 350°F

NUTRITION FACTS per serving:

CALORIES 181
TOTAL FAT 6 g (1 g sat. fat)
CHOLESTEROL 0 mg
PROTEIN 5 g
CARBOHYDRATE 28 g
FIBER 1 g
SODIUM 177 mg

EXCHANGES 1 Starch, 1 Other Carbohydrates, 1 Fat

1 cup all-purpose flour

¾ cup white whole wheat flour or whole wheat flour

2½ teaspoons pumpkin pie spice

1 teaspoon baking powder

¼ teaspoon baking soda

¼ teaspoon salt

2 eggs

¾ cup packed brown sugar

¾ cup canned pumpkin

⅓ cup fat-free milk

¼ cup canola oil

1 teaspoon vanilla

⅓ cup golden raisins

Pumpkin Bread

PREP: 15 minutes   **BAKE:** 50 minutes

COOL: 10 minutes   **STAND:** overnight

OVEN: 350°F

NUTRITION FACTS per serving:

CALORIES 191

TOTAL FAT 6 g (1 g sat. fat)

CHOLESTEROL 35 mg

PROTEIN 6 g

CARBOHYDRATE 32 g

FIBER 2 g

SODIUM 127 mg

EXCHANGES 2 Starch, 1 Fat

1 Preheat oven to 350°F. Grease the bottom and ½ inch up the sides of an 8×4×2-inch loaf pan; set aside.

2 In a large bowl combine all-purpose flour, whole wheat flour, pumpkin pie spice, baking powder, baking soda, and salt. In a medium bowl beat eggs with a fork. Stir in brown sugar, pumpkin, milk, oil, and vanilla. Add egg mixture all at once to flour mixture; stir just until moistened. Fold in raisins. Spoon batter into prepared loaf pan.

3 Bake for 50 to 55 minutes or until a toothpick inserted near center comes out clean. Cool in pan on a wire rack for 10 minutes. Remove bread from pan. Cool on wire rack. Wrap and store overnight before slicing. Makes 1 loaf (12 servings).

1¼   cups all-purpose flour

¼   cup flaxseed meal or toasted wheat germ

1½   teaspoons baking powder

1   teaspoon apple pie spice

¼   teaspoon salt

2   egg whites

1   cup finely shredded zucchini

⅔   cup sugar

¼   cup canola oil

1   teaspoon finely shredded orange peel

⅓   cup snipped dried cranberries

1 Preheat oven to 350°F. Grease the bottom and ½ inch up the sides of an 8×4×2-inch loaf pan; set aside. In a large bowl stir together flour, flaxseed meal, baking powder, apple pie spice, and salt. Make a well in the center of flour mixture; set aside.

2 In a medium bowl beat egg whites with a fork. Stir in zucchini, sugar, oil, and orange peel. Add zucchini mixture all at once to flour mixture; stir just until moistened (batter should be lumpy). Fold in dried cranberries. Spoon batter into prepared loaf pan.

3 Bake for 50 to 55 minutes or until a toothpick inserted near center comes out clean. Cool in pan on a wire rack for 10 minutes. Remove bread from pan. Cool on wire rack. Wrap and store overnight before slicing. Makes 1 loaf (12 servings).

Cranberry and Orange Zucchini Bread

PREP: 25 minutes   **BAKE:** 50 minutes

COOL: 2 hours   **STAND:** overnight

OVEN: 350°F

NUTRITION FACTS per serving:

CALORIES 159
TOTAL FAT 6 g (0 g sat. fat)
CHOLESTEROL 0 mg
PROTEIN 3 g
CARBOHYDRATE 25 g
FIBER 1 g
SODIUM 105 mg

EXCHANGES 1 Starch, 0.5 Other Carbohydrates, 1 Fat

NUTRITION NOTE

Wheat germ, the embryo of a wheat kernel, is loaded with nutrients such as B vitamins, vitamin E, folate, magnesium, phosphorus, potassium, iron, and zinc. The germ also contains protein, fiber, and some fat.

Nonstick cooking spray

1½	cups all-purpose flour
1	cup whole bran cereal
2	tablespoons grated Parmesan cheese
1	tablespoon sugar
1	tablespoon snipped fresh basil, dill, rosemary, thyme, sage, or chives
½	teaspoon baking powder
¼	teaspoon baking soda
1	egg
1	cup buttermilk or sour fat-free milk*
¼	cup canola oil

Herb-Bran Muffins

PREP: 20 minutes   **BAKE:** 18 minutes

COOL: 5 minutes   **OVEN:** 400°F

NUTRITION FACTS per muffin:

CALORIES 132
TOTAL FAT 6 g (1 g sat. fat)
CHOLESTEROL 19 mg
PROTEIN 4 g
CARBOHYDRATE 18 g
FIBER 2 g
SODIUM 90 mg

EXCHANGES 1 Starch, 1 Fat

NUTRITION NOTE

Wheat bran, a concentrated source of fiber, is a good source of insoluble fiber, the type of fiber that contributes to digestive health.

1 Preheat oven to 400°F. Coat twelve 2½-inch muffin cups with nonstick cooking spray; set aside. In a large bowl stir together flour, bran cereal, Parmesan cheese, sugar, basil, baking powder, and baking soda. Make a well in the center of flour mixture; set aside.

2 In a medium bowl whisk together egg, buttermilk, and oil. Add egg mixture all at once to flour mixture; stir just until moistened (batter should be lumpy).

3 Spoon batter into prepared muffin cups, filling each two-thirds full. Bake for 18 to 20 minutes or until golden brown. Cool in muffin cups on a wire rack for 5 minutes. Remove muffins from muffin cups. Serve warm. Makes 12 muffins.

*To make 1 cup sour fat-free milk, place 1 tablespoon lemon juice or vinegar in a glass measuring cup. Add enough fat-free milk to make 1 cup total liquid; stir. Let stand for 5 minutes before using.

COOK'S TIP

Refrigerate extra muffins for another meal. To reheat, place a muffin on a microwave-safe plate. Microwave, uncovered, on 100% power (high) about 15 seconds or until warm.

1 cup all-purpose flour
¾ cup white whole wheat flour or whole wheat flour
2 teaspoons baking powder
1 to 2 teaspoons chili powder
¼ teaspoon salt
¼ teaspoon dried oregano, crushed
1 8-ounce carton light dairy sour cream
⅓ cup fat-free milk
Chili powder (optional)

1 Preheat oven to 425°F. Lightly grease a large baking sheet or line with parchment paper; set aside. In a medium bowl stir together all-purpose flour, whole wheat flour, baking powder, 1 to 2 teaspoons chili powder, salt, and oregano. Make a well in the center of the flour mixture.

2 In a small bowl whisk together sour cream and milk until smooth. Add sour cream mixture all at once to flour mixture; stir just until combined.

3 Using about ⅓ cup dough for each biscuit, drop dough into eight mounds onto prepared baking sheet, leaving about 2 inches between mounds. If desired, sprinkle with additional chili powder. Bake for 14 to 16 minutes or until golden brown. Serve warm. Makes 8 biscuits.

Southwestern Drop Biscuits

PREP: 20 minutes   **BAKE:** 14 minutes
OVEN: 425°F

NUTRITION FACTS per biscuit:

CALORIES 138
TOTAL FAT 3 g (2 g sat. fat)
CHOLESTEROL 10 mg
PROTEIN 4 g
CARBOHYDRATE 23 g
FIBER 1 g
SODIUM 191 mg

EXCHANGES 1.5 Starch, 0.5 Fat

Two-Cheese Garlic 'n' Herb Biscuits

PREP: 20 minutes   **BAKE:** 10 minutes
OVEN: 450°F

NUTRITION FACTS per biscuit:

CALORIES 127
TOTAL FAT 5 g (3 g sat. fat)
CHOLESTEROL 12 mg
PROTEIN 5 g
CARBOHYDRATE 17 g
FIBER 1 g
SODIUM 171 mg

EXCHANGES 1 Starch, 0.5 Medium-Fat Meat, 0.5 Fat

1	cup all-purpose flour
½	cup white whole wheat flour or whole wheat flour
1	tablespoon snipped fresh basil or 1 teaspoon dried basil, crushed
2	teaspoons baking powder
2	cloves garlic, minced
¼	teaspoon cream of tartar
⅛	teaspoon salt
2	ounces soft goat cheese (chèvre) or reduced-fat cream cheese (Neufchâtel)
2	tablespoons butter
¼	cup finely shredded Parmesan cheese (1 ounce)
½	cup fat-free milk

1 Preheat oven to 450°F. In a medium bowl stir together all-purpose flour, whole wheat flour, basil, baking powder, garlic, cream of tartar, and salt. Using a pastry blender, cut in goat cheese and butter until mixture resembles coarse crumbs. Stir in 3 tablespoons of the Parmesan cheese. Make a well in the center of the flour mixture. Add milk all at once; stir just until dough clings together.

2 Turn out dough on a lightly floured surface. Knead by folding and gently pressing dough for four to six strokes or until nearly smooth. Pat or lightly roll dough into an 8×6-inch rectangle.

3 Cut dough into nine rectangles. Sprinkle tops with remaining 1 tablespoon Parmesan cheese. Place rectangles 1 inch apart on an ungreased baking sheet. Bake for 10 to 12 minutes or until golden brown. Serve warm. Makes 9 biscuits.

Nonstick cooking spray

1   cup yellow cornmeal

¾   cup white whole wheat flour or
     whole wheat flour

2   tablespoons snipped fresh chives

2½ teaspoons baking powder

¾   teaspoon salt

2   eggs

1   cup fat-free milk

2   tablespoons honey

¾   cup coarsely shredded carrot
     (2 to 3 small)

½   cup finely chopped red
     sweet pepper

1 Preheat oven to 400°F. Lightly coat a 2-quart square baking dish with nonstick cooking spray; set aside. In a large bowl stir together cornmeal, flour, chives, baking powder, and salt; set aside.

2 In a medium bowl whisk together eggs, milk, and honey. Add egg mixture all at once to flour mixture; stir just until moistened. Fold in carrot and sweet pepper. Pour batter into prepared baking dish.

3 Bake for 25 to 30 minutes or until a toothpick inserted near center comes out clean. Cool in pan on a wire rack for 20 minutes. Serve warm. Makes 9 servings.

Garden Veggie Corn Bread

PREP: 20 minutes   **BAKE:** 25 minutes
COOL: 20 minutes   **OVEN:** 400°F

NUTRITION FACTS per serving:

CALORIES 139
TOTAL FAT 1 g (0 g sat. fat)
CHOLESTEROL 48 mg
PROTEIN 5 g
CARBOHYDRATE 31 g
FIBER 2 g
SODIUM 328 mg

EXCHANGES 2 Starch

NUTRITION NOTE

Cornmeal is available in several colors. Yellow cornmeal contains a bit more vitamin A thanks to beta-carotene, which also gives cornmeal its yellow color.

Nonstick cooking spray
¾ cup all-purpose flour
¾ cup cornmeal
¼ cup whole wheat flour
2 tablespoons sugar
2½ teaspoons baking powder
½ teaspoon salt
½ teaspoon ground cumin
½ of a 15-ounce can (¾ cup) cut sweet potatoes, lightly rinsed and drained
¾ cup fat-free milk
2 eggs
¼ cup canola oil
½ to 1 small canned chipotle chile pepper in adobo sauce*

Spicy Sweet Potato Corn Bread

PREP: 20 minutes **BAKE:** 20 minutes
COOL: 15 minutes **OVEN:** 400°F

NUTRITION FACTS per serving:

CALORIES 177
TOTAL FAT 7 g (1 g sat. fat)
CHOLESTEROL 43 mg
PROTEIN 4 g
CARBOHYDRATE 25 g
FIBER 2 g
SODIUM 207 mg

EXCHANGES 1.5 Starch, 1 Fat

1 Preheat oven to 400°F. Lightly coat a 9×1½-inch round baking pan or unheated 9- to 10-inch cast-iron skillet with nonstick cooking spray; set aside. In a large bowl stir together all-purpose flour, cornmeal, whole wheat flour, sugar, baking powder, salt, and cumin. Make a well in the center of flour mixture; set aside.

2 In a blender combine sweet potatoes, milk, eggs, oil, and chipotle pepper. Cover and blend until smooth. Add sweet potato mixture all at once to flour mixture; stir just until moistened. Pour batter into prepared baking pan.

3 Bake for 20 to 25 minutes or until a toothpick inserted near center comes out clean. Cool in pan on a wire rack about 15 minutes. Cut into wedges. Serve warm. Makes 10 servings.

*See handling note, p. 103.

Maple Sweet Potato Corn Bread: Prepare as directed, except omit the sugar, cumin, and chipotle chile pepper. Add 2 tablespoons pure maple syrup or maple-flavor syrup and ¼ teaspoon maple flavoring to the sweet potato mixture.

Per serving: 178 cal., 7 g total fat (1 g sat. fat), 43 mg chol., 205 mg sodium, 25 g carbo., 1 g fiber, 3 g pro. Exchanges: 1.5 Starch, 1 Fat

Citrus Sweet Potato Corn Bread: Prepare as directed, except omit the cumin and chipotle chile pepper. Add 1 teaspoon finely shredded orange peel and 1 teaspoon finely shredded lemon peel to the flour mixture.

Per serving: 177 cal., 7 g total fat (1 g sat. fat), 43 mg chol., 205 mg sodium, 25 g carbo., 2 g fiber, 3 g pro. Exchanges: 1.5 Starch, 1 Fat

1½ cups all-purpose flour
1 tablespoon sugar
1 package active dry yeast
2 teaspoons caraway seeds
1 teaspoon salt
½ teaspoon dried dill
¾ cup warm water (120°F to 130°F)
1 egg, lightly beaten
1 tablespoon butter, melted
¾ cup rye flour
  Water (optional)
  Caraway seeds (optional)

Caraway-Rye Batter Bread

PREP: 20 minutes **RISE:** 50 minutes
BAKE: 25 minutes **COOL:** 2 hours
OVEN: 375°F

NUTRITION FACTS per serving:

CALORIES 121
TOTAL FAT 2 g (1 g sat. fat)
CHOLESTEROL 24 mg
PROTEIN 4 g
CARBOHYDRATE 22 g
FIBER 2 g
SODIUM 249 mg

EXCHANGES 1.5 Starch

1 Grease a 1-quart casserole or an 8×1½-inch round baking pan; set aside. In a large bowl stir together 1 cup all-purpose flour, sugar, yeast, 2 teaspoons caraway seeds, salt, and dill. Add ¾ cup warm water, egg, and butter.

2 Beat with an electric mixer on low to medium speed for 30 seconds, scraping side of bowl constantly. Beat on high speed for 3 minutes. Using a wooden spoon, stir in rye flour and remaining ½ cup all-purpose flour (batter will be stiff).

3 Spoon batter into the prepared casserole, spreading to edge. Cover and let rise in a warm place until double in size (50 to 60 minutes). If desired, lightly brush top of loaf with water and sprinkle with additional caraway seeds.

4 Preheat oven to 375°F. Bake about 25 minutes or until bread is golden brown and sounds hollow when lightly tapped. Immediately remove bread from pan. Cool on a wire rack. Makes 1 loaf (10 servings).

COOK'S TIP

Rye flour contains less gluten than whole wheat or all-purpose flour. When baking with rye flour, combine it with a high-gluten flour so the bread will rise adequately.

Easy Oatmeal Bread

PREP: 25 minutes   **RISE:** 1¼ hours
BAKE: 40 minutes   **COOL:** 2 hours
OVEN: 350°F

NUTRITION FACTS per serving:

CALORIES 156
TOTAL FAT 2 g (0 g sat. fat)
CHOLESTEROL 18 mg
PROTEIN 5 g
CARBOHYDRATE 29 g
FIBER 2 g
SODIUM 113 mg

EXCHANGES 2 Starch

1   cup warm fat-free milk
     (105°F to 115°F)
¼   cup honey or packed brown sugar
1   package active dry yeast
½   teaspoon salt
1¾ cups bread flour or
     all-purpose flour
1   egg, lightly beaten
1   tablespoon canola oil
¾   cup whole wheat flour
½   cup rolled oats
     Nonstick cooking spray
     Water (optional)
     Rolled oats (optional)

1 In a large bowl combine milk, honey or brown sugar, yeast, and salt, stirring to dissolve yeast. Let stand for 5 minutes.

2 Add bread flour, egg, and oil to yeast mixture. Beat with an electric mixer on low to medium speed until combined. Beat on high speed for 3 minutes, scraping side of bowl occasionally. Using a wooden spoon, stir in whole wheat flour and ½ cup oats until combined. Cover and let rise in a warm place until double in size (45 to 60 minutes).

3 Lightly coat a 9×5×3-inch loaf pan with nonstick cooking spray. Stir down dough and spoon into prepared loaf pan. Cover and let rise in a warm place until double in size (about 30 minutes). If desired, lightly brush top of loaf with water and sprinkle with additional rolled oats.

4 Preheat oven to 350°F. Bake about 40 minutes or until bread is golden brown and sounds hollow when lightly tapped. Immediately remove bread from pan. Cool on a wire rack. Makes 12 servings.

1 cup Sourdough Starter (see page 86)
3½ to 4 cups all-purpose flour
1 package active dry yeast
1½ cups water
¼ cup honey
3 tablespoons canola oil
1½ teaspoons salt
1½ cups white whole wheat flour or whole wheat flour
¼ cup flaxseed meal or toasted wheat germ
2 teaspoons flaxseeds
½ teaspoon baking soda
   Water (optional)
   Flaxseeds (optional)
   Flaxseed meal (optional)

Honey-Flax Sourdough Bread

See page 86 for Sourdough Starter recipe.

PREP: 45 minutes   **STAND:** 30 minutes
RISE: 1¼ hours   **REST:** 10 minutes
BAKE: 30 minutes   **COOL:** 2 hours
OVEN: 375°F

NUTRITION FACTS per serving:

CALORIES 140
TOTAL FAT 2 g (0 g sat. fat)
CHOLESTEROL 0 mg
PROTEIN 4 g
CARBOHYDRATE 26 g
FIBER 2 g
SODIUM 173 mg

EXCHANGES 1.5 Starch

1 Measure Sourdough Starter; let stand at room temperature for 30 minutes. In a large bowl combine 2½ cups all-purpose flour and yeast; set aside. In a medium saucepan heat and stir 1½ cups water, honey, oil, and salt just until warm (120°F to 130°F). Add water mixture to yeast mixture; add Sourdough Starter. Beat with an electric mixer on low to medium speed for 30 seconds, scraping side of bowl constantly. Beat on high speed for 3 minutes. In a medium bowl combine ½ cup remaining all-purpose flour, whole wheat flour, ¼ cup flaxseed meal, 2 teaspoons flaxseeds, and baking soda; add to yeast mixture. Using a wooden spoon, stir until combined. Stir in as much of the remaining all-purpose flour as you can.

2 Turn out dough on a lightly floured surface. Knead in enough of the remaining all-purpose flour to make a moderately stiff dough that is smooth and elastic (6 to 8 minutes total). Shape dough into a ball. Place in a lightly greased bowl, turning once to grease surface. Cover and let rise in a warm place until double in size (45 to 60 minutes). Punch down dough. Turn out on a lightly floured surface. Divide dough in half. Cover; let rest for 10 minutes. Meanwhile, lightly grease two baking sheets.

3 Shape each dough portion by gently pulling it into a ball, tucking edges underneath. Place dough balls on prepared baking sheets. Flatten each dough ball slightly to about 6 inches in diameter. Using a sharp knife, make crisscross slashes across tops of loaves. Cover; let rise in a warm place until nearly double in size (about 30 minutes). If desired, lightly brush tops of loaves with water and sprinkle with additional flaxseeds and flaxseed meal.

4 Preheat oven to 375°F. Bake for 30 to 35 minutes or until bread sounds hollow when lightly tapped. (If necessary to prevent overbrowning, cover loosely with foil for the last 10 minutes of baking.) Remove bread from baking sheets. Cool on wire racks. Makes 2 loaves (24 servings).

Parmesan-Rosemary Baguettes

PREP: 25 minutes   **STAND:** 10 minutes

REST: 10 minutes   **RISE:** 30 minutes

BAKE: 10 minutes   **COOL:** 2 hours

OVEN: 375°F

NUTRITION FACTS per serving:

CALORIES 121

TOTAL FAT 2 g (1 g sat. fat)

CHOLESTEROL 1 mg

PROTEIN 4 g

CARBOHYDRATE 21 g

FIBER 1 g

SODIUM 175 mg

EXCHANGES 1.5 Starch

*If you don't have baguette pans, grease two 8×4×2-inch loaf pans. Shape each portion of dough by gently patting and pinching it into a loaf, tucking edges under (use floured hands if dough is too sticky). Continue as directed, except bake loaves for 30 to 35 minutes.

2 cups warm water (105°F to 115°F)

2 packages active dry yeast

1 tablespoon sugar

2 cups white whole wheat flour or whole wheat flour

½ cup finely shredded Parmesan cheese (2 ounces)

3 tablespoons olive oil

1 tablespoon snipped fresh rosemary or 1 teaspoon dried rosemary, crushed

1½ teaspoons salt

3 to 3½ cups bread flour

  Water (optional)

  Finely shredded Parmesan cheese (optional)

  Snipped fresh rosemary (optional)

1 In a large bowl combine 2 cups warm water, yeast, and sugar. Let stand about 10 minutes or until foamy. Meanwhile, grease two baguette pans;* set aside.

2 Using a wooden spoon, stir whole wheat flour, ½ cup Parmesan cheese, oil, 1 tablespoon rosemary, and salt into yeast mixture. Stir in as much of the bread flour as you can. Turn out dough onto a lightly floured surface. Knead in enough of the remaining bread flour to make a moderately soft dough that is smooth and elastic (3 to 5 minutes total). Divide dough in half. Cover; let rest for 10 minutes.

3 Using floured hands, gently shape each dough portion into a 16-inch-long baguette. If desired, pinch and slightly pull ends to taper them. Place shaped dough, seam sides down, in baguette pans. Cover loosely and let rise in a warm place until nearly double in size (about 30 minutes). If desired, lightly brush loaves with additional water and sprinkle with additional Parmesan cheese and rosemary.

4 Preheat oven to 375°F. Using a sharp knife, make three or four diagonal cuts about ¼ inch deep across top of each loaf. Bake for 28 to 30 minutes or until bread sounds hollow when lightly tapped. (If necessary to prevent overbrowning, cover loosely with foil for the last 5 to 10 minutes of baking.) Immediately remove bread from pans. Cool on wire racks. Makes 2 loaves (24 servings).

3 to 3½ cups all-purpose flour

1 package active dry yeast

1 teaspoon salt

1¼ cups warm water (120°F to 130°F)

2 tablespoons olive oil

½ cup white whole wheat flour or whole wheat flour

⅔ cup finely shredded Swiss cheese

⅓ cup sliced almonds

½ teaspoon coarse sea salt

½ teaspoon cracked black pepper

1 In a large bowl stir together 1¼ cups all-purpose flour, yeast, and 1 teaspoon salt. Add the warm water and 1 tablespoon oil. Beat with an electric mixer on low to medium speed for 30 seconds, scraping side of bowl constantly. Beat on high speed for 3 minutes. Using a wooden spoon, stir in whole wheat flour and as much of the remaining all-purpose flour as you can.

2 Turn out dough on a lightly floured surface. Knead in enough of the remaining all-purpose flour to make a stiff dough that is smooth and elastic (8 to 10 minutes total). Shape dough into a ball. Place in a lightly greased bowl, turning once to grease surface. Cover and let rise in a warm place until double in size (about 1 hour).

3 Lightly grease two baking sheets; set aside. Punch down dough. Turn out on a lightly floured surface. Divide dough in half. Shape each dough portion into a ball. Place on prepared baking sheets. Cover; let rest for 10 minutes. Flatten each ball into a circle about 9 inches in diameter. Using your fingers, make ½-inch-deep indentations every 2 inches in dough (dust your fingers with flour if necessary). Brush with remaining 1 tablespoon oil. Sprinkle with Swiss cheese, almonds, coarse salt, and pepper. Cover; let rise in a warm place until nearly double in size (about 20 minutes).

4 Preheat oven to 375°F. Bake for 25 to 30 minutes or until golden brown. Remove bread from baking sheets. Cool on wire racks. Makes 2 rounds (24 servings).

Swiss Cheese-Almond Flatbread

PREP: 40 minutes   **RISE:** 1 hour 20 minutes

REST: 10 minutes   **BAKE:** 25 minutes

OVEN: 375°F   **COOL:** 1 hour

NUTRITION FACTS per serving:

CALORIES 97
TOTAL FAT 3 g (1 g sat. fat)
CHOLESTEROL 3 mg
PROTEIN 3 g
CARBOHYDRATE 14 g
FIBER 1 g
SODIUM 138 mg

EXCHANGES 1 Starch, 0.5 Fat

2¾ to 3¼ cups all-purpose flour
½ cup warm water (105°F to 115°F)
1 teaspoon active dry yeast
1 cup warm water (120°F to 130°F)
⅓ cup snipped dried tomatoes (not oil pack)
1 cup white whole wheat flour or whole wheat flour
½ cup crumbled reduced-fat feta cheese (2 ounces)
1 clove garlic, minced
1 teaspoon salt
1 tablespoon olive oil
1 tablespoon grated Parmesan cheese

Dried Tomato-Feta Focaccia

PREP: 35 minutes **STAND:** 8 hours
RISE: 1 hour **REST:** 30 minutes
BAKE: 15 minutes **COOL:** 15 minutes
OVEN: 475°F

NUTRITION FACTS per serving:

CALORIES 166
TOTAL FAT 2 g (1 g sat. fat)
CHOLESTEROL 2 mg
PROTEIN 6 g
CARBOHYDRATE 30 g
FIBER 2 g
SODIUM 311 mg

EXCHANGES 2 Starch

1 In a large bowl combine ½ cup all-purpose flour, ½ cup warm water, and yeast. Beat with a wooden spoon until smooth. Cover loosely with plastic wrap. Let stand at room temperature for at least 8 hours or overnight to ferment.

2 In a small bowl combine 1 cup warm water and dried tomatoes. Let stand for 5 minutes. Gradually stir tomato mixture into the yeast mixture. Stir in whole wheat flour, feta cheese, garlic, and salt. Stir in as much of the remaining all-purpose flour as you can. Turn out dough onto a lightly floured surface. Knead in enough of the remaining all-purpose flour to make a stiff dough that is smooth and elastic (8 to 10 minutes total). Shape dough into a ball. Place in a lightly greased bowl, turning once to grease surface. Cover and let rise in a warm place until double in size (about 1 hour).

3 Punch down dough. Turn out on a well-floured baking sheet. Place a large bowl upside down over dough to cover it; let rest for 30 minutes.

4 Preheat oven and a bread stone* to 475°F. Shape dough on the baking sheet into an 11-inch circle by gently pulling and pressing with your fingertips, taking care to keep dough air bubbles intact. Using your fingers, make ½-inch-deep indentations every 2 inches in dough (dust your fingers with flour if necessary). Brush dough with oil; sprinkle with Parmesan cheese. Carefully slide dough from baking sheet to preheated bread stone.

*If you don't have a bread stone, preheat a greased baking sheet in the oven for 5 minutes (do not preheat longer). Carefully transfer the shaped dough to the preheated baking sheet.

5 Bake about 15 minutes or until golden brown, checking after 8 minutes and using a sharp knife to pop any large air bubbles. Using a large spatula, transfer focaccia to a wire rack. Cool about 15 minutes. Cut into 12 wedges. Serve warm. Makes 12 servings.

Nonstick cooking spray

1 medium tomato, seeded and chopped (⅔ cup)

⅓ cup reduced-fat shredded mozzarella cheese

1 clove garlic, minced

½ teaspoon dried basil or Italian seasoning, crushed

1 16-ounce loaf frozen whole wheat bread dough, thawed

Fat-free milk

2 tablespoons finely shredded Parmesan cheese

1 Lightly coat an 8×8×2-inch baking pan with nonstick cooking spray; set aside. In a small bowl combine tomato, mozzarella cheese, garlic, and basil; set aside.

2 Divide bread dough into 12 portions. On a lightly floured surface flatten each dough portion to a 3-inch round. Spoon about 1 tablespoon of the tomato mixture into center of each dough round; shape dough around tomato mixture into a ball, pinching the dough together to seal.

3 Place rolls, seam sides down, in the prepared baking pan. Cover and let rise in a warm place until nearly double in size (30 to 45 minutes). Lightly brush tops of rolls with milk and sprinkle with Parmesan cheese.

4 Preheat oven to 375°F. Bake about 20 minutes or until tops are golden brown. Cool in pan on a wire rack for 20 minutes. Serve warm. Makes 12 rolls.

See page 86 for recipe variations (Seeded Pull-Apart Rolls and Gremolata-Stuffed Parker House Rolls).

Italian-Style Dinner Rolls

PREP: 25 minutes **RISE:** 30 minutes

BAKE: 20 minutes **COOL:** 20 minutes

OVEN: 375°F

NUTRITION FACTS per roll:

CALORIES 110
TOTAL FAT 2 g (0 g sat. fat)
CHOLESTEROL 2 mg
PROTEIN 5 g
CARBOHYDRATE 19 g
FIBER 2 g
SODIUM 243 mg

EXCHANGES 1.5 Starch

Berry-Cream Tea Braid

PREP: 30 minutes **RISE:** 45 minutes
BAKE: 25 minutes **COOL:** 15 minutes
OVEN: 350°F

NUTRITION FACTS per serving:

CALORIES 111
TOTAL FAT 2 g (1 g sat. fat)
CHOLESTEROL 4 mg
PROTEIN 5 g
CARBOHYDRATE 19 g
FIBER 2 g
SODIUM 214 mg
EXCHANGES 1.5 Starch

COOK'S TIP

When selecting berries look for bright color. Avoid those with mold, soft spots, or discoloration. When berries come in a box, tip the box to see whether the berries move freely; if they stick together, chances are they're moldy.

1 16-ounce loaf frozen whole wheat bread dough, thawed
½ of an 8-ounce tub light cream cheese spread with strawberries, softened
½ cup fresh pitted tart red or dark sweet cherries
½ cup fresh blueberries
½ cup fresh raspberries
1 egg white
1 tablespoon water
1 recipe Orange Glaze (optional)

1 Line a large baking sheet with parchment paper or foil. If using foil, lightly grease foil. Set aside.

2 On a lightly floured surface roll bread dough into a 16×9-inch rectangle. If dough is difficult to roll out, let it rest for 5 to 10 minutes. Transfer dough rectangle to prepared baking sheet. Spread cream cheese lengthwise down the center third of the dough, leaving ½ inch unfilled along each end. Top cream cheese with cherries, blueberries, and raspberries.

3 On both long sides make 3-inch cuts from the edges toward the center, spacing the cuts 1 inch apart. Starting at an end, alternately fold opposite strips of dough, at an angle, across the filling. Slightly press ends together in center to seal. Cover and let rise in a warm place for 45 minutes.

4 Preheat oven to 350°F. In a small bowl whisk together egg white and water; brush mixture over braid. Bake for 25 to 30 minutes or until top and bottom are golden brown. Cool on baking sheet on a wire rack for 15 minutes. Cut crosswise into slices. If desired, drizzle with Orange Glaze. Serve warm.
Makes 14 to 16 servings.

Orange Glaze: In a small bowl stir together ¾ cup powdered sugar and ¼ teaspoon finely shredded orange peel. Stir in enough orange juice or fat-free milk (3 to 4 teaspoons) to make drizzling consistency.

- 2½ to 2¾ cups all-purpose flour
- 1 package active dry yeast
- 1¼ cups water
- 5 tablespoons sugar
- 3 tablespoons pareve margarine
- 1 teaspoon salt
- 2 eggs
- 1½ cups white whole wheat flour
- 1 tablespoon shredded orange peel
- 3 tablespoons unsweetened cocoa powder
  Nonstick cooking spray
- 1 egg white, lightly beaten
- 1 recipe Orange Drizzle

1 In a large bowl stir together 2 cups all-purpose flour and yeast; set aside. In a small saucepan heat and stir water, 2 tablespoons sugar, margarine, and salt just until warm (120°F to 130°F) and margarine almost melts. Add water mixture to yeast mixture; add 2 eggs. Beat with an electric mixer on low to medium speed for 30 seconds, scraping side of bowl constantly. Beat on high speed for 3 minutes. Using a wooden spoon, stir in whole wheat flour.

2 Transfer half of the batter to a medium bowl; stir in orange peel. Turn out onto a lightly floured surface. Knead in enough of the remaining all-purpose flour (you will not use all of the flour) to make a moderately soft dough that is smooth and elastic (3 to 5 minutes total). Shape dough into a ball. Place in a lightly greased small bowl, turning once to grease surface. Cover and set aside.

3 To the remaining batter stir in 3 tablespoons sugar and cocoa powder. Turn out onto a lightly floured surface. Knead in enough all-purpose flour to make a moderately soft dough that is smooth and elastic (3 to 5 minutes total). Shape dough into a ball. Place in a lightly greased small bowl, turning once. Cover dough. Let both portions of dough rise in a warm place until double in size (1 to 1¼ hours).

4 Punch down dough. Turn out on a lightly floured surface. Cover; let rest for 10 minutes. Lightly coat a large baking sheet with nonstick cooking spray; set aside.

5 Roll each dough portion into a 22-inch-long rope. Place ropes side by side. Twist ropes together several times. Place twist on prepared baking sheet. Shape twist into a circle, leaving a 3-inch hole in center. Pinch ends together to seal. Crumple a piece of foil into a 2-inch ball; lightly coat with nonstick cooking spray. Place foil ball in the center of the dough ring. Cover and let rise in a warm place until nearly double in size (30 to 40 minutes).

6 Preheat oven to 375°F. Brush bread with egg white. Bake for 25 to 30 minutes or until bread sounds hollow when lightly tapped. (If necessary to prevent overbrowning, cover loosely with foil for the last 10 minutes of baking.) Immediately remove ball of foil. Remove bread from baking sheet. Cool on a wire rack. Before serving, top with Orange Drizzle. Makes 24 servings.

Chocolate-Orange Challah Wreath

PREP: 45 minutes **RISE:** 1½ hours
REST: 10 minutes **BAKE:** 25 minutes
COOL: 2 hours **OVEN:** 375°F

NUTRITION FACTS per serving:

CALORIES 120
TOTAL FAT 2 g (0 g sat. fat)
CHOLESTEROL 18 mg
PROTEIN 3 g
CARBOHYDRATE 22 g
FIBER 1 g
SODIUM 123 mg
EXCHANGES 1.5 Starch

Orange Drizzle: In a small bowl stir together ¾ cup powdered sugar and enough orange juice or fat-free milk (3 to 4 teaspoons) to reach drizzling consistency.

Cranberry-Maple Cinnamon Rolls

PREP: 30 minutes   **STAND:** 10 minutes
RISE: 1½ hours   **REST:** 10 minutes
BAKE: 25 minutes   **COOL:** 5 minutes
OVEN: 375°F

NUTRITION FACTS per roll:

CALORIES 180
TOTAL FAT 4 g (1 g sat. fat)
CHOLESTEROL 18 mg
PROTEIN 5 g
CARBOHYDRATE 33 g
FIBER 2 g
SODIUM 180 mg

EXCHANGES 2 Starch, 0.5 Fat

Maple-Brown Sugar Icing: In a small bowl combine 2 tablespoons packed brown sugar and 1 tablespoon very hot water; stir to dissolve brown sugar. Stir in ¾ cup powdered sugar and ¼ teaspoon maple flavoring. Stir in enough fat-free milk (1 to 2 teaspoons) to make drizzling consistency.

1   cup fat-free milk
2   tablespoons pure maple syrup
2   tablespoons butter
1   teaspoon salt
¼   cup warm water (110°F to 115°F)
1   package active dry yeast
1   egg, lightly beaten
1¼   cups white whole wheat flour or whole wheat flour
2½   to 3 cups all-purpose flour
⅓   cup packed brown sugar
2   teaspoons ground cinnamon
¼   cup snipped dried cranberries
¼   cup chopped pecans, toasted
1   recipe Maple-Brown Sugar Icing (optional)

1 In a small saucepan heat and stir milk, maple syrup, butter, and salt just until warm (110°F to 115°F); set aside. In a large bowl combine warm water and yeast; let stand for 10 minutes. Add milk mixture and egg to yeast mixture. Stir in whole wheat flour. Stir in as much of the all-purpose flour as you can.

2 Turn out dough on a lightly floured surface. Knead in enough all-purpose flour to make a moderately soft dough that is smooth and elastic (3 to 5 minutes total). Shape dough into a ball. Place in a lightly greased bowl, turning once to grease surface. Cover and let rise in a warm place until double in size (about 1 hour). Punch down dough. Turn out on a lightly floured surface. Cover; let rest for 10 minutes.

3 Meanwhile, lightly grease a 13×9×2-inch baking pan; set aside. In a small bowl combine brown sugar and cinnamon. Stir in dried cranberries and pecans.

4 Roll dough into a 15×8-inch rectangle. Sprinkle with pecan mixture, leaving 1 inch unfilled along one of the long sides. Starting from the long filled side, roll up rectangle. Pinch dough to seal seam; slice into 15 equal pieces. Arrange pieces, cut sides up, in prepared baking pan. Cover and let rise in a warm place until nearly double in size (about 30 minutes).

5 Preheat oven to 375°F. Bake for 25 minutes or until golden brown. Cool in pan on a wire rack for 5 minutes. Remove rolls from pan. If desired, drizzle with Maple-Brown Sugar Icing. Serve warm. Makes 15 rolls.

Nonstick cooking spray

¼ cup flaxseed meal or toasted wheat germ

3 tablespoons sugar

2 teaspoons ground cinnamon

1 16-ounce loaf frozen whole wheat bread dough, thawed

½ cup Cream Cheese Frosting

1 Line a large baking sheet with foil. Lightly coat foil with nonstick cooking spray; set aside. In a small bowl combine flaxseed meal, sugar, and cinnamon. Spread sugar mixture on a piece of waxed paper; set aside.

2 Divide bread dough into 24 portions. On a lightly floured surface, roll each dough portion into an 8-inch-long rope.* Lightly brush dough ropes with a little water. Roll dough ropes in sugar mixture to coat.

3 Place two ropes side by side on prepared baking sheet. Twist ropes together several times and pinch ends together to seal. Repeat with remaining ropes to make 12 twists, placing twists 2 inches apart on baking sheet. Cover and let rise in a warm place until nearly double in size and dough feels light when touched (30 to 45 minutes).

4 Preheat oven to 375°F. Bake for 12 to 15 minutes or until golden brown. Remove twists from baking sheet. Cool on a wire rack for 5 minutes. Frost or drizzle** with Cream Cheese Frosting. Serve warm. Makes 12 sticks.

*Dough ropes will shrink after shaping. Roll all of the ropes, letting each one rest while rolling the others. Then reroll each rope to desired length.

**To drizzle frosting, place it in a resealable heavy plastic bag; seal. Cut a small piece off of one corner of the bag; pipe frosting.

Cinnamon Buns: Prepare as directed, except do not twist dough ropes together. For each bun, place two ropes side by side on prepared baking sheet. Coil ropes together into a flat spiral. Pinch ends of ropes to seal. Continue as directed.

Frosted Cinnamon Sticks

PREP: 40 minutes   **RISE:** 30 minutes

BAKE: 12 minutes   **COOL:** 5 minutes

OVEN: 375°F

NUTRITION FACTS per stick:

CALORIES 171
TOTAL FAT 3 g (1 g sat. fat)
CHOLESTEROL 2 mg
PROTEIN 5 g
CARBOHYDRATE 32 g
FIBER 2 g
SODIUM 224 mg

EXCHANGES 1.5 Starch, 0.5 Other Carbohydrates

Cream Cheese Frosting: In a medium bowl combine one-fourth of an 8-ounce package reduced-fat cream cheese (Neufchâtel), softened; ½ teaspoon vanilla; and, if desired, ¼ teaspoon butter flavoring. Beat with an electric mixer on medium speed until smooth. Gradually beat in 1½ cups powdered sugar. Beat in 1 to 2 teaspoons fat-free milk to make frosting of drizzling consistency. Makes about ¾ cup.

Continued from page 81

Italian-Style Dinner Roll Variations

Seeded Pull-Apart Rolls: Lightly grease a 10-inch fluted tube pan; set aside. In a shallow dish combine 1 egg white and 1 tablespoon water. In a small bowl combine ¼ cup flaxseeds; 3 tablespoons sesame seeds, toasted; 2 tablespoons poppy seeds; and 1 tablespoon cumin seeds, toasted.

Divide one 16-ounce loaf frozen whole wheat bread dough, thawed, into 36 portions. Roll each portion of dough into a ball. Roll each ball in egg white mixture, allowing excess to drip off. Roll in seed mixture to coat. Place coated rolls in prepared tube pan. Cover and let rise in a warm place until nearly double in size (30 to 60 minutes).

Preheat oven to 375°F. Bake for 20 to 25 minutes or until rolls sound hollow when lightly tapped. Invert onto a wire rack. Serve slightly warm or cool. Makes 12 servings.

Per roll: 140 cal., 5 g total fat (0 g sat. fat), 0 mg chol., 216 mg sodium, 20 g carbo., 3 g fiber, 6 g pro.

Exchanges: 1.5 Starch, 0.5 Fat

Gremolata-Stuffed Parker House Rolls: Lightly grease a baking sheet; set aside. In a small bowl combine ½ cup snipped fresh flat-leaf parsley, 2 tablespoons finely chopped walnuts or pecans, 1 tablespoon finely shredded lemon peel, and 4 to 6 cloves garlic, minced; set aside.

Divide one 16-ounce loaf frozen whole wheat bread dough, thawed, into 16 portions. On a lightly floured surface flatten each dough portion to a 3-inch round. Using the dull edge of a table knife, make an off-center crease in each dough round. Spoon about 2 teaspoons of the parsley mixture onto the small side of each round. Fold larger side over parsley mixture along the crease; press folded edge firmly. Place rolls, large halves up, 2 to 3 inches apart on prepared baking sheet. Cover and let rise in a warm place until nearly double in size (30 to 45 minutes).

Preheat oven to 375°F. Bake for 12 to 15 minutes or until golden brown. Serve warm. Makes 16 rolls.

Per roll: 83 cal., 2 g total fat (0 g sat. fat), 0 mg chol., 159 mg sodium, 14 g carbo., 1 g fiber, 4 g pro.

Exchanges: 1 Starch

Continued from page 77

Honey-Flax Sourdough Bread

Sourdough Starter: Dissolve 1 package active dry yeast in ½ cup warm water (105°F to 115°F). Add 2 cups all-purpose flour, 2 cups warm water (105°F to 115°F), and 1 tablespoon honey. Using a wooden spoon, beat until smooth. Cover with 100%-cotton cheesecloth. Let stand at room temperature (75°F to 85°F) for 5 to 10 days or until mixture has a fermented aroma and vigorous bubbling stops, stirring two or three times a day. (Fermentation time depends on room temperature; a warmer room will hasten the fermentation process.) To store, transfer Sourdough Starter to a 1-quart plastic container. Cover and chill.

To use, stir starter. Measure amount of cold starter called for in recipe; bring to room temperature. Replenish starter after each use. For each 1 cup starter removed, stir ¾ cup all-purpose flour, ¾ cup water, and 1 teaspoon honey into remaining starter. Cover with cheesecloth; let stand at room temperature about 1 day or until bubbly. Cover with lid; chill for later use. If starter is not used within 10 days, stir in 1 teaspoon honey. Continue to add 1 teaspoon honey every 10 days unless starter is replenished.

Sandwiches & Wraps

4   6-inch whole wheat
       hoagie rolls, split
     Olive oil nonstick cooking spray
10   ounces thinly sliced cooked
       roast beef
½   cup fresh basil leaves or fresh
       baby spinach
12   refrigerated mango slices,
       well drained
1   teaspoon black pepper
¼   cup semisoft goat cheese (chèvre)
       or 4 ounces provolone cheese,
       sliced

1 To assemble sandwiches, lightly coat outsides
of hoagie rolls with nonstick cooking spray.
Turn roll bottoms coated sides down; divide roast
beef among roll bottoms. Top each with some
basil and 3 mango slices. Sprinkle with pepper.
Turn roll tops coated sides down; spread each
with goat cheese. Place on sandwiches, cheese
sides down.

2 Preheat an electric sandwich press, panini
griddle, or covered indoor grill according to
manufacturer's directions. (Or coat an unheated
grill pan or large skillet with nonstick cooking
spray. Preheat over low to medium-low heat for
1 to 2 minutes.) Add sandwiches in batches, if
necessary. If using sandwich press, panini griddle,
or covered indoor grill, close lid and grill for 4 or
5 minutes or until rolls are toasted and cheese
melts. (If using grill pan or skillet, place a heavy
skillet on sandwiches. Cook over medium-low heat
for 7 to 10 minutes or until bottoms are toasted.
Carefully remove top skillet, which may be hot.
Turn sandwiches and top again with the skillet.
Cook for 7 to 10 minutes more or until rolls are
toasted and cheese melts.) Makes 4 servings.

Turkey-Sweet Pepper Panini: Prepare as
above, except substitute thinly sliced turkey
breast for the roast beef and ½ cup bottled
roasted red sweet peppers, drained and cut
into strips, for the mango.

Per serving: 306 cal., 6 g total fat (2 g sat. fat),
42 mg chol., 1,277 mg sodium, 47 g carbo., 3 g
fiber, 17 g pro. Exchanges: 3 Starch,
2 Very Lean Meat

Roast Beef-Mango Panini

PREP: 20 minutes

COOK: 4 minutes per batch

NUTRITION FACTS per serving:

- -

CALORIES 381
TOTAL FAT 5 g (3 g sat. fat)
CHOLESTEROL 35 mg
PROTEIN 20 g
CARBOHYDRATE 61 g
FIBER 2 g
SODIUM 1,042 mg

EXCHANGES 3 Starch, 1 Fruit, 2 Very Lean Meat

Chipotle-BBQ Steak Sandwiches

PREP: 25 minutes   **MARINATE:** 4 to 6 hours
GRILL: 17 minutes

NUTRITION FACTS per serving:

CALORIES 378
TOTAL FAT 9 g (3 g sat. fat)
CHOLESTEROL 35 mg
PROTEIN 25 g
CARBOHYDRATE 47 g
FIBER 4 g
SODIUM 1,030 mg

EXCHANGES 2 Starch, 2.5 Lean Meat

COOK'S TIP

Avoid marinating meat for longer than the recipe suggests. Overmarinating cuts such as flank steak breaks down the tissue and causes meat to become tough rather than tender.

1 8-ounce can tomato sauce with roasted garlic or one 8-ounce can tomato sauce plus 1 clove garlic, minced
3 tablespoons tomato paste
2 tablespoons water
1 tablespoon Dijon-style mustard
1 tablespoon Worcestershire sauce
2 teaspoons honey
1 teaspoon finely chopped chipotle chile peppers in adobo sauce*
1 12-ounce beef flank steak
1 medium green sweet pepper, seeded and quartered
4 ½-inch-thick slices sweet onion (such as Vidalia, Walla Walla, or Maui)
   Nonstick cooking spray
4 ciabatta rolls, split and toasted

1 For marinade, in a small bowl combine tomato sauce, tomato paste, water, mustard, Worcestershire sauce, honey, and chile peppers. Set aside. Trim fat from steak. Score both sides of steak in a diamond pattern by making shallow diagonal cuts at 1-inch intervals. Place steak in a large resealable plastic bag. Pour marinade over steak in bag. Seal bag; turn to coat steak. Marinate steak in the refrigerator for 4 to 6 hours, turning bag occasionally.

2 Drain steak, reserving marinade. Lightly coat sweet pepper quarters and onion slices with nonstick cooking spray.

3 For a charcoal grill, place steak, sweet pepper quarters, and onion slices on the rack of an uncovered grill directly over medium coals. Grill until steak is medium doneness (160°F) and vegetables are tender, turning all once halfway through grilling. Allow 17 to 21 minutes for the steak and 8 to 12 minutes for the vegetables. (For a gas grill, preheat grill. Reduce heat to medium. Place steak, sweet pepper quarters, and onion slices on grill rack over heat. Cover and grill as above.)

4 Meanwhile, for BBQ sauce, pour reserved marinade into a small saucepan. Bring to boiling; reduce heat. Simmer, uncovered, about 5 minutes or until desired consistency.

5 Thinly slice steak across the grain. Thinly slice sweet pepper quarters lengthwise. Place steak slices and sweet pepper strips on the bottom halves of ciabatta rolls. Top with onion slices. Spoon BBQ sauce on onions. Add ciabatta roll tops. Makes 4 servings.

*See handling note, page 103.

- ½ cup low-fat plain yogurt
- 1 teaspoon lemon juice
- 2 cloves garlic, minced
- ¼ teaspoon salt
- 12 ounces lean ground beef
- 1 tablespoon snipped fresh oregano or 1 teaspoon dried oregano, crushed
- ¾ teaspoon salt
- ⅛ to ¼ teaspoon cayenne pepper
- 4 large whole wheat pita bread rounds
- 8 lettuce leaves
- 2 medium red and/or yellow tomatoes, sliced

1 Preheat oven to 350°F. For sauce, in a small bowl combine yogurt, lemon juice, half of the garlic, and ¼ teaspoon salt. Set aside.

2 For meatballs, in a medium bowl combine ground beef, oregano, ¾ teaspoon salt, cayenne pepper, and remaining garlic; mix well. Form beef mixture into 24 meatballs, each about 1 inch in diameter. Place meatballs in a 15×10×1-inch baking pan.

3 Bake meatballs, uncovered, about 20 minutes or until cooked through.

4 Cut pita rounds in half crosswise; open pita halves to make pockets. Line pita pockets with lettuce leaves. Fill pitas with tomato slices and meatballs. Serve with sauce. Makes 8 servings.

Meatball Pitas

PREP: 25 minutes   **BAKE:** 20 minutes
OVEN: 350°F

NUTRITION FACTS per serving:

CALORIES 180
TOTAL FAT 5 g (2 g sat. fat)
CHOLESTEROL 29 mg
PROTEIN 13 g
CARBOHYDRATE 21 g
FIBER 3 g
SODIUM 508 mg

EXCHANGES 1 Starch, 1.5 Lean Meat, 0.5 Vegetable

NUTRITION NOTE

When shopping for ground beef, look for 95% to 98% lean. Although a little fat is necessary for flavor and moistness, cut it down to the smallest amount possible.

3 tablespoons bottled reduced-calorie Thousand Island salad dressing

1 tablespoon cider vinegar

½ teaspoon caraway seeds

3 cups packaged shredded cabbage with carrot (coleslaw mix)

8 slices pumpernickel or dark rye bread

Nonstick cooking spray

6 ounces thinly sliced deli roast beef

4 slices reduced-fat Swiss cheese (3 to 4 ounces)

Fresh Reubens

PREP: 15 minutes

BROIL: 3 minutes

NUTRITION FACTS per serving:

CALORIES 330
TOTAL FAT 10 g (4 g sat. fat)
CHOLESTEROL 35 mg
PROTEIN 21 g
CARBOHYDRATE 37 g
FIBER 5 g
SODIUM 1,081 mg

EXCHANGES 2.5 Starch, 2 Medium-Fat Meat, 0.5 Vegetable

1 Preheat broiler. In a medium bowl combine salad dressing, vinegar, and caraway seeds. Add cabbage; toss to coat. Set aside.

2 Lightly coat bread slices with nonstick cooking spray; arrange bread slices on a large baking sheet. Broil 4 to 5 inches from heat for 2 to 3 minutes or until bread is toasted, turning once. Transfer 4 of the bread slices to a wire rack; set aside.

3 Arrange beef on bread slices on baking sheet. Top with cheese. Broil for 1 to 2 minutes or until cheese is melted. Spoon cabbage mixture on top of cheese. Top with reserved bread slices. Makes 4 servings.

3 tablespoons light mayonnaise or salad dressing

1 tablespoon balsamic vinegar

1 clove garlic, minced

4 oval multigrain wraps

6 ounces thinly sliced cooked ham

2 cups fresh baby spinach

1 medium pear, cored, quartered, and thinly sliced

1 ounce Parmesan cheese, shaved (optional)

Nonstick cooking spray

1 In a small bowl stir together mayonnaise, balsamic vinegar, and garlic. Spread mayonnaise mixture on one side of each wrap. Divide ham, spinach, pear slices, and, if desired, shaved Parmesan cheese among wraps on top of mayonnaise mixture, arranging ingredients on only one half of each wrap. Fold wraps in half.

2 Lightly coat an unheated electric sandwich press, panini griddle, covered indoor electric grill, grill pan, or large nonstick skillet with nonstick cooking spray. Preheat sandwich press, panini griddle, or grill according to manufacturer's directions. (Or heat grill pan or skillet over medium heat.) Add sandwiches in batches. If using sandwich press, griddle, or covered indoor grill, close lid and grill for 2 to 3 minutes or until bread is toasted. (If using grill pan or skillet, place a heavy skillet on top of sandwiches. Cook over medium heat for 1 to 2 minutes or until bottoms are toasted. Carefully remove top skillet, which may be hot. Turn sandwiches and top again with skillet. Cook for 1 to 2 minutes more or until toasted.) If desired, cut sandwiches in half. Makes 4 servings.

COOK'S TIP

For all the flavor without all the calories, blend flavorful mix-ins such as vinegar and fresh herbs with low-fat mayonnaise.

Pressed Ham Sandwiches with Balsamic Mayo

PREP: 25 minutes

COOK: 2 to 3 minutes per batch

NUTRITION FACTS per serving:

CALORIES 230

TOTAL FAT 10 g (2 g sat. fat)

CHOLESTEROL 28 mg

PROTEIN 17 g

CARBOHYDRATE 27 g

FIBER 11 g

SODIUM 1,078 mg

EXCHANGES 2 Starch, 1.5 Lean Meat, 0.5 Fat

Mushroom and Ham Fold-Overs

PREP: 25 minutes **BAKE:** 8 minutes
OVEN: 375°F

NUTRITION FACTS per serving:

CALORIES 284
TOTAL FAT 13 g (4 g sat. fat)
CHOLESTEROL 34 mg
PROTEIN 25 g
CARBOHYDRATE 26 g
FIBER 11 g
SODIUM 1,232 mg

EXCHANGES 1.5 Starch, 2.5 Medium-Fat
Meat, 1 Vegetable

1	tablespoon olive oil
2	cups sliced fresh mushrooms
1	large red or green sweet pepper, seeded and chopped
2	teaspoons snipped fresh oregano or ½ teaspoon dried oregano, crushed
1	8-ounce can pizza sauce
4	oval multigrain wraps
6	ounces thinly sliced low-sodium cooked ham, coarsely chopped
½	cup shredded reduced-fat cheddar cheese or reduced-fat mozzarella cheese (2 ounces)

1 Preheat oven to 375°F. In a large skillet heat oil over medium heat. Add mushrooms and sweet pepper; cook for 5 to 10 minutes or until vegetables are tender, stirring occasionally. Stir in oregano.

2 Meanwhile, spread some pizza sauce on one side of each wrap, leaving a ½-inch border around the edge. Divide ham among wraps, arranging it on top of sauce on half of each wrap. Top ham with mushroom mixture. Sprinkle with cheese. Fold wraps in half. Place on a large baking sheet. Bake for 8 to 10 minutes or until heated through. Makes 4 servings.

- 1 12-ounce boneless pork top loin roast (single loin)
- 1 small avocado, halved, pitted, and peeled
- 2 tablespoons snipped fresh flat-leaf parsley
- 2 teaspoons lemon juice
- 1 clove garlic, minced
- ¼ teaspoon salt
- ½ teaspoon Greek seasoning
  Nonstick cooking spray
- 4 whole grain hamburger buns, split and toasted
- 1 medium tomato, sliced

1 For easier slicing, wrap and freeze pork for 1 hour. Meanwhile, in a small bowl mash avocado with a fork. Stir in parsley, lemon juice, garlic, and ⅛ teaspoon salt. Cover surface of the mixture with plastic wrap and set aside.

2 Working from one end of the roast, cut pork crosswise into twelve to sixteen ⅛- to ¼-inch-thick slices. Sprinkle pork slices with Greek seasoning and remaining ⅛ teaspoon salt.

3 Coat an unheated large nonstick skillet with nonstick cooking spray. Preheat over medium-high heat. Cook pork slices, half at a time, in hot skillet for 2 to 3 minutes or until pork slices are no longer pink on outside, turning once to brown evenly. Keep cooked pork slices warm while cooking the remaining pork.

4 To serve, layer cooked pork slices on bun bottoms. Top with sliced tomato. Spread avocado mixture on cut sides of bun tops. Place bun tops on tomato, avocado-spread sides down. Makes 4 servings.

Mediterranean Pork Sandwiches with Avocado Spread

PREP: 25 minutes
FREEZE: 1 hour

NUTRITION FACTS per serving:

CALORIES 328
TOTAL FAT 15 g (4 g sat. fat)
CHOLESTEROL 50 mg
PROTEIN 22 g
CARBOHYDRATE 25 g
FIBER 4 g
SODIUM 407 mg

EXCHANGES 1.5 Starch, 2.5 Lean Meat, 1.5 Fat

1 tablespoon olive oil

8 ounces lean boneless pork, cut into thin bite-size strips

1 clove garlic, minced

¾ cup loose-pack frozen whole kernel corn, thawed

½ cup chopped bottled roasted red sweet peppers

¼ cup sliced green onion

3 tablespoons lime juice

½ teaspoon ground cumin

⅛ teaspoon cayenne pepper (optional)

½ cup canned refried black beans*

4 9- or 10-inch whole grain tortillas

½ cup shredded romaine

½ cup chopped tomatoes

Light dairy sour cream (optional)

Mexi-Pork Wraps

START TO FINISH: 35 minutes

NUTRITION FACTS per serving:

- -

CALORIES 316
TOTAL FAT 11 g (3 g sat. fat)
CHOLESTEROL 36 mg
PROTEIN 17 g
CARBOHYDRATE 39 g
FIBER 5 g
SODIUM 484 mg

EXCHANGES 2 Starch, 1.5 Lean Meat, 1 Vegetable, 1 Fat

1 In a large skillet heat oil over medium-high heat. Add pork and garlic; cook for 4 to 5 minutes or until pork is cooked through and juices run clear. Set aside.

2 In a medium bowl stir together corn, roasted red peppers, green onion, 2 tablespoons lime juice, cumin, and, if desired, cayenne pepper. In a small bowl stir together refried black beans and remaining 1 tablespoon lime juice.

3 Spread 2 tablespoons black bean mixture in a 2-inch-wide strip down the center of each tortilla. Top with pork strips, corn mixture, romaine, and tomatoes. Fold bottom edge of each tortilla up and over the filling. Roll tortillas around filling. If desired, serve wraps with sour cream. Makes 4 servings.

*If you can't find refried black beans, rinse and drain half of a 15-ounce can black beans. In a small bowl mash beans; stir in 1 tablespoon lime juice.

Mexi-Chicken Wraps: Prepare as above, except substitute skinless, boneless chicken breast halves, cut into bite-size strips, for the pork.

Per serving: 289 cal., 7 g total fat (1 g sat. fat), 33 mg chol., 483 mg sodium, 39 g carbo., 5 g fiber, 20 g pro.

Exchanges: 2.5 Starch, 1.5 Very Lean Meat, 0.5 Vegetable, 0.5 Fat.

1½	teaspoons garlic powder
1½	teaspoons onion powder
1½	teaspoons black pepper
1	teaspoon celery salt
1	3-pound boneless pork shoulder roast
2	large onions, cut into thin wedges
½	cup water
4	cups packaged shredded broccoli (broccoli slaw mix)
1	cup light mayonnaise or salad dressing
16	whole grain hamburger buns, split and toasted

1 In a small bowl stir together garlic powder, onion powder, pepper, and celery salt. Trim fat from meat. Sprinkle pepper mixture evenly over meat; rub in with your fingers. If necessary, cut meat to fit into a 3½- or 4-quart slow cooker.

2 Place onion in the bottom of the slow cooker. Add meat. Pour water over meat.

3 Cover and cook on low-heat setting for 8 to 10 hours or on high-heat setting for 4 to 5 hours.

4 Remove meat and onions from cooker to a cutting board; discard cooking liquid. Using two forks, pull meat apart into shreds. Return meat to slow cooker to keep warm.

5 In a small bowl combine shredded broccoli and ½ cup mayonnaise. Spread bottoms of the buns with remaining ½ cup mayonnaise. Place meat mixture on bun bottoms. Top with shredded broccoli mixture; add bun tops.
Makes 16 servings.

Shredded Pork Sandwiches

PREP: 20 minutes

COOK: 8 to 10 hours (low) or 4 to 5 hours (high)

NUTRITION FACTS per serving:
- -

CALORIES 294
TOTAL FAT 11 g (2 g sat. fat)
CHOLESTEROL 60 mg
PROTEIN 22 g
CARBOHYDRATE 26 g
FIBER 3 g
SODIUM 506 mg

EXCHANGES 1.5 Starch, 2.5 Lean Meat, 1 Fat

¼ cup light dairy sour cream

1 tablespoon prepared horseradish

4 8-inch whole wheat flour tortillas

4 cups shredded romaine or fresh
   baby spinach

8 ounces cooked pork loin,
   thinly sliced

2 cups bite-size red sweet
   pepper strips

1 In a small bowl combine sour cream and horseradish. Spread sour cream mixture on tortillas. Top with romaine, pork, and sweet pepper strips. Roll up tortillas. Makes 4 servings.

Horseradish Pork Wrap

START TO FINISH: 15 minutes

NUTRITION FACTS per serving:

CALORIES 263
TOTAL FAT 9 g (3 g sat. fat)
CHOLESTEROL 35 mg
PROTEIN 22 g
CARBOHYDRATE 23 g
FIBER 13 g
SODIUM 373 mg

EXCHANGES 1 Starch, 2 Lean Meat, 1.5 Vegetable, 0.5 Fat

NUTRITION NOTE

Horseradish packs abundant flavor in small amounts, with very few calories and no fat! Combining prepared horseradish with light sour cream is healthier than the calorie- and fat-laden horseradish sauce.

1 medium apple or pear
4 whole wheat English muffins, split
2 tablespoons Dijon-style mustard
4 slices Canadian-style bacon
4 slices Swiss cheese

1 Core apple and thinly slice crosswise to form rings. Spread cut sides of muffin halves with mustard.

2 To assemble, top the cut sides of four of the muffin halves with Canadian-style bacon, apple rings, and Swiss cheese. Top with remaining muffin halves, cut sides down.

3 Heat a large nonstick skillet or griddle. Place sandwiches in skillet or on griddle. Cook over medium-low heat for 9 to 10 minutes or until sandwiches are golden brown and cheese starts to melt, turning once. If desired, secure with toothpicks. Makes 4 servings.

Hot Apple and Cheese Sandwiches

START TO FINISH: 25 minutes

NUTRITION FACTS per serving:

CALORIES 303
TOTAL FAT 11 g (6 g sat. fat)
CHOLESTEROL 40 mg
PROTEIN 20 g
CARBOHYDRATE 34 g
FIBER 3 g
SODIUM 851 mg

EXCHANGES 2 Starch, 2 Medium-Fat Meat

NUTRITION NOTE

Canadian bacon is a low-calorie alternative to other pork products such as bacon strips because it comes from the low-fat eye of the loin.

12 ounces skinless, boneless chicken breast strips for stir-frying
¼ teaspoon garlic salt
⅛ teaspoon black pepper
Nonstick cooking spray
2 cups packaged shredded broccoli (broccoli slaw mix)
¼ teaspoon ground ginger
3 10-inch whole wheat flour tortillas, warmed*
1 recipe Peanut Sauce

Thai Chicken-Broccoli Wraps

START TO FINISH: 25 minutes

NUTRITION FACTS per serving:

- -

CALORIES 191
TOTAL FAT 6 g (1 g sat. fat)
CHOLESTEROL 33 mg
PROTEIN 18 g
CARBOHYDRATE 16 g
FIBER 2 g
SODIUM 460 mg

EXCHANGES 1 Starch, 2 Very Lean Meat, 0.5 Vegetable, 0.5 Fat

1 Sprinkle chicken strips with garlic salt and pepper. Coat an unheated large nonstick skillet with nonstick cooking spray. Preheat skillet over medium-high heat. Add seasoned chicken; cook and stir for 2 to 3 minutes or until chicken is no longer pink. Remove chicken from skillet; keep warm. Add broccoli and ginger to skillet. Cook and stir for 2 to 3 minutes or until vegetables are crisp-tender.

2 Spread tortillas with Peanut Sauce. Top with chicken strips and vegetable mixture. Roll up tortillas. Cut each wrap in half. Serve immediately. Makes 6 servings.

*See tortilla warming note, page 101.

Peanut Sauce: In a small saucepan combine 3 tablespoons creamy peanut butter; 2 tablespoons water; 1 tablespoon reduced-sodium soy sauce; 1 clove garlic, minced; and ¼ teaspoon ground ginger. Heat over very low heat until melted and smooth, whisking constantly.

COOK'S TIP

If you're pressed for time and can't make your own peanut sauce, look for organic and/or health-conscious brands of bottled peanut sauces.

- 12 ounces skinless, boneless chicken breast strips for stir-frying
- ½ teaspoon chili powder
- ¼ teaspoon garlic powder

  Nonstick cooking spray
- 2 small red, yellow, and/or green sweet peppers, seeded and cut into thin strips
- 2 tablespoons bottled reduced-calorie ranch salad dressing
- 2 10-inch whole wheat, tomato, or jalapeño flour tortillas, warmed*
- ½ cup purchased deli-style fresh salsa
- ⅓ cup shredded reduced-fat cheddar cheese

1 Sprinkle chicken strips with chili powder and garlic powder. Coat an unheated large nonstick skillet with nonstick cooking spray. Preheat over medium-high heat. Cook chicken in hot skillet over medium heat for 4 to 6 minutes or until chicken is no longer pink. Remove chicken from skillet. Add sweet peppers to skillet; cook about 5 minutes or until peppers are tender. Return chicken to skillet; add salad dressing. Lightly toss to coat.

2 Divide chicken and pepper mixture between warmed tortillas, placing it on one side of each tortilla. Top with salsa and cheese. Fold each tortilla over; cut in half. Makes 4 servings.

*To warm tortillas, preheat oven to 350°F. Wrap tortillas tightly in foil; bake for 5 to 8 minutes or until warm. (Or wrap tortillas in white microwave-safe paper towels; microwave on 100% power [high] for 20 to 30 seconds or until tortillas are softened.)

Fajita-Ranch Chicken Wraps

START TO FINISH: 30 minutes

OVEN: 350°F

NUTRITION FACTS per serving:

CALORIES 267
TOTAL FAT 7 g (2 g sat. fat)
CHOLESTEROL 57 mg
PROTEIN 26 g
CARBOHYDRATE 24 g
FIBER 5 g
SODIUM 706 mg

EXCHANGES 1.5 Starch, 3 Very Lean Meat, 0.5 Vegetable, 0.5 Fat

Grilled Chicken Sandwiches

PREP: 20 minutes

GRILL: 12 minutes

NUTRITION FACTS per serving:

CALORIES 298
TOTAL FAT 7 g (1 g sat. fat)
CHOLESTEROL 71 mg
PROTEIN 31 g
CARBOHYDRATE 27 g
FIBER 3 g
SODIUM 587 mg

EXCHANGES 1.5 Starch, 3.5 Very Lean Meat, 1 Vegetable, 1 Fat

¼ cup light mayonnaise or salad dressing

½ teaspoon finely shredded lime peel or lemon peel

1 medium zucchini or yellow summer squash,* cut lengthwise into ¼-inch-thick slices

3 tablespoons Worcestershire sauce for chicken

4 small skinless, boneless chicken breast halves (1 to 1¼ pounds total)

4 whole wheat hamburger buns, split and toasted

1 medium tomato, thinly sliced

1 For lime dressing, in a small bowl combine mayonnaise and lime peel. Cover and chill until serving time.

2 Brush zucchini slices with 1 tablespoon Worcestershire sauce; set aside. Brush all sides of the chicken with remaining 2 tablespoons Worcestershire sauce.

3 For a charcoal grill, place chicken on the rack of an uncovered grill directly over medium coals. Grill for 12 to 15 minutes or until no longer pink (170°F), turning once halfway through grilling. Add zucchini slices to grill for the last 6 minutes of chicken grilling time, turning once and grilling until zucchini slices are softened and lightly browned. (For a gas grill, preheat grill. Reduce heat to medium. Place chicken on the grill rack. Cover and grill as above, adding zucchini as directed.)

4 To serve, spread lime dressing on cut sides of toasted buns. If desired, halve zucchini slices crosswise. Place chicken, tomato slices, and zucchini slices on bun bottoms; add bun tops. Makes 4 servings.

*For added color, use half of a medium zucchini and half of a medium yellow summer squash.

1 pound uncooked ground chicken breast or turkey breast

2 medium onions, chopped

1 medium green **sweet** pepper, seeded and chopped

½ cup loose-pack frozen whole kernel corn

2 large cloves garlic, minced

1 fresh jalapeño chile pepper, seeded (if desired) and finely chopped*

1 teaspoon chili powder

1 teaspoon ground cumin

1 teaspoon dried oregano, crushed, or 1 tablespoon snipped fresh oregano

¾ cup ketchup

4 teaspoons Worcestershire sauce

8 whole wheat hamburger buns

Dill pickle slices (optional)

Tex-Mex Sloppy Joes

START TO FINISH: 30 minutes

NUTRITION FACTS per serving:

CALORIES 208
TOTAL FAT 6 g (0 g sat. fat)
CHOLESTEROL 0 mg
PROTEIN 13 g
CARBOHYDRATE 26 g
FIBER 4 g
SODIUM 453 mg

EXCHANGES 1.5 Starch, 1.5 Very Lean Meat, 0.5 Vegetable, 0.5 Fat

1 In a large nonstick skillet combine ground chicken breast, onions, sweet pepper, corn, garlic, chile pepper, chili powder, cumin, and oregano. Cook over medium heat until chicken is no longer pink and onions are tender, stirring frequently. Stir in ketchup and Worcestershire sauce; heat through.

2 Divide chicken mixture among buns. If desired, top with pickle slices. Makes 8 servings.

*Because chile peppers contain volatile oils that can burn your skin and eyes, avoid direct contact with them as much as possible. When working with chile peppers, wear plastic or rubber gloves. If your bare hands do touch the peppers, wash your hands and nails well with soap and warm water.

1 recipe Barbecue Sauce
2 cups shredded cooked chicken*
6 whole wheat hamburger buns, split and, if desired, toasted
   Red onion slices (optional)
   Dill pickle slices (optional)

Pulled Chicken Sandwiches

START TO FINISH: 25 minutes

NUTRITION FACTS per serving:

CALORIES 254
TOTAL FAT 8 g (2 g sat. fat)
CHOLESTEROL 42 mg
PROTEIN 19 g
CARBOHYDRATE 27 g
FIBER 1 g
SODIUM 539 mg

EXCHANGES 2 Starch, 2 Lean Meat

1 Prepare Barbecue Sauce. Add shredded chicken to sauce. Heat through, stirring frequently. Serve on split buns. If desired, serve with red onion slices and dill pickle slices. Makes 6 servings.

*For shredded chicken, use a purchased deli-roasted chicken. Pull the meat from the chicken, discarding skin and bones. Use two forks to pull chicken into shreds. Or use leftover cooked chicken breast.

Barbecue Sauce: In a medium saucepan heat 1 tablespoon olive oil over medium heat. Add ¼ cup finely chopped onion; cook for 3 to 5 minutes or until tender, stirring occasionally. Add one 8-ounce can tomato sauce, 2 tablespoons tomato paste, 1 tablespoon Dijon-style mustard, 1 tablespoon Worcestershire sauce, and 1 teaspoon honey. Bring to boiling; reduce heat. Simmer, uncovered, about 5 minutes or until desired consistency. Season to taste with salt and black pepper.

12 ounces skinless, boneless chicken breast halves, cut into ¼-inch-thick slices
1 tablespoon curry powder
1 teaspoon ground coriander
¼ teaspoon salt
¼ teaspoon black pepper
1 tablespoon olive oil
1 cup thinly sliced red onion
1 cup chopped mango
2 cups shredded romaine
1 cup watercress, tough stems removed
2 tablespoons lemon juice
2 teaspoons olive oil
6 7- to 8-inch whole wheat flour tortillas

1 In a medium bowl combine chicken, curry powder, coriander, salt, and pepper. Cover and marinate in the refrigerator for 30 minutes.

2 In a large skillet heat 1 tablespoon olive oil over medium heat. Add chicken and red onion; cook and stir for 4 to 6 minutes or until chicken is tender and no longer pink. Add mango; cook and stir until heated through.

3 Meanwhile, in a medium bowl combine romaine and watercress. Drizzle with lemon juice and 2 teaspoons olive oil; toss gently to coat.

4 To serve, divide the chicken mixture and the romaine mixture among tortillas. Roll up tortillas. Makes 6 servings.

Curried Chicken-Mango Wraps

PREP: 25 minutes

MARINATE: 30 minutes

NUTRITION FACTS per serving:

CALORIES 260
TOTAL FAT 8 g (2 g sat. fat)
CHOLESTEROL 33 mg
PROTEIN 22 g
CARBOHYDRATE 23 g
FIBER 12 g
SODIUM 459 mg

EXCHANGES 1.5 Starch, 2.5 Very Lean Meat, 1 Vegetable, 1 Fat

COOK'S TIP

Watercress is a mustard green that adds savory spicy flavor and vitamins A, C, and K. Thoroughly wash and pat dry watercress before storing it in a plastic bag in the refrigerator.

1 tablespoon olive oil
1 teaspoon lemon juice
¼ teaspoon paprika
Dash salt
Dash black pepper
2 small skinless, boneless chicken breast halves (8 to 12 ounces total)
2 large whole wheat pita bread rounds
1 7-ounce container hummus
¾ cup coarsely chopped plum tomato
½ cup thinly sliced cucumber
⅓ cup plain low-fat yogurt

Chicken and Hummus Pitas

PREP: 20 minutes
BROIL: 12 minutes

NUTRITION FACTS per serving:

CALORIES 289
TOTAL FAT 10 g (2 g sat. fat)
CHOLESTEROL 34 mg
PROTEIN 20 g
CARBOHYDRATE 31 g
FIBER 5 g
SODIUM 380 mg

EXCHANGES 1.5 Starch, 0.5 Other Carbohydrates, 2 Very Lean Meat, 1 Fat

1 Preheat broiler. In a small bowl combine oil, lemon juice, paprika, salt, and pepper. Place chicken on the unheated rack of a broiler pan. Brush all sides of the chicken breast halves with the oil mixture. Broil 4 to 5 inches from heat for 12 to 15 minutes or until chicken is no longer pink (170°F), turning once halfway through broiling. Cool slightly; cut into strips.

2 Cut pita rounds in half crosswise; open pita halves to make pockets. Spread hummus inside pita pockets. Stuff pockets with chicken strips, tomato, cucumber, and yogurt. Makes 4 servings.

NUTRITION NOTE

While striving to include more beans in your diet, remember, they can be added to many dishes in a variety of forms, such as the hummus in this recipe. The main ingredient in hummus is garbanzo beans, which contain manganese, folate, protein, fiber, and iron.

- ½ cup Black Bean-Smoked Chile Dip
- 4 7- or 8-inch whole wheat flour tortillas
- 12 ounces cooked skinless chicken or turkey breast, chopped (about 2⅓ cups)
- 4 cups shredded or torn romaine or whole fresh baby spinach leaves
- 1 cup coarsely snipped fresh cilantro
- ¼ cup purchased salsa

1 Spread Black Bean-Smoked Chile Dip on one side of each tortilla. Top with chicken, romaine, cilantro, and salsa. Roll up tortillas. If desired, secure with toothpicks. Makes 4 servings.

Black Bean-Smoked Chile Dip: In a small saucepan heat 1 tablespoon canola oil over medium heat. Add ¾ cup finely chopped onion, 1 teaspoon ground coriander, and 1 teaspoon ground cumin; cover and cook about 10 minutes or until very tender, stirring occasionally. Remove from heat; stir in ¼ cup snipped fresh cilantro. Transfer onion mixture to a blender or food processor. Add one 15-ounce can black beans, rinsed and drained; ½ cup water; 1 tablespoon lime juice; 1 teaspoon finely chopped chipotle chile pepper in adobo sauce;* and ⅛ teaspoon salt. Cover and blend or process until nearly smooth. Serve immediately or cover and chill for up to 3 days before serving. Makes 1⅔ cups.

*Because chile peppers contain volatile oils that can burn your skin and eyes, avoid direct contact with them as much as possible. When working with chile peppers, wear plastic or rubber gloves. If your bare hands do touch the peppers, wash your hands and nails well with soap and warm water.

Chicken and Black Bean Wraps

START TO FINISH: 10 minutes

NUTRITION FACTS per serving:

CALORIES 324
TOTAL FAT 8 g (2 g sat. fat)
CHOLESTEROL 72 mg
PROTEIN 38 g
CARBOHYDRATE 24 g
FIBER 14 g
SODIUM 600 mg

EXCHANGES 1.5 Starch, 4.5 Very Lean Meat, 1 Vegetable, 1 Fat

Deli Greek-Style Pitas

START TO FINISH: 20 minutes

NUTRITION FACTS per serving:

CALORIES 274
TOTAL FAT 4 g (1 g sat. fat)
CHOLESTEROL 40 mg
PROTEIN 18 g
CARBOHYDRATE 45 g
FIBER 6 g
SODIUM 1,204 mg

EXCHANGES 2.5 Starch, 2 Very Lean Meat, 0.5 Vegetable

NUTRITION NOTE

Cucumbers are more than 90 percent water, so feel free to munch on any extra cucumber that doesn't go in the pita. You'll be consuming very few calories while getting vitamin C and potassium.

¼	cup plain low-fat yogurt
2	teaspoons vinegar
1	teaspoon snipped fresh dill or ¼ teaspoon dried dill
½	teaspoon sugar
1	cup thinly sliced cucumber
½	of a small red onion, halved and thinly sliced
½	cup chopped plum tomato
4	6-inch whole wheat or white pita bread rounds
10	ounces thinly sliced deli cooked turkey, roast beef, or cooked chicken

1 In a medium bowl combine yogurt, vinegar, dill, and sugar. Add cucumber, red onion, and tomato. Toss gently to coat. Set aside.

2 Cut pita rounds in half crosswise; open pita halves to make pockets. Line pita pockets with turkey. Spoon the cucumber mixture into pita pockets. Makes 4 servings.

1 cup chopped cooked chicken
(5 ounces)

⅓ cup chopped cored apple or
finely chopped celery

1 hard-cooked egg, peeled
and chopped

2 tablespoons plain low-fat yogurt

2 tablespoons light mayonnaise or
salad dressing

Salt

Black pepper

8 slices whole wheat bread

4 leaf lettuce or romaine leaves

1 medium tomato, thinly sliced

½ of a small cucumber, thinly sliced
(about ¾ cup)

1 In a medium bowl stir together chicken, apple, and egg. Add yogurt and mayonnaise; stir to combine. Season to taste with salt and pepper.*

2 Top half of the bread slices with a lettuce leaf each. Then add tomato slices, cucumber slices, and some of the chicken mixture to each. Add one of the remaining bread slices to each stack. Cut each sandwich in half. Makes 4 servings.

*If desired, cover and chill the chicken mixture for up to 4 hours before using.

Chicken Salad Sandwiches

START TO FINISH: 25 minutes

NUTRITION FACTS per serving:

CALORIES 248
TOTAL FAT 7 g (2 g sat. fat)
CHOLESTEROL 86 mg
PROTEIN 18 g
CARBOHYDRATE 28 g
FIBER 5 g
SODIUM 447 mg

EXCHANGES 1.5 Starch, 2 Very Lean Meat, 1 Vegetable, 0.5 Fat

NUTRITION NOTE

To cook chicken with the least amount of added calories and for perfectly moist meat, poach it in water. Put chicken in a small saucepan with just enough water to cover, bring to a rolling boil for 2 minutes, remove from heat. Let stand for 20 minutes. Or purchase refrigerated cooked chicken breast from the grocery store to save time.

Turkey-Grilled Veggie Wraps

PREP: 30 minutes

GRILL: 10 minutes

NUTRITION FACTS per serving:

CALORIES 174
TOTAL FAT 8 g (2 g sat. fat)
CHOLESTEROL 21 mg
PROTEIN 11 g
CARBOHYDRATE 17 g
FIBER 4 g
SODIUM 649 mg

EXCHANGES 1 Starch, 1 Very Lean Meat, 1 Vegetable, 1 Fat

1	large red or green sweet pepper, seeded and cut into ½-inch-wide strips
1	medium yellow summer squash, cut lengthwise into ¼-inch-thick slices
1	small red onion, cut into 1-inch-wide wedges
2	teaspoons canola oil
3	tablespoons bottled reduced-calorie ranch salad dressing
3	10-inch whole grain, tomato, or spinach flour tortillas
6	ounces thinly sliced cooked turkey breast
2	ounces reduced-fat Monterey Jack cheese or Monterey Jack cheese with jalapeño chile peppers, cut into thin slices
¼	cup snipped fresh cilantro

1 Brush sweet pepper, squash, and onion with oil. Place vegetables in a grill wok, grill basket, or on a greased grilling tray. For a charcoal grill, place wok, basket, or tray on rack of an uncovered grill directly over medium-hot coals. Grill just until tender, turning occasionally. Allow 6 to 8 minutes for sweet pepper and squash and 10 to 12 minutes for onion. Remove vegetables from grill as they are done; set aside and keep warm. (For a gas grill, preheat grill. Reduce heat to medium-hot. Place wok, basket, or tray on grill rack over heat. Cover and grill as above.)

2 To assemble wraps, spread ranch dressing on one side of each tortilla. Divide turkey among tortillas. Top with cheese. Spoon grilled vegetables over cheese just below center of each tortilla. Top vegetables with snipped cilantro. Fold bottom third of each tortilla partially over the vegetables. Fold in sides. Roll up tortillas. Cut wraps in half diagonally. Makes 6 servings.

12	ounces cooked turkey breast, shredded
1	cup chopped green apple
½	cup chopped celery
½	cup sliced green onion
½	cup chopped fresh flat-leaf parsley
¼	cup chopped walnuts, toasted
¼	cup dried tart cherries
½	cup light dairy sour cream
2	tablespoons lemon juice
½	to 1 teaspoon bottled hot pepper sauce
¼	teaspoon salt
¼	teaspoon freshly ground black pepper
12	butterhead (Boston or Bibb) lettuce leaves

1 In a large bowl combine turkey, apple, celery, green onion, parsley, walnuts, and dried cherries.

2 In a small bowl stir together sour cream, lemon juice, hot pepper sauce, salt, and black pepper. Add the sour cream mixture to the turkey mixture; stir until well mixed.

3 Divide turkey mixture among lettuce leaves, spooning turkey mixture into center of each leaf. Makes 4 servings.

Turkey-Apple Salad Wraps

START TO FINISH: 30 minutes

NUTRITION FACTS per serving:

CALORIES 262
TOTAL FAT 8 g (2 g sat. fat)
CHOLESTEROL 81 mg
PROTEIN 30 g
CARBOHYDRATE 18 g
FIBER 3 g
SODIUM 228 mg

EXCHANGES 0.5 Fruit, 4 Very Lean Meat, 1.5 Vegetable, 1 Fat

Fish Sandwiches with Aïoli

START TO FINISH: 35 minutes

OVEN: 450°F

NUTRITION FACTS per serving:

CALORIES 353
TOTAL FAT 7 g (1 g sat. fat)
CHOLESTEROL 53 mg
PROTEIN 30 g
CARBOHYDRATE 45 g
FIBER 6 g
SODIUM 521 mg

EXCHANGES 3 Starch, 3 Very Lean Meat, 0.5 Fat

4 4-ounce fresh or frozen skinless cod, catfish, or trout fillets, ½ to ¾ inch thick

Nonstick cooking spray

¾ cup soft whole wheat bread crumbs (1 slice)

¼ cup yellow cornmeal

1 teaspoon chili powder or paprika or ½ teaspoon Cajun seasoning

⅛ teaspoon salt

¼ cup fat-free milk

1 recipe Simple Aïoli

4 whole wheat miniature bagel-bread squares, split and toasted

4 lettuce leaves

½ of a medium tomato, cut into 4 slices

1 Thaw fish, if frozen. Rinse fish; pat dry with paper towels. Measure thickness of fish. Preheat oven to 450°F. Coat a large baking sheet with nonstick cooking spray; set aside. Spread bread crumbs in a 15×10×1-inch baking pan; bake for 2 to 4 minutes or until dry and golden brown, stirring twice and watching carefully to prevent burning. Cool slightly.

2 Add cornmeal, chili powder, and salt to bread crumbs in pan; toss to combine. Pour milk into a shallow dish. Dip fish in milk, allowing excess to drip off; coat fish with crumb mixture. Place fish on prepared baking sheet. Coat the top of the fish with nonstick cooking spray.

3 Bake fish for 4 to 6 minutes per ½-inch thickness or until fish flakes easily when tested with a fork. Spread Simple Aïoli on cut sides of bagel-bread squares. Serve fish in bagel-bread with lettuce leaves and tomato slices. Makes 4 servings.

Simple Aïoli: In a small bowl combine 3 tablespoons light mayonnaise or salad dressing, 2 teaspoons lemon juice, and 1 clove garlic, minced.

16 ounces fresh asparagus spears

½ of an 8-ounce tub light cream cheese (½ cup)

2 teaspoons finely shredded lemon peel

2 tablespoons lemon juice

⅛ teaspoon cayenne pepper

8 ounces smoked salmon, coarsely flaked and skin and bones removed

¼ cup snipped fresh basil or 2 teaspoons dried basil, crushed

4 7- to 8-inch whole wheat flour tortillas

1 medium red sweet pepper, seeded and cut into thin bite-size strips

1 Snap off and discard woody bases from asparagus. In a covered large saucepan cook asparagus spears in a small amount of lightly salted boiling water for 3 to 5 minutes or until crisp-tender. Drain and plunge into ice water to cool quickly. Drain again; pat dry with paper towels.

2 In a medium bowl stir together cream cheese, lemon peel, lemon juice, and cayenne pepper. Fold in flaked salmon and basil. Spread on tortillas. Arrange asparagus and sweet pepper strips on salmon mixture on tortillas. Roll up tortillas. If necessary, secure with toothpicks. Makes 4 servings.

Salmon and Asparagus Wraps

START TO FINISH: 30 minutes

NUTRITION FACTS per serving:

CALORIES 290
TOTAL FAT 11 g (5 g sat. fat)
CHOLESTEROL 28 mg
PROTEIN 24 g
CARBOHYDRATE 24 g
FIBER 13 g
SODIUM 918 mg

EXCHANGES 1.5 Starch, 2.5 Lean Meat, 1 Vegetable, 0.5 Fat

1   12-ounce can solid white tuna (water pack), drained and broken into chunks
¼   cup finely chopped red onion
¼   cup thinly sliced celery
¼   cup shredded carrot
1   tablespoon capers, rinsed and drained
2   tablespoons olive oil
2   tablespoons lime juice
1   tablespoon Dijon-style mustard
1   tablespoon champagne vinegar or white wine vinegar
1½ cups torn mixed salad greens
2   large whole wheat pita bread rounds

Tuna Salad Pockets

START TO FINISH: 20 minutes

NUTRITION FACTS per serving:

CALORIES 272
TOTAL FAT 10 g (2 g sat. fat)
CHOLESTEROL 36 mg
PROTEIN 24 g
CARBOHYDRATE 22 g
FIBER 3 g
SODIUM 659 mg

EXCHANGES 1 Starch, 2.5 Very Lean Meat, 2 Vegetable, 2 Fat

1 In a medium bowl combine tuna, red onion, celery, carrot, and capers; set aside. For vinaigrette, in a small screw-top jar combine olive oil, lime juice, mustard, and vinegar. Cover and shake well to combine. Pour vinaigrette over tuna mixture; toss gently to combine. Add greens; toss gently to combine.

2 Cut pita rounds in half crosswise; open pita halves to make pockets. Fill pockets with tuna mixture. Makes 4 servings.

COOK'S TIP

Capers or caper buds, the buds of the caper flower, are salted and pickled. They are extremely salty, so be careful about adding seasoning when using capers.

3   hard-cooked eggs, peeled and chopped

½   cup chopped cucumber

½   cup chopped zucchini or yellow summer squash

¼   cup chopped red onion

¼   cup shredded carrot

2   tablespoons fat-free mayonnaise dressing or light mayonnaise or salad dressing

1   tablespoon Dijon-style mustard

2   teaspoons fat-free milk

½   teaspoon snipped fresh basil or ¼ teaspoon dried basil, crushed

Dash paprika

3   leaf lettuce leaves

3   10-inch whole grain, spinach, or vegetable flour tortillas

1   plum tomato, thinly sliced

1 In a large bowl combine eggs, cucumber, zucchini, red onion, and carrot. For dressing, in a small bowl stir together mayonnaise, mustard, milk, basil, and paprika. Pour dressing over egg mixture; toss gently to coat.

2 For each wrap, place a lettuce leaf on a tortilla. Top with tomato slices, slightly off center. Spoon egg mixture on tomato slices. Fold in two opposite sides of the tortilla; roll up from the bottom. Diagonally cut tortilla roll-ups in quarters. Makes 6 servings.

Egg and Vegetable Salad Wraps

START TO FINISH: 30 minutes

NUTRITION FACTS per serving:

CALORIES 161
TOTAL FAT 5 g (1 g sat. fat)
CHOLESTEROL 107 mg
PROTEIN 7 g
CARBOHYDRATE 21 g
FIBER 4 g
SODIUM 402 mg

EXCHANGES 1.5 Starch, 0.5 Very Lean Meat, 0.5 Vegetable, 0.5 Fat

Tomato-Basil Panini

PREP: 20 minutes

COOK: 2 minutes per batch

NUTRITION FACTS per serving:

CALORIES 174
TOTAL FAT 5 g (2 g sat. fat)
CHOLESTEROL 5 mg
PROTEIN 10 g
CARBOHYDRATE 27 g
FIBER 5 g
SODIUM 597 mg

EXCHANGES 1.5 Starch, 0.5 Lean Meat, 1 Vegetable

Olive oil nonstick cooking spray

8 slices whole wheat bread; four 6-inch whole wheat hoagie rolls, split; or 2 whole wheat pita bread rounds, halved crosswise and split horizontally

4 cups fresh baby spinach leaves

1 medium tomato, cut in 8 slices

⅛ teaspoon salt

⅛ teaspoon black pepper

¼ cup thinly sliced red onion

2 tablespoons shredded fresh basil

½ cup crumbled reduced-fat feta cheese (2 ounces)

1 Lightly coat an unheated electric sandwich press, panini griddle, covered indoor grill, grill pan, or large nonstick skillet with nonstick cooking spray; set aside.

2 Place 4 of the bread slices, roll bottoms, or pita pieces on a work surface; divide half of the spinach leaves among these bread slices, roll bottoms, or pita pieces. Top spinach with tomato; sprinkle lightly with salt and pepper. Add red onion and basil. Top with feta and remaining spinach. Top with remaining bread slices, roll tops, or pita pieces. Press down firmly.

3 Preheat sandwich press, panini griddle, or covered indoor grill according to manufacturer's directions. (Or heat grill pan or skillet over medium heat.) Add sandwiches, in batches if necessary. If using sandwich press, panini griddle, or covered indoor grill, close lid and grill for 2 to 3 minutes or until bread is toasted. (If using grill pan or skillet, place a heavy skillet on top of sandwiches. Cook over medium heat for 1 to 2 minutes or until bottoms are toasted. Carefully remove top skillet, which may be hot. Turn sandwiches and top again with the skillet. Cook for 1 to 2 minutes more or until bread is toasted.) Makes 4 servings.

- ½ of an 8-ounce tub light cream cheese (½ cup)
- 1 tablespoon snipped fresh dill or 1 teaspoon dried dill
- ¼ teaspoon salt
- ⅛ teaspoon black pepper
- 4 whole wheat bagel halves, toasted, or 4 slices whole wheat bread, toasted
- ½ of a medium cucumber, thinly sliced
- ½ of a medium onion, thinly sliced
- ½ of a medium avocado, halved, seeded, peeled, and thinly sliced
- ¾ cup bottled roasted red sweet peppers, drained and cut into thin strips

  Snipped fresh dill (optional)

1 In a small bowl stir together cream cheese, 1 tablespoon snipped dill, salt, and black pepper. Spread bagel halves or bread slices with cream cheese mixture. Top with cucumber, onion, avocado, and red pepper. If desired, top with additional snipped fresh dill. Makes 4 servings.

Savory Vegetable Open-Face Sandwiches

START TO FINISH: 30 minutes

NUTRITION FACTS per serving:

CALORIES 222
TOTAL FAT 8 g (3 g sat. fat)
CHOLESTEROL 13 mg
PROTEIN 9 g
CARBOHYDRATE 31 g
FIBER 5 g
SODIUM 301 mg

EXCHANGES 1.5 Starch, 1 Vegetable, 1.5 Fat

1 cup chopped yellow summer
squash and/or zucchini

¾ cup chopped broccoli

2 plum tomatoes, seeded and
chopped (about ⅔ cup)

8 pitted kalamata or ripe olives,
chopped

2 tablespoons snipped fresh flat-leaf
parsley or regular parsley

2 tablespoons bottled fat-free
Italian salad dressing

2 6- to 7-inch whole wheat pita
bread rounds or four 6- to 7-inch
whole wheat flour tortillas

½ cup Spicy Navy Bean Hummus

Veggie Salad in a Pocket

PREP: 20 minutes

CHILL: 2 to 24 hours

NUTRITION FACTS per serving:

CALORIES 166
TOTAL FAT 2 g (0 g sat. fat)
CHOLESTEROL 0 mg
PROTEIN 7 g
CARBOHYDRATE 31 g
FIBER 6 g
SODIUM 599 mg
EXCHANGES 1 Starch, 0.5 Other
Carbohydrates, 1 Vegetable

1 In a medium bowl combine squash, broccoli, tomato, olives, and parsley; toss with salad dressing. Cover and chill for 2 to 24 hours.

2 If using pita bread, cut rounds in half crosswise; open pita halves to make pockets. Spread the inside of each pita bread pocket or one side of each tortilla with 2 tablespoons Spicy Navy Bean Hummus.

3 Spoon chilled vegetable mixture into pita pockets or onto tortillas. If using tortillas, fold or roll them. Makes 4 servings.

Spicy Navy Bean Hummus: In a food processor combine one 15- to 19-ounce can navy or cannellini beans (white kidney beans), rinsed and drained; ¼ cup bottled fat-free Italian salad dressing; and 1 tablespoon spicy brown mustard. Cover and process until smooth and spreadable. (Or mash beans with a potato masher or fork. Stir in salad dressing and mustard.) Transfer to an airtight storage container. Cover and chill for up to 1 week. Makes 1⅓ cups.

Chapter 5

Salads

On the divider: Spinach and Lentil Salad with Toasted Walnuts (*see recipe, page 133*)

12 ounces beef flank steak or boneless beef top sirloin steak, cut 1 inch thick

⅛ teaspoon salt

⅛ teaspoon black pepper

⅓ cup lime juice

2 tablespoons olive oil

2 tablespoons snipped fresh cilantro

1 tablespoon honey

2 cloves garlic, minced

8 cups torn romaine

5 ounces jicama, peeled and cut into thin bite-size strips (1 cup)

1 medium mango, seeded, peeled, and sliced

1 small red onion, cut into thin wedges

Mango-Steak Salad with Lime Dressing

PREP: 25 minutes

GRILL: 17 minutes

NUTRITION FACTS per serving:

CALORIES 195
TOTAL FAT 9 g (2 g sat. fat)
CHOLESTEROL 23 mg
PROTEIN 14 g
CARBOHYDRATE 17 g
FIBER 3 g
SODIUM 87 mg

EXCHANGES 0.5 Fruit, 1.5 Lean Meat, 1.5 Vegetable, 1 Fat

1 Trim fat from steak. If using flank steak, score both sides of steak in a diamond pattern by making shallow diagonal cuts at 1-inch intervals. Sprinkle steak with salt and pepper.

2 For a charcoal grill, place steak on the rack of an uncovered grill directly over medium coals. Grill until medium doneness (160°F), turning once halfway through grilling time. Allow 17 to 21 minutes for flank steak or 18 to 22 minutes for top sirloin steak. (For a gas grill, preheat grill. Reduce heat to medium. Place steak on grill rack over heat. Cover and grill as above.) Thinly slice steak diagonally across the grain.

3 Meanwhile, for dressing, in a small bowl whisk together lime juice, oil, cilantro, honey, and garlic.

4 To serve, divide romaine among six serving plates. Top with steak slices, jicama, mango, and red onion. Drizzle dressing over salads. Makes 6 servings.

Broiler Directions: Preheat broiler. Place steak on the unheated rack of a broiler pan. Broil 3 to 4 inches from heat until medium doneness (160°F), turning once halfway through broiling time. Allow 15 to 18 minutes for flank steak or 20 to 22 minutes for sirloin steak.

Spinach and Basil Salad with Beef

START TO FINISH: 25 minutes

NUTRITION FACTS per serving:

CALORIES 311
TOTAL FAT 15 g (3 g sat. fat)
CHOLESTEROL 49 mg
PROTEIN 30 g
CARBOHYDRATE 14 g
FIBER 4 g
SODIUM 92 mg

EXCHANGES 0.5 Fruit, 4 Lean Meat, 1.5 Vegetable, 0.5 Fat

NUTRITION NOTE

Oranges are known for high levels of the antioxidant vitamin C, an important vitamin for bones, teeth, and wound healing. Once oranges are squeezed or cut, the level of vitamin C diminishes quickly. Eat them shortly after cutting or squeezing.

¼   cup pear nectar
2   tablespoons canola oil
2   tablespoons white wine vinegar
½   teaspoon Worcestershire sauce for chicken
⅛   teaspoon black pepper
4   cups fresh baby spinach
2   cups sliced fresh mushrooms
½   cup lightly packed fresh basil leaves
12 ounces sliced cooked beef sirloin steak, cut into thin strips*
2   medium oranges, peeled and sectioned
¼   cup sliced almonds, toasted

1 For dressing, in a screw-top jar combine pear nectar, oil, vinegar, Worcestershire sauce, and pepper. Cover and shake well.

2 In a bowl toss together spinach, mushrooms, and basil leaves. Divide mixture among four serving plates. Top with beef strips; add orange sections. Drizzle with dressing and sprinkle with almonds. Makes 4 servings.

*If you are cooking your own beef, start with 1 to 1¼ pounds boneless beef top sirloin steak, cut 1 inch thick. Preheat broiler. Place steak on the unheated rack of a broiler pan and broil 3 to 4 inches from heat to desired doneness, turning once halfway through broiling. Allow 15 to 17 minutes for medium-rare doneness (145°F) or 20 to 22 minutes for medium doneness (160°F).

1 pound boneless beef top sirloin steak, cut 1 inch thick

1 cup reduced-calorie balsamic vinaigrette salad dressing

½ of a 1-pound loaf whole grain crusty bread, cut into 1-inch-thick slices

2 medium yellow, green, and/or red sweet peppers, quartered

   Nonstick cooking spray

2 cups cherry or grape tomatoes, halved if large

3 ounces part-skim mozzarella cheese, cubed

1 tablespoon snipped fresh mint

   Fresh mint leaves (optional)

1 Place steak in a large resealable plastic bag set in a shallow dish. Add ½ cup vinaigrette. Seal bag; turn to coat beef. Marinate in the refrigerator for 1 to 2 hours, turning bag occasionally.

2 Coat bread slices and pepper quarters with nonstick cooking spray. Set aside. Drain steak, discarding marinade.

3 For a charcoal grill, place steak, bread, and pepper quarters on the rack of an uncovered grill directly over medium coals. Grill bread for 3 to 4 minutes or until lightly browned, turning once. Grill peppers for 8 to 10 minutes or until crisp-tender, turning once halfway through grilling. Grill beef until desired doneness, turning once halfway through grilling. Allow 14 to 18 minutes for medium-rare doneness (145°F) or 18 to 22 minutes for medium doneness (160°F). Remove items from the grill as they are done. (For a gas grill, preheat grill. Reduce heat to medium. Place steak, bread, and pepper quarters on grill rack over heat. Cover and grill as above.)

4 To serve, cut bread into cubes. Cut pepper quarters into bite-size strips. Cut steak into bite-size strips. In a very large bowl toss together bread, peppers, steak, tomatoes, and mozzarella cheese. Stir the snipped mint into remaining ½ cup vinaigrette. Add to steak mixture; toss to coat. If desired, garnish with fresh mint leaves. Serve immediately. Makes 6 servings.

Grilled Beef Panzanella

PREP: 25 minutes   **MARINATE:** 1 to 2 hours
GRILL: 14 minutes

NUTRITION FACTS per serving:

CALORIES 302
TOTAL FAT 11 g (3 g sat. fat)
CHOLESTEROL 55 mg
PROTEIN 27 g
CARBOHYDRATE 24 g
FIBER 5 g
SODIUM 722 mg

EXCHANGES 1.5 Starch, 3 Lean Meat, 0.5 Vegetable

12 ounces boneless beef sirloin steak, cut 1 inch thick

⅛ teaspoon salt

⅛ teaspoon black pepper

1 cup fresh raspberries

2 tablespoons white wine vinegar or cider vinegar

1 tablespoon canola oil

2 teaspoons honey

1 teaspoon chopped canned chipotle chile peppers in adobo sauce*

Dash salt

6 cups arugula leaves

1 4-ounce package goat cheese (chèvre), cut up or crumbled

Beef and Arugula with Raspberry-Chipotle Dressing

PREP: 15 minutes

GRILL: 14 minutes

NUTRITION FACTS per serving:

CALORIES 281

TOTAL FAT 16 g (7 g sat. fat)

CHOLESTEROL 74 mg

PROTEIN 25 g

CARBOHYDRATE 9 g

FIBER 3 g

SODIUM 319 mg

EXCHANGES 3 Lean Meat, 1.5 Vegetable, 1.5 Fat

NUTRITION NOTE

A rich source of vitamins A and C and iron, arugula is a nice complement to the sweet, salty, and spicy flavors of this dish. If the flavor of arugula is too sharp, substitute spinach, watercress, or Belgian endive.

1 Trim fat from steak; sprinkle ⅛ teaspoon salt and pepper over steak. For a charcoal grill, place steak on the rack of an uncovered grill directly over medium coals. Grill until desired doneness, turning once halfway through grilling. Allow 14 to 18 minutes for medium-rare doneness (145°F) or 18 to 22 minutes for medium doneness (160°F). (For a gas grill, preheat grill. Reduce heat to medium. Place steak on grill rack over heat. Cover and grill as above.) Thinly slice beef.

2 Meanwhile, for raspberry dressing, in a blender combine raspberries, vinegar, oil, honey, chipotle peppers, and dash salt. Cover and blend until smooth. Set aside.

3 Divide arugula among four serving plates. Top with grilled steak and goat cheese. Drizzle with raspberry dressing. Makes 4 servings.

*Because chile peppers contain volatile oils that can burn your skin and eyes, avoid direct contact with them as much as possible. When working with chile peppers, wear plastic or rubber gloves. If your bare hands do touch the peppers, wash your hands and nails well with soap and warm water.

- 12 ounces beef flank steak
- ½ cup bottled reduced-calorie clear Italian salad dressing
- ½ teaspoon finely shredded lemon peel
- ¼ cup lemon juice
- 2 tablespoons snipped fresh cilantro
- ¼ cup chopped onion
- ¼ teaspoon salt
- ¼ teaspoon black pepper
- 6 cups torn mixed salad greens
- 2 small red and/or yellow tomatoes, cut into wedges
- 1 small avocado, halved, seeded, peeled, and sliced (optional)

1 Score both sides of steak in a diamond pattern by making shallow diagonal cuts at 1-inch intervals. Place steak in a resealable plastic bag set in a shallow dish. Set aside.

2 In a screw-top jar combine salad dressing, lemon peel, lemon juice, and cilantro. Cover and shake well. Pour half of the salad dressing mixture into a small bowl; cover and chill until serving time. Add onion to remaining salad dressing mixture in jar. Cover and shake well; pour mixture over steak in bag. Seal bag; turn to coat steak. Marinate in the refrigerator for 24 hours, turning bag occasionally.

3 Drain steak, discarding marinade. Sprinkle steak with salt and pepper. For a charcoal grill, place steak on the rack of an uncovered grill directly over medium coals. Grill for 17 to 21 minutes or until medium doneness (160°F), turning once halfway through grilling. (For a gas grill, preheat grill. Reduce heat to medium. Place steak on grill rack over heat. Cover and grill as above.)

4 To serve, thinly slice steak across grain. Arrange salad greens, tomatoes, and, if desired, avocado on four serving plates. Top with sliced steak. Drizzle reserved salad dressing mixture over individual salads. Makes 4 servings.

Broiler Directions: Preheat broiler. Place steak on the unheated rack of a broiler pan. Broil 3 to 4 inches from heat for 15 to 18 minutes for medium doneness (160°F), turning once halfway through broiling.

Grilled Beef Salad with Cilantro Vinaigrette

PREP: 25 minutes   **MARINATE:** 24 hours
GRILL: 17 minutes

NUTRITION FACTS per serving:

CALORIES 186
TOTAL FAT 8 g (3 g sat. fat)
CHOLESTEROL 36 mg
PROTEIN 21 g
CARBOHYDRATE 8 g
FIBER 2 g
SODIUM 622 mg

EXCHANGES 3 Lean Meat, 1.5 Vegetable

3 tablespoons apple juice

3 tablespoons canola oil

1 tablespoon red or white wine vinegar or cider vinegar

4 to 6 cups torn mixed salad greens

2 medium apples or pears, cored and cut into wedges

8 ounces lean cooked beef, ham, chicken breast, or turkey breast, cut into thin bite-size strips (about 1½ cups)

2 medium carrots, cut into thin bite-size strips

1 cup thinly sliced, halved yellow summer squash

1 For dressing, in a screw-top jar combine apple juice, oil, and vinegar. Cover and shake well.

2 Divide salad greens, apples, beef, carrots, and squash among four serving plates. Drizzle dressing over salads. Makes 4 servings.

Super-Crunchy Supper Salad

START TO FINISH: 35 minutes

NUTRITION FACTS per serving:

- -

CALORIES 272
TOTAL FAT 15 g (3 g sat. fat)
CHOLESTEROL 50 mg
PROTEIN 20 g
CARBOHYDRATE 16 g
FIBER 4 g
SODIUM 67 mg

EXCHANGES 0.5 Fruit, 2.5 Lean Meat, 1 Vegetable, 2 Fat

- ⅓ cup buttermilk
- 2 tablespoons light mayonnaise or salad dressing
- 2 tablespoons crumbled blue cheese
- 1 green onion, thinly sliced
- 2 boneless pork loin chops (about 12 ounces total), cut ¾ inch thick
- 2 teaspoons snipped fresh thyme or 1 teaspoon dried thyme, crushed
- ¼ teaspoon ground black pepper
- 8 cups torn mixed salad greens
- 2 medium apples and/or pears, cored and thinly sliced
- ¼ cup coarsely chopped walnuts, toasted (optional)
- Cracked black pepper (optional)

1 For dressing, in a small bowl whisk together buttermilk and mayonnaise until smooth. Stir in blue cheese and green onion. Set aside.

2 Preheat broiler. Trim fat from chops. Sprinkle thyme and ground black pepper evenly over all sides of chops; rub in with your fingers. Place chops on the unheated rack of a broiler pan. Broil 3 to 4 inches from heat for 9 to 11 minutes or until no pink remains (160°F) and juices run clear, turning once halfway through broiling. Slice chops.

3 Serve salad greens with apple slices and sliced pork; drizzle with dressing. If desired, sprinkle with walnuts and cracked black pepper. Makes 4 servings.

Pork and Apple Salad with Blue Cheese Dressing

PREP: 25 minutes
BROIL: 9 minutes

NUTRITION FACTS per serving:

CALORIES 234
TOTAL FAT 11 g (4 g sat. fat)
CHOLESTEROL 61 mg
PROTEIN 21 g
CARBOHYDRATE 14 g
FIBER 3 g
SODIUM 203 mg

EXCHANGES 0.5 Fruit, 2.5 Lean Meat, 2 Vegetable, 1 Fat

Pork with Warm Herbed Grain Salad

PREP: 20 minutes

COOK: 40 minutes

NUTRITION FACTS per serving:

CALORIES 271
TOTAL FAT 6 g (1 g sat. fat)
CHOLESTEROL 42 mg
PROTEIN 22 g
CARBOHYDRATE 32 g
FIBER 4 g
SODIUM 275 mg

EXCHANGES 1.5 Starch, 0.5 Fruit,
2.5 Very Lean Meat, 0.5 Vegetable, 0.5 Fat

NUTRITION NOTE

Wild rice is generally more expensive than white rice, but it contains double the protein of white rice. It also has fewer calories and expands 3 to 4 times its original size when cooked, so you don't need as much of it.

3 cups water
¾ cup wild rice, rinsed and drained
¼ cup barley
4 boneless pork loin chops, cut ½ inch thick (1 to 1¼ pounds total)
¼ teaspoon salt
⅛ teaspoon black pepper
1 tablespoon canola oil or olive oil
¼ cup rice wine vinegar or white wine vinegar
¼ cup reduced-sodium chicken broth
¼ cup snipped fresh basil or 1 tablespoon dried basil, crushed
1 tablespoon snipped fresh oregano, rosemary, and/or thyme or ½ teaspoon dried oregano, rosemary, and/or thyme, crushed
½ cup dried cranberries
3 cups shredded red cabbage
2 tablespoons chopped pecans, toasted

1 In a large saucepan bring water to boiling; stir in uncooked wild rice and barley. Return to boiling; reduce heat. Cover and simmer for 40 to 45 minutes or until wild rice and barley are tender. Drain and return to hot saucepan; cover and keep warm.

2 Meanwhile, trim fat from pork. Cut pork into thin bite-size strips. Sprinkle pork strips with salt and pepper. In a large skillet heat oil over medium heat. Add pork strips; cook for 3 to 5 minutes or just until pork is no longer pink. Stir in vinegar, chicken broth, basil, and oregano. Add pork mixture and dried cranberries to rice mixture; toss to combine.

3 Divide red cabbage among six serving plates. Top cabbage with rice mixture; sprinkle with pecans. Serve warm. Makes 6 servings.

12 ounces boneless pork top loin roast or pork tenderloin, trimmed and cut into thin bite-size strips

½ teaspoon dried sage, crushed

¼ teaspoon salt

¼ teaspoon black pepper

Nonstick cooking spray

¼ cup coarsely chopped hazelnuts (filberts) or almonds

⅓ cup pear nectar

1 tablespoon olive oil

2 teaspoons Dijon-style mustard or chipotle chile pepper-style mustard

6 cups torn mixed salad greens

2 medium pears, cored and sliced

1 Sprinkle pork strips with sage, salt, and pepper. Coat an unheated large nonstick skillet with nonstick cooking spray. Preheat over medium-high heat. Add pork to hot skillet. Cook and stir for 2 to 3 minutes or until pork is slightly pink in the center. Add nuts. Cook and stir for 30 seconds more. Remove pork mixture. Cover and keep warm.

2 For dressing, carefully add pear nectar, oil, and mustard to hot skillet. Cook and stir just until blended, scraping up any crusty browned bits from bottom of skillet.

3 Divide salad greens and pear slices among four serving plates. Top with pork mixture; drizzle with warm dressing. Serve immediately. Makes 4 servings.

Sauteed Pork and Pear Salad

START TO FINISH: 30 minutes

NUTRITION FACTS per serving:

CALORIES 278
TOTAL FAT 13 g (2 g sat. fat)
CHOLESTEROL 47 mg
PROTEIN 21 g
CARBOHYDRATE 20 g
FIBER 5 g
SODIUM 256 mg

EXCHANGES 0.5 Other Carbohydrates, 0.5 Fruit, 2.5 Lean Meat, 1.5 Vegetable, 1 Fat

NUTRITION NOTE

Hazelnuts, like other nuts, are cholesterol-free. These nuts contain fiber, calcium, the antioxidant vitamin E, and a good dose of protein.

Roast Pork Salad with Ginger-Pineapple Dressing

PREP: 25 minutes   **ROAST:** 25 minutes
OVEN: 425°F

NUTRITION FACTS per serving:

CALORIES 240
TOTAL FAT 8 g (2 g sat. fat)
CHOLESTEROL 60 mg
PROTEIN 19 g
CARBOHYDRATE 22 g
FIBER 3 g
SODIUM 219 mg

EXCHANGES 1 Fruit, 2.5 Very Lean Meat, 1 Vegetable, 1.5 Fat

12   ounces pork tenderloin
⅛   teaspoon salt
⅛   teaspoon black pepper
2   tablespoons honey mustard
6   cups torn romaine and/or fresh spinach
2   cups fresh or canned pineapple chunks and/or sliced fresh nectarines or peaches
     Cracked black pepper (optional)
1   recipe Ginger-Pineapple Dressing

1 Preheat oven to 425°F. Trim fat from pork tenderloin; sprinkle pork with salt and ground black pepper. Place pork tenderloin on a rack in a shallow roasting pan. Roast for 20 minutes.

2 Spoon honey mustard on pork tenderloin. Roast for 5 to 10 minutes more or until an instant-read thermometer inserted in the thickest part of the tenderloin registers 160°F.

3 To serve, thinly slice pork tenderloin. On four serving plates arrange romaine, pork, and fruit. If desired, sprinkle salads with cracked black pepper. Stir Ginger-Pineapple Dressing; drizzle onto salads. Makes 4 servings.

Make-Ahead Directions: Make Ginger-Pineapple Dressing; cover and chill for up to 24 hours.

Ginger-Pineapple Dressing: In a small bowl combine ¼ cup low-fat mayonnaise dressing, ¼ cup unsweetened pineapple juice or orange juice, 1 tablespoon honey mustard, and 1 teaspoon grated fresh ginger. Cover; chill until serving time.

1 small cantaloupe, halved, peeled, and seeded

4 cups torn romaine

8 ounces lean cooked ham, cut into bite-size strips (about 1½ cups)

1 small cucumber, sliced

1 cup torn fresh spinach

2 green onions, thinly sliced

¼ cup unsweetened pineapple juice

1 tablespoon white wine vinegar

1 tablespoon canola oil

1½ teaspoons snipped fresh mint or ½ teaspoon dried mint, crushed

¼ cup sliced almonds, toasted (optional)

1 Coarsely chop one-quarter of the melon; slice remaining melon. In a large bowl combine chopped melon, romaine, ham, cucumber, spinach, and green onion.

2 In a screw-top jar combine pineapple juice, white wine vinegar, oil, and mint. Cover and shake well.

3 Arrange melon slices on four serving plates. Drizzle dressing over greens mixture; toss lightly to coat. Divide greens mixture among plates with melon slices. If desired, sprinkle with almonds. Makes 4 servings.

COOK'S TIP

When choosing any type of melon, pick those that feel heavy for their size and have no cracks or bruises. When cantaloupe is ripe, the area between the webbing will be light gold.

Ham and Cantaloupe Salad

START TO FINISH: 25 minutes

NUTRITION FACTS per serving:

CALORIES 155
TOTAL FAT 5 g (1 g sat. fat)
CHOLESTEROL 27 mg
PROTEIN 12 g
CARBOHYDRATE 16 g
FIBER 3 g
SODIUM 655 mg

EXCHANGES 0.5 Fruit, 2 Lean Meat, 1.5 Vegetable

Caesar Salad with Grilled Portobello Mushrooms

PREP: 25 minutes   **BAKE:** 10 minutes
GRILL: 12 minutes   **OVEN:** 350°F

NUTRITION FACTS per serving:

CALORIES 304
TOTAL FAT 13 g (3 g sat. fat)
CHOLESTEROL 79 mg
PROTEIN 32 g
CARBOHYDRATE 16 g
FIBER 4 g
SODIUM 612 mg

EXCHANGES 0.5 Starch, 4 Very Lean Meat, 2 Vegetable, 2 Fat

2   fresh portobello mushrooms (about 4 ounces each)
1   pound skinless, boneless chicken breast halves
    Nonstick cooking spray
¼   teaspoon salt
¼   teaspoon black pepper
1   tablespoon lemon juice
1   tablespoon red wine vinegar
2   teaspoons Dijon-style mustard
1   teaspoon Worcestershire sauce
1   clove garlic, minced
⅛   teaspoon black pepper
½   cup light mayonnaise or salad dressing
8   cups torn romaine
1   recipe Whole Wheat Croutons or ½ cup packaged whole wheat croutons
2   tablespoons shredded Parmesan cheese

1 Wipe mushrooms clean with a damp cloth. Remove stems and gills from mushrooms. Lightly coat both sides of mushrooms and chicken breast halves with nonstick cooking spray; sprinkle chicken with salt and ¼ teaspoon pepper.

2 For a charcoal grill, place mushrooms and chicken on the rack of an uncovered grill directly over medium coals. Grill mushrooms for 10 to 12 minutes or until tender. Grill chicken for 12 to 15 minutes or until no longer pink (170°F), turning once halfway through grilling. (For a gas grill, preheat grill. Reduce heat to medium. Place mushrooms and chicken on grill rack over heat. Cover and grill as above.)

3 Meanwhile, for dressing, in a small bowl combine lemon juice, red wine vinegar, Dijon-style mustard, Worcestershire sauce, garlic, and ⅛ teaspoon pepper. Whisk in mayonnaise.

4 Divide lettuce among four serving plates. Slice grilled mushrooms and chicken. Arrange on lettuce. Spoon dressing over salads. Sprinkle with Whole Wheat Croutons and Parmesan cheese. Makes 4 servings.

Whole Wheat Croutons: Preheat oven to 350°F. Cut 2 slices whole wheat bread into ½- to 1-inch pieces. Spread pieces in an even layer in a shallow baking pan. Lightly coat bread cubes with nonstick cooking spray; toss to turn pieces. Spread evenly and lightly coat again with nonstick cooking spray. Bake about 10 minutes or until bread cubes are lightly browned and crisp. Cool completely.

- 1 cup water
- ½ cup dry brown or French lentils, rinsed and drained
- ½ cup chopped red sweet pepper
- ⅓ cup chopped green onion
- ¼ cup snipped fresh flat-leaf parsley
- 2 tablespoons chopped walnuts, toasted
- 6 cups torn mixed salad greens
- 12 ounces cooked chicken breast, sliced
- 1 recipe Red Wine Vinaigrette

1 In a small saucepan combine water and lentils. Bring to boiling; reduce heat. Cover and simmer for 20 to 25 minutes or until lentils are tender and most of the liquid is absorbed. Drain lentils and place in a medium bowl. Stir in sweet pepper, green onion, parsley, and walnuts.

2 Place salad greens on a serving platter. Top with lentil mixture and chicken. Drizzle with Red Wine Vinaigrette. Makes 4 servings.

Red Wine Vinaigrette: In a small bowl combine 2 tablespoons red wine vinegar and 1 tablespoon finely chopped shallot. Let stand for 5 minutes. Whisk in 1½ teaspoons Dijon-style mustard. Add 2 tablespoons olive oil in a thin steady stream, whisking constantly until combined. Stir in ⅛ teaspoon salt and ⅛ teaspoon black pepper. Makes about ⅓ cup.

Spinach and Lentil Salad with Toasted Walnuts

PREP: 20 minutes
COOK: 20 minutes

NUTRITION FACTS per serving:

CALORIES 336
TOTAL FAT 13 g (2 g sat. fat)
CHOLESTEROL 72 mg
PROTEIN 35 g
CARBOHYDRATE 20 g
FIBER 9 g
SODIUM 192 mg

EXCHANGES 1 Starch, 4 Very Lean Meat, 1.5 Vegetable, 2 Fat

⅓ cup apple jelly

3 tablespoons horseradish mustard

4 skinless, boneless chicken breast halves (about 1 pound total)

4 cups mesclun or torn mixed salad greens

2 tart medium apples, cored and sliced

¼ cup coarsely chopped walnuts, toasted

1 tablespoon cider vinegar

1 tablespoon canola oil

1 In a small saucepan melt apple jelly over low heat. Remove from heat; stir in mustard. Set aside 2 tablespoons of the jelly mixture to brush on chicken. Reserve remaining jelly mixture for dressing.

2 For a charcoal grill, place chicken on the rack of an uncovered grill directly over medium coals. Grill for 12 to 15 minutes or until no longer pink (170°F), turning once halfway through grilling. (For a gas grill, preheat grill. Reduce heat to medium. Place chicken on grill rack over heat. Cover and grill as above.) Brush chicken with 2 tablespoons jelly mixture. Transfer chicken to a cutting board; cool slightly and cut into bite-size pieces.

3 Meanwhile, in a large bowl toss together mesclun, apples, and walnuts. For dressing, whisk together reserved jelly mixture, cider vinegar, and oil. Divide greens mixture among four serving plates. Arrange chicken on the greens; drizzle with dressing. Makes 4 servings.

Apple and Chicken Salad

PREP: 20 minutes

GRILL: 12 minutes

NUTRITION FACTS per serving:

CALORIES 330
TOTAL FAT 10 g (1 g sat. fat)
CHOLESTEROL 66 mg
PROTEIN 29 g
CARBOHYDRATE 32 g
FIBER 3 g
SODIUM 176 mg

EXCHANGES 0.5 Other Carbohydrates, 0.5 Fruit, 4 Very Lean Meat, 1 Vegetable, 1 Fat

COOK'S TIP

Mesclun may sound like a foreign ingredient, but it is just a mix of young salad greens, herbs, and sometimes edible flowers. It's also called mesculum, field greens, spring mix, and gourmet mix.

1½ cups water

½ cup bulgur

2 medium tomatoes, chopped

1 cup finely chopped, seeded cucumber

1 cup finely chopped fresh flat-leaf parsley

⅓ cup thinly sliced green onion

¼ cup snipped fresh mint or 1 tablespoon dried mint, crushed

⅓ to ½ cup lemon juice

¼ cup olive oil

½ teaspoon salt

½ teaspoon black pepper

12 large leaves romaine and/or butterhead lettuce (Boston or Bibb)

18 ounces grilled or broiled skinless, boneless chicken breast halves,* sliced

Mediterranean Tabbouleh Salad with Chicken

PREP: 30 minutes **CHILL:** 4 to 24 hours
STAND: 30 minutes

NUTRITION FACTS per serving:

- -

CALORIES 294
TOTAL FAT 13 g (2 g sat. fat)
CHOLESTEROL 72 mg
PROTEIN 30 g
CARBOHYDRATE 16 g
FIBER 5 g
SODIUM 276 mg

EXCHANGES 0.5 Starch, 3 Very Lean Meat, 2 Vegetable, 2 Fat

1 In a large bowl combine water and bulgur. Let stand for 30 minutes. Drain bulgur through a fine sieve, using a large spoon to press out excess water. Return bulgur to bowl. Stir in tomato, cucumber, parsley, green onion, and mint.

2 For dressing, in a screw-top jar combine lemon juice, oil, salt, and pepper. Cover and shake well. Pour dressing over the bulgur mixture. Toss lightly to coat. Cover and chill for 4 to 24 hours, stirring occasionally. Bring to room temperature before serving.

3 Serve romaine with bulgur mixture and cooked chicken. Makes 6 servings.

*To grill chicken breast halves, lightly sprinkle chicken with salt and black pepper. For a charcoal grill, place chicken on the rack of an uncovered grill directly over medium coals. Grill for 12 to 15 minutes or until chicken is no longer pink (170°F), turning once halfway through grilling. (For a gas grill, preheat grill. Reduce heat to medium. Place chicken on grill rack over heat. Cover and grill as above.)

To broil chicken breast halves, preheat broiler. Lightly sprinkle chicken with salt and black pepper. Place chicken on the unheated rack of a broiler pan. Broil chicken 4 to 5 inches from heat for 12 to 15 minutes or until chicken is no longer pink (170°F), turning once halfway through broiling.

4   skinless, boneless chicken breast
      halves (about 1 pound total)
¾   cup bottled reduced-calorie
      balsamic vinaigrette
      salad dressing
3   cloves garlic, minced
¼   teaspoon crushed red pepper
8   cups torn mixed salad greens

1 Place chicken breast halves in a resealable
      plastic bag set in a shallow dish. For marinade,
stir together ⅓ cup vinaigrette, garlic, and crushed
red pepper. Pour marinade over chicken. Seal bag;
turn to coat chicken. Marinate in the refrigerator
for 1 to 4 hours, turning bag occasionally.

2 Preheat broiler. Drain chicken, reserving
      marinade. Place chicken on the unheated
rack of a broiler pan. Broil 4 to 5 inches from
heat for 12 to 15 minutes or until chicken is no
longer pink (170°F), turning once and brushing
with reserved marinade halfway through
broiling. Discard any remaining marinade.

3 Divide greens among four serving plates.
      Slice chicken. Place chicken on greens. Serve
with remaining vinaigrette. Makes 4 servings.

Balsamic Chicken over Greens

PREP: 15 minutes   **MARINATE:** 1 to 4 hours
BROIL: 12 minutes

NUTRITION FACTS per serving:

CALORIES 203
TOTAL FAT 7 g (1 g sat. fat)
CHOLESTEROL 66 mg
PROTEIN 28 g
CARBOHYDRATE 6 g
FIBER 1 g
SODIUM 703 mg

EXCHANGES 3.5 Very Lean Meat,
1.5 Vegetable, 1 Fat

NUTRITION NOTE

Broiling is a healthful choice for cooking
meats and fish because no fat is added.
If a broiler pan is not available, place a wire
baking rack in a pan to catch drippings.
For easy cleanup, line the pan with
aluminum foil.

2 cups shredded cooked chicken breast*

2 cups peeled, seeded, and cubed cantaloupe and/or halved seedless red grapes

1 cup chopped cucumber

⅓ cup orange juice

3 tablespoons canola oil

1 tablespoon snipped fresh mint or cilantro

Salt

Black pepper

4 cups shredded romaine or leaf lettuce

1 In a large bowl toss together chicken, cantaloupe and/or grapes, and cucumber.

2 For dressing, in a screw-top jar combine orange juice, oil, and mint. Cover and shake well. Season to taste with salt and pepper. Drizzle over chicken mixture; toss lightly to coat.

3 Divide romaine among four serving plates. Top with chicken mixture. Serve immediately. Makes 4 servings.

*For 2 cups shredded cooked chicken breast, purchase a deli-roasted chicken. Using two forks, shred enough of the chicken breast to make 2 cups, discarding the skin. (Or cut up a 9-ounce package thawed frozen cooked chicken breast strips.) If you have more time, in a covered saucepan cook 12 ounces skinless, boneless chicken breast in 1½ cups water about 15 minutes or until no longer pink (170°F). Drain well. Cool slightly and shred.

Crunchy Cucumber Chicken Salad

START TO FINISH: 25 minutes

NUTRITION FACTS per serving:

CALORIES 256
TOTAL FAT 13 g (2 g sat. fat)
CHOLESTEROL 60 mg
PROTEIN 23 g
CARBOHYDRATE 11 g
FIBER 2 g
SODIUM 105 mg

EXCHANGES 0.5 Fruit, 3 Very Lean Meat, 1.5 Vegetable, 2 Fat

6 cups cut-up romaine or napa
    cabbage

2 cups chopped cooked chicken
    breast (about 10 ounces)

1 small apple, cored and
    cut into chunks

½ cup green and/or red seedless
    grapes, halved

3 tablespoons water

2 tablespoons reduced-fat
    peanut butter

2 teaspoons reduced-sodium
    soy sauce

¼ teaspoon ground ginger

1 On four serving plates stack romaine, chicken, apple, and grapes.

2 For dressing, in a small bowl whisk together the water, peanut butter, soy sauce, and ginger; drizzle over arranged salads. Makes 4 servings.

Apple-Grape Chicken Salad

START TO FINISH: 30 minutes

NUTRITION FACTS per serving:

- -

CALORIES 205
TOTAL FAT 6 g (1 g sat. fat)
CHOLESTEROL 60 mg
PROTEIN 25 g
CARBOHYDRATE 14 g
FIBER 3 g
SODIUM 218 mg

EXCHANGES 0.5 Fruit, 3 Very Lean Meat,
1.5 Vegetable, 0.5 Fat

3   tablespoons canola oil

½   teaspoon finely shredded
    lime peel

2   tablespoons lime juice

1   tablespoon water

8   cups torn butterhead lettuce
    (Boston or Bibb)

2   medium mangoes, seeded, peeled,
    and thinly sliced

12 ounces cooked smoked turkey or
    chicken breast, cut into
    bite-size pieces

¼   cup chopped green onion

2   tablespoons snipped fresh cilantro
    Lime wedges (optional)

1 For lime vinaigrette, in a screw-top jar combine oil, lime peel, lime juice, and water. Cover and shake well.

2 Divide lettuce among four salad plates. Arrange mangoes, smoked turkey, and green onion on lettuce. Sprinkle individual servings with cilantro and drizzle with lime vinaigrette. If desired, serve salads with lime wedges. Makes 4 servings.

Make-Ahead Directions: Prepare lime vinaigrette as above in step 1. Cover and chill for up to 4 hours. Shake the dressing before drizzling over salad.

COOK'S TIP
The tough skin of mangoes is not intended to be eaten. For some people the skin causes an allergic reaction.

Mango Salad with Turkey

START TO FINISH: 30 minutes

NUTRITION FACTS per serving:

CALORIES 256
TOTAL FAT 12 g (1 g sat. fat)
CHOLESTEROL 37 mg
PROTEIN 19 g
CARBOHYDRATE 23 g
FIBER 3 g
SODIUM 1,031 mg

EXCHANGES 0.5 Fruit, 3 Very Lean Meat, 2 Vegetable, 2 Fat

Turkey Taco Salad

START TO FINISH: 25 minutes

NUTRITION FACTS per serving:

- -

CALORIES 228
TOTAL FAT 4 g (1 g sat. fat)
CHOLESTEROL 39 mg
PROTEIN 26 g
CARBOHYDRATE 27 g
FIBER 4 g
SODIUM 611 mg

EXCHANGES 1.5 Starch, 3 Very Lean Meat,
1 Vegetable

Nonstick cooking spray
12 ounces ground uncooked
     turkey breast
1   15-ounce can pinto beans, rinsed
     and drained (optional)
1   cup loose-pack frozen whole
     kernel corn
1   cup purchased salsa
¼   cup water
4   to 6 cups shredded romaine
¼   cup shredded reduced-fat
     cheddar cheese (1 ounce)
2   ounces purchased baked
     tortilla chips

1 Lightly coat an unheated large nonstick
skillet with nonstick cooking spray. Preheat
over medium heat. Add ground turkey to hot
skillet; cook about 5 minutes or until no longer
pink. Drain off fat. Stir in beans (if desired),
corn, salsa, and water. Bring to boiling; reduce
heat. Cover and simmer for 2 to 3 minutes to
blend flavors.

2 Line four salad bowls or serving plates
with romaine. Top with hot turkey mixture.
Sprinkle with cheese. Serve with tortilla chips.
Makes 4 servings.

- 3 tablespoons water
- 2 tablespoons balsamic vinegar
- 1 tablespoon powdered fruit pectin
- 2 tablespoons snipped fresh oregano, thyme, and/or basil or 2 teaspoons dried oregano, thyme, and/or basil, crushed
- 1 tablespoon lime juice
- 1 tablespoon honey
- ½ teaspoon salt
- 4 fresh or frozen skinless salmon fillets, cut 1 inch thick (1 to 1¼ pounds total)

  Nonstick cooking spray
- 6 cups torn mixed salad greens
- ¾ cup bottled roasted red sweet peppers, drained and cut into thin strips

Herbed Salmon with Greens

PREP: 20 minutes **CHILL:** 30 minutes to 3 days
GRILL: 8 minutes

NUTRITION FACTS per serving:

CALORIES 255
TOTAL FAT 13 g (3 g sat. fat)
CHOLESTEROL 67 mg
PROTEIN 24 g
CARBOHYDRATE 11 g
FIBER 2 g
SODIUM 371 mg

EXCHANGES 3 Lean Meat, 1.5 Vegetable, 1 Fat

1 For dressing, in a screw-top jar combine water, balsamic vinegar, pectin, half of the fresh or dried herb, lime juice, honey, and ¼ teaspoon salt. Cover and shake well. Chill for 30 minutes to 3 days.

2 Thaw salmon, if frozen. Rinse salmon; pat dry with paper towels. Coat salmon on all sides with nonstick cooking spray. Sprinkle salmon with remaining fresh or dried herbs and remaining ¼ teaspoon salt. For a charcoal grill, place salmon on the greased rack of an uncovered grill directly over medium coals. Grill for 8 to 12 minutes or until salmon flakes easily when tested with a fork, turning once halfway through grilling. (For a gas grill, preheat grill. Reduce heat to medium. Place salmon on greased grill rack over heat. Cover and grill as above.)

3 Divide salad greens and roasted red peppers among four serving plates. Top with salmon. Shake dressing; drizzle over salads. Makes 4 servings.

Shrimp Salad

PREP: 25 minutes

CHILL: 4 hours

NUTRITION FACTS per serving:

CALORIES 244
TOTAL FAT 9 g (1 g sat. fat)
CHOLESTEROL 129 mg
PROTEIN 20 g
CARBOHYDRATE 23 g
FIBER 5 g
SODIUM 177 mg

EXCHANGES 0.5 Starch, 0.5 Fruit, 2.5 Very Lean Meat, 1.5 Vegetable, 1 Fat

NUTRITION NOTE

With so many protein sources available, most Americans easily meet their daily protein requirements. Choose low-fat protein foods such as shrimp, which is lower in saturated fat than many other protein sources.

2   tablespoons finely snipped dried tomatoes (not oil pack)
¼   cup balsamic vinegar
2   tablespoons olive oil
1   tablespoon snipped fresh basil
2   cloves garlic, minced
⅛   teaspoon black pepper
12   ounces fresh or frozen peeled, deveined shrimp (leave tails intact if desired)*
4   cups water
1   clove garlic
8   ounces fresh asparagus, trimmed and cut into 2-inch-long pieces
6   cups torn mixed salad greens
2   medium pears, thinly sliced

1 For dressing, in a small bowl pour enough boiling water over dried tomatoes to cover; let stand for 2 minutes. Drain. In the same small bowl whisk together tomatoes, balsamic vinegar, oil, basil, 2 cloves garlic, and pepper. Set aside.

2 Rinse shrimp; pat dry with paper towels. Set aside. In a large saucepan combine water and 1 clove garlic; bring to boiling. Add asparagus. Return to boiling; reduce heat. Simmer, uncovered, for 4 minutes. Add shrimp. Return to boiling; reduce heat. Simmer, uncovered, for 1 to 3 minutes more or until shrimp are opaque. Drain, discarding garlic. Rinse under cold running water; drain well. Cover and chill for 4 hours.

3 To serve, divide greens and pears among four serving plates. Top with shrimp and asparagus. Shake dressing; drizzle over salads. Makes 4 servings.

*Thaw and drain shrimp, if frozen.

Make-Ahead Directions: Prepare as above through step 2. Chill dressing and shrimp separately for up to 24 hours. Serve as above in step 3.

1   medium fennel bulb

12 fresh or frozen sea scallops
    (1 to 1½ pounds total)

⅛   teaspoon salt

⅛   teaspoon black pepper

⅓   cup plain low-fat yogurt

1   to 1½ teaspoons grated fresh
    ginger or ⅛ to ¼ teaspoon
    ground ginger

½   teaspoon finely shredded
    orange peel

1   teaspoon orange juice

1   teaspoon honey

2   medium oranges, peeled and
    thinly sliced crosswise

4   cups watercress,
    tough stems removed

1 Preheat broiler. Cut off and discard upper stalks from fennel bulb. Remove any wilted outer layers and cut and discard a thin slice from fennel base. Cut fennel bulb into very thin slices.* Set aside.

2 Thaw scallops, if frozen. Rinse scallops; pat dry with paper towels. Sprinkle scallops with salt and pepper. Place scallops on the unheated rack of a broiler pan. Broil 4 inches from the heat about 8 minutes or until scallops are opaque, turning once halfway through broiling.

3 Meanwhile, for dressing, in a small bowl whisk together yogurt, ginger, orange peel, orange juice, and honey. Set aside.

4 Cut orange slices in half. Divide sliced fennel and watercress among four serving plates. Top with scallops and orange slices. Drizzle with dressing. Makes 4 servings.

*Use a mandoline to slice fennel very thinly.

Scallops with Watercress and Fennel

START TO FINISH: 25 minutes

NUTRITION FACTS per serving:

CALORIES 172
TOTAL FAT 1 g (0 g sat. fat)
CHOLESTEROL 39 mg
PROTEIN 22 g
CARBOHYDRATE 18 g
FIBER 4 g
SODIUM 314 mg

EXCHANGES 0.5 Other Carbohydrates, 0.5 Fruit, 3 Very Lean Meat, 1 Vegetable

Shrimply Delicious Salad

PREP: 30 minutes   **MARINATE:** 1 hour
GRILL: 5 minutes

NUTRITION FACTS per serving:

CALORIES 331
TOTAL FAT 13 g (1 g sat. fat)
CHOLESTEROL 172 mg
PROTEIN 27 g
CARBOHYDRATE 30 g
FIBER 4 g
SODIUM 192 mg

EXCHANGES 1 Fruit, 3 Very Lean Meat,
2.5 Vegetable, 2 Fat

16	ounces fresh or frozen peeled, deveined large shrimp (leave tails intact if desired)
¼	cup orange juice
¼	cup lime juice
¾	to 1 teaspoon bottled hot pepper sauce
2	tablespoons canola oil
1	tablespoon sugar
2	teaspoons red wine vinegar
1	teaspoon toasted sesame oil
8	cups torn mixed salad greens
2	11-ounce cans mandarin orange sections, drained
2	medium red, green, and/or yellow sweet peppers, cut into bite-size strips
½	cup thinly sliced red onion
2	tablespoons sesame seeds, toasted

1 If using wooden skewers, soak skewers in warm water for 30 minutes.

2 Thaw shrimp, if frozen. Rinse shrimp; pat dry with paper towels. In a screw-top jar combine orange juice, lime juice, and hot pepper sauce. Cover and shake well. Place ¼ cup of the juice mixture in a medium bowl. Add shrimp and toss to coat. Cover and marinate in the refrigerator for 1 hour.

3 For dressing, add canola oil, sugar, red wine vinegar, and toasted sesame oil to remaining juice mixture in screw-top jar. Cover and shake well; set aside.

4 Drain shrimp, discarding marinade. Thread shrimp onto skewers, leaving a ¼-inch space between shrimp.

5 For a charcoal grill, place skewers on the greased rack of an uncovered grill directly over medium coals. Grill for 5 to 8 minutes or until shrimp are opaque, turning once halfway through grilling. (For a gas grill, preheat grill. Reduce heat to medium. Place skewers on grill rack over heat. Cover and grill as above.)

6 In a large bowl combine salad greens, orange sections, sweet peppers, and red onion. Add dressing; toss gently to coat. Divide among four serving plates. Arrange shrimp on greens mixture. Sprinkle with sesame seeds. Makes 4 servings.

3 medium red potatoes
(about 1 pound)

½ cup light mayonnaise or
salad dressing

½ cup plain fat-free yogurt

1 tablespoon snipped fresh dill or
1 teaspoon dried dill

1 tablespoon fat-free milk

½ teaspoon finely shredded
lemon peel

¼ teaspoon salt

1 clove garlic, minced

1 cup chopped cucumber

¼ cup sliced green onion

¼ cup coarsely chopped radishes

1 9-ounce can chunk white tuna
(water pack), drained and
broken into chunks

2 hard-cooked eggs, chopped

12 leaves savoy cabbage or
napa cabbage

Fresh dill sprigs (optional)

1 Scrub potatoes; cut into ½-inch cubes. In a covered medium saucepan cook potatoes in a small amount of boiling water for 10 to 12 minutes or just until tender. Drain and cool slightly.

2 Meanwhile, in a large bowl stir together mayonnaise, yogurt, snipped dill, milk, lemon peel, salt, and garlic. Stir in cucumber, green onion, and radishes. Add cooked potatoes, tuna, and chopped eggs; toss gently to coat. Cover and chill for 4 to 6 hours.

3 To serve, line six serving bowls with cabbage leaves. Gently stir tuna mixture; spoon on cabbage. If desired, garnish with fresh dill. Makes 6 servings.

Dilled Tuna and Potato Salad

PREP: 25 minutes

CHILL: 4 to 6 hours

NUTRITION FACTS per serving:

CALORIES 243
TOTAL FAT 10 g (2 g sat. fat)
CHOLESTEROL 96 mg
PROTEIN 18 g
CARBOHYDRATE 22 g
FIBER 5 g
SODIUM 461 mg

EXCHANGES 1 Starch, 2 Very Lean Meat, 1.5 Vegetable, 1.5 Fat

Salad Niçoise

START TO FINISH: 35 minutes

NUTRITION FACTS per serving:

CALORIES 232
TOTAL FAT 14 g (3 g sat. fat)
CHOLESTEROL 124 mg
PROTEIN 16 g
CARBOHYDRATE 12 g
FIBER 5 g
SODIUM 595 mg

EXCHANGES 1.5 Lean Meat, 2.5 Vegetable, 2 Fat

NUTRITION NOTE

Choose water-packed over oil-packed tuna. Water-packed tuna contains less fat than oil-packed and offers more healthful omega-3 fatty acids.

4	ounces fresh green beans
5	cups packaged European-style torn mixed salad greens
1	6-ounce can chunk white tuna (water pack), drained and broken into chunks
4	medium tomatoes, quartered
2	hard-cooked eggs, quartered
¾	cup pitted ripe olives
½	cup snipped fresh flat-leaf parsley
3	green onions, cut into ½-inch-long pieces
4	anchovy fillets, drained, rinsed, and patted dry (optional)
1	recipe Niçoise Dressing

1 Leave beans whole or snap in half. In a covered medium saucepan cook green beans in a small amount of lightly salted boiling water about 5 minutes or just until tender. Drain and place in ice water until chilled; drain well. If desired, cover and chill for 2 to 24 hours.

2 In four salad bowls arrange greens, green beans, tuna, tomatoes, eggs, and olives. Sprinkle with parsley and green onion. If desired, top with anchovy fillets. Drizzle Niçoise Dressing over salads. Makes 4 servings.

Niçoise Dressing: In a small bowl combine 2 tablespoons olive oil, 2 tablespoons white wine vinegar, ½ teaspoon Dijon-style mustard, ¼ teaspoon salt, and ⅛ teaspoon black pepper. Whisk together until combined.

2½   cups water
1   cup wheat berries, rinsed
2   tablespoons lemon juice
2   tablespoons canola oil
1   tablespoon maple-flavored syrup
¼   teaspoon ground cinnamon
¼   teaspoon salt
¼   teaspoon black pepper
1   medium apple, cored, peeled, and sliced
1   large carrot, shredded
2   green onions, sliced
6   cups fresh baby spinach
¼   cup snipped dried apricots

1 In a small saucepan bring water to boiling. Add wheat berries to boiling water. Return to boiling; reduce heat. Cover and simmer for 40 to 50 minutes or until tender. Drain and transfer to a large bowl. Let cool for 1 hour.

2 In a small bowl whisk together lemon juice, oil, syrup, cinnamon, salt, and pepper. Drizzle dressing over cooled wheat berries. Add apple, carrot, and green onion; toss to coat. Serve wheat berry mixture with baby spinach; sprinkle with dried apricots. Makes 4 servings.

Wheat Berry Salad

PREP: 20 minutes   **COOK:** 40 minutes
COOL: 1 hour

NUTRITION FACTS per serving:

CALORIES 284
TOTAL FAT 8 g (1 g sat. fat)
CHOLESTEROL 0 mg
PROTEIN 8 g
CARBOHYDRATE 50 g
FIBER 12 g
SODIUM 217 mg

EXCHANGES 2 Starch, 0.5 Fruit, 2 Vegetable, 1.5 Fat

1   15-ounce can black beans, rinsed and drained

6   cups packaged shredded cabbage with carrot (coleslaw mix)

2   medium green apples, cored and chopped

1   large red sweet pepper, cut into strips

¼   cup cider vinegar

2   tablespoons reduced-sodium soy sauce

2   tablespoons peanut oil

2   teaspoons grated fresh ginger

2   teaspoons honey

¼   teaspoon black pepper

Black Bean Slaw with Soy-Ginger Dressing

START TO FINISH: 20 minutes

NUTRITION FACTS per serving:

CALORIES 217
TOTAL FAT 7 g (1 g sat. fat)
CHOLESTEROL 0 mg
PROTEIN 9 g
CARBOHYDRATE 36 g
FIBER 9 g
SODIUM 577 mg

EXCHANGES 1 Starch, 0.5 Fruit, 0.5 Very Lean Meat, 2 Vegetable, 1 Fat

1 In a large bowl combine black beans, shredded cabbage with carrot, apple, and sweet pepper. In a small screw-top jar combine cider vinegar, soy sauce, peanut oil, ginger, honey, and black pepper; cover and shake well. Pour over cabbage mixture. Toss to coat. Makes 4 servings.

Make-Ahead and Toting Directions:
Prepare slaw as above. Divide among four airtight storage containers. Cover and chill overnight. For each serving, pack a storage container of salad in an insulated container with at least two ice packs. Serve within 5 hours.

COOK'S TIP

Because the skin on fresh ginger is very thin, it is often used unpeeled. To grate the root, grate across the grain with a ginger grater or Microplane.

1 cup water
½ cup bulgur
2 cups fresh or frozen shelled sweet soybeans (edamame), thawed
1 medium red sweet pepper, seeded and cut into thin bite-size strips
½ cup coarsely shredded carrot
½ cup thinly sliced red onion
2 tablespoons snipped fresh cilantro
4 cups fresh spinach leaves
1 recipe Thai Peanut Dressing
¼ cup chopped peanuts (optional)

1 In a medium saucepan bring water to boiling; add uncooked bulgur. Return to boiling; reduce heat. Cover and simmer about 15 minutes or until bulgur is tender and most of the liquid is absorbed. Drain, if necessary. Transfer to a large bowl; stir in soybeans, sweet pepper, carrot, red onion, and cilantro.

2 Divide spinach among four serving plates. Top with bulgur mixture; drizzle with Thai Peanut Dressing. If desired, sprinkle with peanuts. Makes 4 servings.

Thai Peanut Dressing: In a small saucepan combine ⅓ cup water, ¼ cup creamy peanut butter, 2 tablespoons reduced-sodium soy sauce, 1 teaspoon sugar, ¼ teaspoon ground ginger, ⅛ teaspoon crushed red pepper, and 1 clove garlic, minced. Whisk constantly over medium-low heat about 3 minutes or until smooth and slightly thickened (mixture will appear curdled at first but will become smooth as it is whisked over the heat). Makes ⅔ cup.

Thai Bulgur Salad

PREP: 25 minutes
COOK: 15 minutes

NUTRITION FACTS per serving:

CALORIES 381
TOTAL FAT 17 g (3 g sat. fat)
CHOLESTEROL 0 mg
PROTEIN 25 g
CARBOHYDRATE 38 g
FIBER 12 g
SODIUM 420 mg

EXCHANGES 2 Starch, 2.5 Very Lean Meat, 1 Vegetable, 2.5 Fat

2 cups chopped romaine lettuce

2 cups cooked brown rice, chilled

1 15-ounce can black beans, rinsed
and drained

2 cups chopped tomato

1 cup chopped green, yellow, and/or
red sweet pepper

1 cup loose-pack frozen whole
kernel corn, thawed

2 green onions, thinly sliced

2 tablespoons snipped fresh cilantro

1 cup purchased picante sauce
or salsa

4 ounces Monterey Jack cheese
with jalapeño chile peppers, cut
into ¼-inch cubes (optional)

½ cup light dairy sour cream

Salsa, Black Bean, and Rice Salad

START TO FINISH: 25 minutes

NUTRITION FACTS per serving:

CALORIES 201
TOTAL FAT 3 g (1 g sat. fat)
CHOLESTEROL 6 mg
PROTEIN 9 g
CARBOHYDRATE 39 g
FIBER 7 g
SODIUM 469 mg

EXCHANGES 2 Starch, 1 Vegetable

1 In a large bowl stir together lettuce, chilled rice, black beans, tomato, sweet pepper, corn, green onion, and cilantro; add picante sauce or salsa. Toss to coat. If desired, stir in cheese. Serve with sour cream. Makes 6 servings.

Chapter 6

Soups

On the divider: Roasted Tomato-Vegetable Soup *(see recipe, page 177)*

- 2¼ cups water
- 1 14½-ounce can diced tomatoes with onion and garlic, undrained
- 1 cup lower-sodium beef broth
- ½ teaspoon dried Italian seasoning, crushed
- ½ cup dried multigrain or whole wheat elbow macaroni
- 2 cups loose-pack frozen Italian-blend vegetables
- ½ of a 16-ounce package frozen bite-size Italian-style cooked meatballs (16)
- 2 tablespoons shredded or grated Parmesan cheese (optional)

1 In a large saucepan stir together water, undrained tomatoes, beef broth, and Italian seasoning. Bring to boiling. Add uncooked pasta and frozen vegetables. Return to boiling; reduce heat. Cover and simmer about 10 minutes or until pasta and vegetables are tender.

2 Meanwhile, place meatballs in a medium microwave-safe bowl. Microwave, uncovered, on 100% power (high) for 2½ to 3 minutes or until heated through. Drain meatballs; pat dry with paper towels. If desired, halve meatballs. Stir meatballs into soup mixture.

3 If desired, sprinkle individual servings with Parmesan cheese.
Makes 4 (1¾-cup) servings.

Italian Meatball Soup

START TO FINISH: 25 minutes

NUTRITION FACTS per serving:

CALORIES 268
TOTAL FAT 13 g (6 g sat. fat)
CHOLESTEROL 37 mg
PROTEIN 14 g
CARBOHYDRATE 22 g
FIBER 5 g
SODIUM 1,052 mg

EXCHANGES 1 Starch, 1.5 High-Fat Meat, 1.5 Vegetable

2 pounds boneless beef chuck roast
Nonstick cooking spray
12 ounces tiny new potatoes, quartered
4 medium carrots, cut into ½-inch pieces
1 medium onion, cut into wedges
1 10¾-ounce can reduced-fat and reduced-sodium condensed cream of mushroom soup
1 cup lower-sodium beef broth
1 teaspoon dried marjoram or dried thyme, crushed
2 cups loose-pack frozen cut green beans (9 ounces)

Super-Simple Beef Stew

PREP: 30 minutes

COOK: 8 to 9 hours (low) or
4 to 4½ hours (high); plus 30 minutes (high)

NUTRITION FACTS per serving:

CALORIES 317
TOTAL FAT 9 g (3 g sat. fat)
CHOLESTEROL 92 mg
PROTEIN 35 g
CARBOHYDRATE 22 g
FIBER 4 g
SODIUM 396 mg

EXCHANGES 1 Starch, 4 Lean Meat,
1 Vegetable

1 Trim fat from beef; cut beef into 1-inch cubes. Coat an unheated large skillet with nonstick cooking spray. Preheat over medium-high heat. Add half of the beef cubes. Cook and stir until browned; remove from skillet. Add remaining beef cubes; cook and stir until browned. Drain off fat from beef.

2 Place beef in a 3½- or 4-quart slow cooker. Add potatoes, carrots, onion, cream of mushroom soup, beef broth, and marjoram. Stir to combine. Cover and cook on low-heat setting for 8 to 9 hours or on high-heat setting for 4 to 4½ hours.

3 If using low-heat setting, turn to high-heat setting. Stir in green beans. Cover and cook about 30 minutes more or just until green beans are tender. Makes 6 (1⅓-cup) servings.

Nonstick cooking spray

- 8 ounces extra-lean ground beef, uncooked ground chicken breast, or uncooked ground turkey breast
- 1 cup chopped onion
- 1½ teaspoons ground cumin
- 2 14½-ounce cans stewed tomatoes, undrained, cut up
- 1 15-ounce can red beans, rinsed and drained
- 1½ cups coarsely chopped red and/or yellow sweet pepper
- ½ cup water
- 2 to 3 teaspoons chopped canned chipotle chile peppers in adobo sauce*
- 1 tablespoon snipped fresh oregano
- ¼ cup shredded reduced-fat cheddar cheese

Lime wedges (optional)

Baked tortilla chips (optional)

Chipotle Chili with Beans

START TO FINISH: 25 minutes

NUTRITION FACTS per serving:

CALORIES 398
TOTAL FAT 14 g (6 g sat. fat)
CHOLESTEROL 57 mg
PROTEIN 27 g
CARBOHYDRATE 40 g
FIBER 10 g
SODIUM 1,030 mg

EXCHANGES 2.5 Starch, 2.5 Lean Meat, 0.5 Vegetable, 1 Fat

1 Lightly coat an unheated large saucepan with nonstick cooking spray. Preheat over medium heat. Add ground beef and onion; cook until browned. If necessary, drain off fat. Stir cumin into beef mixture in skillet; cook and stir for 1 minute more. Add undrained tomatoes, red beans, sweet pepper, water, and chile peppers. Bring to boiling; reduce heat. Cover and simmer for 5 minutes. Stir in oregano.

2 Spoon chili into serving bowls. Sprinkle individual servings with cheese. If desired, serve with lime wedges and tortilla chips. Makes 4 (1½-cup) servings.

*Because chile peppers contain volatile oils that can burn your skin and eyes, avoid direct contact with them as much as possible. When working with chile peppers, wear plastic or rubber gloves. If your bare hands do touch the peppers, wash your hands and nails well with soap and warm water.

COOK'S TIP

Chipotles in adobo sauce are smoked jalapeño peppers stewed in tomatoes, garlic, vinegar, salt, and spices. One pepper goes a long way, so don't overdo it.

Vegetable Beef Stew

PREP: 25 minutes

COOK: 8 to 10 hours (low) or 4 to 5 hours high); plus 15 minutes (high)

NUTRITION FACTS per serving:

CALORIES 220
TOTAL FAT 5 g (1 g sat. fat)
CHOLESTEROL 67 mg
PROTEIN 27 g
CARBOHYDRATE 18 g
FIBER 3 g
SODIUM 465 mg

EXCHANGES 1 Starch, 3 Lean Meat, 1 Vegetable

1	1½-pound boneless beef chuck pot roast
1	pound butternut squash, peeled, seeded, and cut into 1-inch pieces (about 2½ cups)
2	small onions, cut into wedges
2	cloves garlic, minced
1	14-ounce can lower-sodium beef broth
1	8-ounce can tomato sauce
2	tablespoons Worcestershire sauce
1	teaspoon dry mustard
¼	teaspoon black pepper
⅛	teaspoon ground allspice
2	tablespoons cold water
4	teaspoons cornstarch
1	9-ounce package frozen Italian green beans

1 Trim fat from meat. Cut meat into 1-inch pieces. Place meat in a 3½- to 4½-quart slow cooker. Add squash, onions, and garlic. Stir in beef broth, tomato sauce, Worcestershire sauce, dry mustard, pepper, and allspice.

2 Cover and cook on low-heat setting for 8 to 10 hours or on high-heat setting for 4 to 5 hours.

3 If using low-heat setting, turn to high-heat setting. In a small bowl combine cold water and cornstarch. Stir cornstarch mixture and green beans into mixture in slow cooker. Cover and cook about 15 minutes more or until thickened. Makes 6 (1⅓-cup) servings.

COOK'S TIP

Use cold water to mix with cornstarch, stirring until it resembles a smooth paste. Cornstarch mixed with hot water becomes lumpy.

1 tablespoon olive oil

12 ounces pork tenderloin or lean boneless pork, cut into bite-size pieces

1 cup chopped red onion

4 cloves garlic, minced

1 10-ounce package frozen whole kernel corn

2 14-ounce cans reduced-sodium chicken broth

1 cup purchased chipotle-style salsa or regular salsa

1 cup chopped red and/or yellow sweet pepper

½ cup chopped tomato

¼ cup snipped fresh cilantro

Light dairy sour cream (optional)

1 In a large saucepan heat oil over medium-high heat. Add pork strips; cook and stir for 4 to 5 minutes or until brown and juices run clear. Remove pork strips from saucepan; set aside. Add red onion and garlic to saucepan. Cook and stir for 3 to 4 minutes or until onion is tender.

2 Add corn to saucepan. Cook and stir for 4 minutes. Stir in chicken broth, salsa, and sweet pepper. Bring to boiling; reduce heat. Simmer, uncovered, for 10 minutes. Return pork strips to saucepan; heat through. Remove saucepan from heat; stir in tomato and cilantro. If desired, top individual servings with sour cream. Makes 5 (about 1⅓-cup) servings.

Tex-Mex Chicken and Corn Soup: Prepare as above, except omit the pork and use 12 ounces skinless, boneless chicken breast halves, cut into 1-inch pieces.

Tex-Mex Pork and Corn Soup

START TO FINISH: 40 minutes

NUTRITION FACTS per serving:

CALORIES 204
TOTAL FAT 6 g (1 g sat. fat)
CHOLESTEROL 44 mg
PROTEIN 20 g
CARBOHYDRATE 21 g
FIBER 3 g
SODIUM 725 mg

EXCHANGES 1.5 Starch, 2 Lean Meat, 0.5 Vegetable

Asian Pork Soup

START TO FINISH: 25 minutes

NUTRITION FACTS per serving:

CALORIES 160
TOTAL FAT 6 g (1 g sat. fat)
CHOLESTEROL 31 mg
PROTEIN 16 g
CARBOHYDRATE 10 g
FIBER 1 g
SODIUM 691 mg

EXCHANGES 2 Lean Meat, 0.5 Vegetable

1	tablespoon canola oil
12	ounces lean boneless pork, cut into thin bite-size strips
2	cups sliced fresh shiitake mushrooms
2	cloves garlic, minced
3	14-ounce cans reduced-sodium chicken broth
2	tablespoons dry sherry
2	tablespoons reduced-sodium soy sauce
2	teaspoons grated fresh ginger or ½ teaspoon ground ginger
¼	teaspoon crushed red pepper
2	cups shredded napa cabbage
1	green onion, thinly sliced
	Fresh cilantro sprigs (optional)

1 In a large saucepan heat oil over medium heat. Add pork; cook and stir for 2 to 3 minutes or until pork is slightly pink in center. Remove from pan; set aside. Add mushrooms and garlic to saucepan; cook until tender.

2 Stir in chicken broth, sherry, soy sauce, ginger, and crushed red pepper. Bring to boiling. Stir in pork, napa cabbage, and green onion; heat through. If desired, garnish individual servings with cilantro. Makes 6 (about 1-cup) servings.

COOK'S TIP

To clean mushrooms, wipe them with a damp paper towel. Avoid washing/rinsing them under running water, which causes them to absorb excess liquid.

1	tablespoon olive oil
2	cups chopped onion
6	cloves garlic, minced
1	tablespoon snipped fresh rosemary or 1 teaspoon dried rosemary, crushed
6	ounces cooked ham, chopped (about 1 cup)
1	cup sliced celery
¾	cup regular barley (not quick-cooking), rinsed
5	cups reduced-sodium chicken broth
3	cups water
1½	cups sliced carrot
2	teaspoons snipped fresh marjoram or ½ teaspoon dried marjoram, crushed
2	teaspoons snipped fresh oregano or ½ teaspoon dried oregano, crushed
1	tablespoon lemon juice
2	tablespoons shredded Parmesan cheese (optional)
	Cracked or freshly ground black pepper (optional)

Ham and Barley Soup

PREP: 30 minutes

COOK: 45 minutes

NUTRITION FACTS per serving:

CALORIES 182
TOTAL FAT 4 g (1 g sat. fat)
CHOLESTEROL 13 mg
PROTEIN 12 g
CARBOHYDRATE 27 g
FIBER 6 g
SODIUM 985 mg

EXCHANGES 1.5 Starch, 1 Lean Meat, 0.5 Vegetable

1 In a 4- to 6-quart Dutch oven heat oil over medium heat. Add onion; cook about 5 minutes or until tender, stirring occasionally. Add garlic and rosemary; cook and stir for 1 minute. Add ham, celery, and uncooked barley; cook for 4 minutes, stirring occasionally.

2 Add chicken broth and water. Bring to boiling; reduce heat. Cover and simmer for 30 minutes. Stir in carrot, marjoram, and oregano. Cover and simmer for 15 to 20 minutes more or until carrot and barley are tender.

3 Stir in lemon juice. If desired, sprinkle individual servings with Parmesan cheese and black pepper. Makes 6 (1¾-cup) servings.

3   14-ounce cans reduced-sodium chicken broth

1½ cups water

1   cup chopped celery

6   ounces cooked ham, chopped (about 1 cup)

¾   cup wild rice, rinsed and drained

1   medium onion, cut into thin wedges

1½ teaspoons dried thyme, crushed

2   medium red sweet peppers, seeded and cut into bite-size pieces

4   cups shredded fresh spinach

Wild Rice-Ham Soup

PREP: 20 minutes

COOK: 6 to 7 hours (low) or

3 to 3½ hours (high); plus 30 minutes (high)

NUTRITION FACTS per serving:

CALORIES 140

TOTAL FAT 1 g (0 g sat. fat)

CHOLESTEROL 14 mg

PROTEIN 12 g

CARBOHYDRATE 21 g

FIBER 3 g

SODIUM 927 mg

EXCHANGES 1 Starch, 1 Lean Meat, 1.5 Vegetable

1 In a 4- to 5-quart slow cooker combine chicken broth, water, celery, ham, uncooked wild rice, onion, and thyme.

2 Cover and cook on low-heat setting for 6 to 7 hours or on high-heat setting for 3 to 3½ hours.

3 If using low-heat setting, turn to high-heat setting. Stir in sweet pepper; cover and cook for 30 minutes more. Just before serving, stir in spinach. Makes 6 (1½-cup) servings.

COOK'S TIP

Leftover celery can be stored in a plastic bag in the refrigerator for up to two weeks.

1	tablespoon olive oil
1	cup sliced carrot
½	cup chopped celery
½	cup chopped onion
3	14-ounce cans reduced-sodium chicken broth
2	15-ounce cans cannellini beans (white kidney beans), rinsed and drained
8	ounces skinless, boneless chicken breast, cut into bite-size pieces
1	cup fresh green beans cut into ½-inch pieces (4 ounces)
¼	teaspoon black pepper
1	cup dried bow tie pasta
1	medium zucchini, quartered lengthwise and cut into ½-inch-thick slices
1	14½-ounce can diced tomatoes with basil, garlic, and oregano, undrained

1 In a 5- to 6-quart Dutch oven heat oil over medium heat. Add carrot, celery, and onion; cook for 5 minutes, stirring frequently. Add chicken broth, cannellini beans, chicken, green beans, and pepper. Bring to boiling; add uncooked pasta. Reduce heat. Simmer, uncovered, for 5 minutes.

2 Stir in zucchini. Return to boiling; reduce heat. Simmer, uncovered, for 8 to 10 minutes more or until pasta is tender and green beans are crisp-tender. Stir in undrained tomatoes; heat through. Makes 8 (about 1⅓-cup) servings.

Chicken Minestrone Soup

START TO FINISH: 45 minutes

NUTRITION FACTS per serving:

CALORIES 173
TOTAL FAT 3 g (0 g sat. fat)
CHOLESTEROL 16 mg
PROTEIN 17 g
CARBOHYDRATE 27 g
FIBER 7 g
SODIUM 818 mg

EXCHANGES 1.5 Starch, 1.5 Very Lean Meat, 1 Vegetable

2 teaspoons olive oil

12 ounces skinless, boneless chicken breast halves, cut into ¾-inch pieces

3 cloves garlic, minced

3 cups sliced fresh mushrooms (about 8 ounces)

2 14-ounce cans reduced-sodium chicken broth

1 ¾ cups water

1 9-ounce package refrigerated cheese-filled tortellini

2 medium carrots, cut into thin bite-size strips

2 cups torn fresh baby spinach

1 tablespoon snipped fresh tarragon

Chicken-Tortellini Soup

START TO FINISH: 40 minutes

NUTRITION FACTS per serving:

CALORIES 265
TOTAL FAT 6 g (2 g sat. fat)
CHOLESTEROL 53 mg
PROTEIN 24 g
CARBOHYDRATE 30 g
FIBER 3 g
SODIUM 618 mg

EXCHANGES 2 Starch, 2 Very Lean Meat, 1 Vegetable, 0.5 Fat

1 In a 4- to 6-quart Dutch oven heat olive oil over medium-high heat. Add chicken and garlic; cook and stir about 4 minutes or until outsides of chicken pieces are no longer pink. Using a slotted spoon, remove chicken from Dutch oven. Add mushrooms to the same Dutch oven. Cook about 5 minutes or just until tender, stirring frequently. Carefully add chicken broth and water; bring to boiling.

2 Add tortellini, carrot strips, and partially cooked chicken to broth mixture. Return to boiling; reduce heat. Cover and simmer for 7 to 9 minutes or until tortellini are tender, stirring occasionally. Stir in spinach and tarragon. Makes 6 (1⅓-cup) servings.

- 2 14-ounce cans reduced-sodium chicken broth
- 2 cups loose-pack frozen yellow, green, and red peppers and onion stir-fry vegetables
- 1 14½-ounce can Mexican-style stewed tomatoes, undrained
- 2 cups chopped cooked chicken breast (10 ounces)
- 2 cups packaged baked tortilla chips

  Chopped avocado (optional)

1 In a large saucepan combine chicken broth, frozen vegetables, and undrained tomatoes. Bring to boiling; reduce heat. Cover and simmer for 3 to 5 minutes or until vegetables are tender. Stir in chicken; heat through.

2 Ladle soup into warm soup bowls. Serve individual servings with tortilla chips. If desired, top with avocado. Makes 4 (about 1½-cup) servings.

Chicken Tortilla Soup

START TO FINISH: 20 minutes

NUTRITION FACTS per serving:

CALORIES 287
TOTAL FAT 4 g (1 g sat. fat)
CHOLESTEROL 60 mg
PROTEIN 29 g
CARBOHYDRATE 32 g
FIBER 4 g
SODIUM 870 mg

EXCHANGES 2 Starch, 3 Very Lean Meat, 1 Vegetable

Wild Rice Chicken Soup

PREP: 30 minutes

COOK: 45 minutes

NUTRITION FACTS per serving:

CALORIES 218

TOTAL FAT 3 g (1 g sat. fat)

CHOLESTEROL 40 mg

PROTEIN 21 g

CARBOHYDRATE 29 g

FIBER 3 g

SODIUM 361 mg

EXCHANGES 1.5 Starch, 2 Very Lean Meat, 1 Vegetable

2 cups water

½ cup wild rice, rinsed and drained

½ cup long grain brown rice

2 14-ounce cans reduced-sodium chicken broth

4 cloves garlic, minced

4 cups chopped fresh tomatoes or two 14½-ounce cans diced tomatoes, undrained

2 cups chopped cooked chicken breast (10 ounces)

1 cup finely chopped zucchini

¼ teaspoon freshly ground black pepper

1 tablespoon snipped fresh thyme or 1 teaspoon dried thyme, crushed

1 tablespoon Madeira or dry sherry (optional)

1 In a large saucepan bring water to boiling. Add uncooked wild rice and brown rice. Return to boiling; reduce heat. Cover and simmer for 40 to 45 minutes or until rice is tender and most of the liquid is absorbed. Remove from heat; set aside.

2 Meanwhile, in a 4-quart Dutch oven combine chicken broth and garlic; bring to boiling. Stir in tomatoes, cooked chicken, zucchini, and pepper. Return to boiling; reduce heat. Cover and simmer for 5 minutes. Stir in cooked rice, thyme, and, if desired, Madeira. Heat through. Makes 6 (1⅓-cup) servings.

- 1 pound skinless, boneless chicken breast halves, cut into 1-inch pieces
- 1 tablespoon canola oil
- 3 medium carrots, sliced
- 3 14-ounce cans reduced-sodium chicken broth
- 1 cup water
- 2 tablespoons rice vinegar
- 1 tablespoon reduced-sodium soy sauce
- 2 to 3 teaspoons grated fresh ginger or ½ to ¾ teaspoon ground ginger
- ¼ teaspoon black pepper
- 2 ounces soba (buckwheat noodles), coarsely broken
- 1 6-ounce package frozen pea pods, thawed and halved diagonally
- Reduced-sodium soy sauce (optional)

Ginger Chicken Noodle Soup

PREP: 20 minutes

COOK: 28 minutes

NUTRITION FACTS per serving:

CALORIES 218
TOTAL FAT 4 g (1 g sat. fat)
CHOLESTEROL 53 mg
PROTEIN 27 g
CARBOHYDRATE 16 g
FIBER 2 g
SODIUM 846 mg

EXCHANGES 1 Starch, 3.5 Very Lean Meat, 0.5 Vegetable

NUTRITION NOTE

Ginger, a source of magnesium, copper, potassium, and vitamin B_6, has long been used to help relieve gastrointestinal distress.

1 In a Dutch oven cook chicken, half at a time, in hot oil just until browned. Drain off fat. Return all of the chicken to Dutch oven. Add carrots, chicken broth, water, rice vinegar, soy sauce, ginger, and pepper. Bring to boiling; reduce heat. Cover and simmer for 20 minutes.

2 Add uncooked noodles to soup. Return to boiling; reduce heat. Simmer, uncovered, for 8 to 10 minutes or until noodles are tender, adding pea pods for the last 2 minutes of cooking time. If desired, serve with additional soy sauce. Makes 5 (1½-cup) servings.

Slow Cooker Directions: In a large skillet cook chicken, half at a time, in hot oil just until browned. Using a slotted spoon, transfer chicken to a 3½- or 4-quart slow cooker. Add carrots, chicken broth, water, rice vinegar, soy sauce, ginger, and pepper. Cover and cook on low-heat setting for 4 to 6 hours or on high-heat setting for 2 to 3 hours.

If using low-heat setting, turn to high-heat setting. Stir in uncooked noodles and pea pods. Cover and cook for 10 to 15 minutes more or until noodles are tender. Serve as above.

Kale, Lentil, and Chicken Soup

PREP: 30 minutes

COOK: 25 minutes

NUTRITION FACTS per serving:

CALORIES 248
TOTAL FAT 5 g (1 g sat. fat)
CHOLESTEROL 40 mg
PROTEIN 25 g
CARBOHYDRATE 27 g
FIBER 9 g
SODIUM 752 mg

EXCHANGES 1 Starch, 2.5 Very Lean Meat, 1.5 Vegetable, 0.5 Fat

NUTRITION NOTE

A single cup of kale provides a whopping dose of vitamin K and more than 10 percent of the daily fiber recommendation.

1 tablespoon olive oil
1 cup chopped onion
1 cup coarsely chopped carrot
2 cloves garlic, minced
6 cups reduced-sodium chicken broth
⅔ cup dry brown lentils
1 tablespoon snipped fresh basil or 1 teaspoon dried basil, crushed
4 cups coarsely chopped fresh kale
¼ teaspoon black pepper
2 cups cubed cooked chicken (10 ounces)
1 14½-ounce can diced tomatoes, undrained

1 In a 4-quart Dutch oven heat oil over medium heat. Add onion, carrot, and garlic. Cover and cook for 5 to 7 minutes or until vegetables are nearly tender, stirring occasionally.

2 Add chicken broth, lentils, and dried basil (if using) to vegetable mixture. Bring to boiling; reduce heat. Cover and simmer for 10 minutes. Stir in kale and pepper. Return to boiling; reduce heat. Cover and simmer for 10 minutes.

3 Stir in cooked chicken and undrained tomatoes. Cover and simmer for 5 to 10 minutes more or until kale and lentils are tender. Stir in fresh basil (if using). Makes 6 (1⅔-cup) servings.

2	teaspoons canola oil
1	large onion, chopped
1	large red sweet pepper, seeded and chopped
1½	teaspoons chili powder
1	teaspoon ground cumin
3	14-ounce cans reduced-sodium chicken broth
1½	cups peeled and seeded winter squash cut into ½-inch pieces
1	14½-ounce can Mexican-style stewed tomatoes, undrained, cut up
2	cups chopped cooked chicken or turkey (10 ounces)
1	cup loose-pack frozen whole kernel corn
¼	cup snipped fresh cilantro (optional)

1 In a 4-quart Dutch oven heat oil over medium heat. Add onion and sweet pepper; cook about 5 minutes or until tender, stirring occasionally. Stir in chili powder and cumin; cook and stir for 30 seconds.

2 Add chicken broth, squash, and undrained tomatoes. Bring to boiling; reduce heat. Cover and simmer about 20 minutes or until squash is tender, stirring occasionally. Stir in chicken and corn. Heat through. If desired, sprinkle with cilantro. Makes 6 (1⅔-cup) servings.

Mexican-Style Chicken Soup

PREP: 30 minutes

COOK: 20 minutes

NUTRITION FACTS per serving:

CALORIES 183
TOTAL FAT 4 g (1 g sat. fat)
CHOLESTEROL 40 mg
PROTEIN 19 g
CARBOHYDRATE 20 g
FIBER 2 g
SODIUM 751 mg

EXCHANGES 1 Starch, 2 Very Lean Meat, 1 Vegetable

1 tablespoon olive oil
1 cup chopped onion
1 cup chopped green sweet pepper
1 cup sliced fresh mushrooms
1 small zucchini, halved lengthwise
   and sliced
1 14½-ounce can diced tomatoes
   with basil, garlic, and oregano,
   undrained
1 8-ounce can no-salt-added
   tomato sauce
1 cup water
¾ cup lower-sodium beef broth
4 ounces smoked turkey sausage,
   halved lengthwise and
   thinly sliced
½ teaspoon pizza seasoning
¼ cup shredded part-skim
   mozzarella cheese (1 ounce)

Pizza Soup

START TO FINISH: 35 minutes

NUTRITION FACTS per serving:

CALORIES 192
TOTAL FAT 8 g (2 g sat. fat)
CHOLESTEROL 24 mg
PROTEIN 11 g
CARBOHYDRATE 22 g
FIBER 3 g
SODIUM 957 mg

EXCHANGES 1 Lean Meat, 3 Vegetable, 1 Fat

1 In a large saucepan heat oil over medium heat. Add onion, sweet pepper, mushrooms, and zucchini; cook and stir about 5 minutes or until vegetables are lightly golden brown. Stir in undrained tomatoes, tomato sauce, water, beef broth, sausage, and pizza seasoning. Return to boiling; reduce heat. Simmer, uncovered, for 5 to 10 minutes more or until vegetables are tender. Top individual servings with cheese. Makes 4 servings.

8   ounces smoked turkey sausage, halved lengthwise and cut into ½-inch-thick slices

1   cup reduced-sodium chicken broth

¾   cup water

1   tablespoon snipped fresh rosemary or 1 teaspoon dried rosemary, crushed

3   cups torn fresh escarole, Swiss chard, kale, and/or spinach

1   15-ounce can cannellini beans (white kidney beans), rinsed and drained

1   medium yellow summer squash, coarsely chopped

1   cup packaged fresh julienned carrots

    Freshly ground black pepper

1 In a large saucepan combine sausage, chicken broth, water, and rosemary. Bring to boiling; reduce heat. Cover and simmer for 5 minutes. Stir in escarole, cannellini beans, squash, and carrots. Return to boiling; reduce heat. Cover and simmer about 5 minutes more or until vegetables are tender.

2 Season to taste with pepper. Makes 4 (1-cup) servings.

Sausage and Greens Ragout

START TO FINISH: 25 minutes

NUTRITION FACTS per serving:

CALORIES 174
TOTAL FAT 5 g (1 g sat. fat)
CHOLESTEROL 38 mg
PROTEIN 17 g
CARBOHYDRATE 21 g
FIBER 7 g
SODIUM 836 mg

EXCHANGES 1 Starch, 1.5 Lean Meat, 1.5 Vegetable

NUTRITION NOTE

The darker the greens, the healthier they are. Deeply colored greens such as kale and escarole have more vitamins and fiber than lighter greens such as iceberg lettuce.

Curried Corn Soup

START TO FINISH: 45 minutes

NUTRITION FACTS per serving:

CALORIES 271
TOTAL FAT 5 g (1 g sat. fat)
CHOLESTEROL 115 mg
PROTEIN 24 g
CARBOHYDRATE 36 g
FIBER 4 g
SODIUM 528 mg

EXCHANGES 1.5 Starch, 1 Milk,
2 Very Lean Meat

COOK'S TIP

To chop fragile herbs such as cilantro,
remove the stems, then place the leaves
in a small bowl. Using a pair of small sharp
kitchen shears, snip away.

2   teaspoons canola oil
1   cup finely chopped green and/or
      red sweet pepper
¼   cup finely chopped onion
2   teaspoons curry powder
¼   teaspoon salt
¼   teaspoon black pepper
3   cups fresh corn kernels or one
      16-ounce package frozen whole
      kernel corn, thawed (about 3 cups)
1   cup reduced-sodium chicken broth
3   cups fat-free milk or plain
      light soymilk
8   ounces peeled and deveined
      cooked medium shrimp*
2   tablespoons snipped fresh cilantro
⅓   cup plain low-fat yogurt or plain
      soy yogurt
     Fresh cilantro sprigs

1 In a large saucepan heat oil over medium-high heat. Add sweet pepper and onion; cook about 4 minutes or until tender, stirring occasionally. Add curry powder, salt, and pepper; cook and stir for 1 minute.

2 Stir in corn and chicken broth. Bring to boiling; reduce heat. Cover and cook about 5 minutes or until corn is tender. Cool about 10 minutes.

3 Transfer the corn mixture to a blender or food processor.** Add ½ cup of milk. Cover and blend or process until mixture is nearly smooth. Return pureed mixture to saucepan; stir in remaining 2½ cups milk and shrimp. Heat through (do not boil). Stir in snipped cilantro.

4 To serve, spoon soup into soup bowls. Top individual servings with yogurt and cilantro sprigs. Makes 4 (1¾-cup) servings.

*Thaw and drain shrimp, if frozen. If desired, cut each shrimp in half.

**If using a food processor, process mixture half at a time using ¼ cup milk with each half.

12 ounces fresh or frozen peeled and deveined shrimp (tails intact if desired)

2 14-ounce cans reduced-sodium chicken broth

1 cup water

2 stalks lemongrass (white part only), cut into ½-inch-thick slices

2 medium fresh jalapeño chile peppers, halved lengthwise and seeded*

1 cup stemmed and sliced fresh shiitake and/or button mushrooms or ½ of a 15-ounce can whole straw mushrooms, drained

1 cup chopped red sweet pepper

1 cup sliced carrot

2 tablespoons lime juice

2 tablespoons rice vinegar or white wine vinegar

1 tablespoon packed brown sugar

1 tablespoon bottled fish sauce

¼ cup slivered fresh basil

1 Thaw shrimp, if frozen. Rinse shrimp; pat dry with paper towels. Set aside.

2 In a large saucepan combine chicken broth and water; bring to boiling. Add lemongrass and chile peppers. Return to boiling; reduce heat. Cover and simmer for 10 minutes. Use a slotted spoon to remove lemongrass and chile peppers; discard.

3 Stir mushrooms, sweet pepper, carrot, lime juice, rice vinegar, brown sugar, and fish sauce into liquid in saucepan. Bring to boiling; reduce heat. Cover and simmer for 10 to 15 minutes or until vegetables are crisp-tender. Add shrimp. Cook, covered, for 2 to 4 minutes more or until shrimp are opaque. Sprinkle individual servings with basil. Makes 4 (1½-cup) servings.

*See handling note, page 155.

Thai Tofu Soup: Prepare as above, except omit shrimp and use 12 ounces firm, silken-style tofu (fresh bean curd), cut into bite-size pieces.

Thai Shrimp Soup

PREP: 30 minutes
COOK: 22 minutes

NUTRITION FACTS per serving:

CALORIES 170
TOTAL FAT 2 g (0 g sat. fat)
CHOLESTEROL 129 mg
PROTEIN 21 g
CARBOHYDRATE 17 g
FIBER 3 g
SODIUM 971 mg

EXCHANGES 1 Starch, 2.5 Very Lean Meat, 1 Vegetable

COOK'S TIP

When cooking with lemongrass, use something heavy such as a rolling pin to pound the lemongrass briefly before cutting it. The pressure causes it to release its oils and intensifies the flavor.

12 ounces fresh or frozen halibut steaks, cut 1 inch thick

2 teaspoons canola oil

¼ teaspoon cumin seeds

1 medium onion, chopped

2 to 3 teaspoons grated fresh ginger

1 fresh serrano chile pepper, seeded and finely chopped*

2 medium plum tomatoes, chopped

¾ cup water

½ teaspoon ground coriander

¼ teaspoon ground turmeric

¼ teaspoon salt

Hot 'n' Spicy Fish Soup

START TO FINISH: 35 minutes

NUTRITION FACTS per serving:

CALORIES 270
TOTAL FAT 9 g (1 g sat. fat)
CHOLESTEROL 54 mg
PROTEIN 37 g
CARBOHYDRATE 10 g
FIBER 2 g
SODIUM 393 mg

EXCHANGES 0.5 Starch, 5 Very Lean Meat, 1 Vegetable, 1 Fat

1 Thaw fish, if frozen. Rinse fish; pat dry with paper towels. Remove and discard skin and bones. Cut fish into 1-inch pieces; set aside.

2 In a medium saucepan heat oil over medium heat. Add cumin seeds; cook and stir about 1 minute or until toasted. Add onion; cook and stir for 4 to 5 minutes or until tender. Add ginger and chile pepper; cook and stir for 1 minute more. Add chopped tomato; cook and stir for 2 to 3 minutes more or until tomatoes have softened. Stir in water, coriander, turmeric, and salt. Bring just to boiling; reduce heat. Stir in fish pieces.

3 Cover and cook about 5 minutes or just until fish pieces flake easily when tested with a fork. Serve immediately. Makes 2 (1-cup) servings.

*Because chile peppers contain volatile oils that can burn your skin and eyes, avoid direct contact with them as much as possible. When working with chile peppers, wear plastic or rubber gloves. If your bare hands do touch the peppers, wash your hands and nails well with soap and warm water.

Nonstick cooking spray

2 leeks, thinly sliced (⅔ cup)

2 cloves garlic, minced

1 small sweet potato, peeled and chopped (1 cup)

2 cups peeled, chopped assorted root vegetables (such as parsnips, turnips, rutabagas, and/or carrots)

1 14-ounce can reduced-sodium chicken broth

1 12-ounce can evaporated fat-free milk

¼ teaspoon fennel seeds, crushed

⅛ teaspoon black pepper

1 Lightly coat an unheated medium saucepan with nonstick cooking spray. Preheat over medium heat. Add leeks and garlic; cook and stir until tender. Add sweet potato, assorted root vegetables, and chicken broth. Bring to boiling; reduce heat. Cover and simmer about 20 minutes or until vegetables are tender.

2 Stir in evaporated milk, fennel seeds, and pepper. Heat through but do not boil. Makes 4 (1-cup) servings.

Root Vegetable Chowder

PREP: 30 minutes
COOK: 20 minutes

NUTRITION FACTS per serving:

CALORIES 161
TOTAL FAT 0 g (0 g sat. fat)
CHOLESTEROL 3 mg
PROTEIN 10 g
CARBOHYDRATE 31 g
FIBER 4 g
SODIUM 388 mg

EXCHANGES 1.5 Starch, 0.5 Milk, 0.5 Vegetable

1 tablespoon canola oil

1 large onion, sliced

1 large red sweet pepper, seeded and chopped

½ teaspoon crushed red pepper

2 14-ounce cans lower-sodium beef broth

1 cup chopped unsalted peanuts

6 tiny new potatoes, cut into 1-inch pieces

1 medium sweet potato, peeled and cut into 1-inch pieces

1 19-ounce can fava beans, rinsed and drained

1 14½-ounce can diced tomatoes, undrained

Light dairy sour cream (optional)

Snipped fresh chives (optional)

Hot African Stew

PREP: 20 minutes

COOK: 30 minutes

NUTRITION FACTS per serving:

CALORIES 296
TOTAL FAT 15 g (2 g sat. fat)
CHOLESTEROL 0 mg
PROTEIN 13 g
CARBOHYDRATE 30 g
FIBER 11 g
SODIUM 669 mg

EXCHANGES 1.5 Starch, 1 High-Fat Meat, 1 Vegetable, 1 Fat

1 In a large saucepan or Dutch oven heat oil over medium heat. Add onion and sweet pepper; cook until golden and tender, stirring occasionally. Stir in crushed red pepper; cook for 1 minute. Add beef broth and peanuts. Bring to boiling.

2 Stir in new potatoes and sweet potato; return to boiling. Reduce heat. Cover and simmer about 25 minutes or until potatoes are tender, stirring occasionally. Stir in beans and undrained tomatoes; heat through. If desired, top individual servings with sour cream and chives. Makes 6 servings.

2 teaspoons canola oil

1 cup chopped onion

3 cloves garlic, minced

1 14-ounce can vegetable broth

2 tablespoons tomato paste

1 teaspoon snipped fresh oregano or ¼ teaspoon dried oregano, crushed

1 teaspoon adobo sauce from canned chipotle peppers in adobo sauce or ½ teaspoon adobo seasoning*

1 15- to 16-ounce can red kidney beans, rinsed and drained

1 tablespoon snipped fresh cilantro

2 cups hot cooked brown rice

Lime wedges (optional)

1 In a large saucepan heat oil over medium heat. Add onion and garlic; cook and stir for 4 to 5 minutes or until onion is tender. Add vegetable broth, tomato paste, dried oregano (if using), and adobo sauce. Stir in kidney beans. Mash mixture slightly with a potato masher or with the back of a wooden spoon. Bring to boiling; reduce heat. Simmer, uncovered, for 5 minutes, stirring occasionally. Stir in cilantro and fresh oregano (if using).

2 Serve stew with rice. If desired, serve with lime wedges. Makes 4 servings.

*Look for adobo seasoning at a market that specializes in Hispanic foods.

Red Bean Stew

START TO FINISH: 25 minutes

NUTRITION FACTS per serving:

CALORIES 246
TOTAL FAT 4 g (0 g sat. fat)
CHOLESTEROL 0 mg
PROTEIN 11 g
CARBOHYDRATE 48 g
FIBER 9 g
SODIUM 641 mg

EXCHANGES 3 Starch, 0.5 Very Lean Meat

1 medium eggplant, cut into ½-inch cubes (5 to 6 cups)

2 14-ounce cans vegetable broth

1 pound tiny new potatoes, cut into 1-inch pieces

2 cups chopped tomatoes or one 14½-ounce can no-salt-added diced tomatoes, undrained

1 15-ounce can garbanzo beans (chickpeas), rinsed and drained

2 teaspoons grated fresh ginger or ½ teaspoon ground ginger

1½ teaspoons curry powder

1 teaspoon ground coriander

¼ teaspoon salt

¼ teaspoon black pepper

2 tablespoons snipped fresh cilantro (optional)

Indian Vegetable Soup

PREP: 30 minutes

COOK: 9 to 10 hours (low) or 4½ to 5 hours (high)

NUTRITION FACTS per serving:

CALORIES 186
TOTAL FAT 1 g (0 g sat. fat)
CHOLESTEROL 0 mg
PROTEIN 7 g
CARBOHYDRATE 39 g
FIBER 9 g
SODIUM 837 mg

EXCHANGES 2 Starch, 1.5 Vegetable

1 In a 5- to 6-quart slow cooker combine eggplant, vegetable broth, potatoes, tomatoes, garbanzo beans, ginger, curry powder, coriander, salt, and pepper.

2 Cover and cook on low-heat setting for 9 to 10 hours or on high-heat setting for 4½ to 5 hours. If desired, sprinkle individual servings with cilantro. Makes 6 (1½-cup) servings.

COOK'S TIP

Choose eggplants that are firm and heavy for their size. The skin should be smooth and shiny and free of discoloration, scars, and bruises, which usually indicate that the flesh has been damaged.

1	tablespoon olive oil
½	cup chopped onion
½	cup chopped celery
½	cup chopped carrot
2	cloves garlic, minced
3	14-ounce cans reduced-sodium chicken broth
2	cups peeled, seeded, and coarsely chopped butternut squash
1	14½-ounce can fire-roasted diced tomatoes, undrained
1	15- to 19-ounce can cannellini beans (white kidney beans), rinsed and drained
1	small zucchini, halved lengthwise and sliced
1	cup broccoli and/or cauliflower florets
1	tablespoon snipped fresh oregano or 1 teaspoon dried oregano, crushed
¼	teaspoon salt
¼	teaspoon freshly ground black pepper
	Freshly shredded Parmesan cheese (optional)

Roasted Tomato-Vegetable Soup

PREP: 35 minutes

COOK: 25 minutes

NUTRITION FACTS per serving:

CALORIES 131
TOTAL FAT 3 g (0 g sat. fat)
CHOLESTEROL 0 mg
PROTEIN 9 g
CARBOHYDRATE 24 g
FIBER 5 g
SODIUM 855 mg

EXCHANGES 1 Starch, 0.5 Very Lean Meat, 1.5 Vegetable

1 In a 4-quart Dutch oven heat oil over medium heat. Add onion, celery, carrot, and garlic; cook and stir for 5 minutes.

2 Stir in chicken broth, squash, and undrained tomatoes. Bring to boiling; reduce heat. Cover and simmer for 20 minutes. Add cannellini beans, zucchini, broccoli, oregano, salt, and pepper; cook for 5 minutes more. If desired, sprinkle individual servings with Parmesan cheese. Makes 6 servings.

Slow Cooker Directions: Omit olive oil. In a 3½- to 4-quart slow cooker combine onion, celery, carrot, garlic, chicken broth, squash, undrained tomatoes, cannellini beans, and dried oregano (if using). Cover and cook on low-heat setting for 7 to 8 hours or on high-heat setting for 3½ to 4 hours. If using low-heat setting, turn to high-heat setting. Add zucchini, broccoli, fresh oregano (if using), salt, and pepper. Cover and cook for 30 minutes more. Serve as above.

1   tablespoon olive oil

12   cloves garlic, minced
       (2 tablespoons minced)

1   medium onion, chopped

3   15-ounce cans Great Northern
       beans, rinsed and drained

2   14-ounce cans reduced-sodium
       chicken broth

2   tablespoons snipped fresh sage or
       2 teaspoons dried sage, crushed

¼   teaspoon black pepper

1   recipe Sage French Bread Toasts
       (optional)

     Fresh sage leaves (optional)

Sage-White Bean Soup

PREP: 20 minutes

COOK: 25 minutes

NUTRITION FACTS per serving:

CALORIES 286

TOTAL FAT 3 g (1 g sat. fat)

CHOLESTEROL 0 mg

PROTEIN 18 g

CARBOHYDRATE 49 g

FIBER 11 g

SODIUM 325 mg

EXCHANGES 3 Starch, 1 Very Lean Meat, 0.5 Fat

1 In a 3- to 4-quart saucepan or Dutch oven heat oil over medium heat. Add garlic and onion; cook and stir over medium heat about 5 minutes or until onion is tender. Stir in Great Northern beans, chicken broth, dried sage (if using), and pepper. Bring to boiling; reduce heat. Cover and simmer for 20 minutes.

2 Stir in snipped fresh sage (if using). Remove from heat. Mash bean mixture slightly with a potato masher or with the back of a wooden spoon. If desired, top individual servings with Sage French Bread Toasts and fresh sage leaves. Makes 6 (1-cup) servings.

Sage French Bread Toasts: Preheat oven to 425°F. Lightly coat both sides of eight ½-inch-thick slices whole grain baguette-style French bread with olive oil nonstick cooking spray. Sprinkle all sides of bread slices with 1 tablespoon snipped fresh sage or 1 teaspoon dried sage, crushed. Arrange on an ungreased baking sheet. Bake for 5 to 7 minutes or until lightly browned and crisp, turning once.

COOK'S TIP

Whole garlic bulbs can be stored in a cool, dry, and dark area for several months. Once cloves have been removed from the bulb, they will keep for 3 to 10 days under the same conditions, or they can be frozen in an airtight container for several months.

2 tablespoons olive oil

3 large red, yellow, and/or green sweet peppers, seeded and chopped

1 large onion, sliced

2 stalks celery, sliced

½ of a small eggplant, cubed (2 cups)

2 cloves garlic, minced

3 large tomatoes, chopped

¼ to ½ cup tomato juice*

1 15-ounce can garbanzo beans (chickpeas), rinsed and drained

2 teaspoons snipped fresh thyme or 1 teaspoon dried thyme, crushed

½ teaspoon crushed red pepper

¼ teaspoon salt

¼ teaspoon black pepper

4 ounces feta cheese, crumbled (optional)

Snipped fresh thyme (optional)

Spicy Veggie Stew

START TO FINISH: 40 minutes

NUTRITION FACTS per serving:

CALORIES 232
TOTAL FAT 9 g (1 g sat. fat)
CHOLESTEROL 0 mg
PROTEIN 11 g
CARBOHYDRATE 34 g
FIBER 10 g
SODIUM 579 mg

EXCHANGES 1.5 Starch, 0.5 Very Lean Meat, 2 Vegetable, 1.5 Fat

1 In a very large skillet heat oil over medium heat. Add sweet pepper, onion, celery, and eggplant; cook for 10 to 15 minutes or until tender, stirring occasionally. Add garlic; cook and stir for 1 minute more.

2 Add tomatoes, tomato juice, garbanzo beans, snipped dried thyme (if using), and crushed red pepper to mixture in skillet. Cover and cook for 5 to 10 minutes or until heated through, stirring occasionally. Stir in 2 teaspoons snipped fresh thyme (if using), salt, and black pepper. If desired, sprinkle individual servings with feta cheese and additional snipped fresh thyme. Makes 4 (about 1½-cup) servings.

*If you have very juicy tomatoes, you may need less tomato juice. If you have less-juicy tomatoes, you may need more tomato juice.

Squash and Lentil Soup

PREP: 25 minutes

COOK: 8 to 9 hours (low)
or 4 to 4½ hours (high)

NUTRITION FACTS per serving:

CALORIES 260
TOTAL FAT 1 g (0 g sat. fat)
CHOLESTEROL 0 mg
PROTEIN 14 g
CARBOHYDRATE 51 g
FIBER 19 g
SODIUM 824 mg

EXCHANGES 3 Starch, 1 Vegetable

NUTRITION NOTE

Boost iron intake with lentils. Unlike red meat, also a source of iron, lentils are low in fat and calories.

1	cup dry brown lentils
2	14-ounce cans vegetable broth
1	pound butternut squash, halved, seeded, peeled, and cut into ¾-inch pieces
1½	cups water
2	medium carrots, chopped
2	stalks celery, sliced
1	medium onion, chopped
2	cloves garlic, minced
1	teaspoon garam masala

1 Rinse and drain lentils. In a 3½- or 4-quart slow cooker combine lentils, vegetable broth, squash, water, carrot, celery, onion, garlic, and garam masala.

2 Cover and cook on low-heat setting for 8 to 9 hours or on high-heat setting for 4 to 4½ hours. Makes 4 (1¾-cup) servings.

COOK'S TIP

A staple in Indian cooking, garam masala lends warm, exotic flavors to your dish. Look for it in the spice aisle of your grocery store or at a local Indian market.

1   14-ounce can vegetable broth

1¾ cups water

¾   cup quick-cooking barley

¾   cup thinly sliced carrot*

1   teaspoon dried thyme, crushed

⅛   teaspoon black pepper

1   19-ounce can ready-to-serve
    tomato-basil soup

2   cups coarsely chopped zucchini*
    and/or yellow summer squash

1   cup loose-pack frozen cut
    green beans*

1 In a large saucepan combine vegetable broth, water, uncooked barley, carrot, thyme, and pepper. Bring to boiling; reduce heat. Cover and simmer for 10 minutes, stirring occasionally.

2 Stir in tomato-basil soup, zucchini, and green beans. Return to boiling; reduce heat. Cover and simmer for 8 to 10 minutes more or until vegetables and barley are tender, stirring occasionally. Makes 4 (1¾-cup) servings.

*You can substitute one 16-ounce package of your favorite frozen vegetable blend for the carrot, zucchini, and green beans, adding it with the tomato-basil soup.

COOK'S TIP

Over time spices and herbs lose color, flavor, and aroma. Store them in a cool, dry place away from light, heat, moisture, and oxygen. Replace ground spices after 6 months and whole spices after 1 year.

Tomato-Barley Soup with Garden Vegetables

PREP: 15 minutes

COOK: 18 minutes

NUTRITION FACTS per serving:

CALORIES 243
TOTAL FAT 3 g (0 g sat. fat)
CHOLESTEROL 0 mg
PROTEIN 7 g
CARBOHYDRATE 49 g
FIBER 9 g
SODIUM 988 mg

EXCHANGES 2.5 Starch, 1.5 Vegetable

Zesty Gazpacho

PREP: 30 minutes

CHILL: 2 to 24 hours

NUTRITION FACTS per serving:

CALORIES 152
TOTAL FAT 1 g (0 g sat. fat)
CHOLESTEROL 0 mg
PROTEIN 11 g
CARBOHYDRATE 35 g
FIBER 10 g
SODIUM 861 mg

EXCHANGES 1 Starch, 3.5 Vegetable

1	19-ounce can cannellini beans (white kidney beans), rinsed and drained
1	14½-ounce can Italian- or Mexican-style stewed tomatoes, undrained, cut up
2	cups tiny red pear-shape tomatoes, halved, and/or cherry tomatoes, halved or quartered
1¼	cups vegetable juice
1	cup lower-sodium beef broth
1	cup coarsely chopped seeded cucumber
½	cup coarsely chopped yellow and/or red sweet pepper
¼	cup coarsely chopped red onion
¼	cup snipped fresh cilantro
3	tablespoons lime juice or lemon juice
2	cloves garlic, minced
¼	to ½ teaspoon bottled hot pepper sauce
	Lime wedges (optional)

1 In a large bowl combine cannellini beans, undrained stewed tomatoes, fresh tomatoes, vegetable juice, beef broth, cucumber, sweet pepper, red onion, cilantro, lime juice, garlic, and hot pepper sauce. Cover and chill for 2 to 24 hours. If desired, serve individual servings with lime wedges. Makes 4 (2-cup) servings.

Chapter 7

Beef, Veal & Lamb

On the divider: Beef-Broccoli Stir-Fry *(see recipe, page 191)*

- 8 cloves garlic, peeled
- 1 teaspoon salt
- 1 tablespoon chili powder
- 1 tablespoon five-spice powder
- 2 teaspoons ground ginger
- 1 teaspoon black pepper
- 2 1-pound boneless beef top sirloin steaks, cut 1 inch thick

1 On a cutting board, chop garlic with salt; press with the side of a large knife to form a chunky paste. In a small bowl combine garlic paste, chili powder, five-spice powder, ginger, and pepper; set aside.

2 Sprinkle garlic mixture on all sides of the steaks; rub in with your fingers. Place steaks in a large resealable plastic bag; seal bag. Chill for 2 hours.

3 For a charcoal grill, place steaks on the rack of an uncovered grill directly over medium coals. Grill until desired doneness, turning once halfway through grilling. Allow 14 to 18 minutes for medium-rare doneness (145°F) or 18 to 22 minutes for medium doneness (160°F). (For a gas grill, preheat grill. Reduce heat to medium. Place steaks on grill rack over heat. Cover and grill as above.) Makes 8 servings.

Spicy Sirloin Steaks

PREP: 20 minutes   **CHILL:** 2 hours
GRILL: 14 minutes

NUTRITION FACTS per serving:
- -

CALORIES 153
TOTAL FAT 4 g (1 g sat. fat)
CHOLESTEROL 53 mg
PROTEIN 25 g
CARBOHYDRATE 3 g
FIBER 1 g
SODIUM 362 mg

EXCHANGES 3.5 Very Lean Meat

1 pound boneless beef top sirloin steak, cut 1 inch thick

¼ teaspoon salt

¼ teaspoon black pepper

1 teaspoon canola oil

2 medium red and/or green sweet peppers, seeded and cut into thin strips

1 medium onion, coarsely chopped

1 tablespoon curry powder

1 cup water

¾ cup apple juice or apple cider

2 teaspoons instant beef bouillon granules

1 cup whole wheat couscous

1 medium tart green apple (such as Granny Smith), cored and coarsely chopped

⅓ cup chopped dry roasted peanuts

Curried Beef with Apple Couscous

PREP: 25 minutes

GRILL: 14 minutes

NUTRITION FACTS per serving:

CALORIES 340

TOTAL FAT 9 g (2 g sat. fat)

CHOLESTEROL 46 mg

PROTEIN 25 g

CARBOHYDRATE 44 g

FIBER 7 g

SODIUM 430 mg

EXCHANGES 2 Starch, 2.5 Very Lean Meat, 0.5 Vegetable, 0.5 Fat

1 Trim fat from steak. Lightly sprinkle steak with salt and black pepper.

2 For a charcoal grill, place steak on the rack of an uncovered grill directly over medium coals. Grill until desired doneness, turning once halfway thorough grilling. Allow 14 to 18 minutes for medium-rare doneness (145°F) or 18 to 22 minutes for medium doneness (160°F). (For a gas grill, preheat grill. Reduce heat to medium. Place steak on grill rack over heat. Cover and grill as above.)

3 Meanwhile, in a large nonstick skillet heat oil over medium heat. Add sweet pepper and onion; cook for 5 minutes. Add curry powder. Cook and stir for 1 minute. Add the water, apple juice, and bouillon granules. Bring to boiling. Stir in couscous and apple; remove from heat. Cover and let stand about 5 minutes or until liquid is absorbed.

4 To serve, fluff couscous mixture with a fork. Thinly slice steak across the grain. Serve steak slices over couscous mixture. Sprinkle with peanuts. Makes 6 servings.

Broiler Directions: Preheat broiler. Place steak on the unheated rack of a broiler pan. Broil 3 to 4 inches from heat until desired doneness, turning once halfway through broiling. Allow 15 to 17 minutes for medium-rare doneness (145°F) or 20 to 22 minutes for medium doneness (160°F).

- ¼ cup lime juice
- ¼ cup bottled steak sauce
- ¼ cup purchased mild, medium, or hot salsa
- 1 tablespoon canola oil
- 1 clove garlic, minced
- ½ teaspoon coarsely ground black pepper
- 1 pound boneless beef top sirloin steak, cut 1-inch thick

  Whole wheat flour tortillas, warmed (optional)

  Purchased salsa (optional)

1 For marinade, in a small saucepan combine lime juice, steak sauce, ¼ cup salsa, oil, garlic, and pepper. Bring to boiling; reduce heat. Simmer, uncovered, for 5 minutes, stirring occasionally; cool.

2 Place steak in a resealable plastic bag set in a shallow dish. Pour marinade over steak. Seal bag; turn to coat steak. Marinate in the refrigerator for 8 to 24 hours, turning bag occasionally.

3 Preheat indoor electric grill. Drain steak, discarding marinade. Place steak on the grill rack. If using a covered grill, close lid. Grill steak until desired doneness. For a covered grill, allow 5 to 7 minutes for medium-rare doneness (145°F) or 7 to 9 minutes for medium doneness (160°F). For an uncovered grill, allow 12 to 15 minutes for medium-rare doneness (145°F) or 15 to 18 minutes for medium doneness (160°F), turning once halfway through grilling.

4 To serve, thinly slice steak across grain. If desired, serve with warmed tortillas and additional salsa. Makes 4 servings.

Southwest Steak

PREP: 20 minutes **MARINATE:** 8 to 24 hours

GRILL: 5 minutes (covered indoor grill) or 12 minutes (uncovered indoor grill)

NUTRITION FACTS per serving:

CALORIES 200
TOTAL FAT 9 g (2 g sat. fat)
CHOLESTEROL 69 mg
PROTEIN 25 g
CARBOHYDRATE 5 g
FIBER 1 g
SODIUM 385 mg

EXCHANGES 3.5 Lean Meat

NUTRITION NOTE

Top sirloin steak is one of the 29 cuts of beef that meet government guidelines for lean or extra lean. Like all beef, it is an excellent source of protein, zinc, and vitamin B_{12}.

1/3   cup balsamic vinegar

2   tablespoons olive oil

6   cloves garlic, minced

1   teaspoon black pepper

1   teaspoon snipped fresh rosemary or 1/4 teaspoon dried rosemary, crushed

1   teaspoon snipped fresh thyme or 1/4 teaspoon dried thyme, crushed

1   pound boneless beef sirloin steak, trimmed and cut into 1 1/4-inch cubes

1   medium red onion, cut into 1-inch pieces

2   medium red and/or yellow sweet peppers, seeded and cut into 1-inch pieces

8   yellow or red cherry tomatoes

Pepper-Beef Kabobs

PREP: 30 minutes   **MARINATE:** 2 to 6 hours

GRILL: 12 minutes

NUTRITION FACTS per serving:

CALORIES 233
TOTAL FAT 9 g (2 g sat. fat)
CHOLESTEROL 53 mg
PROTEIN 26 g
CARBOHYDRATE 11 g
FIBER 2 g
SODIUM 71 mg

EXCHANGES 3.5 Lean Meat, 1.5 Vegetable

NUTRITION NOTE

Grilling veggies brings out natural flavor and sweetness without adding sugar or additional calories.

1 For marinade, in a small bowl combine balsamic vinegar, oil, garlic, black pepper, rosemary, and thyme.

2 Place beef cubes in a resealable plastic bag set in a medium bowl. Pour marinade over beef cubes. Seal bag; turn to coat beef cubes. Marinate in the refrigerator for 2 to 6 hours, turning bag occasionally.

3 Drain beef cubes, discarding marinade. On eight long metal skewers, alternately thread beef cubes, onion pieces, and sweet pepper pieces, leaving a 1/4-inch space between pieces.

4 For a charcoal grill, place the skewers on the rack of an uncovered grill directly over medium coals. Grill for 12 to 14 minutes or until beef is desired doneness, turning occasionally to brown evenly. (For a gas grill, preheat grill. Reduce heat to medium. Place the skewers on grill rack over heat. Cover and grill as above.)

5 To serve, add a cherry tomato to the end of each skewer. Makes 4 (2-skewer) servings.

8 ounces fresh green beans, trimmed and halved crosswise

½ cup orange juice

2 tablespoons reduced-sodium soy sauce

1 tablespoon toasted sesame oil

1 teaspoon cornstarch

½ teaspoon finely shredded orange peel

Nonstick cooking spray

½ cup bias-sliced green onion

1 tablespoon grated fresh ginger or 1 teaspoon ground ginger

2 cloves garlic, minced

1 teaspoon canola oil

12 ounces boneless beef sirloin steak, thinly sliced

2 cups hot cooked brown rice

2 teaspoons sesame seeds, toasted

2 oranges, peeled and sectioned or thinly sliced crosswise

Sesame-Orange Beef

START TO FINISH: 30 minutes

NUTRITION FACTS per serving:

CALORIES 350
TOTAL FAT 11 g (2 g sat. fat)
CHOLESTEROL 52 mg
PROTEIN 24 g
CARBOHYDRATE 41 g
FIBER 6 g
SODIUM 348 mg

EXCHANGES 2 Starch, 0.5 Fruit, 2.5 Lean Meat, 0.5 Vegetable, 0.5 Fat

1 In a covered medium saucepan cook green beans in a small amount of boiling water for 6 to 8 minutes or until crisp-tender. Drain; set aside.

2 For sauce, in a small bowl combine orange juice, soy sauce, toasted sesame oil, cornstarch, and orange peel; set aside.

3 Coat an unheated large nonstick skillet with nonstick cooking spray. Preheat over medium-high heat. Add green onion, ginger, and garlic to hot skillet; cook and stir for 1 minute. Add precooked green beans; cook and stir for 2 minutes. Remove vegetables from skillet.

4 Carefully add canola oil to the hot skillet. Add beef; cook and stir about 3 minutes or until desired doneness. Remove from skillet.

5 Stir sauce; add to skillet. Cook and stir until thickened and bubbly; cook and stir for 2 minutes more. Return meat and vegetables to skillet. Heat through, stirring to coat all ingredients with sauce. Serve over hot cooked brown rice. Sprinkle with toasted sesame seeds. Serve with orange slices. Makes 4 servings.

1   6-ounce carton plain fat-free or
    low-fat yogurt
¼   cup coarsely shredded
    unpeeled cucumber
1   tablespoon finely chopped
    red onion
1   tablespoon snipped fresh mint
¼   teaspoon sugar
¼   teaspoon salt
⅛   teaspoon black pepper
1   pound boneless beef sirloin steak,
    cut 1-inch thick
½   teaspoon Greek seasoning

Beef with Cucumber Raita

PREP: 20 minutes

GRILL: 15 minutes

NUTRITION FACTS per serving:

CALORIES 176
TOTAL FAT 5 g (2 g sat. fat)
CHOLESTEROL 48 mg
PROTEIN 28 g
CARBOHYDRATE 4 g
FIBER 0 g
SODIUM 252 mg

EXCHANGES 4 Very Lean Meat, 1 Fat

NUTRITION NOTE

Keep the peel on cucumbers to give food bright color and more fiber and minerals than peeled cucumbers.

1 For raita, in a small bowl combine yogurt, cucumber, red onion, snipped mint, sugar, salt, and pepper; set aside.

2 Trim fat from steak. Sprinkle steak with Greek seasoning. For a charcoal grill, place steak on the rack of an uncovered grill directly over medium coals. Grill until desired doneness, turning once halfway through grilling. Allow 15 to 17 minutes for medium-rare doneness (145°F) or 20 to 22 minutes for medium doneness (160°F). (For a gas grill, preheat grill. Reduce heat to medium. Place steak on grill rack over heat. Cover and grill as above.)

3 Thinly slice steak across the grain. Serve sliced steak with raita. Makes 4 servings.

- ¾ cup lower-sodium beef broth
- 2 tablespoons reduced-sodium soy sauce
- 1 tablespoon rice vinegar or white vinegar
- 2 teaspoons cornstarch
- 2 teaspoons grated fresh ginger or ½ teaspoon ground ginger
- 2 cloves garlic, minced
- ¼ teaspoon crushed red pepper
- 1 pound broccoli
- 12 ounces boneless beef top sirloin steak
- 2 teaspoons canola oil
- 2 medium carrots, sliced
- 4 green onions, sliced
- 6 ounces dried soba (buckwheat noodles) or multigrain spaghetti, cooked according to package directions

Beef-Broccoli Stir-Fry

START TO FINISH: 30 minutes

NUTRITION FACTS per serving:

- -

CALORIES 351
TOTAL FAT 7 g (2 g sat. fat)
CHOLESTEROL 40 mg
PROTEIN 30 g
CARBOHYDRATE 46 g
FIBER 6 g
SODIUM 793 mg

EXCHANGES 2 Starch, 3 Very Lean Meat, 2 Vegetable, 1 Fat

1 For sauce, in a small bowl combine beef broth, soy sauce, vinegar, cornstarch, ginger, garlic, and crushed red pepper; set aside.

2 Cut broccoli florets from stems. If desired, peel stems. Cut stems into ¼-inch-thick slices. Set aside. Trim fat from meat. Cut meat across the grain into thin slices; set aside.

3 In a wok or large skillet heat 1 teaspoon of oil over medium-high heat. Add broccoli and carrot. Cook and stir for 5 to 6 minutes or until crisp-tender; remove from wok or skillet.

4 Add remaining 1 teaspoon oil to hot wok or skillet. Add beef. Cook and stir for 2 to 3 minutes or until desired doneness. Push meat from center of wok or skillet. Stir sauce; add to wok or skillet. Cook and stir until thickened and bubbly. Return vegetables to wok or skillet; add green onion. Stir to coat all ingredients with sauce. Cook and stir until heated through.

5 Serve beef mixture over hot cooked soba or spaghetti. Makes 4 servings.

Italian Beef Skillet

PREP: 30 minutes

COOK: 1¼ hours

NUTRITION FACTS per serving:

CALORIES 269
TOTAL FAT 5 g (2 g sat. fat)
CHOLESTEROL 51 mg
PROTEIN 24 g
CARBOHYDRATE 32 g
FIBER 3 g
SODIUM 431 mg

EXCHANGES 1.5 Starch, 2.5 Very Lean Meat, 1.5 Vegetable, 0.5 Fat

---

1   pound boneless beef round steak
    Nonstick cooking spray
2   cups sliced fresh mushrooms
2   medium onions, chopped
1   medium green sweet pepper, seeded and chopped
1   stalk celery, chopped
1   14½-ounce can diced tomatoes with basil, garlic, and oregano, undrained
2   tablespoons water
⅛   to ¼ teaspoon crushed red pepper
6   ounces dried whole wheat or multigrain pasta, cooked according to package directions
    Snipped fresh parsley (optional)
2   tablespoons grated Parmesan cheese

1 Trim fat from meat. Cut meat into six serving-size pieces. Lightly coat an unheated large nonstick skillet with nonstick cooking spray. Preheat over medium heat. Add meat and cook until brown, turning to brown evenly. Remove meat from skillet; set aside.

2 Add mushrooms, onion, sweet pepper, and celery to skillet. Cook about 5 minutes or until vegetables are nearly tender, stirring occasionally. Stir in undrained tomatoes, water, and crushed red pepper. Return meat to skillet, spooning vegetable mixture over meat. Bring to boiling; reduce heat. Cover and simmer about 1¼ hours or until meat is tender, stirring occasionally.

3 Place steak on hot cooked pasta. Spoon vegetable mixture over steak. If desired, sprinkle with parsley. Serve with Parmesan cheese. Makes 6 servings.

COOK'S TIP

Braising or slow cooking meat in a small amount of liquid for a long time is an ideal method for cooking slightly tough cuts. It tenderizes the meat and develops great flavor.

1	2-pound boneless beef round steak, cut ¾- to 1-inch thick
½	teaspoon salt
¼	teaspoon black pepper
1	14½-ounce can Cajun-, Mexican-, or Italian-style stewed tomatoes, undrained
⅓	cup tomato paste
½	teaspoon bottled hot pepper sauce (optional)
1	16-ounce package frozen yellow, green, and red peppers and onion stir-fry vegetables
4	cups hot cooked whole wheat pasta (optional)

1 Trim fat from steak. Cut steak into six serving-size pieces. Sprinkle meat with salt and black pepper. Place in a 3½- or 4-quart slow cooker. In a medium bowl combine undrained tomatoes, tomato paste, and, if desired, hot pepper sauce. Pour over meat in cooker. Top with frozen vegetables.

2 Cover and cook on low-heat setting for 9 to 10 hours or on high-heat setting for 4½ to 5 hours. If desired, serve with hot cooked pasta. Makes 6 servings.

So-Easy Pepper Steak

PREP: 15 minutes

COOK: 9 to 10 hours (low) or

4½ to 5 hours (high)

NUTRITION FACTS per serving:

CALORIES 257
TOTAL FAT 6 g (2 g sat. fat)
CHOLESTEROL 83 mg
PROTEIN 37 g
CARBOHYDRATE 12 g
FIBER 3 g
SODIUM 655 mg

EXCHANGES 4.5 Very Lean Meat, 2 Vegetable, 1 Fat

Beef and Chipotle Burritos

PREP: 35 minutes

COOK: 8 to 10 hours (low) or 4 to 5 hours (high)

NUTRITION FACTS per serving:

CALORIES 328
TOTAL FAT 11 g (4 g sat. fat)
CHOLESTEROL 65 mg
PROTEIN 32 g
CARBOHYDRATE 24 g
FIBER 11 g
SODIUM 969 mg

EXCHANGES 1 Starch, 4 Lean Meat, 1 Vegetable

NUTRITION NOTE

The nutritional content of tortillas can vary greatly from brand to brand. Read the package labels and choose tortillas high in fiber and protein and low in calories and fat.

---

1   recipe Pico de Gallo Salsa

1½   pounds boneless beef round steak, cut ¾ inch thick

2   14½-ounce cans diced tomatoes with garlic and onion, undrained

2   canned chipotle chile peppers in adobo sauce, finely chopped*

1   teaspoon dried oregano, crushed

¼   teaspoon ground cumin

8   7- to 8-inch whole wheat flour tortillas, warmed**

¾   cup shredded reduced-fat cheddar cheese (3 ounces)

1 Prepare Pico de Gallo Salsa. Trim fat from meat. Place meat in a 3½- or 4-quart slow cooker. Add undrained tomatoes, chile pepper, oregano, and cumin.

2 Cover and cook on low-heat setting for 8 to 10 hours or on high-heat setting for 4 to 5 hours.

3 Using a slotted spoon, transfer meat and tomatoes to a large bowl; reserve cooking liquid in slow cooker. Using two forks, pull meat apart into shreds. Stir enough reserved cooking liquid into meat to moisten.

4 To serve, spoon meat mixture just below centers of tortillas. Top with cheese and Pico de Gallo Salsa. Roll up tortillas. Makes 8 servings.

Pico de Gallo Salsa: In a small bowl combine 1 cup finely chopped tomato; 2 tablespoons finely chopped onion; 2 tablespoons snipped fresh cilantro; and 1 fresh serrano chile pepper, seeded and finely chopped.* Stir in ½ cup chopped peeled jicama and ¼ cup radishes cut into thin bite-size strips. Cover and chill for several hours before serving.

*Because chile peppers contain volatile oils that can burn your skin and eyes, avoid direct contact with them as much as possible. When working with chile peppers, wear plastic or rubber gloves. If your bare hands do touch the peppers, wash your hands and nails well with soap and warm water.

**See tortilla warming note, page 101.

- 1½ pounds boneless beef round steak, cut ¾- to 1-inch thick
- ¼ teaspoon black pepper
- ⅛ teaspoon salt
- 2 cups packaged peeled baby carrots
- 2 cups sliced fresh mushrooms
- 1 large onion, cut into wedges
- 1 14½-ounce can diced tomatoes with basil, garlic, and oregano, undrained
- 3 tablespoons tomato paste with Italian seasonings
- 1 tablespoon Worcestershire sauce
- 1 medium zucchini, halved lengthwise and sliced

1 Trim fat from steak. Cut steak into four serving-size pieces; season with pepper and salt. Place meat in a 3½- or 4-quart slow cooker. Top with carrots, mushrooms, and onion.

2 In a medium bowl stir together undrained tomatoes, tomato paste, and Worcestershire sauce. Pour tomato mixture over vegetables.

3 Cover and cook on low-heat setting for 8 to 9 hours or on high-heat setting for 4 to 4½ hours, adding zucchini for the last 20 minutes of cooking. Makes 4 servings.

Round Steak with Vegetables

PREP: 20 minutes

COOK: 8 to 9 hours (low) or 4 to 4½ hours (high)

NUTRITION FACTS per serving:

CALORIES 335
TOTAL FAT 6 g (2 g sat. fat)
CHOLESTEROL 78 mg
PROTEIN 44 g
CARBOHYDRATE 26 g
FIBER 4 g
SODIUM 901 mg

EXCHANGES 5.5 Very Lean Meat, 3 Vegetable, 1.5 Fat

2   10- to 12-ounce beef ribeye steaks, cut 1-inch thick
1½   teaspoons paprika
1½   teaspoons garlic salt
1   teaspoon dried thyme, crushed
1   teaspoon dried oregano, crushed
½   teaspoon lemon-pepper seasoning
¼   to ½ teaspoon cayenne pepper
1   recipe Grilled Peppers

Peppered Ribeye Steaks with Grilled Sweet Peppers

PREP: 20 minutes   **CHILL:** 1 hour
GRILL: 10 minutes

NUTRITION FACTS per serving:

CALORIES 249
TOTAL FAT 11 g (4 g sat. fat)
CHOLESTEROL 83 mg
PROTEIN 30 g
CARBOHYDRATE 6 g
FIBER 2 g
SODIUM 764 mg

EXCHANGES 4 Lean Meat, 1 Vegetable

1 Trim fat from steaks. In a small bowl combine paprika, garlic salt, thyme, oregano, lemon-pepper seasoning, and cayenne pepper. Evenly sprinkle paprika mixture over steaks; rub in with your fingers. Cover steaks; chill for 1 hour. Meanwhile, prepare Grilled Peppers.

2 For a charcoal grill, place steaks on the rack of an uncovered grill directly over medium coals. Grill for 10 to 12 minutes for medium-rare doneness (145°F) or 12 to 15 minutes for medium doneness (160°F), turning once halfway through grilling. (For a gas grill, preheat grill. Reduce heat to medium. Place steaks on grill rack over heat. Cover and grill as above.)

3 Cut each steak in half. Serve with Grilled Peppers. Makes 4 servings.

Grilled Peppers: Seed and quarter 3 green, red, yellow, and/or orange sweet peppers. For a charcoal grill, place pepper quarters on the rack of an uncovered grill directly over medium coals. Grill for 12 to 15 minutes or until peppers are crisp-tender and lightly browned, turning once halfway through grilling. (For a gas grill, preheat grill. Reduce heat to medium. Place pepper quarters on grill rack over heat. Cover and grill as above.) Remove peppers from grill; cool slightly. Cut peppers into wide strips. Place peppers in bowl. Add 1 tablespoon snipped fresh basil or 1 teaspoon dried basil, crushed, and 1 tablespoon balsamic vinegar; toss well. Serve immediately or cool to room temperature.

- 1 1-pound beef flank steak
- ⅓ cup orange juice
- ¼ cup snipped fresh cilantro
- 2 tablespoons red wine vinegar
- 1 tablespoon olive oil
- 4 cloves garlic, minced
- 2 teaspoons ground cumin
- 1 teaspoon ground coriander
- ¼ teaspoon salt
- ¼ teaspoon crushed red pepper
- 2 red and/or green sweet peppers, halved, stemmed, and seeded
- 1 red onion, cut into ½-inch-thick slices

Spicy Cilantro Flank Steak

PREP: 25 minutes **MARINATE:** 4 to 6 hours
GRILL: 17 minutes

NUTRITION FACTS per serving:

CALORIES 244
TOTAL FAT 11 g (3 g sat. fat)
CHOLESTEROL 47 mg
PROTEIN 26 g
CARBOHYDRATE 10 g
FIBER 2 g
SODIUM 209 mg

EXCHANGES 3.5 Lean Meat, 1 Vegetable, 0.5 Fat

1 Trim fat from steak. Score both sides of steak in a diamond pattern by making shallow diagonal cuts at 1-inch intervals. Place steak in a resealable plastic bag set in a shallow dish.

2 For marinade, in a small bowl stir together orange juice, cilantro, vinegar, oil, garlic, cumin, coriander, salt, and crushed red pepper. Pour over steak. Seal bag; turn to coat steak. Marinate in the refrigerator for 4 to 6 hours, turning bag occasionally.

3 Drain steak, reserving marinade. Brush sweet peppers and onion with reserved marinade; discard any remaining marinade. Set vegetables aside. For a charcoal grill, place steak on the rack of an uncovered grill directly over medium coals. Grill for 8 minutes. Turn steak. Place vegetables, cut sides down, on grill rack with steak. Grill steak and vegetables for 9 to 13 minutes or until steak is medium doneness (160°F) and vegetables are crisp-tender, turning vegetables occasionally to brown evenly. (For a gas grill, preheat grill. Reduce heat to medium. Place steak, then vegetables on grill rack over heat. Cover and grill as above.)

4 To serve, thinly slice steak across the grain and cut sweet peppers into strips. Serve with grilled onion. Makes 4 servings.

COOK'S TIP

Store onions up to one month in a cool, dry place in a container such as a wire basket so air can circulate around them.

Spicy Steak and Beans

PREP: 25 minutes

COOK: 7 to 9 hours (low) or
3 ½ to 4 ½ hours (high); plus 30 minutes (high)

NUTRITION FACTS per serving:

CALORIES 372
TOTAL FAT 8 g (3 g sat. fat)
CHOLESTEROL 48 mg
PROTEIN 33 g
CARBOHYDRATE 41 g
FIBER 7 g
SODIUM 604 mg

EXCHANGES 2.5 Starch, 3 Lean Meat,
1 Vegetable

1½	pounds beef flank steak
1	14½-ounce can diced tomatoes and green chile peppers, undrained
1	medium onion, chopped
2	cloves garlic, minced
1½	to 2 teaspoons chili powder
1	teaspoon dried oregano, crushed
1	teaspoon ground cumin
¼	to ½ teaspoon black pepper
2	medium green, red, and/or yellow sweet peppers, seeded and cut into strips
1	15-ounce can pinto beans, rinsed and drained
3	cups hot cooked brown rice
1	ounce crumbled queso fresco or reduced-fat feta cheese (optional)

1 Trim fat from steak. Cut steak to fit in a 3½- or 4-quart slow cooker; add steak to cooker. In a medium bowl stir together undrained tomatoes, onion, garlic, chili powder, oregano, cumin, and black pepper. Pour over steak.

2 Cover and cook on low-heat setting for 7 to 9 hours or on high-heat setting for 3½ to 4½ hours.

3 If using low-heat setting, turn to high-heat setting. Stir in sweet pepper and pinto beans. Cover and cook for 30 minutes. Remove steak; cool slightly. Shred or thinly slice steak across the grain.

4 Divide rice among six serving plates. Arrange meat on rice. Spoon bean mixture over meat. If desired, sprinkle with cheese. Makes 6 servings.

1¼   to 1½ pounds beef flank steak
2   green onions, sliced
¼   cup water
¼   cup dry red wine
¼   cup reduced-sodium soy sauce
3   tablespoons lemon juice
2   tablespoons canola oil
2   cloves garlic, minced
½   teaspoon celery seeds
½   teaspoon black pepper

1 Score both sides of steak in a diamond pattern by making shallow diagonal cuts at 1-inch intervals. Place steak in a resealable plastic bag set in a shallow dish. For marinade, in a small bowl combine green onion, water, wine, soy sauce, lemon juice, oil, garlic, celery seeds, and pepper. Pour marinade over steak in bag. Seal bag; turn to coat steak. Marinate in the refrigerator for 6 to 24 hours, turning bag occasionally.

2 Drain steak, discarding marinade. For a charcoal grill, place steak on the rack of an uncovered grill directly over medium coals. Grill for 17 to 21 minutes or until medium doneness (160°F), turning once halfway through grilling. (For a gas grill, preheat grill. Reduce heat to medium. Place steak on grill rack over heat. Cover and grill as above.)

3 Thinly slice steak diagonally across the grain. Makes 4 servings.

Lemon-Soy Marinated Flank Steak

PREP: 15 minutes   **MARINATE:** 6 to 24 hours
GRILL: 17 minutes

NUTRITION FACTS per serving:

CALORIES 253
TOTAL FAT 12 g (4 g sat. fat)
CHOLESTEROL 57 mg
PROTEIN 31 g
CARBOHYDRATE 2 g
FIBER 0 g
SODIUM 292 mg

EXCHANGES 4.5 Very Lean Meat

Five-Spice Steak

PREP: 20 minutes
MARINATE: 30 minutes to 4 hours
GRILL: 17 minutes

NUTRITION FACTS per serving:

CALORIES 231
TOTAL FAT 8 g (3 g sat. fat)
CHOLESTEROL 47 mg
PROTEIN 26 g
CARBOHYDRATE 13 g
FIBER 2 g
SODIUM 381 mg

EXCHANGES 0.5 Fruit, 3.5 Lean Meat, 0.5 Vegetable

1	pound beef flank steak
2	tablespoons reduced-sodium soy sauce
1	tablespoon sweet rice wine (mirin)
1	tablespoon lemon juice
4	cloves garlic, minced
2	teaspoons five-spice powder
2	teaspoons ground coriander
1	teaspoon toasted sesame oil
¼	teaspoon fennel seeds, crushed
⅛	teaspoon cayenne pepper
½	of a cored and peeled fresh pineapple, cut crosswise into 4 slices
2	cups shredded napa cabbage

1 Trim fat from steak. Score both sides of steak in a diamond pattern by making shallow diagonal cuts at 1-inch intervals. Place steak in a large resealable plastic bag set in a shallow dish.

2 For marinade, in a small bowl combine soy sauce, sweet rice wine, lemon juice, garlic, five-spice powder, coriander, toasted sesame oil, fennel seeds, and cayenne pepper. Pour marinade over steak. Seal bag; turn to coat steak. Marinate in the refrigerator for 30 minutes to 4 hours, turning bag occasionally.

3 Drain steak, discarding marinade. For a charcoal grill, place steak on the rack of an uncovered grill directly over medium coals. Grill for 17 to 21 minutes or until medium doneness (160°F), turning once halfway through grilling. Add pineapple slices to grill with steak for the last 5 minutes of grilling; turn pineapple after 2 to 3 minutes and remove pineapple when it is lightly browned. (For a gas grill, preheat grill. Reduce heat to medium. Place steak on grill rack over heat. Cover and grill as above, adding pineapple slices as directed.)

4 To serve, thinly slice steak across the grain. Serve with pineapple and cabbage. Makes 4 servings.

1 pound beef flank steak

¼ cup water

¼ cup lime juice

6 cloves garlic, minced

2 tablespoons snipped fresh cilantro

2 teaspoons snipped fresh oregano or
   ½ teaspoon dried oregano, crushed

¼ teaspoon chipotle chili powder or
   regular chili powder

1 recipe Avocado-Poblano Pico de Gallo

¼ teaspoon salt

⅛ teaspoon black pepper

   Lime wedges and/or fresh cilantro
   (optional)

Lime-Marinated Flank Steak

PREP: 35 minutes **MARINATE:** 1 to 2 hours

GRILL: 17 minutes

NUTRITION FACTS per serving:

CALORIES 212
TOTAL FAT 9 g (3 g sat. fat)
CHOLESTEROL 47 mg
PROTEIN 27 g
CARBOHYDRATE 8 g
FIBER 2 g
SODIUM 282 mg

EXCHANGES 3.5 Lean Meat, 0.5 Vegetable

1 Trim fat from steak. Score both sides of steak in a diamond pattern by making shallow diagonal cuts at 1-inch intervals. Place steak in a resealable plastic bag set in a shallow dish.

2 For marinade, in a small bowl stir together water, lime juice, garlic, cilantro, oregano, and chili powder. Pour marinade over steak in bag. Seal bag; turn to coat steak. Marinate in the refrigerator for 1 to 2 hours, turning bag occasionally.

3 Prepare Avocado-Poblano Pico de Gallo. Drain steak, reserving marinade. Sprinkle steak with salt and black pepper. For a charcoal grill, place steak on the rack of an uncovered grill directly over medium coals. Grill for 17 to 21 minutes or until medium doneness (160°F), turning once and brushing with the reserved marinade halfway through grilling. Discard any remaining marinade. (For a gas grill, preheat grill. Reduce heat to medium. Place steak on grill rack over heat. Cover and grill as above.)

4 To serve, thinly slice beef across the grain; divide among four serving plates. Top with Avocado-Poblano Pico de Gallo. If desired, garnish with lime wedges and/or cilantro. Makes 4 servings.

Avocado-Poblano Pico de Gallo: Preheat broiler. Arrange 1 fresh poblano chile pepper* or 1 sweet pepper on a foil-lined baking sheet. Broil 4 to 5 inches from heat for 8 to 10 minutes or until skin is bubbly and blackened, turning occasionally. Carefully bring the foil up and around the pepper to enclose. Let stand about 15 minutes or until cool enough to handle. Using a paring knife, pull off the skin gently and slowly. Discard skin. Remove pepper stem, seeds, and membranes; chop the pepper.

In a medium bowl combine chopped pepper; 1 small tomato, chopped; 3 tablespoons finely chopped red onion; 1 tablespoon snipped fresh cilantro; ¼ teaspoon finely shredded lime peel; 1½ teaspoons lime juice; and ⅛ teaspoon salt. Stir in ½ of a small avocado, halved, seeded, peeled, and chopped. Makes about 1½ cups.

*Because chile peppers contain volatile oils that can burn your skin and eyes, avoid direct contact with them as much as possible. When working with chile peppers, wear plastic or rubber gloves. If your bare hands do touch the peppers, wash your hands and nails well with soap and warm water.

Flat-Iron Steak with Balsamic Tomatoes

PREP: 20 minutes   **CHILL:** 2 to 24 hours

GRILL: 7 minutes

NUTRITION FACTS per serving:

CALORIES 232

TOTAL FAT 12 g (3 g sat. fat)

CHOLESTEROL 59 mg

PROTEIN 24 g

CARBOHYDRATE 6 g

FIBER 1 g

SODIUM 274 mg

EXCHANGES 3 Lean Meat, 1 Vegetable, 1 Fat

COOK'S TIP

Arugula, with its peppery mustard flavor, is growing in popularity and availability. It's usually sold in small bunches with roots attached. Choose bright green arugula that looks fresh.

1   recipe Balsamic Tomatoes

1   tablespoon dried marjoram, crushed

½   teaspoon garlic salt

½   teaspoon freshly ground black pepper

4   beef shoulder top blade (flat-iron) steaks, cut ¾ inch thick (about 1½ pounds)

4   cups torn spinach or arugula

1 Prepare Balsamic Tomatoes. For rub, in a small bowl combine marjoram, garlic salt, and pepper. Sprinkle rub evenly over all sides of the steaks; rub in with your fingers. If desired, cover and chill for 2 to 24 hours.

2 For a charcoal grill, place steaks on the rack of an uncovered grill directly over medium coals. Grill until desired doneness, turning once halfway through grilling. Allow 7 to 9 minutes for medium-rare doneness (145°F) or 10 to 12 minutes for medium doneness (160°F). (For a gas grill, preheat grill. Reduce heat to medium. Place steaks on grill rack over heat. Cover and grill as above.)

3 Thinly slice steaks across the grain. Serve with spinach and Balsamic Tomatoes. Drizzle with marinade from Balsamic Tomatoes. Makes 6 servings.

Balsamic Tomatoes: Remove the cores from 2 medium tomatoes. Trim off ends. Cut tomatoes crosswise into ¾-inch-thick slices. Arrange tomato slices in a shallow dish; sprinkle lightly with salt and black pepper. Pour ⅓ cup balsamic vinegar over tomatoes. Drizzle with 2 tablespoons olive oil. Cover and chill for 2 to 24 hours, turning occasionally.

Using a slotted spoon, remove tomatoes, reserving marinade. For a charcoal grill, place tomatoes on the rack of an uncovered grill directly over medium coals. Grill about 4 minutes or until lightly charred and slightly soft, turning once halfway through grilling. (For a gas grill, preheat grill. Reduce heat to medium. Place tomatoes on grill rack over heat. Cover and grill as above.)

- 4 beef shoulder top blade (flat-iron) steaks or boneless beef top sirloin steaks, cut ¾ inch thick (about 1½ pounds total)
- 2 teaspoons packed brown sugar
- 1 teaspoon chili powder
- ½ teaspoon garlic salt
- ½ teaspoon black pepper
- 4 ounces fresh tomatillos, husked and quartered (2 small)
- 2 tablespoons water
- 1 ounce reduced-fat cream cheese (Neufchâtel)
- 1 medium avocado, halved, seeded, peeled, and cut up
- ½ of a medium fresh jalapeño chile pepper, seeded and cut up*
- ¼ teaspoon salt

Flat-Iron Steak with Tomatillo Sauce

PREP: 25 minutes   **CHILL:** 30 minutes
GRILL: 7 minutes

NUTRITION FACTS per serving:

CALORIES 286
TOTAL FAT 18 g (6 g sat. fat)
CHOLESTEROL 76 mg
PROTEIN 23 g
CARBOHYDRATE 7 g
FIBER 3 g
SODIUM 315 mg

EXCHANGES 0.5 Other Carbohydrates, 3.5 Lean Meat, 1.5 Fat

1 Trim fat from steaks. For rub, in a small bowl combine brown sugar, chili powder, garlic salt, and black pepper. Sprinkle rub evenly over all sides of the steaks; rub in with your fingers. Cover and chill for 30 minutes.

2 Meanwhile, for sauce, in a small saucepan combine tomatillo quarters and water. Bring to boiling; reduce heat. Cover and simmer for 5 to 7 minutes or until tomatillos are soft. Add cream cheese; stir until melted. Cool mixture slightly. In a food processor or blender combine tomatillo mixture, avocado, chile pepper, and salt; cover and process or blend until smooth. Transfer sauce to a serving bowl.

3 For a charcoal grill, place steaks on the rack of an uncovered grill directly over medium coals. Grill until desired doneness, turning once halfway through grilling. For flat-iron steaks, allow 7 to 10 minutes for medium-rare doneness (145°F) or 10 to 12 minutes for medium doneness (160°F). For top sirloin steaks, allow 12 to 15 minutes for medium-rare doneness (145°F) or 15 to 18 minutes for medium doneness (160°F). (For a gas grill, preheat grill. Reduce heat to medium. Place steaks on grill rack over heat. Cover and grill as above.) Serve steaks with sauce. Makes 6 servings.

*Because chile peppers contain volatile oils that can burn your skin and eyes, avoid direct contact with them as much as possible. When working with chile peppers, wear plastic or rubber gloves. If your bare hands do touch the peppers, wash your hands and nails well with soap and warm water.

1   to 2 teaspoons cracked
     black pepper

4   beef tenderloin steaks, cut 1-inch
     thick (1 to 1¼ pounds total)

1   tablespoon olive oil

½   cup finely chopped onion

1   medium shallot, finely chopped

1   tablespoon snipped fresh thyme
     or 1 teaspoon dried thyme,
     crushed

½   cup Merlot or other dry red wine
     or lower-sodium beef broth

2   tablespoons lower-sodium
     beef broth or water

1   tablespoon balsamic vinegar

⅛   teaspoon salt

Tenderloin Steaks with Merlot Sauce

START TO FINISH: 30 minutes

NUTRITION FACTS per serving:

CALORIES 249
TOTAL FAT 12 g (4 g sat. fat)
CHOLESTEROL 70 mg
PROTEIN 24 g
CARBOHYDRATE 5 g
FIBER 1 g
SODIUM 142 mg

EXCHANGES 3.5 Lean Meat, 0.5 Fat

1 Use your fingers to press pepper onto all sides of the steaks. In a large skillet heat oil over medium heat. Add steaks to skillet; cook until desired doneness, turning once. Allow 10 to 13 minutes for medium-rare doneness (145°F) to medium doneness (160°F). Transfer steaks to a serving platter; keep warm.

2 For sauce, add onion, shallot, and dried thyme (if using) to drippings in skillet. Cook and stir for 4 to 6 minutes or until onion is tender. Add Merlot and broth. Bring to boiling; reduce heat. Boil gently for 3 to 5 minutes or until mixture is reduced by about half. Stir in balsamic vinegar, salt, and fresh thyme (if using). Spoon sauce over steaks. Makes 4 servings.

¼	cup coarse-grain mustard
2	teaspoons honey
1	teaspoon black pepper
¾	teaspoon dry mustard
½	teaspoon salt
½	teaspoon finely shredded orange peel
½	teaspoon finely shredded lemon peel
1	tablespoon olive oil
1	1-pound beef tenderloin roast

1 Preheat oven to 425°F. In a small bowl combine coarse-grain mustard, honey, pepper, dry mustard, salt, orange peel, and lemon peel; set aside.

2 In a heavy large skillet heat oil over medium-high heat. Quickly brown roast on all sides in hot oil (about 2 minutes total). Transfer meat to a rack set in a shallow roasting pan. Spread mustard mixture over top and sides of roast. Insert an oven-going meat thermometer into center of roast.

3 Roast beef for 35 to 45 minutes or until meat thermometer registers 140°F. Cover meat with foil; let stand for 10 minutes before slicing. The temperature of the meat after standing should be 145°F. Makes 4 servings.

Mustard-Crusted Beef Tenderloin

PREP: 20 minutes   **ROAST:** 35 minutes
STAND: 10 minutes   **OVEN:** 425°F

NUTRITION FACTS per serving:

CALORIES 235
TOTAL FAT 12 g (4 g sat. fat)
CHOLESTEROL 70 mg
PROTEIN 24 g
CARBOHYDRATE 3 g
FIBER 0 g
SODIUM 703 mg

EXCHANGES 3.5 Lean Meat, 0.5 Fat

Southwestern Tri-Tip Roast

PREP: 15 minutes   **CHILL:** 6 to 24 hours

ROAST: 30 minutes   **STAND:** 15 minutes

OVEN: 425°F

NUTRITION FACTS per serving:

CALORIES 156
TOTAL FAT 7 g (2 g sat. fat)
CHOLESTEROL 45 mg
PROTEIN 20 g
CARBOHYDRATE 1 g
FIBER 0 g
SODIUM 260 mg

EXCHANGES 3 Lean Meat

1 tablespoon finely chopped canned chipotle chile peppers in adobo sauce*

1 tablespoon snipped fresh oregano or 1 teaspoon dried oregano, crushed

1 tablespoon olive oil

1 teaspoon ground cumin

½ teaspoon salt

2 cloves garlic, minced

1 1½- to 2-pound boneless beef tri-tip roast (bottom sirloin)

Avocado slices (optional)

Purchased pico de gallo (optional)

1 For rub, combine chile peppers, oregano, oil, cumin, salt, and garlic. Spread on surface of roast, rubbing in with glove-covered hands. Cover and chill for 6 to 24 hours.

2 Preheat oven to 425°F. Place roast on a rack in a shallow roasting pan. Insert an oven-going meat thermometer into center of roast. For medium-rare doneness, roast for 30 to 35 minutes or until meat thermometer registers 140°F. Cover with foil and let stand for 15 minutes. The temperature of the meat after standing should be 145°F. (For medium doneness, roast for 40 to 45 minutes or until meat thermometer registers 155°F. Cover and let stand for 15 minutes. The temperature of the meat after standing should be 160°F.)

3 Thinly slice roast across the grain. If desired, serve with avocado and pico de gallo. Makes 6 servings.

*Because chile peppers contain volatile oils that can burn your skin and eyes, avoid direct contact with them as much as possible. When working with chile peppers, wear plastic or rubber gloves. If your bare hands do touch the peppers, wash your hands and nails well with soap and warm water.

- 6 ounces lean ground beef or lamb
- ¼ cup finely chopped onion
- 2 cloves garlic, minced
- 1 8-ounce can tomato sauce
- 1 teaspoon snipped fresh rosemary or ¼ teaspoon dried rosemary, crushed
- 2 6-inch whole wheat or white pita bread rounds
- ½ cup shredded reduced-fat mozzarella cheese (2 ounces)
- ½ cup shredded fresh spinach
- 1 medium tomato, seeded and chopped
- ¼ cup crumbled reduced-fat feta cheese (1 ounce)
- 12 pitted kalamata or ripe olives, quartered

1 Preheat oven to 400°F. In a medium nonstick skillet cook ground beef, onion, and garlic until meat is browned; drain off fat. Stir tomato sauce and rosemary into meat mixture in skillet. Bring to boiling; reduce heat. Simmer, uncovered, for 2 minutes.

2 Carefully split pita bread rounds in half horizontally; place pita halves, rough sides up, in a single layer on a large baking sheet. Bake for 3 to 4 minutes or until lightly toasted.

3 Top toasted pita bread with meat mixture; sprinkle with mozzarella cheese. Bake for 2 to 3 minutes more or until cheese is melted. Remove from oven. Top with spinach, tomato, feta cheese, and olives; serve immediately. Makes 4 servings.

Greek Pita Pizzas

START TO FINISH: 35 minutes

OVEN: 400°F

NUTRITION FACTS per serving:

CALORIES 256
TOTAL FAT 10 g (4 g sat. fat)
CHOLESTEROL 40 mg
PROTEIN 18 g
CARBOHYDRATE 25 g
FIBER 5 g
SODIUM 842 mg

EXCHANGES 1.5 Starch, 1.5 Lean Meat, 0.5 Vegetable, 1 Fat

COOK'S TIP

Uncooked ground beef can be stored in the freezer for 6 to 12 months and in the refrigerator for 2 or 3 days. Leftover cooked beef should be stored in the refrigerator no more than 3 or 4 days.

¼ cup finely chopped onion

¼ cup snipped fresh parsley or
   ½ teaspoon dried dill

2 cloves garlic, minced

½ teaspoon salt

1 pound lean ground beef

⅓ cup plain low-fat yogurt

1 tablespoon stone-ground mustard
   or Dijon-style mustard

1 tablespoon snipped fresh dill or
   1 teaspoon dried dill

1 teaspoon balsamic vinegar

¼ cup chopped seeded cucumber

Cucumber slices (optional)

Tomato slices (optional)

Red onion slices (optional)

Fresh spinach leaves (optional)

Burgers with Dill Sauce

PREP: 20 minutes

BROIL: 12 minutes

NUTRITION FACTS per serving:

CALORIES 234
TOTAL FAT 12 g (5 g sat. fat)
CHOLESTEROL 75 mg
PROTEIN 25 g
CARBOHYDRATE 6 g
FIBER 1 g
SODIUM 474 mg

EXCHANGES 3.5 Lean Meat, 0.5 Vegetable, 0.5 Fat

1 Preheat broiler. In a large bowl combine chopped onion, parsley, garlic, and salt. Add beef; mix well. Shape into four ¾-inch-thick patties.

2 Place patties on the unheated rack of a broiler pan. Broil 3 to 4 inches from heat for 12 to 14 minutes or until done (160°F),* turning once halfway through broiling.

3 Meanwhile, for sauce, in a small bowl combine yogurt, mustard, dill, and balsamic vinegar. Stir in chopped cucumber. Spoon sauce over burgers. If desired, serve with cucumber slices, tomato slices, red onion slices, and spinach. Makes 4 servings.

*The internal color of a burger is not a reliable doneness indicator. A beef patty cooked to 160°F is safe, regardless of color. To measure the doneness of a patty, insert an instant-read thermometer through the side of the patty to a depth of 2 to 3 inches.

COOK'S TIP

Dillweed loses its fragrance quickly when heated. When you cook with it, be sure to add it at the end of the cooking time.

1	lemon
6	ounces dried whole wheat orzo (about 1 cup)
1	cup cherry tomatoes, halved
¼	cup capers, rinsed and drained
2	teaspoons snipped fresh rosemary or ½ teaspoon dried rosemary, crushed
1	tablespoon olive oil
1	pound veal scaloppine (about ¼ inch thick)
¼	teaspoon salt
¼	teaspoon black pepper
¼	cup dry white wine or lower-sodium beef broth
1	tablespoon snipped fresh flat-leaf parsley
	Fresh rosemary sprigs (optional)
	Lemon wedges (optional)

1 Finely shred peel from the lemon. Squeeze juice from lemon; set peel and juice aside separately. Cook orzo in lightly salted boiling water according to package directions; drain. Stir in half of the lemon peel, half of the lemon juice, cherry tomatoes, half of the capers, and snipped or dried rosemary. Cover and let stand until serving time.

2 Meanwhile, in a very large skillet heat oil over medium-high heat. Sprinkle veal with salt and pepper. Add veal to skillet. Cook about 4 minutes or until no longer pink, turning veal occasionally to brown evenly. Transfer veal to a serving platter; cover and keep warm.

3 Add remaining lemon peel, remaining lemon juice, remaining capers, and white wine to the skillet. Bring to boiling, scraping the browned bits from the bottom of the pan.

4 Pour wine mixture over veal. Serve with cooked orzo. Sprinkle orzo mixture with parsley. If desired, garnish with rosemary sprigs and serve with lemon wedges. Makes 4 servings.

Veal Piccata

START TO FINISH: 25 minutes

NUTRITION FACTS per serving:

CALORIES 329
TOTAL FAT 7 g (1 g sat. fat)
CHOLESTEROL 89 mg
PROTEIN 30 g
CARBOHYDRATE 35 g
FIBER 9 g
SODIUM 481 mg

EXCHANGES 2 Starch, 3 Lean Meat, 0.5 Vegetable

COOK'S TIP

Orzo is a rice-shape pasta, generally found in the pasta aisle of grocery stores. If you have trouble finding the whole wheat variety, look for it at health or specialty markets or ask your grocer to carry it.

Veal Chops with Pesto-Stuffed Mushrooms

PREP: 15 minutes   **MARINATE:** 2 to 6 hours

GRILL: 11 minutes

NUTRITION FACTS per serving:

CALORIES 286
TOTAL FAT 12 g (3 g sat. fat)
CHOLESTEROL 134 mg
PROTEIN 36 g
CARBOHYDRATE 5 g
FIBER 1 g
SODIUM 294 mg

EXCHANGES 0.5 Lean Meat, 0.5 Vegetable

¼ cup dry white wine or reduced-sodium chicken broth

1 tablespoon snipped fresh sage or thyme or 1 teaspoon dried sage or thyme, crushed

1 tablespoon olive oil

1 tablespoon Worcestershire sauce for chicken

3 cloves garlic, minced

¼ teaspoon black pepper

4 bone-in veal loin chops, cut ¾ inch thick (about 2½ pounds total) or 1 pound boneless beef top sirloin steak, cut into 4 serving-size pieces

8 large fresh mushrooms (2 to 2½ inches in diameter), stems removed

3 tablespoons purchased refrigerated reduced-fat basil pesto

Fresh flat-leaf parsley sprigs (optional)

1 For marinade, in a small bowl combine wine, sage, oil, Worcestershire sauce, garlic, and pepper. Place meat and mushrooms in a resealable plastic bag set in a shallow dish. Pour marinade into bag. Seal bag; turn to coat meat and mushrooms. Marinate in the refrigerator for 2 to 6 hours, turning bag occasionally.

2 For a charcoal grill, place meat on the rack of an uncovered grill directly over medium coals. Grill until desired doneness, turning once halfway through grilling. For veal, allow 11 to 13 minutes for medium doneness (160°F). For beef top sirloin, allow 14 to 18 minutes for medium-rare doneness (145°F) or 18 to 22 minutes for medium doneness (160°F).

3 Meanwhile, place mushrooms, stemmed sides down, on grill rack. Grill for 4 minutes. Turn mushrooms stemmed sides up; spoon some of the pesto into each mushroom. Grill about 4 minutes more or until heated through. (For a gas grill, preheat grill. Reduce heat to medium. Place meat, then mushrooms on grill rack over heat. Cover and grill as above.)

4 Serve chops with mushrooms. If desired, garnish with parsley. Makes 4 servings.

12 ounces boneless veal leg round steak or veal leg sirloin steak, cut ¼ inch thick and trimmed of fat

¼ teaspoon salt

¼ teaspoon black pepper

1 medium onion, chopped

¼ cup water

2 cloves garlic, minced

1 14½-ounce can no-salt-added diced tomatoes, undrained

3 tablespoons dry white wine or reduced-sodium chicken broth

1 tablespoon snipped fresh oregano or 1 teaspoon dried oregano, crushed

1 tablespoon capers, rinsed and drained (optional)

Nonstick cooking spray

2 cups hot cooked whole wheat pasta

Veal Scaloppine

START TO FINISH: 35 minutes

NUTRITION FACTS per serving:

CALORIES 219
TOTAL FAT 2 g (1 g sat. fat)
CHOLESTEROL 66 mg
PROTEIN 23 g
CARBOHYDRATE 26 g
FIBER 4 g
SODIUM 244 mg

EXCHANGES 1.5 Starch, 2.5 Very Lean Meat, 1 Vegetable

1 Cut meat into eight pieces. Place each piece of meat between two pieces of plastic wrap. Working from center to edges, pound with flat side of a meat mallet to about an ⅛-inch thickness. Remove plastic wrap. Sprinkle meat with salt and ⅛ teaspoon pepper. Set aside.

2 For sauce, in a medium saucepan combine onion, water, and garlic. Cover and cook until onion is tender. Stir in undrained tomatoes, wine, oregano, capers (if using), and remaining ⅛ teaspoon pepper. Bring to boiling; reduce heat. Simmer, uncovered, about 15 minutes or until desired consistency. Keep warm.

3 Meanwhile, lightly coat an unheated large skillet with nonstick cooking spray. Preheat over medium-high heat. Cook veal, half at a time, for 2 to 4 minutes or until desired doneness, turning once. Transfer veal to a serving platter. Keep warm.

4 To serve, spoon sauce over veal. Serve with pasta. Makes 4 servings.

COOK'S TIP

The veal in this recipe takes only a few minutes to cook through because it is flattened beforehand. Pay attention to the meat while it cooks because veal can quickly overcook and dry out.

8   lamb rib chops, cut about 1 inch
     thick (2 to 2½ pounds total)
4   cloves garlic, minced
1½ teaspoons fennel seeds, crushed
1½ teaspoons ground cumin
½   teaspoon ground coriander
½   teaspoon salt
½   teaspoon cracked black pepper

1 Trim fat from lamb chops; set chops aside. In a small bowl combine garlic, fennel seeds, cumin, coriander, salt, and pepper. Sprinkle evenly over all sides of lamb chops; rub in with your fingers. Place lamb chops on a plate; cover with plastic wrap. Chill for 30 minutes to 24 hours.

2 For a charcoal grill, place lamb chops on the rack of an uncovered grill directly over medium coals. Grill until desired doneness, turning once halfway through grilling. Allow 12 to 14 minutes for medium-rare doneness (145°F) or 15 to 17 minutes for medium doneness (160°F). (For a gas grill, preheat grill. Reduce heat to medium. Place chops on grill rack over heat. Cover and grill as above.) Makes 4 servings.

Garlic-Fennel Lamb Chops

PREP: 15 minutes

CHILL: 30 minutes to 24 hours

GRILL: 12 minutes

NUTRITION FACTS per serving:

CALORIES 249
TOTAL FAT 8 g (3 g sat. fat)
CHOLESTEROL 119 mg
PROTEIN 39 g
CARBOHYDRATE 2 g
FIBER 1 g
SODIUM 384 mg

EXCHANGES 5.5 Very Lean Meat, 1 Fat

NUTRITION NOTE

Lamb has less fat marbling than other meats; most visible fat is on the outer edges of the cuts. To reduce saturated fat and cholesterol, trim the fat.

8	lamb loin chops, cut 1 inch thick (about 2 pounds total)
1	tablespoon snipped fresh thyme or 1 teaspoon dried thyme, crushed
¼	teaspoon salt
¼	teaspoon black pepper
3	medium tomatoes, chopped
1	medium cucumber, chopped
1	medium yellow sweet pepper, seeded and chopped
½	of a medium red onion, chopped
1	teaspoon snipped fresh oregano or ½ teaspoon dried oregano, crushed
2	tablespoons balsamic vinegar
1	tablespoon olive oil
	Fresh romaine leaves (optional)

1 Trim fat from chops. Sprinkle chops with 2 teaspoons fresh thyme or ¾ teaspoon dried thyme, ⅛ teaspoon salt, and ⅛ teaspoon black pepper. For a charcoal grill, place chops on the rack of an uncovered grill directly over medium coals. Grill until desired doneness, turning once halfway through grilling. Allow 12 to 14 minutes for medium-rare doneness (145°F) or 15 to 17 minutes for medium doneness (160°F). (For a gas grill, preheat grill. Reduce heat to medium. Place chops on grill rack over heat. Cover and grill as above.)

2 Meanwhile, for salad, in a large bowl combine tomato, cucumber, sweet pepper, red onion, oregano, remaining 1 teaspoon fresh thyme or ¼ teaspoon dried thyme, and remaining ⅛ teaspoon salt and ⅛ teaspoon black pepper. Drizzle with balsamic vinegar and oil. Toss gently to combine. If desired, spoon onto romaine leaves.

3 Serve grilled lamb chops with salad. Makes 4 servings.

Lamb Chops with Fresh Greek Salad

PREP: 25 minutes

GRILL: 12 minutes

NUTRITION FACTS per serving:

CALORIES 325
TOTAL FAT 12 g (4 g sat. fat)
CHOLESTEROL 119 mg
PROTEIN 43 g
CARBOHYDRATE 13 g
FIBER 2 g
SODIUM 245 mg

EXCHANGES 5.5 Very Lean Meat, 2 Vegetable, 2 Fat

On the divider: Apple-Glazed Tenderloin (see recipe, page 219)

- 1 1-pound pork tenderloin
- ¼ cup balsamic vinegar
- 2 tablespoons olive oil
- 1 tablespoon snipped fresh rosemary or ½ teaspoon dried rosemary, crushed
- 2 cloves garlic, minced
- ¾ teaspoon black pepper
- ⅛ teaspoon salt
- 1 recipe Balsamic Glaze

1 Place tenderloin in large resealable plastic bag set in a shallow dish. For marinade, in a small bowl combine balsamic vinegar, oil, rosemary, garlic, pepper, and salt. Pour over tenderloin. Seal bag; turn to coat tenderloin. Marinate in the refrigerator for 1 hour, turning bag occasionally.

2 Remove tenderloin from marinade, discarding marinade. For a charcoal grill, arrange hot coals around a drip pan. Test for medium-hot heat above the pan. Place tenderloin on grill rack over drip pan. Cover and grill for 30 to 35 minutes or until an instant-read thermometer inserted into the thickest part of the tenderloin registers 155°F. (For a gas grill, preheat grill. Reduce heat to medium-high. Adjust for indirect cooking. Place tenderloin on grill rack over burner that is off. Grill as above.)

3 Brush tenderloin on all sides with Balsamic Glaze. Grill for 1 minute more. Remove from grill. Cover tightly with foil; let stand for 15 minutes before slicing. The temperature of the meat after standing should be 160°F. Makes 4 servings.

Balsamic Glaze: In a small saucepan bring ½ cup balsamic vinegar to boiling. Reduce heat; boil gently for 5 minutes. Makes about ¼ cup.

Balsamic Pork Tenderloin

PREP: 20 minutes **MARINATE:** 1 hour
GRILL: 31 minutes **STAND:** 15 minutes

NUTRITION FACTS per serving:

CALORIES 189
TOTAL FAT 7 g (2 g sat. fat)
CHOLESTEROL 73 mg
PROTEIN 24 g
CARBOHYDRATE 5 g
FIBER 0 g
SODIUM 81 mg

EXCHANGES 3.5 Very Lean Meat, 1.5 Fat

COOK'S TIP

When selecting pork, choose a pale pink cut that has little marbling. The fat that is present should be white, not yellow, or you will not be getting the freshest product.

1 pound boneless pork loin
¼ cup bottled plum sauce
1 tablespoon reduced-sodium
  soy sauce
1 tablespoon lime juice
2 teaspoons honey
⅛ teaspoon ground ginger
½ of a cored peeled pineapple, cut
  into 1½-inch chunks
1 medium red sweet pepper, seeded
  and cut into 1-inch pieces

Pork and Pineapple Kabobs

PREP: 25 minutes **MARINATE:** 30 to 60 minutes
GRILL: 18 minutes

NUTRITION FACTS per serving:

CALORIES 218
TOTAL FAT 5 g (2 g sat. fat)
CHOLESTEROL 71 mg
PROTEIN 25 g
CARBOHYDRATE 18 g
FIBER 2 g
SODIUM 244 mg

EXCHANGES 0.5 Other Carbohydrates,
0.5 Fruit, 3.5 Very Lean Meat, 0.5 Fat

1 Trim fat from pork; cut pork into 1½-inch cubes. Place pork cubes in a large resealable plastic bag set in a shallow dish. For marinade, in a small bowl whisk together plum sauce, soy sauce, lime juice, honey, and ginger. Pour marinade over pork cubes in bag. Seal bag; turn to coat pork cubes. Marinate in the refrigerator for 30 to 60 minutes, turning bag occasionally.

2 Drain pork, discarding marinade. On two or three 10- to 12-inch metal skewers, thread pork cubes, leaving a ¼-inch space between cubes. On two more 10- to 12-inch metal skewers, alternately thread pineapple and sweet pepper pieces, leaving a ¼-inch space between pieces.

3 For a charcoal grill, place skewers on the rack of an uncovered grill directly over medium coals. Grill for 8 to 10 minutes for pineapple and sweet pepper or until pineapple is lightly browned and 18 to 20 minutes for pork or until no pink remains, turning skewers to brown evenly. (For a gas grill, preheat grill. Reduce heat to medium. Place skewers on grill rack over heat. Cover and grill as above.)

4 Serve pork with pineapple and sweet pepper. Makes 4 servings.

COOK'S TIP

To peel a pineapple, begin by cutting off the crown and the bottom. With the pineapple upright, cut in strips, following the contour of the fruit, to remove the skin.

2 cups apple or hickory wood chips

1 1-pound pork tenderloin

½ teaspoon coarsely ground
   black pepper

¼ teaspoon salt

2 tablespoons apple jelly, melted

¼ teaspoon ground cinnamon

1 recipe Apple-Onion Spice Packet
   (optional)

1 At least 1 hour before grilling, soak wood chips in enough water to cover. Drain chips before using. Trim fat from tenderloin. Sprinkle tenderloin with pepper and salt. In a small bowl stir together apple jelly and cinnamon; set aside.

2 For a charcoal grill, arrange medium-hot coals around a drip pan. Pour 1 inch of water into the drip pan. Test for medium heat above the pan. Sprinkle wood chips over the coals. Place tenderloin on grill rack over the drip pan. Place Apple-Onion Spice Packet (if using) directly over the coals. Cover and grill the pork for 35 to 40 minutes or until an instant-read thermometer inserted in the thickest part of the tenderloin registers 155°F. Brush tenderloin with the apple jelly mixture for the last 10 minutes of grilling. If using spice packet, turn packet after 10 minutes and continue grilling for 10 minutes more. Remove packet from grill and let stand while pork continues to cook. (For a gas grill, preheat grill. Reduce heat to medium. Adjust for indirect cooking. Place tenderloin over burner that is off and spice packet [if using] on grill rack over burner that is on. Cover and grill as above.)

3 Remove from grill. Cover tightly with foil; let stand for 15 minutes. The temperature of meat after standing should be 160°F. If using Apple-Onion Spice Packet, serve with pork. Makes 4 servings.

Apple-Onion Spice Packet: Fold a 36×18-inch piece of heavy foil in half to make an 18-inch square; set aside. Core 2 medium cooking apples; cut into thin wedges. Cut 1 medium sweet onion (such as Vidalia, Walla Walla, or Maui) into thin wedges. Place apple and onion wedges in the center of the foil. Top with 2 tablespoons apple jelly and sprinkle with ¼ teaspoon ground cinnamon. Bring up two opposite edges of the foil square and seal with a double fold. Fold remaining edges to enclose apple and onion, leaving space for steam to build.

Apple-Glazed Tenderloin

PREP: 20 minutes **SOAK:** 1 hour
GRILL: 35 minutes **STAND:** 15 minutes

NUTRITION FACTS per serving:

CALORIES 189
TOTAL FAT 6 g (2 g sat. fat)
CHOLESTEROL 62 mg
PROTEIN 25 g
CARBOHYDRATE 8 g
FIBER 0 g
SODIUM 200 mg

EXCHANGES 0.5 Other Carbohydrates,
3.5 Lean Meat

NUTRITION NOTE

When a craving for pork hits, pork tenderloin is a good choice. It's one of the lowest fat cuts of meat available, and very little of the fat is saturated.

1   1-pound pork tenderloin

¾   teaspoon Greek seasoning

1   large red sweet pepper, stemmed, seeded, and quartered

2   tablespoons balsamic vinegar

⅛   teaspoon salt

1 ¼   cups water

¾   cup whole wheat couscous

2   cups shredded or coarsely chopped fresh spinach

Greek Pork Tenderloin with Red Pepper Sauce

PREP: 25 minutes   **GRILL:** 35 minutes
STAND: 15 minutes

NUTRITION FACTS per serving:

CALORIES 314
TOTAL FAT 5 g (1 g sat. fat)
CHOLESTEROL 74 mg
PROTEIN 31 g
CARBOHYDRATE 38 g
FIBER 6 g
SODIUM 162 mg

EXCHANGES 2 Starch, 3 Very Lean Meat, 1 Vegetable

1 Trim fat from tenderloin. Sprinkle tenderloin with ½ teaspoon Greek seasoning. For a charcoal grill, arrange medium-hot coals around a drip pan. Test for medium heat above the pan. Place tenderloin on the grill rack over the drip pan. Place pepper quarters on the grill rack over the coals. Cover and grill until peppers are tender and an instant-read thermometer inserted in the thickest part of the tenderloin registers 155°F. Turn peppers once halfway through grilling. Allow 12 to 15 minutes for peppers and 35 to 40 minutes for tenderloin. (For a gas grill, preheat grill. Reduce heat to medium. Adjust for indirect cooking. Place tenderloin on grill rack over burner that is off and peppers on grill rack over burner that is on. Grill as above.)

2 Remove tenderloin from grill. Cover tightly with foil; let stand for 15 minutes before slicing. The temperature of the meat after standing should be 160°F.

3 When peppers are done, remove from grill and cool slightly. For red pepper sauce, place peppers in a blender or food processor. Add balsamic vinegar and salt. Cover and blend or process until smooth. Keep warm.

4 In a medium saucepan bring water and remaining ¼ teaspoon Greek seasoning to boiling. Add couscous; remove from heat. Cover and let stand for 5 minutes. Stir in spinach.

5 To serve, slice tenderloin. Serve with couscous mixture and red pepper sauce. Makes 4 servings.

- 1 1-pound pork tenderloin
- 2 cloves garlic, minced
- ¼ teaspoon salt
- ¼ teaspoon black pepper
- 1 medium mango, seeded, peeled, and chopped
- ½ of a medium red sweet pepper, seeded and cut into bite-size strips
- ½ of an avocado, seeded, peeled, and chopped
- ½ cup chopped jicama
- ¼ cup snipped fresh cilantro
- 1½ teaspoons finely shredded lime peel
- ⅛ teaspoon salt
     Lime wedges (optional)

1 Preheat oven to 425°F. Trim fat from tenderloin. Rub garlic onto tenderloin. Sprinkle tenderloin with ¼ teaspoon salt and black pepper. Place tenderloin on a rack in a shallow roasting pan. Roast for 25 to 35 minutes or until an instant-read thermometer inserted into thickest part of the tenderloin registers 155°F.

2 Remove tenderloin from oven. Cover tightly with foil; let stand for 15 minutes before slicing. The temperature of the meat after standing should be 160°F.

3 Meanwhile, in a medium bowl gently stir together mango, sweet pepper, avocado, jicama, cilantro, lime peel, and ⅛ teaspoon salt. Slice pork and serve with mango mixture. If desired, serve with lime wedges. Makes 4 servings.

Roasted Pork with Crunchy Mango Salad

PREP: 25 minutes **ROAST:** 25 minutes
STAND: 15 minutes **OVEN:** 425°F

NUTRITION FACTS per serving:

CALORIES 211
TOTAL FAT 7 g (2 g sat. fat)
CHOLESTEROL 74 mg
PROTEIN 25 g
CARBOHYDRATE 13 g
FIBER 3 g
SODIUM 281 mg

EXCHANGES 0.5 Fruit, 3.5 Very Lean Meat, 1.5 Fat

NUTRITION NOTE

Fresh mangoes are sweet summer treats that are loaded with vitamins A and C. Mangoes pair deliciously with pork and are flavorful additions to sorbets, smoothies, and fruit salads.

2 teaspoons chili powder
1 teaspoon garlic powder
1 teaspoon dried oregano, crushed
½ teaspoon salt
½ teaspoon black pepper
½ teaspoon ground cumin
¼ teaspoon cayenne pepper
2 1-pound pork tenderloins

1 Preheat oven to 425°F. For rub, in a small bowl combine chili powder, garlic powder, oregano, salt, black pepper, cumin, and cayenne pepper. Sprinkle rub evenly over all sides of tenderloins; rub in with your fingers.

2 Place tenderloins on a rack in a shallow roasting pan. Roast for 25 to 35 minutes or until an instant-read thermometer inserted into thickest part of the tenderloins registers 155°F.

3 Remove tenderloins from oven. Cover tightly with foil; let stand for 15 minutes before slicing. The temperature of the meat after standing should be 160°F. Makes 8 servings.

Latin-Spiced Pork Tenderloins

PREP: 10 minutes   **ROAST:** 25 minutes
STAND: 15 minutes   **OVEN:** 425°F

NUTRITION FACTS per serving:

CALORIES 138
TOTAL FAT 3 g (1 g sat. fat)
CHOLESTEROL 73 mg
PROTEIN 24 g
CARBOHYDRATE 1 g
FIBER 0 g
SODIUM 198 mg
EXCHANGES 3.5 Very Lean Meat, 0.5 Fat

COOK'S TIP

Garlic powder and garlic salt may seem similar enough, but they should not be substituted for each other. Garlic powder is concentrated, so more garlic salt would be required to achieve the same flavor, resulting in too much added salt in the recipe.

- ¼ cup yellow cornmeal
- ¼ cup finely chopped pecans
- 1 teaspoon paprika
- ½ teaspoon ground cumin
- ½ teaspoon garlic powder
- ¼ teaspoon salt
- ¼ teaspoon black pepper
- 1 egg, lightly beaten
- 1 tablespoon water
- 1 1-pound pork tenderloin
  Nonstick cooking spray

1 Preheat oven to 425°F. In a shallow dish combine cornmeal, pecans, paprika, cumin, garlic powder, salt, and pepper. In another shallow dish combine egg and water. Dip pork tenderloin in egg mixture, turning to coat; allow excess to drip off. Dip tenderloin in cornmeal mixture, turning to coat. Place tenderloin on a rack in a shallow roasting pan. Lightly coat pork with nonstick cooking spray.

2 Roast pork for 25 to 35 minutes or until an instant-read thermometer inserted into thickest part of the tenderloin registers 155°F.

3 Remove tenderloin from oven. Cover tightly with foil; let stand for 15 minutes before slicing. The temperature of the meat after standing should be 160°F. Makes 4 servings.

Pecan-Cornmeal-Crusted Pork

PREP: 15 minutes   **ROAST:** 25 minutes
STAND: 15 minutes   **OVEN:** 425°F

NUTRITION FACTS per serving:
- -

CALORIES 233
TOTAL FAT 10 g (2 g sat. fat)
CHOLESTEROL 127 mg
PROTEIN 27 g
CARBOHYDRATE 8 g
FIBER 2 g
SODIUM 224 mg

EXCHANGES 0.5 Starch, 3.5 Very Lean Meat, 1.5 Fat

2 tablespoons bottled chili sauce or 1 tablespoon Asian chili sauce
1 tablespoon reduced-sodium teriyaki sauce
2 cloves garlic, minced
½ teaspoon grated fresh ginger or ⅛ teaspoon ground ginger
1 12- to 16-ounce pork tenderloin
1 teaspoon sesame seeds
2 teaspoons olive oil
⅛ teaspoon salt
⅛ teaspoon black pepper
4 cups packaged shredded broccoli (broccoli slaw mix)

Sesame Pork Tenderloin

PREP: 25 minutes   **ROAST:** 25 minutes
STAND: 10 minutes   **OVEN:** 425°F

NUTRITION FACTS per serving:

CALORIES 167
TOTAL FAT 6 g (1 g sat. fat)
CHOLESTEROL 55 mg
PROTEIN 21 g
CARBOHYDRATE 8 g
FIBER 3 g
SODIUM 365 mg

EXCHANGES 3 Lean Meat, 1 Vegetable

1 Preheat oven to 425°F. For sauce, in a small bowl stir together chili sauce, teriyaki sauce, half of the garlic, and ginger.

2 Place tenderloin on a rack in a shallow roasting pan. Spread half of the sauce on tenderloin. Roast, uncovered, for 15 minutes. Spread remaining sauce on tenderloin; sprinkle tenderloin with sesame seeds. Roast, uncovered, for 10 to 20 minutes more or until an instant-read thermometer inserted in the thickest part of the tenderloin registers 155°F.

3 Remove from oven. Cover tightly with foil; let stand for 10 minutes before serving. The temperature of the meat after standing should be 160°F.

4 Meanwhile, in a 4-quart Dutch oven heat oil over medium heat. Add remaining garlic, salt, and pepper; cook and stir for 15 seconds. Add broccoli. Cook and toss for 1 to 2 minutes or until broccoli is heated through.

5 To serve, slice tenderloin and serve with broccoli. Makes 4 servings.

1 pound boneless pork loin

⅓ cup lime juice

2 tablespoons honey

1 fresh jalapeño chile pepper, seeded and finely chopped*

¼ cup snipped fresh cilantro

½ teaspoon salt

3 fresh ears of corn or 1½ cups loose-pack frozen whole kernel corn, thawed

2 cups coarsely chopped fresh arugula or spinach

1 medium red sweet pepper, seeded and chopped

Pork Kabobs with Corn Salad

PREP: 20 minutes   **MARINATE:** 1 hour
GRILL: 18 minutes

NUTRITION FACTS per serving:

CALORIES 286
TOTAL FAT 10 g (3 g sat. fat)
CHOLESTEROL 73 mg
PROTEIN 25 g
CARBOHYDRATE 26 g
FIBER 3 g
SODIUM 384 mg

EXCHANGES 1.5 Starch, 3 Lean Meat, 0.5 Vegetable

1 Trim fat from pork; cut pork into 1½-inch cubes. Place pork cubes in a large resealable plastic bag set in a shallow dish. For marinade, in a small bowl whisk together lime juice and honey. Stir in chile pepper, cilantro, and salt. Add ¼ cup of the lime juice mixture to pork cubes in bag. Seal bag; turn to coat pork cubes. Marinate in the refrigerator for 1 hour, turning bag occasionally.

2 Drain pork, discarding marinade. Thread pork onto eight 8-inch skewers,** leaving a ¼-inch space between cubes. For a charcoal grill, place skewers on the rack of an uncovered grill directly over medium coals. Grill for 18 to 20 minutes or until no pink remains, turning skewers to brown evenly. (For a gas grill, preheat grill. Reduce heat to medium. Place skewers on grill rack over heat. Cover and grill as above.)

3 Meanwhile, if using fresh corn, carefully cut corn kernels off the cobs. For corn salad, in a medium bowl combine corn kernels, arugula, and sweet pepper. Add remaining lime juice mixture; toss to coat. Serve pork with corn salad. Makes 4 servings.

*Because chile peppers contain volatile oils that can burn your skin and eyes, avoid direct contact with them as much as possible. When working with chile peppers, wear plastic or rubber gloves. If your bare hands do touch the peppers, wash your hands and nails well with soap and warm water.

**If using wooden skewers, soak in enough water to cover for 30 minutes.

COOK'S TIP

Store chile peppers, such as jalapeño peppers, unwashed and wrapped in paper towels in a plastic bag in the refrigerator for up to 10 days.

Asian Pork Stir-Fry

START TO FINISH: 30 minutes

NUTRITION FACTS per serving:

CALORIES 304
TOTAL FAT 11 g (2 g sat. fat)
CHOLESTEROL 71 mg
PROTEIN 28 g
CARBOHYDRATE 23 g
FIBER 4 g
SODIUM 487 mg

EXCHANGES 1 Starch, 3 Lean Meat, 2 Vegetable, 0.5 Fat

⅓ cup low-sugar apricot preserves

3 tablespoons reduced-sodium soy sauce

2 teaspoons cornstarch

½ teaspoon ground ginger

¼ to ½ teaspoon crushed red pepper

4 teaspoons canola oil

2 large carrots, thinly bias-sliced

½ of a 16-ounce package frozen (yellow, green, and red) peppers and onion stir-fry vegetables (2 cups)

1 pound lean boneless pork, cut into thin bite-size strips

3 cups packaged shredded broccoli (broccoli slaw mix) or shredded napa cabbage

2 tablespoons chopped almonds, toasted, or peanuts

1 For sauce, in a small bowl stir together preserves, soy sauce, cornstarch, ginger, and crushed red pepper. Set sauce aside.

2 In a wok or large nonstick skillet heat 2 teaspoons oil over medium-high heat. Add carrot; cook and stir for 3 to 5 minutes or until crisp-tender. Add frozen stir-fry vegetables; cook and stir until heated through. Remove vegetables from wok or skillet; set aside.

3 Add remaining 2 teaspoons oil and half of the pork to wok or skillet. Cook and stir for 2 to 4 minutes or until no pink remains. Remove pork from wok or skillet; set aside. Add remaining pork to wok or skillet. Cook and stir for 2 to 4 minutes or until no pink remains. Return all of the pork to wok or skillet. Push pork to the edge of the wok or skillet.

4 Stir sauce; add to wok or skillet. Cook and stir until thickened and bubbly. Return vegetables to wok or skillet; stir gently to coat all ingredients with sauce. Heat through. Serve pork mixture over broccoli; sprinkle with almonds. Makes 4 servings.

Nonstick cooking spray

1 pound lean boneless pork, cut into thin bite-size strips

2 cups sliced fresh mushrooms

½ cup chopped onion

2 tablespoons canola oil or olive oil

¼ cup all-purpose flour

½ teaspoon salt

½ teaspoon dried sage, crushed

¼ teaspoon black pepper

2 cups fat-free milk

4 cups chopped, stemmed fresh kale or Swiss chard

2 cups cooked wild rice

1 tablespoon finely shredded lemon peel

1 Preheat oven to 350°F. Coat an unheated very large skillet with nonstick cooking spray. Preheat skillet over medium-high heat. Add pork to hot skillet; cook and stir for 2 to 4 minutes or until no pink remains. Remove pork from skillet; set aside.

2 Add mushrooms, onion, and oil to the same skillet. Cook about 5 minutes or until mushrooms are tender, stirring occasionally. Stir in flour, salt, sage, and pepper. Add milk all at once; cook and stir until thickened and bubbly. Stir in pork, kale, cooked wild rice, and lemon peel.

3 Spoon mixture into a 1½- to 2-quart rectangular or oval baking dish. Bake, uncovered, for 30 to 35 minutes or until heated through. Let stand for 10 minutes before serving. Makes 6 servings.

COOK'S TIP

With the exception of spinach, all greens, including kale, should be thoroughly washed before storage. Shake off excess water, wrap the greens in paper towels, put them in a plastic bag, and store in the refrigerator for up to three days.

Pork Casserole with Mushrooms and Kale

PREP: 25 minutes **BAKE:** 30 minutes
STAND: 10 minutes **OVEN:** 350°F

NUTRITION FACTS per serving:

CALORIES 285
TOTAL FAT 10 g (2 g sat. fat),
CHOLESTEROL 49 mg
PROTEIN 24 g
CARBOHYDRATE 27 g
FIBER 3 g
SODIUM 305 mg

EXCHANGES 1.5 Starch, 2.5 Lean Meat, 1 Vegetable, 0.5 Fat

Smoked Jerk Pork Roast with Warm Mango Sauce

PREP: 20 minutes   **SOAK:** 1 hour
GRILL: 1 hour   **STAND:** 10 minutes

NUTRITION FACTS per serving:

CALORIES 195
TOTAL FAT 6 g (2 g sat. fat)
CHOLESTEROL 62 mg
PROTEIN 25 g
CARBOHYDRATE 9 g
FIBER 1 g
SODIUM 163 mg

EXCHANGES 0.5 Starch, 3.5 Lean Meat

4	cups apple or hickory wood chips
1	2- to 3-pound boneless pork top loin roast (single loin)
2	teaspoons Jamaican jerk seasoning
2	medium mangoes, seeded, peeled, and coarsely chopped (about 2 cups)
¼	teaspoon ground ginger
¼	teaspoon crushed red pepper (optional)
⅛	teaspoon salt
½	teaspoon finely shredded lime peel
2	tablespoons lime juice

1 At least 1 hour before grilling, soak wood chips in enough water to cover. Drain before using. Trim fat from pork. Sprinkle jerk seasoning evenly over pork.

2 For a charcoal grill, arrange medium coals around a drip pan. Pour 1 inch of water into drip pan. Test for medium-low heat above the pan. Sprinkle half of the drained wood chips over the coals. Place meat on grill rack over drip pan. Cover and grill for 1 to 1½ hours or until juices run clear (150°F). Add remaining wood chips as needed and additional coals as necessary to maintain heat. (For a gas grill, preheat grill. Reduce heat to medium-low. Adjust for indirect cooking. Add drained wood chips according to manufacturer's directions. Place pork on grill rack over burner that is off. Grill as above.)

3 Remove pork from grill. Cover tightly with foil; let stand for 10 minutes before slicing. The temperature of the meat after standing should be 160°F.

4 Meanwhile, place mangoes in a blender or food processor. Cover and blend or process until smooth. Transfer to a small saucepan. Stir in ginger, crushed red pepper (if using), and salt. Heat through. Stir in lime peel and lime juice. Serve with sliced pork. Makes 8 to 10 servings.

1 tablespoon ground cumin

1 tablespoon packed brown sugar

2 teaspoons chili powder

2 teaspoons ground coriander

1 teaspoon ground cinnamon

1 teaspoon crushed red pepper

1 teaspoon black pepper

1 2-pound boneless pork top loin roast (single loin)

1 For spice rub, in a small screw-top jar combine cumin, brown sugar, chili powder, coriander, cinnamon, crushed red pepper, and black pepper. Cover and shake well to combine. Use 2 tablespoons rub for this recipe. Store remaining spice rub, covered, at room temperature for up to 1 month.

2 Preheat oven to 325°F. Trim fat from pork. Sprinkle 2 tablespoons spice rub on all surfaces of the pork roast; rub in with your fingers. Place roast on a rack in a shallow roasting pan and insert an oven-going meat thermometer. Roast for 1 to 1½ hours or until thermometer registers 155°F.

3 Remove roast from oven. Cover tightly with foil; let stand for 15 minutes before slicing. The temperature of the roast after standing should be 160°F. Makes 8 servings.

Spice-Rubbed Pork Loin Roast

PREP: 15 minutes   **ROAST:** 1 hour
STAND: 15 minutes **OVEN:** 325°F

NUTRITION FACTS per serving:

CALORIES 172
TOTAL FAT 6 g (2 g sat. fat)
CHOLESTEROL 62 mg
PROTEIN 25 g
CARBOHYDRATE 2 g
FIBER 1 g
SODIUM 60 mg

EXCHANGES 3.5 Very Lean Meat, 1 Fat

NUTRITION NOTE

Although cinnamon is added as a spice to enhance foods, it contains a few nutrients such as manganese, calcium, and iron.

Mustard-Maple Pork Roast

PREP: 20 minutes **ROAST:** 1¼ hours
STAND: 15 minutes **OVEN:** 325°F

NUTRITION FACTS per serving:

CALORIES 290
TOTAL FAT 9 g (3 g sat. fat)
CHOLESTEROL 62 mg
PROTEIN 27 g
CARBOHYDRATE 22 g
FIBER 3 g
SODIUM 301 mg

EXCHANGES 1 Starch, 3.5 Very Lean Meat, 1 Vegetable, 1 Fat

1 2- to 2½-pound boneless pork top loin roast (single loin)
2 tablespoons Dijon-style mustard
1 tablespoon maple-flavored syrup
2 teaspoons dried sage, crushed
1 teaspoon finely shredded orange peel
¼ teaspoon black pepper
⅛ teaspoon salt
20 to 24 tiny new potatoes, 1½ to 2 inches in diameter (about 1¾ pounds)*
1 1-pound package peeled baby carrots
1 tablespoon olive oil
¼ teaspoon salt

1 Preheat oven to 325°F. Trim fat from roast. Place roast, fat side up, on a rack in a shallow roasting pan. In a small bowl stir together mustard, syrup, sage, orange peel, pepper, and ⅛ teaspoon salt. Spoon mixture over roast, spreading evenly over the top. Insert an oven-going meat thermometer into center of roast. Roast for 30 minutes.

2 Meanwhile, peel a strip of skin from the center of each potato. In a covered 4-quart Dutch oven cook potatoes in enough boiling lightly salted water to cover for 5 minutes. Add carrots; cook for 5 minutes more. Drain. Return to Dutch oven. Add oil and ¼ teaspoon salt; toss gently to coat.

3 Place potatoes and carrots in pan around roast. Roast for 45 to 60 minutes more or until meat thermometer registers 155°F.

4 Remove roast from oven. Cover tightly with foil; let stand for 15 minutes before slicing. The temperature of the meat after standing should be 160°F. Serve roast with potatoes and carrots. Makes 8 servings.

*Note: If your potatoes are larger, use enough potatoes to make 1¾ pounds and cut any large potatoes in half.

- 1 tablespoon snipped fresh thyme or ¾ teaspoon dried thyme, crushed
- 1 tablespoon snipped fresh sage or ¾ teaspoon dried sage, crushed
- 1 tablespoon snipped fresh rosemary or ¾ teaspoon dried rosemary, crushed
- 2 cloves garlic, minced
- 1½ teaspoons coarsely ground black pepper
- 1 teaspoon coarse salt
- ½ teaspoon crushed red pepper
- 1 2- to 2½-pound boneless pork top loin roast (single loin)

1 For rub, in a small bowl combine thyme, sage, rosemary, garlic, black pepper, coarse salt, and crushed red pepper. Sprinkle rub over all sides of roast; rub in with your fingers. Place roast in a baking dish. Cover tightly and chill for 4 to 24 hours.

2 For a charcoal grill, arrange medium coals around a drip pan. Test for medium-low heat above pan. Insert an oven-going meat thermometer into center of the roast. Place roast on grill rack over drip pan. Cover and grill for 1 to 1¼ hours or until thermometer registers 150°F. (For a gas grill, preheat grill. Reduce heat to medium-low. Adjust for indirect cooking. Place roast on grill rack over burner that is off. Grill as above.)

3 Remove roast from grill. Cover tightly with foil; let stand for 15 minutes before slicing. The temperature of the meat after standing should be 160°F. Makes 6 servings.

Herb-Cured Pork

PREP: 15 minutes   **CHILL:** 4 to 24 hours
GRILL: 1 hour   **STAND:** 15 minutes

NUTRITION FACTS per serving:

CALORIES 175
TOTAL FAT 6 g (2 g sat. fat)
CHOLESTEROL 67 mg
PROTEIN 27 g
CARBOHYDRATE 1 g
FIBER 0 g
SODIUM 377 mg

EXCHANGES 4 Very Lean Meat, 0.5 Fat

Chili-Glazed Pork Roast

PREP: 20 minutes   **ROAST:** 1¼ hours
STAND: 15 minutes   **OVEN:** 325°F

NUTRITION FACTS per serving:

CALORIES 134
TOTAL FAT 4 g (2 g sat. fat)
CHOLESTEROL 50 mg
PROTEIN 20 g
CARBOHYDRATE 2 g
FIBER 0 g
SODIUM 37 mg

EXCHANGES 3 Very Lean Meat, 0.5 Fat

1   tablespoon packed brown sugar
1   tablespoon snipped fresh thyme
     or 1 teaspoon dried thyme,
     crushed
1   teaspoon chili powder
1   teaspoon snipped fresh rosemary
     or ¼ teaspoon dried rosemary,
     crushed
⅛   teaspoon cayenne pepper
1   2- to 2½-pound boneless pork top
     loin roast (single loin)
     Fresh rosemary sprigs (optional)

1 Preheat oven to 325°F. In a small bowl combine brown sugar, thyme, chili powder, snipped or dried rosemary, and cayenne pepper. Sprinkle brown sugar mixture evenly over roast; rub in with your fingers.

2 Place roast on a rack in a shallow roasting pan. Insert an oven-going meat thermometer into center of roast. Roast for 1¼ to 1½ hours or until thermometer registers 155°F.

3 Remove roast from oven. Cover tightly with foil; let stand for 15 minutes before slicing. The temperature of the meat after standing should be 160°F. If desired, garnish with rosemary sprigs. Makes 8 servings.

Make-Ahead Directions: Prepare as above through step 1. Cover and chill for up to 24 hours. Preheat oven to 325°F. Continue as above in steps 2 and 3.

COOK'S TIP
Covering the pork with foil after cooking prevents the surface of the meat from cooling too quickly, allowing the entire roast to reach the same temperature. Use this method with all meats to ensure safety and highest quality.

2	pork shoulder steaks, cut ¾ inch thick (1 to 1¼ pounds total)
¼	cup soy sauce
¼	cup dry red wine or lower-sodium beef broth
¼	cup lemon juice
2	tablespoons chopped onion
1½	teaspoons grated fresh ginger
2	cloves garlic, minced
¼	teaspoon black pepper

1 Place pork in a resealable plastic bag set in a shallow dish. For marinade, in a small bowl stir together soy sauce, wine, lemon juice, onion, ginger, garlic, and pepper. Pour marinade over pork. Seal bag; turn to coat pork. Marinate in the refrigerator for 4 to 24 hours, turning bag occasionally.

2 Drain pork, discarding marinade. For a charcoal grill, place pork on the rack of an uncovered grill directly over medium coals. Grill for 12 to 15 minutes or until no pink remains (160°F) and juices run clear, turning once halfway through grilling. (For a gas grill, preheat grill. Reduce heat to medium. Place pork on grill rack over heat. Cover and grill as above.)

3 To serve, cut pork steaks in half. Makes 4 servings.

Asian-Style Pork Steaks

PREP: 15 minutes **MARINATE:** 4 to 24 hours
GRILL: 12 minutes

NUTRITION FACTS per serving:

CALORIES 164
TOTAL FAT 6 g (2 g sat. fat)
CHOLESTEROL 73 mg
PROTEIN 23 g
CARBOHYDRATE 1 g
FIBER 0 g
SODIUM 379 mg

EXCHANGES 3 Lean Meat

3   4-ounce fresh portobello
    mushroom caps

    Nonstick cooking spray

4   small pork loin chops, cut ½ inch
    thick (about 1¼ pounds total)

2   teaspoons snipped fresh sage or
    ½ teaspoon dried sage, crushed

¼   teaspoon salt

⅛   teaspoon black pepper

1   tablespoon olive oil

2   medium cooking apples (such as
    Rome Beauty, Granny Smith, or
    Jonathan), cored, halved, and
    cut into ¼ inch-thick slices

⅓   cup reduced-sodium chicken broth

2   tablespoons maple syrup

    Fresh sage leaves (optional)

Apple-Mushroom Pork Chops

PREP: 25 minutes

COOK: 15 minutes

NUTRITION FACTS per serving:

CALORIES 281
TOTAL FAT 7 g (2 g sat. fat)
CHOLESTEROL 78 mg
PROTEIN 34 g
CARBOHYDRATE 21 g
FIBER 3 g
SODIUM 461 mg

EXCHANGES 0.5 Other Carbohydrates,
0.5 Fruit, 4 Lean Meat, 1 Vegetable

1 Remove stems and gills from mushrooms. Slice mushrooms; set aside. Coat an unheated large nonstick skillet with nonstick cooking spray. Preheat skillet over medium heat. Sprinkle pork with 1 teaspoon snipped fresh sage or ¼ teaspoon dried sage, salt, and pepper. Add pork chops to hot skillet. Cook for 6 to 8 minutes or until pork is slightly pink in the center and juices run clear, turning once halfway through cooking. Remove pork from skillet; set aside.

2 Add oil and mushroom slices to hot skillet. Cook, uncovered, for 5 minutes, stirring occasionally. Add apple slices, chicken broth, and maple syrup. Cook, uncovered, for 3 to 5 minutes or until apples are tender and juices are slightly thickened, stirring occasionally. Stir in remaining 1 teaspoon snipped fresh sage or ¼ teaspoon dried sage.

3 Return pork chops to skillet; cover and cook about 1 minute or until heated through. To serve, transfer pork chops to serving plates; spoon mushroom mixture over pork chops. If desired, garnish individual servings with fresh sage leaves. Makes 4 servings.

COOK'S TIP

Remove mushroom gills by scooping them out with a spoon. Removing the gills eliminates an unattractive dark gray color that they give off while cooking.

- 4 boneless pork top loin chops, cut ¾-inch thick (about 1 pound total)
- ½ teaspoon Cajun seasoning
- 1 medium red or orange sweet pepper, stemmed, seeded, and quartered
- 1 medium fresh poblano chile pepper, stemmed, seeded, and quartered*
- 1 medium fresh jalapeño chile pepper, stemmed, seeded, and halved*
  Nonstick cooking spray
- 1 cup reduced-sodium chicken broth
- ⅔ cup whole wheat couscous
- ½ cup sliced almonds, toasted

Chops with Nutty Triple-Pepper Couscous

PREP: 15 minutes   **GRILL:** 7 minutes
STAND: 5 minutes

NUTRITION FACTS per serving:

CALORIES 375
TOTAL FAT 10 g (1 g sat. fat)
CHOLESTEROL 62 mg
PROTEIN 35 g
CARBOHYDRATE 37 g
FIBER 7 g
SODIUM 377 mg

EXCHANGES 2.5 Starch, 4 Very Lean Meat, 0.5 Vegetable, 1 Fat

1 Trim fat from pork chops. Sprinkle all sides of the chops with Cajun seasoning. Coat peppers with nonstick cooking spray; set aside.

2 For a charcoal grill, place pork chops, sweet pepper quarters, and poblano pepper quarters on the rack of an uncovered grill directly over medium coals. Grill for 7 to 9 minutes or until chops are slightly pink in the center (160°F) and peppers are crisp-tender, turning once halfway through grilling. Add jalapeño pepper to the grill for the last 2 to 3 minutes of grilling. (For a gas grill, preheat grill. Reduce heat to medium. Place chops, sweet pepper quarters, and poblano pepper quarters on grill rack over heat. Cover and grill as above, adding jalapeño pepper to grill as above.)

3 Meanwhile, in a medium saucepan bring chicken broth to boiling; add couscous. Remove from heat. Cover and let stand for 5 minutes. Slice sweet pepper and poblano pepper quarters into bite-size strips. Finely chop jalapeño pepper halves. Stir peppers and almonds into couscous. Serve couscous mixture with pork chops. Makes 4 servings.

*Because chile peppers contain volatile oils that can burn your skin and eyes, avoid direct contact with them as much as possible. When working with chile peppers, wear plastic or rubber gloves. If your bare hands do touch the peppers, wash your hands and nails well with soap and warm water.

COOK'S TIP

Some jalapeño peppers have white lengthwise streaks or cracks at the stem ends. Some cooks look for these cracks as an indication that the pepper has fully developed flavor.

4 boneless pork top loin chops, cut
   ¾-inch thick
   (1 to 1½ pounds total)

⅓ cup low-sugar orange marmalade

1 fresh jalapeño chile pepper,
   seeded and finely chopped*

2 tablespoons tequila or lime juice

½ teaspoon grated fresh ginger or
   ¼ teaspoon ground ginger

¼ cup snipped fresh cilantro

1 Trim fat from pork. For glaze, in a small bowl stir together orange marmalade, chile pepper, tequila, and ginger.

2 For a charcoal grill, place chops on the rack of an uncovered grill directly over medium coals. Grill for 7 to 9 minutes or until no pink remains (160°F) and juices run clear, turning once halfway through grilling and spooning glaze over chops frequently during the last 2 minutes of grilling. (For a gas grill, preheat grill. Reduce heat to medium. Place chops on grill rack over heat. Cover and grill as above.)

3 To serve, sprinkle pork chops with cilantro. Makes 4 servings.

*Because chile peppers contain volatile oils that can burn your skin and eyes, avoid direct contact with them as much as possible. When working with chile peppers, wear plastic or rubber gloves. If your bare hands do touch the peppers, wash your hands and nails well with soap and warm water.

Margarita-Glazed Pork Chops

PREP: 10 minutes

GRILL: 7 minutes

NUTRITION FACTS per serving:

CALORIES 184
TOTAL FAT 3 g (1 g sat. fat)
CHOLESTEROL 62 mg
PROTEIN 26 g
CARBOHYDRATE 8 g
FIBER 0 g
SODIUM 211 mg

EXCHANGES 0.5 Other Carbohydrates,
3.5 Very Lean Meat

- 4 boneless or bone-in pork loin chops, cut ½ inch thick (1 to 1½ pounds total)
- ¼ teaspoon salt
- ¼ teaspoon freshly ground black pepper
- 1 tablespoon finely snipped fresh rosemary or 1 teaspoon dried rosemary, crushed
- 3 cloves garlic, minced

1 Preheat oven to 425°F. Sprinkle all sides of chops with salt and pepper; set aside. In a small bowl combine rosemary and garlic. Sprinkle rosemary mixture evenly over all sides of the chops; rub in with your fingers.

2 Place chops on a rack in a shallow roasting pan. Roast chops for 10 minutes. Reduce oven temperature to 350°F and continue roasting about 25 minutes or until no pink remains (160°F) and juices run clear. Makes 4 servings.

Mediterranean Pork Chops

PREP: 10 minutes   **ROAST:** 35 minutes
OVEN: 425°F/350°F

NUTRITION FACTS per serving:

CALORIES 161
TOTAL FAT 5 g (2 g sat. fat)
CHOLESTEROL 62 mg
PROTEIN 25 g
CARBOHYDRATE 1 g
FIBER 0 g
SODIUM 192 mg

EXCHANGES 3.5 Very Lean Meat, 1 Fat

Pork Chops with Apricot Quinoa

START TO FINISH: 30 minutes
OVEN: 375°F

NUTRITION FACTS per serving:

CALORIES 364
TOTAL FAT 10 g (2 g sat. fat)
CHOLESTEROL 78 mg
PROTEIN 38 g
CARBOHYDRATE 31 g
FIBER 5 g
SODIUM 452 mg

EXCHANGES 1 Starch, 0.5 Fruit, 5 Very
Lean Meat, 1 Vegetable, 1 Fat

4	boneless pork loin chops, cut ½- to ¾-inch thick (about 1¼ pounds total)
½	teaspoon five-spice powder
¼	teaspoon black pepper
2	teaspoons olive oil
1	medium fennel bulb, trimmed and chopped (about 1 cup)
½	cup quinoa
1	cup reduced-sodium chicken broth
2	cups coarsely chopped fresh spinach
½	cup finely snipped dried apricots
¼	cup chopped almonds, toasted

1 Preheat oven to 375°F. Trim fat from chops. Arrange chops in a foil-lined 15×10×1-inch baking pan. Sprinkle all sides of chops with five-spice powder and pepper. Bake about 25 minutes or until juices run clear and an instant-read thermometer inserted in centers of chops registers 160°F.

2 Meanwhile, in a medium saucepan heat oil over medium heat. Add fennel; cook about 5 minutes or just until tender, stirring occasionally. Add uncooked quinoa; cook and stir about 2 minutes or until quinoa is lightly browned. Add chicken broth. Bring to boiling; reduce heat. Cover and simmer about 15 minutes or until most of the liquid is absorbed. Stir in spinach, apricots, and almonds. Serve with chops. Makes 4 servings.

COOK'S TIP

To prepare fennel, wash it in cold water and cut off the feathery greenery. Remove the greenery to use as a garnish, if desired. Trim the fennel at the base of the bulb, removing any brown layers, then chop.

- 2 tablespoons olive oil
- 1 pound fresh mushrooms (such as stemmed shiitake, cremini, and/or button), sliced
- ½ cup finely chopped onion
- 6 cloves garlic, minced
- 1 tablespoon snipped fresh thyme or ½ teaspoon dried thyme, crushed
- ½ cup dry white wine or chicken broth
- 1 tablespoon grated Parmesan cheese
- ¼ teaspoon salt
- ¼ teaspoon black pepper
- 4 boneless pork loin chops (about 1¼ pounds total)
- 1 cup chicken broth

Pork with Mushrooms

START TO FINISH: 40 minutes

NUTRITION FACTS per serving:

CALORIES 300
TOTAL FAT 11 g (2 g sat. fat)
CHOLESTEROL 80 mg
PROTEIN 36 g
CARBOHYDRATE 9 g
FIBER 1 g
SODIUM 675 mg

EXCHANGES 5 Very Lean Meat, 1 Vegetable, 2 Fat

1 In a large skillet heat 1 tablespoon oil over medium-high heat. Add mushrooms; cook about 5 minutes or until tender and starting to brown, stirring occasionally. Add onion; cook and stir about 4 minutes or until onion is tender. Add garlic and thyme; cook and stir for 1 minute more. Carefully add wine to skillet. Bring to boiling; reduce heat. Boil gently, uncovered, for 2 to 3 minutes or until most of the liquid has evaporated. Remove from heat; transfer to a medium bowl. Stir in Parmesan cheese, ⅛ teaspoon salt, and ⅛ teaspoon pepper.

2 Season chops with remaining ⅛ teaspoon salt and remaining ⅛ teaspoon pepper. In the same skillet heat remaining 1 tablespoon oil over medium-high heat. Add chops; cook for 6 minutes, turning once to brown evenly. Add mushroom mixture and chicken broth to skillet around the chops. Bring to boiling; reduce heat. Cover and simmer for 7 to 10 minutes or until pork is done (160°F) and juices run clear. Transfer chops to a serving platter; cover and keep warm.

3 Bring mushroom mixture in skillet to boiling; reduce heat. Boil gently, uncovered, for 5 minutes. Spoon some of the mushroom mixture over chops; pass remaining mushroom mixture. Makes 4 servings.

2 medium red, green, and/or yellow
  sweet peppers, cut into strips*
1 cup thinly sliced celery
½ cup chopped onion
8 bone-in pork loin chops,
  cut ¾-inch thick (about
  3 pounds)
½ teaspoon garlic salt
¼ teaspoon black pepper
2 tablespoons canola oil
¼ cup reduced-sodium chicken broth
¼ cup orange juice
1 tablespoon chopped canned
  chipotle chile peppers in
  adobo sauce**
½ teaspoon dried oregano, crushed

Sassy Pork Chops

PREP: 25 minutes

COOK: 6 to 7 hours (low) or 3 to 3½ hours (high)

NUTRITION FACTS per serving:

CALORIES 215
TOTAL FAT 7 g (1 g sat. fat)
CHOLESTEROL 78 mg
PROTEIN 33 g
CARBOHYDRATE 4 g
FIBER 1 g
SODIUM 363 mg

EXCHANGES 4 Lean Meat, 1 Vegetable

NUTRITION NOTE

Sweet peppers, also called bell peppers, are excellent sources of vitamin C, a potent antioxidant. It's better to eat these peppers raw because cooking quickly destroys the vitamin C.

1 In a 4- to 5-quart slow cooker combine sweet peppe, celery, and onion; set aside. Season chops with garlic salt and black pepper. In a 12-inch skillet heat oil over medium heat. Add chops, half at a time; cook until brown on both sides. Add chops to slow cooker. In a small bowl combine chicken broth, orange juice, chile peppers, and oregano. Pour broth mixture over mixture in cooker.

2 Cover and cook on low-heat setting for 6 to 7 hours or on high-heat setting for 3 to 3½ hours. Using a slotted spoon, transfer chops and vegetables to a serving platter; discard cooking liquid. Makes 8 servings.

*To add more color to this dish, use three small peppers of different colors.

**Because chile peppers contain volatile oils that can burn your skin and eyes, avoid direct contact with them as much as possible. When working with chile peppers, wear plastic or rubber gloves. If your bare hands do touch the peppers, wash your hands and nails well with soap and warm water.

4	bone-in pork rib chops, cut ¾ inch thick (about 1¾ pounds total)
¼	cup lime juice
1	tablespoon chili powder
1	tablespoon olive oil
2	cloves garlic, minced
2	teaspoons ground cumin
1	teaspoon ground cinnamon
½	teaspoon bottled hot pepper sauce
¼	teaspoon salt
	Lettuce leaves (optional)
	Sliced mango (optional)
	Sliced fresh chile pepper* (optional)

1 Trim fat from chops. Place chops in a resealable plastic bag set in a shallow dish. For marinade, in a small bowl stir together lime juice, chili powder, oil, garlic, cumin, cinnamon, hot pepper sauce, and salt; pour over chops. Seal bag; turn to coat chops. Marinate in the refrigerator for 4 to 24 hours, turning bag occasionally.

2 Drain chops, discarding marinade. For a charcoal grill, place chops on the rack of an uncovered grill directly over medium coals. Grill for 11 to 14 minutes or until juices run clear (160°F), turning once. (For a gas grill, preheat grill. Reduce heat to medium. Place chops on grill rack over heat. Cover and grill as above.) If desired, garnish with lettuce leaves, mango and chile pepper. Makes 4 servings.

*Because chile peppers contain volatile oils that can burn your skin and eyes, avoid direct contact with them as much as possible. When working with chile peppers, wear plastic or rubber gloves. If your bare hands do touch the peppers, wash your hands and nails well with soap and warm water.

Spicy Grilled Pork Chops

PREP: 15 minutes **MARINATE:** 4 to 24 hours
GRILL: 11 minutes

NUTRITION FACTS per serving:

CALORIES 196
TOTAL FAT 9 g (2 g sat. fat)
CHOLESTEROL 61 mg
PROTEIN 25 g
CARBOHYDRATE 3 g
FIBER 1 g
SODIUM 159 mg

EXCHANGES 3.5 Lean Meat

3   bone-in pork rib chops, cut ¾ inch thick (about 12 ounces total)

1   tablespoon snipped fresh thyme or ½ teaspoon dried thyme or Italian seasoning, crushed

⅛   teaspoon salt

⅛   teaspoon black pepper

    Nonstick cooking spray

4   cups cauliflower florets

1   medium onion, cut into wedges

1   tablespoon olive oil

⅛   teaspoon salt

⅛   teaspoon black pepper

Thyme Pork Chops with Roasted Cauliflower

START TO FINISH: 30 minutes

NUTRITION FACTS per serving:

CALORIES 255
TOTAL FAT 11 g (3 g sat. fat)
CHOLESTEROL 62 mg
PROTEIN 28 g
CARBOHYDRATE 11 g
FIBER 4 g
SODIUM 282 mg

EXCHANGES 0.5 Starch, 3 Lean Meat, 1.5 Vegetable, 0.5 Fat

1 Trim fat from chops. In a small bowl stir together thyme, ⅛ teaspoon salt, and ⅛ teaspoon pepper; sprinkle evenly on all sides of chops; rub in with your fingers. Set chops aside.

2 Coat an unheated very large nonstick skillet with nonstick cooking spray. Preheat over medium-high heat. Add cauliflower and onion to hot skillet; sprinkle with ⅛ teaspoon salt and ⅛ teaspoon pepper. Cook and stir about 5 minutes or until almost tender. Remove skillet from heat. Push cauliflower and onion to the edge of the skillet.

3 Add oil to the skillet. Arrange the seasoned chops in a single layer in skillet. Cook over medium heat for 10 to 15 minutes or until no pink remains in chops (160°F) and vegetables are tender. Turn chops to brown evenly and stir the vegetable mixture often.

4 Transfer chops and vegetable mixture to serving plates. Makes 3 servings.

COOK'S TIP
Select cauliflower that is firm with compact florets. Raw cauliflower can be refrigerated, tightly wrapped, for 3 to 5 days.

8	ounces ground pork
½	cup thinly sliced celery
1	14½-ounce can diced tomatoes with onion and garlic, undrained
1⅓	cups cooked brown rice
1	medium fresh jalapeño chile pepper, seeded and finely chopped*
½	teaspoon Cajun seasoning
⅛	teaspoon salt
4	large green, red, and/or yellow sweet peppers

1 In a large skillet cook pork and celery over medium heat until pork is brown, stirring to break up pork as it cooks. Drain tomatoes, reserving liquid. Add half of the tomatoes, cooked brown rice, chile pepper, Cajun seasoning, and salt to pork mixture. Remove tops, membranes, and seeds from sweet peppers. Spoon pork mixture into peppers. Pour reserved tomato liquid and remaining tomatoes into the bottom of a 5- to 6-quart slow cooker. Place peppers, filled sides up, on top of tomatoes in cooker.

2 Cover and cook on low-heat setting for 6 to 7 hours or on high-heat setting for 3 to 3½ hours. Transfer peppers to a serving plate. Serve with tomatoes from slow cooker. Makes 4 servings.

*Because chile peppers contain volatile oils that can burn your skin and eyes, avoid direct contact with them as much as possible. When working with chile peppers, wear plastic or rubber gloves. If your bare hands do touch the peppers, wash your hands and nails well with soap and warm water.

Jambalaya-Style Stuffed Peppers

PREP: 25 minutes

COOK: 6 to 7 hours (low) or 3 to 3½ hours (high)

NUTRITION FACTS per serving:

CALORIES 294
TOTAL FAT 13 g (5 g sat. fat)
CHOLESTEROL 41 mg
PROTEIN 13 g
CARBOHYDRATE 32 g
FIBER 5 g
SODIUM 592 mg

EXCHANGES 1.5 Starch, 1.5 High-Fat Meat, 1.5 Vegetable

Tamale Pie

PREP: 35 minutes   **COOK:** 10 minutes
BAKE: 30 minutes   **OVEN:** 350°F

NUTRITION FACTS per serving:

CALORIES 246
TOTAL FAT 11 g (4 g sat. fat)
CHOLESTEROL 34 mg
PROTEIN 12 g
CARBOHYDRATE 26 g
FIBER 4 g
SODIUM 812 mg

EXCHANGES 1.5 Starch, 1 Medium-Fat
Meat, 1 Vegetable, 1 Fat

Nonstick cooking spray
1⅓ cups water
½ cup yellow cornmeal
½ cup cold water
½ teaspoon salt
8 ounces ground pork
½ cup chopped green and/or red
    sweet pepper
1 tablespoon chili powder
1 14½-ounce can diced tomatoes
    with onion and garlic, drained
1 11-ounce can whole kernel corn,
    drained
2 tablespoons tomato paste
½ cup shredded reduced-fat
    cheddar cheese (2 ounces)
2 tablespoons snipped fresh cilantro

1 Preheat oven to 350°F. Lightly coat a 2-quart square baking dish with nonstick cooking spray; set aside. In a small saucepan bring 1⅓ cups water to boiling. Meanwhile, in a small bowl stir together cornmeal, ½ cup cold water, and ¼ teaspoon salt. Slowly add the cornmeal mixture to boiling water, stirring constantly. Cook and stir until mixture returns to boiling; reduce heat. Cook over low heat about 10 minutes or until mixture is very thick, stirring frequently.

2 Spoon hot cornmeal mixture into the prepared baking dish. Cover and chill while preparing filling.

3 For filling, in a large skillet cook pork and sweet pepper until meat is brown. Drain off fat. Stir chili powder and remaining ¼ teaspoon salt into meat mixture in skillet; cook for 1 minute. Stir in drained tomatoes, corn, and tomato paste. Spoon the meat mixture on chilled cornmeal mixture in baking dish.

4 Bake, uncovered, about 30 minutes or until heated through. Sprinkle with cheese and cilantro. Makes 6 servings.

- 1 pound tiny new potatoes, halved
- 4 large carrots, cut into 1-inch pieces
- 1 large fennel bulb, trimmed and cut in ½-inch-thick wedges, or 1 medium onion, cut in ½-inch-thick wedges
- 1 tablespoon olive oil
- ½ teaspoon dried dill
- ½ teaspoon cracked black pepper
- 1 2- to 3-pound cooked boneless ham
- 1 8-ounce carton light dairy sour cream
- ¼ cup fat-free milk
- 2 tablespoons country Dijon-style mustard
- 1 tablespoon prepared horseradish

1 Preheat oven to 425°F. In a large bowl combine potatoes, carrot pieces, and fennel; add oil, ¼ teaspoon dill, and cracked black pepper. Arrange vegetables in a shallow roasting pan. Roast for 20 minutes.

2 Reduce oven temperature to 325°F. Push vegetables to sides of pan. Place a meat rack in center of pan; place ham on rack. Roast for 1 to 1¼ hours or until ham is hot (140°F) and vegetables are tender, stirring vegetables once.

3 Meanwhile, in a small bowl combine remaining ¼ teaspoon dill, sour cream, milk, mustard, and horseradish.

4 To serve, transfer ham and vegetables to a serving platter. Serve with sour cream mixture. Makes 8 servings.

COOK'S TIP

Most potatoes should be stored in dark, cool, well-ventilated areas for no more than two weeks. New potatoes should be used within three days of purchase.

Roasted Ham and Vegetables with Horseradish Sauce

PREP: 20 minutes   **ROAST:** 1 hour 20 minutes
OVEN: 425°F/325°F

NUTRITION FACTS per serving:

CALORIES 318
TOTAL FAT 15 g (5 g sat. fat)
CHOLESTEROL 75 mg
PROTEIN 22 g
CARBOHYDRATE 24 g
FIBER 5 g
SODIUM 1,650 mg

EXCHANGES 1.5 Starch, 2 Medium-Fat Meat, 1 Vegetable, 1 Fat

Pomegranate-Glazed Ham with Pistachio Barley

PREP: 20 minutes   **BAKE:** 1¼ hours
OVEN: 325°F

NUTRITION FACTS per serving:

- -

CALORIES 423
TOTAL FAT 15 g (4 g sat. fat)
CHOLESTEROL 65 mg
PROTEIN 26 g
CARBOHYDRATE 48 g
FIBER 9 g
SODIUM 1,680 mg

EXCHANGES 3 Starch, 2.5 Medium-Fat Meat

1½- to 2-pound cooked boneless ham
1 recipe Pomegranate Glaze
2 teaspoons canola oil or olive oil
½ cup finely chopped shallot or onion
2 cups reduced-sodium chicken broth
1¼ cups quick-cooking barley
2 teaspoons snipped fresh thyme or ½ teaspoon dried thyme, crushed
¼ cup coarsely chopped pistachio nuts
¼ cup coarsely chopped dried cranberries or cherries
Fresh thyme sprigs (optional)

1 Preheat oven to 325°F. Line a shallow baking pan with foil; set aside. Score ham in a diamond pattern by making shallow diagonal cuts at 1-inch intervals. Place ham on a rack in prepared pan. Insert an oven-going meat thermometer into center of ham. Bake, uncovered, about 1¼ hours or until thermometer registers 140°F, brushing with ¼ cup Pomegranate Glaze during the last 20 minutes of baking.

2 Meanwhile, in a medium saucepan heat oil over medium-high heat. Add shallot; cook until tender. Add chicken broth, barley, and dried thyme (if using). Bring to boiling; reduce heat. Cover and simmer for 10 to 12 minutes or until most of the liquid is absorbed and barley is tender. Stir in snipped fresh thyme (if using), pistachio nuts, and dried cranberries.

3 Slice ham and serve with barley mixture. If desired, garnish with fresh thyme sprigs. Pass the remaining Pomegranate Glaze. Makes 6 servings.

Pomegranate Glaze: In a small saucepan combine ¾ cup pomegranate juice or cranberry juice, ¼ cup balsamic vinegar, and 2 teaspoons cornstarch. Cook and stir over medium heat until thickened and bubbly. Cook and stir for 2 minutes more.

Chapter 9

Chicken & Turkey

On the divider: Apricot Chicken Kabobs *(see recipe, page 255)*

Nonstick cooking spray

1 cup finely crushed multigrain tortilla chips

½ teaspoon dried oregano, crushed

¼ teaspoon ground cumin

¼ teaspoon black pepper

1 egg

4 skinless, boneless chicken breast halves (about 1¼ pounds total)

Shredded romaine (optional)

Purchased salsa (optional)

Avocado slices (optional)

1 Preheat oven to 375°F. Coat a 15×10×1-inch baking pan with nonstick cooking spray; set aside. In a shallow dish combine tortilla chips, oregano, cumin, and pepper. Place egg in another shallow dish; beat lightly. Dip chicken in beaten egg, then coat with tortilla chip mixture.

2 Arrange chicken in prepared baking pan. Bake about 25 minutes or until chicken is no longer pink (170°F). If desired, serve chicken on a bed of shredded romaine with salsa and avocado slices. Makes 4 servings.

Tortilla-Crusted Chicken

PREP: 10 minutes   **BAKE:** 25 minutes
OVEN: 375°F

NUTRITION FACTS per serving:

CALORIES 230
TOTAL FAT 6 g (1 g sat. fat)
CHOLESTEROL 135 mg
PROTEIN 35 g
CARBOHYDRATE 7 g
FIBER 1 g
SODIUM 143 mg

EXCHANGES 0.5 Starch, 4.5 Very Lean Meat, 1 Fat

4 skinless, boneless chicken breast halves (1 to 1¼ pounds total)
¼ cup fat-free milk
⅔ cup fine dry bread crumbs
2 teaspoons adobo seasoning*
2 tablespoons canola oil
1¾ cups water
1 clove garlic, minced
4 teaspoons lemon juice
1 tablespoon snipped fresh parsley
Lemon peel strips (optional)

Adobo-Lemon Chicken

PREP: 20 minutes

COOK: 15 minutes

NUTRITION FACTS per serving:

CALORIES 266
TOTAL FAT 9 g (1 g sat. fat)
CHOLESTEROL 66 mg
PROTEIN 29 g
CARBOHYDRATE 15 g
FIBER 1 g
SODIUM 936 mg

EXCHANGES 1 Starch, 4 Very Lean Meat, 1 Fat

1 Split chicken breast halves in half horizontally. Place milk in a shallow bowl. In a shallow dish combine bread crumbs and adobo seasoning. Dip chicken pieces into milk, allowing excess to drip off. Dip chicken pieces into crumb mixture, turning to coat evenly.

2 In a 12-inch nonstick skillet heat oil over medium heat. Add chicken to skillet; cook about 5 minutes or until browned, turning occasionally.

3 Add water and garlic to skillet. Sprinkle lemon juice on chicken. Bring to boiling; reduce heat. Simmer, uncovered, about 15 minutes or until sauce is thickened, stirring occasionally.

4 Sprinkle chicken with parsley and, if desired, lemon peel. Makes 4 servings.

*Look for this seasoning blend at a market that specializes in Hispanic foods.

NUTRITION NOTE

Canola oil is called for in recipes for this book because it has less saturated fat and more omega-3 fatty acids than any other oil, and more monounsaturated fat than all other oils except olive oil. Its mild flavor is perfect for cooking and making salad dressings.

- 1 6-ounce carton plain fat-free yogurt
- ½ cup chopped red onion
- 2 tablespoons crumbled Roquefort or other blue cheese
- 1 tablespoon snipped fresh chives
- ⅛ teaspoon black pepper
- 2 medium pears, halved lengthwise, cored, and stemmed
-    Lemon juice
- 4 skinless, boneless chicken breast halves (1 to 1¼ pounds total)
- ½ teaspoon dried Italian seasoning, crushed
- ¼ teaspoon salt

1 For sauce, in a small bowl combine yogurt, red onion, Roquefort cheese, chives, and pepper. Cover and chill until ready to serve. Brush cut sides of pears with lemon juice. Set aside.

2 Sprinkle chicken with Italian seasoning and salt. For a charcoal grill, place chicken on the rack of an uncovered grill directly over medium coals. Grill for 5 minutes. Turn chicken. Place pears on grill, cut sides down. Grill chicken and pears for 7 to 10 minutes more or until chicken is no longer pink (170°F) and pears are just tender. (For a gas grill, preheat grill. Reduce heat to medium. Place chicken and later pears on grill rack over heat. Cover and grill as above.) Serve sauce with chicken and pears. Makes 4 servings.

Chicken with Roquefort

PREP: 20 minutes

GRILL: 12 minutes

NUTRITION FACTS per serving:

CALORIES 218
TOTAL FAT 3 g (1 g sat. fat)
CHOLESTEROL 70 mg
PROTEIN 30 g
CARBOHYDRATE 18 g
FIBER 3 g
SODIUM 297 mg

EXCHANGES 1 Fruit, 4 Very Lean Meat

Apple-Glazed Chicken with Spinach

START TO FINISH: 30 minutes

NUTRITION FACTS per serving:

CALORIES 306
TOTAL FAT 2 g (0 g sat. fat)
CHOLESTEROL 66 mg
PROTEIN 31 g
CARBOHYDRATE 45 g
FIBER 4 g
SODIUM 592 mg

EXCHANGES 2 Starch, 0.5 Fruit, 3 Very Lean Meat, 2 Vegetable

½ cup apple jelly
2 tablespoons reduced-sodium soy sauce
1 tablespoon snipped fresh thyme or 1 teaspoon dried thyme, crushed
1 teaspoon finely shredded lemon peel
1 teaspoon grated fresh ginger
4 skinless, boneless chicken breast halves (1 to 1¼ pounds total)
¼ teaspoon salt
¼ teaspoon black pepper
Nonstick cooking spray
2 medium apples, cored and coarsely chopped
½ cup sliced onion
2 cloves garlic, minced
12 cups packaged fresh baby spinach

1 Preheat broiler. For glaze, in a small microwave-safe bowl combine apple jelly, soy sauce, thyme, lemon peel, and ginger. Microwave, uncovered, on 100% power (high) for 1 to 1¼ minutes or just until jelly is melted, stirring once. Set aside ¼ cup glaze.

2 Season chicken with half of the salt and half of the pepper. Place chicken on the unheated rack of a broiler pan. Broil 4 to 5 inches from heat for 12 to 15 minutes or until chicken is tender and no longer pink (170°F). Turn once and brush with remaining glaze during the last 5 minutes of broiling.

3 Meanwhile, lightly coat an unheated large saucepan with nonstick cooking spray. Preheat over medium heat. Add apple, onion, and garlic; cook and stir for 3 minutes. Stir in reserved ¼ cup glaze; bring to boiling. Add spinach; toss just until wilted. Sprinkle with remaining salt and pepper.

4 Serve chicken with spinach mixture. Makes 4 servings.

1   recipe Pineapple Salsa
1¼ cups water
¾   cup whole wheat couscous
4   skinless, boneless chicken breast
    halves (1 to 1¼ pounds total)
1   teaspoon Jamaican jerk seasoning
1   tablespoon canola oil
    Lime slices (optional)

1 Prepare Pineapple Salsa; cover and set aside. In a small saucepan bring water to boiling. Stir in uncooked couscous. Remove from heat. Cover and let stand while preparing chicken.

2 Sprinkle all sides of chicken with jerk seasoning. In a large skillet heat oil over medium heat. Add chicken; cook for 8 to 12 minutes or until chicken is no longer pink (170°F), turning once halfway through cooking.

3 Fluff couscous with a fork. Serve chicken with couscous, Pineapple Salsa, and, if desired, lime slices. Makes 4 servings.

Pineapple Salsa: In a medium bowl combine 1 cup coarsely chopped, peeled, and cored pineapple; 1 red sweet pepper, seeded and chopped; and ¼ cup snipped fresh cilantro. Makes about 1¾ cups.

Jamaican Jerk Chicken with Pineapple Salsa

START TO FINISH: 30 minutes

NUTRITION FACTS per serving:

CALORIES 339
TOTAL FAT 6 g (1 g sat. fat)
CHOLESTEROL 66 mg
PROTEIN 33 g
CARBOHYDRATE 41 g
FIBER 7 g
SODIUM 139 mg

EXCHANGES 2 Starch, 0.5 Fruit, 3.5 Very Lean Meat, 0.5 Vegetable

NUTRITION NOTE

Chicken breast is the leanest part of the chicken and contributes protein, iron, and niacin to the diet. When you eat other cuts, choose skinless and white meat for less fat and fewer calories than pieces with skin and dark meat.

Herbed Balsamic Chicken

PREP: 20 minutes

COOK: 4½ hours (low) or 2 hours (high);
plus 30 minutes (high)

NUTRITION FACTS per serving:

CALORIES 234
TOTAL FAT 2 g (1 g sat. fat)
CHOLESTEROL 100 mg
PROTEIN 41 g
CARBOHYDRATE 10 g
FIBER 2 g
SODIUM 308 mg

EXCHANGES 5.5 Very Lean Meat,
1 Vegetable

1 medium onion, cut into
   thin wedges
1 tablespoon quick-cooking tapioca,
   crushed
6 bone-in chicken breast halves
   (3½ to 4 pounds total), skinned
1 teaspoon dried rosemary, crushed
1 teaspoon dried thyme, crushed
½ teaspoon salt
¼ teaspoon black pepper
¼ cup balsamic vinegar
2 tablespoons chicken broth
1 9-ounce package frozen Italian
   green beans
1 medium red sweet pepper, seeded
   and cut into bite-size strips

1 Place onion in a 3½- or 4-quart slow cooker.
Sprinkle with tapioca. Add chicken. Sprinkle
with rosemary, thyme, salt, and black pepper.
Pour balsamic vinegar and chicken broth over all.

2 Cover and cook on low-heat setting for
4½ hours or on high-heat setting for
2 hours.

3 If using low-heat setting, turn to high-heat
setting. Add green beans and sweet pepper.
Cover and cook for 30 minutes more.

4 Using a slotted spoon, transfer chicken and
vegetables to a serving platter. Spoon some
of the sauce over chicken and vegetables. Pass
remaining sauce. Makes 6 servings.

1 pound skinless, boneless chicken breasts, cut into 1-inch pieces

1½ teaspoons Jamaican jerk seasoning

1 cup fresh sugar snap peas or pea pods, strings and tips removed

1 cup fresh or canned pineapple chunks

1 medium red sweet pepper, seeded and cut into 1-inch pieces

¼ cup apricot spreadable fruit

1 Sprinkle chicken with half of the jerk seasoning; toss gently to coat. Cut any large pea pods in half crosswise.

2 On metal skewers, alternately thread chicken, sugar snap peas, pineapple, and sweet pepper, leaving a ¼-inch space between pieces.

3 For sauce, in a small saucepan combine remaining jerk seasoning and spreadable fruit. Cook and stir just until spreadable fruit is melted; set aside.

4 For a charcoal grill, place kabobs on the rack of an uncovered grill directly over medium coals. Grill for 8 to 12 minutes or until chicken is no longer pink and vegetables are crisp-tender, turning once and brushing occasionally with sauce during the last 3 minutes of grilling. (For a gas grill, preheat grill. Reduce heat to medium. Place kabobs on grill rack over heat. Cover and grill as above.) Makes 4 servings.

Apricot Chicken Kabobs

PREP: 20 minutes

GRILL: 8 minutes

NUTRITION FACTS per serving:

CALORIES 199
TOTAL FAT 2 g (0 g sat. fat)
CHOLESTEROL 66 mg
PROTEIN 27 g
CARBOHYDRATE 20 g
FIBER 2 g
SODIUM 173 mg

EXCHANGES 1 Starch, 3 Very Lean Meat, 0.5 Vegetable

Grilled Chicken with Cucumber-Yogurt Sauce

PREP: 20 minutes
GRILL: 12 minutes

NUTRITION FACTS per serving:

CALORIES 159
TOTAL FAT 2 g (1 g sat. fat)
CHOLESTEROL 68 mg
PROTEIN 29 g
CARBOHYDRATE 5 g
FIBER 0 g
SODIUM 251 mg
EXCHANGES 4 Very Lean Meat

NUTRITION NOTE

Prebiotics and probiotics promote the growth of healthy bacteria in the digestive tract. Yogurt has long been known for its probiotic health benefits, such as stimulating the immune system and helping with digestion and absorption.

1 | 6-ounce carton plain low-fat yogurt
¼ | cup thinly sliced green onions
2 | teaspoons snipped fresh mint or ½ teaspoon dried mint, crushed
½ | teaspoon ground cumin
¼ | teaspoon salt
⅛ | teaspoon black pepper
1 | cup chopped, seeded cucumber
4 | skinless, boneless chicken breast halves (1 to 1¼ pounds total)
⅛ | teaspoon black pepper
| Fresh mint leaves (optional)

1 In a medium bowl combine yogurt, green onion, snipped or dried mint, cumin, salt, and ⅛ teaspoon pepper. Transfer half of the yogurt mixture to a small bowl; set aside. For cucumber-yogurt sauce, stir cucumber into remaining yogurt mixture.

2 Sprinkle chicken breasts with ⅛ teaspoon pepper.

3 For a charcoal grill, place chicken on the rack of an uncovered grill directly over medium coals. Grill for 12 to 15 minutes or until chicken is no longer pink (170°F), turning once halfway through grilling and brushing with reserved yogurt mixture during the last half of grilling. Discard any remaining yogurt mixture. (For a gas grill, preheat grill. Reduce heat to medium. Place chicken on grill rack over heat. Cover and grill as above.)

4 Serve chicken with the cucumber-yogurt sauce. If desired, garnish with fresh mint. Makes 4 servings.

8   ounces dried whole wheat or multigrain penne pasta (about 2½ cups)

3   cups broccoli florets

1   pound skinless, boneless chicken breasts, cut into bite-size pieces

1   teaspoon adobo seasoning*

2   tablespoons olive oil

1   clove garlic, minced

¼   cup light mayonnaise or salad dressing

⅛   teaspoon black pepper

2   tablespoons shaved Parmesan cheese

1 In a Dutch oven cook pasta according to package directions, adding broccoli for the last 5 minutes of cooking. Drain well. Return to hot Dutch oven.

2 Meanwhile, in a medium bowl combine chicken pieces and adobo seasoning; toss to coat. In a large skillet heat oil over medium-high heat. Add garlic; cook and stir for 30 seconds. Add chicken; cook for 3 to 4 minutes or until chicken is no longer pink, stirring occasionally.

3 Add chicken to drained pasta and broccoli in Dutch oven. Stir in mayonnaise and pepper. Cook over low heat until heated through, stirring occasionally.

4 To serve, sprinkle with Parmesan cheese. Makes 6 servings.

*Look for this seasoning blend at markets that specialize in Hispanic foods.

Penne with Chicken and Broccoli

START TO FINISH: 30 minutes

NUTRITION FACTS per serving:

CALORIES 316
TOTAL FAT 10 g (1 g sat. fat)
CHOLESTEROL 48 mg
PROTEIN 24 g
CARBOHYDRATE 33 g
FIBER 3 g
SODIUM 383 mg

EXCHANGES 2 Starch, 2.5 Very Lean Meat, 0.5 Vegetable, 1 Fat

Nonstick cooking spray

1 large onion, chopped

2 teaspoons curry powder

1⅓ cups water

⅔ cup whole wheat couscous

2 cups chopped cooked chicken breast (about 12 ounces)

1 cup loose-pack frozen peas

1 large red sweet pepper, seeded and chopped

½ cup light mayonnaise or salad dressing

3 tablespoons bottled mango chutney

Curried Chicken Skillet

START TO FINISH: 25 minutes

NUTRITION FACTS per serving:

CALORIES 287
TOTAL FAT 9 g (2 g sat. fat)
CHOLESTEROL 47 mg
PROTEIN 20 g
CARBOHYDRATE 33 g
FIBER 5 g
SODIUM 244 mg

EXCHANGES 2 Starch, 2 Very Lean Meat, 0.5 Vegetable, 1 Fat

1 Lightly coat an unheated large skillet with nonstick cooking spray. Preheat skillet over medium heat. Add onion; cook and stir until onion is crisp-tender. Stir in curry powder; cook for 1 minute more. Add water and couscous to skillet; bring to boiling. Stir in chicken, peas, sweet pepper, mayonnaise, and chutney; return to boiling. Remove from heat. Cover and let stand for 5 minutes. Makes 6 servings.

COOK'S TIP

Curry powder is a blend of about 20 spices, herbs, and seeds. Because it loses its pungency quickly, store it in an airtight container for no longer than two months.

1 12-inch whole wheat bread shell (such as Boboli brand)

½ cup pizza sauce

1 cup coarsely chopped or shredded cooked chicken breast (about 6 ounces)

½ of a 14-ounce can artichoke hearts, drained and coarsely chopped

1 cup bottled roasted red sweet peppers, drained and cut into strips

¼ cup sliced green onion or chopped red onion

¾ cup shredded reduced-fat mozzarella cheese (3 ounces)

2 ounces semisoft goat cheese (chèvre), crumbled

1 Preheat oven to 425°F. Place bread shell on a large baking sheet.

2 Spread pizza sauce evenly on crust. Top with chicken, artichokes, roasted red peppers, and green onion. Top with mozzarella cheese and goat cheese.

3 Bake for 13 to 15 minutes or until toppings are hot and cheese is melted. Makes 4 servings.

Roasted Pepper and Artichoke Pizza

PREP: 25 minutes   **BAKE:** 13 minutes
OVEN: 425°F

NUTRITION FACTS per serving:

CALORIES 383
TOTAL FAT 12 g (6 g sat. fat)
CHOLESTEROL 52 mg
PROTEIN 28 g
CARBOHYDRATE 43 g
FIBER 8 g
SODIUM 935 mg

EXCHANGES 2.5 Starch, 2.5 Lean Meat, 1 Vegetable, 0.5 Fat

NUTRITION NOTE

Artichokes are an excellent food choice for health-conscious consumers. Low in calories and fat-free, they contribute potassium, vitamin C, folate, and fiber.

1 tablespoon canola oil

4 skinless, boneless chicken breast halves (1 to 1¼ pounds total)

3 cloves garlic, peeled and thinly sliced

1 teaspoon finely shredded lime peel

2 tablespoons lime juice

2 teaspoons snipped fresh cilantro

⅛ teaspoon crushed red pepper

1 medium orange

1 In a large skillet heat oil over medium heat. Add chicken and garlic; cook for 8 to 10 minutes or until chicken is no longer pink (170°F), turning chicken once and stirring garlic occasionally.

2 Meanwhile, in a small bowl combine lime peel, lime juice, cilantro, and crushed red pepper; set aside. Peel and coarsely chop orange. Add lime juice mixture to skillet. Place chopped orange on chicken. Cover and cook for 1 to 2 minutes more or until heated through.

3 Serve any pan juices with chicken and chopped orange. Makes 4 servings.

Keys-Style Citrus Chicken

START TO FINISH: 25 minutes

NUTRITION FACTS per serving:

CALORIES 175
TOTAL FAT 5 g (1 g sat. fat)
CHOLESTEROL 66 mg
PROTEIN 26 g
CARBOHYDRATE 5 g
FIBER 1 g
SODIUM 60 mg

EXCHANGES 3.5 Very Lean Meat, 1 Fat

COOK'S TIP

The finer that garlic is cut, the more flavor it gives. Sliced in this recipe, it has mild flavor. Minced and crushed garlic contribute strong flavor to other recipes.

¾ cup smoke-flavored
    barbecue sauce

3 tablespoons bottled light
    teriyaki sauce

1¼ pounds skinless, boneless chicken
    breasts, cut into 1¼-inch pieces

1 medium red onion, cut
    into 1-inch pieces

1 medium green sweet pepper,
    seeded and cut
    into 1-inch pieces

8 ounces whole fresh mushrooms

1 For marinade, in a large resealable plastic bag set in a shallow dish combine barbecue sauce and teriyaki sauce. Add chicken, red onion, sweet pepper, and mushrooms to marinade. Seal bag; turn to coat chicken and vegetables. Marinate in the refrigerator for 30 minutes to 24 hours.

2 Remove chicken and vegetables from marinade, reserving marinade. On eight long metal skewers, alternately thread chicken pieces, red onion pieces, sweet pepper pieces, and mushrooms, leaving a ¼-inch space between pieces.

3 For a charcoal grill, place kabobs on the rack of an uncovered grill directly over medium coals. Grill for 12 to 14 minutes or until chicken is no longer pink, turning occasionally to brown evenly. (For a gas grill, preheat grill. Reduce heat to medium. Place kabobs on grill rack over heat. Cover and grill as above.)

4 Meanwhile, in a small saucepan bring reserved marinade to boiling; reduce heat. Cover and simmer for 3 minutes. Pass with kabobs. Makes 4 servings.

Broiler Directions: Prepare as above through step 2. Preheat broiler. Place kabobs on the unheated rack of a broiler pan. Broil 4 to 5 inches from the heat for 12 to 14 minutes or until chicken is no longer pink, turning occasionally to brown evenly. Continue as directed in step 4.

Smoky Grilled Chicken Kabobs

PREP: 25 minutes

MARINATE: 30 minutes to 24 hours

GRILL: 12 minutes

NUTRITION FACTS per serving:

CALORIES 266
TOTAL FAT 2 g (0 g sat. fat)
CHOLESTEROL 82 mg
PROTEIN 36 g
CARBOHYDRATE 25 g
FIBER 3 g
SODIUM 843 mg

EXCHANGES 1 Other Carbohydrates, 4.5 Very Lean Meat, 1.5 Vegetable

Spicy Chinese Chicken with Eggplant

START TO FINISH: 35 minutes

NUTRITION FACTS per serving:

CALORIES 347
TOTAL FAT 11 g (2 g sat. fat)
CHOLESTEROL 76 mg
PROTEIN 30 g
CARBOHYDRATE 31 g
FIBER 5 g
SODIUM 730 mg

EXCHANGES 2 Starch, 3 Lean Meat,
1 Vegetable, 0.5 Fat

4   cups eggplant cut into thin
      bite-size strips*
      Boiling water
2   tablespoons soy sauce
1   tablespoon cornstarch
1   tablespoon dry sherry
12 ounces cooked chicken breast,
      cut into bite-size strips
1   tablespoon canola oil
4   to 5 red and/or green fresh
      jalapeño chile peppers, seeded
      and thinly sliced**
1   cup reduced-sodium chicken broth
1   tablespoon grated fresh ginger
1   clove garlic, minced
2   cups hot cooked brown rice

1 In a large bowl cover eggplant strips with boiling water; let stand for 5 minutes. Drain and set aside. (Eggplant may darken.)

2 Meanwhile, in a large bowl combine soy sauce, cornstarch, and sherry. Add chicken, stirring to coat; set aside.

3 In a large skillet heat oil over medium-high heat. Add chile pepper slices; cook about 4 minutes or until tender, stirring frequently. Remove chile peppers from skillet. Add chicken mixture to skillet along with chicken broth; cook and stir for 3 to 4 minutes or until chicken is heated through and sauce has thickened. Stir in eggplant, chile peppers, ginger, and garlic. Heat through. Serve with hot cooked rice. Makes 4 servings.

*Peel eggplant, if desired.

**Because chile peppers contain volatile oils that can burn your skin and eyes, avoid direct contact with them as much as possible. When working with chile peppers, wear plastic or rubber gloves. If your bare hands do touch the peppers, wash your hands and nails well with soap and warm water.

½	teaspoon ground cumin
⅛	to ¼ teaspoon crushed red pepper
⅛	teaspoon salt
8	ounces skinless, boneless chicken breasts
1	teaspoon canola oil
4	6-inch corn tortillas, warmed,* or purchased baked tostada shells
2	cups shredded romaine
3	kiwifruits, peeled and chopped, and/or 3 plum tomatoes, seeded and chopped
½	cup shredded reduced-fat Monterey Jack cheese or Monterey Jack cheese with jalapeño chile peppers (2 ounces)

1 In a small bowl combine cumin, crushed red pepper, and salt. Brush all sides of chicken with oil; sprinkle evenly with cumin mixture.

2 For a charcoal grill, place chicken on the rack of an uncovered grill directly over medium coals. Grill for 12 to 15 minutes or until no longer pink (170°F), turning once halfway through grilling. (For a gas grill, preheat grill. Reduce heat to medium. Place chicken on grill rack over heat. Cover and grill as above.)

3 Cut chicken into bite-size strips. Arrange romaine on warmed tortillas. Top with kiwifruit and/or tomato, chicken, and cheese. Makes 4 servings.

*To warm tortillas, preheat oven to 350°F. Wrap tortillas tightly in foil; bake for 5 to 8 minutes or until warm. (Or wrap tortillas in white microwave-safe paper towels; microwave on 100% power [high] for 20 to 30 seconds or until tortillas are softened.)

Kiwifruit Chicken Tostadas

PREP: 20 minutes

GRILL: 12 minutes

NUTRITION FACTS per serving:

CALORIES 208
TOTAL FAT 6 g (2 g sat. fat)
CHOLESTEROL 43 mg
PROTEIN 19 g
CARBOHYDRATE 21 g
FIBER 4 g
SODIUM 238 mg

EXCHANGES 1 Starch, 0.5 Fruit, 2.5 Very Lean Meat, 0.5 Fat

6   ounces dried whole wheat linguine or fettuccine

2   cups broccoli florets

½   cup reduced-sodium chicken broth

2   teaspoons cornstarch

¼   teaspoon lemon-pepper seasoning or black pepper

12   ounces skinless, boneless chicken breasts, cut into bite-size strips

2   teaspoons olive oil or cooking oil

1   tablespoon snipped fresh tarragon or dill or ½ teaspoon dried tarragon or dill, crushed

Tarragon Chicken Linguine

START TO FINISH: 25 minutes

NUTRITION FACTS per serving:

CALORIES 285
TOTAL FAT 4 g (1 g sat. fat)
CHOLESTEROL 49 mg
PROTEIN 28 g
CARBOHYDRATE 36 g
FIBER 1 g
SODIUM 214 mg

EXCHANGES 2 Starch, 3 Very Lean Meat, 0.5 Vegetable

1 Cook pasta according to package directions, adding broccoli for the last 4 minutes of cooking. Drain. Return to hot pan; cover and keep warm.

2 In a small bowl combine chicken broth, cornstarch, and seasoning; set aside.

3 In a large nonstick skillet cook chicken in hot oil about 4 minutes or until no longer pink, stirring often.

4 Stir cornstarch mixture; add to skillet. Cook and stir until thickened. Stir in tarragon; cook for 2 minutes more. Serve over hot cooked pasta. Makes 4 servings.

COOK'S TIP

Defrost chicken in the refrigerator, in cold water, or in the microwave. It's safest to plan ahead and thaw meat in the refrigerator. Boneless chicken breasts usually defrost overnight in the refrigerator. Never defrost meat at room temperature.

4 teaspoons canola oil

1 medium red onion, halved
   lengthwise and sliced

¼ of a medium fresh pineapple,
   peeled, cored, and cut into
   bite-size pieces

¾ cup zucchini cut into thin
   bite-size strips

¾ cup trimmed fresh pea pods

12 ounces skinless, boneless chicken
   breasts, cut into thin
   bite-size strips

3 tablespoons bottled stir-fry sauce

   Cooked brown rice (optional)

1 In a wok or very large skillet heat 2 teaspoons
oil over medium-high heat. Add red onion;
cook and stir for 2 minutes. Add pineapple
pieces, zucchini, and pea pods. Cook and stir for
2 minutes more. Remove mixture from wok.

2 Add remaining 2 teaspoons oil to hot wok.
Add chicken. Cook and stir for 2 to
3 minutes or until chicken is tender and no
longer pink. Return onion mixture to wok. Add
stir-fry sauce. Cook and stir about 1 minute
or until heated through. If desired, serve with
brown rice. Makes 4 servings.

Pineapple-Chicken Stir-Fry

START TO FINISH: 30 minutes

NUTRITION FACTS per serving:

- -

CALORIES 187
TOTAL FAT 6 g (1 g sat. fat)
CHOLESTEROL 49 mg
PROTEIN 21 g
CARBOHYDRATE 11 g
FIBER 1 g
SODIUM 450 mg

EXCHANGES 0.5 Fruit, 3 Very Lean Meat,
0.5 Vegetable, 1 Fat

Pasta and Sweet Peppers

START TO FINISH: 25 minutes

NUTRITION FACTS per serving:

CALORIES 296
TOTAL FAT 7 g (2 g sat. fat)
CHOLESTEROL 36 mg
PROTEIN 22 g
CARBOHYDRATE 37 g
FIBER 4 g
SODIUM 199 mg

EXCHANGES 2 Starch, 2 Very Lean Meat, 1 Vegetable, 1 Fat

8   ounces dried whole wheat or multigrain rotini pasta (about 3¼ cups)
1   16-ounce package frozen yellow, green, and red peppers and onions stir-fry vegetables
    Nonstick cooking spray
12 ounces skinless, boneless chicken breasts, cut into bite-size pieces
4   cloves garlic, minced
1   cup chopped plum tomato
⅓   cup purchased dried tomato pesto
¼   cup snipped fresh basil
¼   cup finely shredded Parmesan cheese (1 ounce)
    Fresh basil leaves (optional)

1 In a 4-quart Dutch oven cook pasta according to package directions, adding stir-fry vegetables for the last 2 minutes of cooking.* Drain well; return to hot Dutch oven. Cover and keep warm.

2 Meanwhile, coat an unheated large nonstick skillet with nonstick cooking spray. Preheat over medium-high heat. Add chicken and garlic to hot skillet. Cook and stir for 3 to 4 minutes or until chicken is no longer pink.

3 Add chicken mixture to cooked pasta mixture along with tomato, pesto, and snipped basil. Toss to coat. Sprinkle with Parmesan cheese. If desired, garnish with fresh basil. Makes 6 servings.

*Slowly add vegetables to pasta to prevent the water from cooling down too quickly. If water does stop boiling, return it to boiling, then begin timing for 2 minutes.

12 ounces tiny whole new potatoes, halved

1 cup baby carrots

1 medium red onion, cut into thin wedges

⅓ cup orange juice

6 cloves garlic, minced

1 tablespoon olive oil

1½ teaspoons dried thyme, crushed

¼ teaspoon salt

4 bone-in chicken breast halves (about 3 pounds total), skinned

1 Preheat oven to 375°F. Place potatoes, carrots, red onion, orange juice, garlic, oil, thyme, and salt in a large resealable plastic bag. Seal bag; turn several times to combine.

2 Using a slotted spoon, transfer vegetables to a shallow roasting pan (reserve bag and juices). Cover and bake for 10 minutes. Meanwhile, add chicken to bag with orange juice mixture. Seal bag; turn to coat chicken. Transfer chicken to roasting pan with vegetables. Bake, uncovered, for 55 to 65 minutes or until chicken is no longer pink (170°F) and vegetables are tender. Makes 4 servings.

Thyme and Garlic Chicken

PREP: 20 minutes   **BAKE:** 65 minutes
OVEN: 375°F

NUTRITION FACTS per serving:

CALORIES 378
TOTAL FAT 6 g (1 g sat. fat)
CHOLESTEROL 128 mg
PROTEIN 53 g
CARBOHYDRATE 24 g
FIBER 3 g
SODIUM 288 mg

EXCHANGES 1 Starch, 7 Very Lean Meat, 1 Vegetable, 0.5 Fat

NUTRITION NOTE

This hearty recipe features tiny new potatoes, which are packed with complex carbohydrates, vitamin C, fiber, potassium, and minerals.

Teriyaki Chicken with Orange Sauce

PREP: 15 minutes

COOK: 4 to 5 hours (low) or
2 to 2½ hours (high)

NUTRITION FACTS per serving:

CALORIES 320
TOTAL FAT 2 g (1 g sat. fat)
CHOLESTEROL 66 mg
PROTEIN 32 g
CARBOHYDRATE 40 g
FIBER 5 g
SODIUM 532 mg

EXCHANGES 2 Starch, 3.5 Very Lean Meat,
1 Vegetable

1   16-ounce package loose-pack frozen broccoli, baby carrots, and water chestnuts

2   tablespoons quick-cooking tapioca

1   pound skinless, boneless chicken breasts or thighs, cut into 1-inch pieces

¾   cup reduced-sodium chicken broth

3   tablespoons low-sugar orange marmalade

2   tablespoons bottled teriyaki sauce

1   teaspoon dry mustard

½   teaspoon ground ginger

2   cups hot cooked brown rice

1 Place frozen vegetables in a 3½- or 4-quart slow cooker. Sprinkle tapioca over vegetables. Stir to combine. Place chicken pieces on vegetable mixture.

2 For sauce, in a small bowl combine chicken broth, orange marmalade, teriyaki sauce, dry mustard, and ginger. Pour sauce over chicken pieces.

3 Cover and cook on low-heat setting for 4 to 5 hours or on high-heat setting for 2 to 2½ hours. Serve with hot cooked brown rice. Makes 4 servings.

COOK'S TIP

Meals prepared in the slow cooker during summer months will keep your kitchen cool and give you time to do other things while your meal cooks.

2 teaspoons peanut oil or canola oil
1 pound chicken breast tenderloins
¼ cup dry-roasted peanuts
1 tablespoon reduced-sodium soy sauce
1 tablespoon rice vinegar
2 teaspoons toasted sesame oil
½ cup fresh cilantro leaves
4 cups sliced napa cabbage
Lime wedges

1 In a large heavy skillet heat oil over medium-high heat. Add chicken; cook and stir for 3 minutes. Add peanuts. Cook and stir about 3 minutes more or until chicken is no longer pink.

2 Add soy sauce, rice vinegar, and toasted sesame oil. Cook and stir for 2 minutes more. Remove from heat. Stir in cilantro leaves.

3 To serve, spoon chicken mixture over cabbage. Serve with lime wedges to squeeze over individual servings. Makes 4 servings.

COOK'S TIP

Napa cabbage is sometimes called Chinese cabbage. Commonly used in raw salads and slaws, it also can be used in any recipe that calls for cabbage.

Cilantro Chicken with Nuts

START TO FINISH: 25 minutes

NUTRITION FACTS per serving:

- -

CALORIES 239
TOTAL FAT 11 g (2 g sat. fat)
CHOLESTEROL 66 mg
PROTEIN 30 g
CARBOHYDRATE 6 g
FIBER 1 g
SODIUM 303 mg

EXCHANGES 4 Very Lean Meat, 1 Vegetable, 2 Fat

1 to 1¼ pounds chicken breast tenderloins

⅛ teaspoon salt

⅛ teaspoon black pepper

Nonstick cooking spray

1 14½-ounce can no-salt-added diced tomatoes, drained

¼ cup snipped fresh basil

1 9- to 10-ounce package fresh spinach

2 tablespoons shredded Parmesan cheese

Basil-Tomato Chicken Skillet

START TO FINISH: 25 minutes

NUTRITION FACTS per serving:

CALORIES 171
TOTAL FAT 2 g (1 g sat. fat)
CHOLESTEROL 68 mg
PROTEIN 30 g
CARBOHYDRATE 7 g
FIBER 3 g
SODIUM 266 mg

EXCHANGES 4 Very Lean Meat, 1 Vegetable

1 Cut any large chicken breast tenderloins in half lengthwise. Sprinkle with salt and pepper. Coat an unheated 12-inch skillet with nonstick cooking spray. Preheat over medium-high heat. Add chicken; cook and stir about 5 minutes or until no longer pink.

2 Add tomatoes and basil to chicken in skillet; heat through. Remove from heat. Add spinach; toss until wilted. Divide among four serving plates. Sprinkle with cheese. Makes 4 servings.

NUTRITION NOTE

Vitamin K is found in large amounts in dark green leafy vegetables. Basil, although an herb, is no exception. It has a healthy dose of this vitamin that is important for blood clotting and bone mineralization.

- 1   9-ounce package frozen Italian-style green beans
- 1   cup fresh mushrooms, quartered
- 1   medium onion, cut into ¼-inch-thick slices
- 12   ounces skinless, boneless chicken thighs, cut into 1-inch pieces
- 1   14½-ounce can Italian-style stewed tomatoes, undrained
- 1   6-ounce can Italian-style tomato paste
- 1   teaspoon dried Italian seasoning, crushed
- 2   cloves garlic, minced
- 6   ounces spinach or whole wheat fettuccine, cooked according to package directions and drained
- 3   tablespoons finely shredded or grated Parmesan cheese

1 In a 3½- or 4-quart slow cooker combine green beans, mushrooms, and onion. Place chicken on vegetables.

2 In a small bowl combine undrained tomatoes, tomato paste, Italian seasoning, and garlic. Pour over chicken.

3 Cover and cook on low-heat setting for 5 to 6 hours or on high-heat setting for 2½ to 3 hours. Serve over hot cooked fettuccine. Sprinkle with Parmesan cheese. Makes 4 servings.

Italian Chicken and Pasta

PREP: 15 minutes

COOK: 5 to 6 hours (low) or 2½ to 3 hours (high)

NUTRITION FACTS per serving:

CALORIES 362
TOTAL FAT 7 g (2 g sat. fat)
CHOLESTEROL 111 mg
PROTEIN 28 g
CARBOHYDRATE 45 g
FIBER 6 g
SODIUM 801 mg

EXCHANGES 2.5 Starch, 2.5 Very Lean Meat, 1.5 Vegetable, 0.5 Fat

Zesty Ginger-Tomato Chicken

PREP: 20 minutes

COOK: 6 to 7 hours (low) or
3 to 3½ hours (high)

NUTRITION FACTS per serving:

CALORIES 281
TOTAL FAT 4 g (1 g sat. fat)
CHOLESTEROL 81 mg
PROTEIN 27 g
CARBOHYDRATE 35 g
FIBER 6 g
SODIUM 542 mg

EXCHANGES 2 Starch, 2.5 Lean Meat,
1 Vegetable

12 chicken drumsticks and/or thighs
 (2½ to 3 pounds total), skinned
2 14½-ounce cans diced tomatoes,
 undrained
2 tablespoons quick-cooking tapioca
1 tablespoon grated fresh ginger
1 tablespoon snipped fresh cilantro
 or parsley
4 cloves garlic, minced
2 teaspoons packed brown sugar
½ teaspoon salt
½ teaspoon crushed red pepper
3 cups hot cooked
 whole wheat couscous
 Snipped fresh parsley (optional)

1 Place chicken pieces in a 3½- or 4-quart
slow cooker.

2 Drain tomatoes, reserving juice from one
can; chop tomatoes. For sauce, in a medium
bowl combine chopped tomatoes and reserved
juice, tapioca, ginger, cilantro, garlic, brown
sugar, salt, and crushed red pepper. Pour sauce
over chicken.

3 Cover and cook on low-heat setting for
6 to 7 hours or on high-heat setting for 3 to
3½ hours. Skim fat from sauce. Serve chicken and
sauce with hot cooked couscous in shallow bowls.
If desired, sprinkle with parsley.
Makes 6 servings.

3 tablespoons olive oil

2½ teaspoons dried tarragon, crushed

2 cloves garlic, minced

½ teaspoon coarsely ground black pepper

¼ teaspoon salt

1 pound red and/or yellow cherry tomatoes

8 shallots

2½ to 3 pounds meaty chicken pieces (breast halves, thighs, and drumsticks), skinned

Fresh tarragon sprigs (optional)

1 Preheat oven to 375°F. In a medium bowl stir together olive oil, dried tarragon, garlic, pepper, and salt. Add cherry tomatoes and shallots; toss gently to coat. Use a slotted spoon to transfer tomatoes and shallots to another bowl, reserving the olive oil mixture.

2 Place chicken in a shallow roasting pan. Brush chicken with the reserved olive oil mixture.

3 Roast chicken for 20 minutes. Add shallots; roast for 15 minutes more. Add tomatoes; roast for 10 to 12 minutes more or until chicken is no longer pink (170°F for breasts; 180°F for thighs and drumsticks) and vegetables are tender. If desired, garnish with fresh tarragon. Makes 6 servings.

Roasted Tarragon Chicken

PREP: 15 minutes   **ROAST:** 45 minutes
OVEN: 375°F

NUTRITION FACTS per serving:

CALORIES 253
TOTAL FAT 13 g (3 g sat. fat)
CHOLESTEROL 77 mg
PROTEIN 26 g
CARBOHYDRATE 8 g
FIBER 1 g
SODIUM 173 mg
EXCHANGES 3.5 Lean Meat, 1 Vegetable, 1 Fat

NUTRITION NOTE

Cooking tomatoes pumps up their natural health benefits by increasing lycopene, a powerful antioxidant.

1   egg, lightly beaten
2   tablespoons fat-free milk
⅓   cup grated Parmesan cheese
⅓   cup fine dry bread crumbs
1   teaspoon dried oregano, crushed
½   teaspoon paprika
⅛   teaspoon black pepper
2½   pounds meaty chicken pieces
    (breast halves, thighs, and
    drumsticks), skinned
    Nonstick cooking spray
    Fresh oregano leaves (optional)

1 Preheat oven to 375°F. Grease a large shallow baking pan; set aside. In a small bowl combine egg and milk. In a shallow dish combine Parmesan cheese, bread crumbs, dried oregano, paprika, and pepper.

2 Dip chicken pieces into egg mixture; coat with crumb mixture. Arrange chicken pieces in prepared baking pan, making sure pieces do not touch. Coat tops of chicken pieces with nonstick cooking spray.

3 Bake for 45 to 55 minutes or until chicken is tender and no longer pink (170°F for breasts; 180°F for thighs and drumsticks). Do not turn chicken pieces during baking. If desired, sprinkle with fresh oregano. Makes 6 servings.

Oven-Fried Parmesan Chicken

PREP: 25 minutes   **BAKE:** 45 minutes
OVEN: 375°F

NUTRITION FACTS per serving:

CALORIES 219
TOTAL FAT 9 g (3 g sat. fat)
CHOLESTEROL 116 mg
PROTEIN 28 g
CARBOHYDRATE 5 g
FIBER 1 g
SODIUM 195 mg

EXCHANGES 4 Lean Meat

- 6 cloves garlic, minced
- 1 teaspoon smoked paprika or paprika
- 1 teaspoon black pepper
- ½ teaspoon salt
- ½ teaspoon onion powder
- ½ teaspoon dried thyme, crushed
- ¼ teaspoon dried sage, crushed
- ¼ teaspoon cayenne pepper
- 1 3½-pound whole roasting chicken
- 1 tablespoon olive oil
  Fresh thyme sprigs (optional)

1 Preheat oven to 450°F. In a small bowl combine garlic, paprika, black pepper, salt, onion powder, dried thyme, sage, and cayenne pepper.

2 Starting at the opening by the leg and thigh, carefully slide your fingertips between the breast and leg meat and the skin to loosen skin from meat. Rub half of the spice mixture between the breast and leg meat and skin. Rub remaining spice mixture on the outside of the chicken. Using 100%-cotton kitchen string, tie legs together. Twist wing tips under back.

3 Place chicken, breast side up, on a rack set in a shallow roasting pan. Brush oil on the outside of the chicken. Insert an oven-going meat thermometer into center of an inside thigh muscle. (The thermometer should not touch bone.)

4 Roast, uncovered, for 15 minutes. Reduce oven temperature to 350°F. Continue roasting about 1 hour more or until drumsticks move easily in their sockets and thermometer registers 180°F (to ensure thighs cook evenly, cut string after 40 minutes of roasting).

5 Remove chicken from oven. Cover chicken with foil and let stand for 10 minutes before carving. If desired, garnish with fresh thyme. While carving, carefully remove and discard chicken skin. Makes 6 servings.

Spice-Rubbed Roasted Chicken

PREP: 20 minutes **ROAST:** 1¼ hours
STAND: 10 minutes **OVEN:** 450°F/350°F

NUTRITION FACTS per serving:

CALORIES 299
TOTAL FAT 13 g (3 g sat. fat)
CHOLESTEROL 127 mg
PROTEIN 42 g
CARBOHYDRATE 2 g
FIBER 0 g
SODIUM 318 mg

EXCHANGES 6 Lean Meat

Turkey and Wild Rice Pilaf

PREP: 25 minutes

COOK: 50 minutes

NUTRITION FACTS per serving:

CALORIES 277
TOTAL FAT 7 g (1 g sat. fat)
CHOLESTEROL 47 mg
PROTEIN 24 g
CARBOHYDRATE 33 g
FIBER 4 g
SODIUM 218 mg

EXCHANGES 1.5 Starch, 0.5 Fruit, 2.5 Very Lean Meat, 0.5 Vegetable, 0.5 Fat

NUTRITION NOTE

About half the fat of turkey and chicken breast meat is contained in the skin. To lower fat, skin the poultry before cooking.

1 | tablespoon olive oil
1 | cup sliced celery
1 | medium onion, chopped
½ | cup wild rice, rinsed and drained
½ | cup regular brown rice
1 | 14-ounce can reduced-sodium chicken broth
¾ | cup water
1 | cup carrots cut into thin bite-size strips
2 | medium red apples, cored and coarsely chopped
12 | ounces cooked turkey breast or chicken breast,* cubed
¼ | cup chopped walnuts, toasted

1 In a large skillet heat oil over medium heat. Add celery and onion; cook about 5 minutes or until tender, stirring occasionally. Add uncooked wild rice and brown rice; cook and stir for 2 minutes. Add chicken broth and water.

2 Bring to boiling; reduce heat. Cover and simmer for 40 minutes. Stir in carrots and chopped apples. Cover and cook for 3 to 5 minutes more or until rice and vegetables are tender.

3 Stir in cubed turkey; heat through. Top individual servings with walnuts. Makes 6 servings.

*For cooked turkey breast or chicken breast, place 1 pound turkey breast tenderloins, halved horizontally, or 1 pound skinless, boneless chicken breasts in a large skillet. Add 1½ cups water. Bring to boiling; reduce heat. Cover and simmer for 12 to 14 minutes or until turkey or chicken is no longer pink (170°F). Drain well.

1 pound turkey breast tenderloins

¾ cup lightly packed fresh cilantro sprigs or fresh basil leaves

3 tablespoons walnuts

2 tablespoons olive oil

2 tablespoons lime juice

1 clove garlic, minced

⅛ teaspoon salt

¼ teaspoon salt

¼ teaspoon black pepper

Lime or lemon wedges (optional)

Turkey Tenderloins with Cilantro Pesto

PREP: 20 minutes

GRILL: 12 minutes

NUTRITION FACTS per serving:

CALORIES 228
TOTAL FAT 11 g (2 g sat. fat)
CHOLESTEROL 70 mg
PROTEIN 29 g
CARBOHYDRATE 2 g
FIBER 1 g
SODIUM 268 mg

EXCHANGES 4 Very Lean Meat, 2 Fat

1 Split each turkey breast tenderloin in half horizontally; set aside. For pesto, in a blender or food processor combine cilantro or basil, walnuts, oil, lime juice, garlic, and ⅛ teaspoon salt. Cover and blend or process until nearly smooth. Cover and store in the refrigerator until ready to use or for up to 2 days.

2 Season turkey with ¼ teaspoon salt and pepper. For a charcoal grill, place turkey on the rack of an uncovered grill directly over medium coals. Grill for 7 minutes; turn. Brush lightly with half of the pesto. Grill for 5 to 8 minutes more or until no longer pink (170°F). (For a gas grill, preheat grill. Reduce heat to medium. Place turkey on grill rack. Cover and grill as above.)

3 Slice into serving-size pieces. Serve with remaining pesto. If desired, serve with lime wedges to squeeze over turkey. Makes 4 servings.

COOK'S TIP

To keep cilantro fresh, wrap it in damp paper towels, place it in a plastic bag, and store it in the refrigerator for up to one week.

Grilled Turkey Mole

PREP: 30 minutes   **MARINATE:** 2 to 4 hours
GRILL: 8 minutes

NUTRITION FACTS per serving:

CALORIES 247
TOTAL FAT 5 g (1 g sat. fat)
CHOLESTEROL 105 mg
PROTEIN 44 g
CARBOHYDRATE 6 g
FIBER 2 g
SODIUM 223 mg

EXCHANGES 6 Very Lean Meat,
0.5 Vegetable, 0.5 Fat

COOK'S TIP

In a pinch, garlic powder can be substituted for fresh garlic cloves. Use ½ teaspoon of garlic powder to equal one clove.

2   turkey breast tenderloins
        (about 1½ pounds total)
¼   cup lime juice
1   tablespoon chili powder
2   teaspoons bottled hot
        pepper sauce
1   tablespoon canola oil
⅓   cup finely chopped onion
1   clove garlic, minced
1   large tomato, chopped
2   tablespoons canned diced green
        chile peppers
1   teaspoon unsweetened
        cocoa powder
1   teaspoon chili powder
⅛   teaspoon salt
        Fat-free dairy sour cream
        (optional)

1 Split each turkey breast tenderloin in half horizontally. Place turkey in a resealable plastic bag set in a shallow dish. For marinade, in a small bowl stir together lime juice, 1 tablespoon chili powder, and hot pepper sauce. Pour over turkey. Seal bag; turn to coat turkey. Marinate in the refrigerator for 2 to 4 hours, turning bag occasionally.

2 For mole sauce, in a small saucepan heat oil over medium heat. Add onion and garlic; cook and stir for 4 to 5 minutes or until onion is tender. Stir in tomato, chile peppers, cocoa powder, 1 teaspoon chili powder, and salt. Bring to boiling; reduce heat. Cover and simmer for 10 minutes. Remove from heat; set aside.

3 Drain turkey, discarding marinade. For a charcoal grill, place turkey on the lightly greased rack of an uncovered grill directly over medium coals. Grill for 8 to 10 minutes or until turkey is tender and no longer pink, turning once halfway through grilling. (For a gas grill, preheat grill. Reduce heat to medium. Place turkey on grill rack over heat. Cover and grill as above.) Serve turkey with mole sauce and, if desired, sour cream. Makes 4 servings.

On the divider: Almond-Herbed Salmon *(see recipe, page 281)*

- 4   5-ounce fresh or frozen skinless salmon fillets, about 1 inch thick
- Nonstick cooking spray
- 1   slice whole wheat bread, torn
- ¼   cup sliced almonds
- 2   tablespoons snipped fresh basil or 2 teaspoons dried basil, crushed
- 2   tablespoons chopped shallot
- 1   tablespoon snipped fresh parsley
- ½   teaspoon salt
- 1   clove garlic, minced
- 2   tablespoons lemon juice
- ¼   teaspoon black pepper
- Fresh basil sprigs (optional)
- Lemon wedges (optional)

1 Thaw fish, if frozen. Preheat oven to 400°F. Rinse fish; pat dry with paper towels. Set aside. Lightly coat a shallow baking pan with nonstick cooking spray; set aside. In a food processor or blender combine bread, almonds, snipped or dried basil, shallot, parsley, ¼ teaspoon salt, and garlic. Cover and process or blend until coarsely chopped.

2 Place fish in prepared baking pan; drizzle with lemon juice. Sprinkle with remaining ¼ teaspoon salt and pepper. Gently pat some of the bread crumb mixture on top of each fish fillet.

3 Bake, uncovered, for 10 to 12 minutes or until fish flakes easily when tested with a fork. If desired, garnish with fresh basil sprigs and serve with lemon wedges. Makes 4 servings.

Almond-Herbed Salmon

PREP: 20 minutes   **BAKE:** 10 minutes
OVEN: 400°F

NUTRITION FACTS per serving:

CALORIES 331
TOTAL FAT 19 g (3 g sat. fat)
CHOLESTEROL 83 mg
PROTEIN 31 g
CARBOHYDRATE 9 g
FIBER 2 g
SODIUM 416 mg

EXCHANGES 0.5 Starch, 4.5 Lean Meat, 1 Fat

NUTRITION NOTE

Salmon is loaded with omega-3 fatty acids, is low in saturated fat and cholesterol, and is a good source of protein.

Grilled Salmon with Citrus Salsa

PREP: 25 minutes   **CHILL:** 8 to 24 hours
GRILL: 14 minutes

NUTRITION FACTS per serving:

CALORIES 249
TOTAL FAT 12 g (2 g sat. fat)
CHOLESTEROL 66 mg
PROTEIN 23 g
CARBOHYDRATE 11 g
FIBER 1 g
SODIUM 457 mg

EXCHANGES 0.5 Fruit, 3.5 Lean Meat, 0.5 Fat

1   1½-pound fresh or frozen salmon fillet (with skin), about 1 inch thick
2   tablespoons sugar
1½ teaspoons finely shredded orange peel
1   teaspoon salt
¼   teaspoon freshly ground black pepper
    Nonstick cooking spray
1   recipe Citrus Salsa

1 Thaw fish, if frozen. Cut into six serving-size portions. Rinse fish; pat dry with paper towels. In a small bowl stir together sugar, orange peel, salt, and pepper. Place salmon pieces, skin sides down, in a glass baking dish. Sprinkle sugar mixture onto salmon pieces; rub in with your fingers. Cover and chill for 8 to 24 hours.

2 Coat an unheated grill rack with nonstick cooking spray. For a charcoal grill, arrange medium-hot coals around a drip pan. Test for medium heat above pan. Drain salmon, discarding liquid. Place salmon pieces, skin sides down, on grill rack over drip pan. Cover and grill for 14 to 18 minutes or until fish flakes easily when tested with a fork. (For a gas grill, preheat grill. Reduce heat to medium. Adjust for indirect cooking. Place salmon pieces, skin sides down, on grill rack over burner that is off. Grill as above.)

3 If desired, carefully slip a metal spatula between fish and skin; lift fish up and away from skin. Discard skin. Serve fish with Citrus Salsa. Makes 6 servings.

Citrus Salsa: In a small bowl combine 1 teaspoon finely shredded orange peel; 2 oranges, peeled, sectioned, and chopped; 1 cup chopped fresh pineapple or canned pineapple tidbits (juice pack), drained; 2 tablespoons snipped fresh cilantro; 1 green onion, sliced; and 1 fresh jalapeño chile pepper, seeded and finely chopped.* Cover and chill until ready to serve or for up to 24 hours.

*Because chile peppers contain volatile oils that can burn your skin and eyes, avoid direct contact with them as much as possible. When working with chile peppers, wear plastic or rubber gloves. If your bare hands do touch the peppers, wash your hands and nails well with soap and warm water.

6   4-ounce fresh or frozen skinless,
    boneless salmon fillets, about
    1 inch thick

1   tablespoon sweet paprika

1   tablespoon smoked paprika or
    ground ancho chile pepper

1   tablespoon chili powder

1   teaspoon garlic powder

1   teaspoon black pepper

½   teaspoon salt

½   teaspoon ground cumin

½   teaspoon dried oregano, crushed

    Nonstick cooking spray

1 Thaw fish, if frozen. Preheat broiler. Rinse
fish; pat dry with paper towels. Measure
thickness of fish. Set aside.

2 In a small bowl combine sweet paprika,
smoked paprika, chili powder, garlic
powder, black pepper, salt, cumin, and oregano.
Transfer spice mixture to a piece of waxed paper.
Gently roll fish fillets in spice mixture to coat.

3 Coat the bottom of a 15×10×1-inch baking
pan with nonstick cooking spray. Place fish
fillets in prepared baking pan. Turn under any
thin portions of fish to make uniform thickness.
Coat tops of fish with nonstick cooking spray.
Broil fish 4 inches from the heat for 4 to
6 minutes per ½-inch thickness of fish or until
fish flakes easily when tested with a fork, carefully
turning once halfway through broiling.
Makes 6 servings.

Broiled BBQ-Spiced Rubbed Salmon

PREP: 15 minutes

BROIL: 4 minutes per ½-inch thickness

NUTRITION FACTS per serving:

CALORIES 220
TOTAL FAT 13 g (3 g sat. fat)
CHOLESTEROL 66 mg
PROTEIN 23 g
CARBOHYDRATE 3 g
FIBER 1 g
SODIUM 276 mg

EXCHANGES 3.5 Lean Meat

NUTRITION NOTE

The American Heart Association
recommends that Americans eat at least
two servings of fish each week, particularly
fatty fish such as tuna, salmon, herring,
mackerel, and lake trout.

Salmon with Tropical Rice

PREP: 15 minutes

BAKE: 4 minutes per ½-inch thickness

OVEN: 450°F

NUTRITION FACTS per serving:

CALORIES 366
TOTAL FAT 13 g (3 g sat. fat)
CHOLESTEROL 66 mg
PROTEIN 26 g
CARBOHYDRATE 35 g
FIBER 3 g
SODIUM 155 mg

EXCHANGES 2 Starch, 0.5 Fruit, 3 Lean Meat

1 1-pound fresh or frozen skinless salmon fillet

Nonstick cooking spray

1 tablespoon coriander seeds, coarsely crushed*

1 tablespoon packed brown sugar

1 teaspoon lemon-pepper seasoning

2 cups hot cooked brown rice

1 medium mango, seeded, peeled, and chopped

1 tablespoon snipped fresh cilantro

1 teaspoon finely shredded lemon peel

Lemon wedges (optional)

Fresh cilantro sprigs (optional)

1 Thaw salmon, if frozen. Preheat oven to 450°F. Coat a shallow baking pan with nonstick cooking spray. Rinse fish; pat dry with paper towels. Measure thickness of fish. Place fish in the prepared baking pan.

2 In a small bowl stir together coriander seeds, brown sugar, and lemon-pepper seasoning. Sprinkle fish evenly with coriander seed mixture; use your fingers to press in slightly. Bake for 4 to 6 minutes per ½-inch thickness of fish or until fish flakes easily when tested with a fork.

3 Meanwhile, in a medium bowl stir together cooked rice, mango, snipped cilantro, and lemon peel. Serve fish on rice mixture. If desired, garnish with lemon wedges and cilantro sprigs. Makes 4 servings.

*You can substitute 1 tablespoon sesame seeds (toasted if desired) and ¼ teaspoon ground cumin for the crushed coriander seeds.

- 4 4- to 5-ounce fresh or frozen skinless salmon fillets, about ¾ inch thick
- ⅓ cup coarsely snipped fresh oregano
- ⅓ cup coarsely snipped fresh cilantro
- ¼ cup sliced green onion
- 1 tablespoon lemon juice
- 2 teaspoons olive oil
- 1 clove garlic
- ¼ teaspoon salt
- ⅛ teaspoon black pepper

1 Thaw fish, if frozen. Rinse fish; pat dry with paper towels. Set aside.

2 In a food processor combine oregano, cilantro, green onion, lemon juice, oil, garlic, salt, and pepper. Cover and process until finely chopped. (Or use a knife to finely chop the oregano, cilantro, green onion, and garlic. Transfer to a shallow bowl. Stir in lemon juice, oil, salt, and pepper.) Generously coat all sides of fish with the herb mixture.

3 For a charcoal grill, place fish on the rack of an uncovered grill directly over medium coals. Grill for 6 to 8 minutes or just until the salmon flakes easily when tested with a fork, turning once halfway through grilling. (For a gas grill, preheat grill. Reduce heat to medium. Place salmon on grill rack over heat. Cover and grill as above.) Makes 4 servings.

COOK'S TIP

Cook fresh fish, such as salmon, the same day of purchase if possible. If you have to wait, loosely wrap the fish in plastic wrap, store it in the coldest part of the refrigerator, and use it within two days.

Grilled Salmon with Herb Crust

PREP: 15 minutes

GRILL: 6 minutes

NUTRITION FACTS per serving:

CALORIES 236
TOTAL FAT 15 g (3 g sat. fat)
CHOLESTEROL 66 mg
PROTEIN 23 g
CARBOHYDRATE 2 g
FIBER 0 g
SODIUM 192 mg

EXCHANGES 3.5 Lean Meat, 0.5 Fat

4   6-ounce fresh or frozen skinless salmon fillets, about 1 inch thick

2   tablespoons honey

1½   teaspoons finely shredded lime peel

¾   teaspoon salt

¼   teaspoon cayenne pepper

1   large mango, seeded, peeled, and cut into thin bite-size strips

½   of a medium cucumber, seeded and cut into thin bite-size strips

2   green onions, sliced

3   tablespoons lime juice

1   tablespoon snipped fresh cilantro or 2 teaspoons snipped fresh mint

1   small fresh jalapeño chile pepper, seeded and chopped*

1   clove garlic, minced

Salmon with Mango Salsa

PREP: 25 minutes   **MARINATE:** 2 to 4 hours
GRILL: 14 minutes

NUTRITION FACTS per serving:

CALORIES 402
TOTAL FAT 19 g (4 g sat. fat)
CHOLESTEROL 100 mg
PROTEIN 35 g
CARBOHYDRATE 24 g
FIBER 2 g
SODIUM 541 mg

EXCHANGES 1.5 Starch, 4 Lean Meat, 0.5 Vegetable, 1 Fat

1 Thaw fish, if frozen. Rinse fish; pat dry. Place fish in a shallow dish. Drizzle with honey, spreading evenly. In a small bowl combine lime peel, ½ teaspoon salt, and cayenne pepper. Sprinkle evenly over fish. Cover and marinate in the refrigerator for 2 to 4 hours.

2 Meanwhile, for salsa, in a medium bowl combine mango, cucumber, green onion, lime juice, cilantro, chile pepper, garlic, and remaining ¼ teaspoon salt. Cover and chill until ready to serve.

3 For a charcoal grill, arrange medium-hot coals around a drip pan. Test for medium heat above the pan. Place fish on greased grill rack over drip pan. Cover and grill for 14 to 18 minutes or until fish begins to flake when tested with a fork, turning once halfway through grilling. (For a gas grill, preheat grill. Reduce heat to medium. Adjust for indirect cooking. Place fish on grill rack over burner that is off. Grill as above.)

4 Serve grilled salmon with salsa. Makes 4 servings.

*Because chile peppers contain volatile oils that can burn your skin and eyes, avoid direct contact with them as much as possible. When working with chile peppers, wear plastic or rubber gloves. If your bare hands do touch the peppers, wash your hands and nails well with soap and warm water.

6   4-ounce fresh or frozen skinless halibut, cod, sole, or other whitefish fillets

¼   teaspoon salt

¼   teaspoon black pepper

⅓   cup orange juice

¼   cup finely chopped red onion or shallot

2   teaspoons white balsamic vinegar or regular balsamic vinegar

1   teaspoon snipped fresh tarragon or rosemary or ½ teaspoon dried tarragon or rosemary, crushed

1   teaspoon olive oil

1   clove garlic, minced

   Dash bottled hot pepper sauce

   Nonstick cooking spray

4   medium tangerines, peeled

2   tablespoons snipped fresh parsley

6   cups torn mixed salad greens (optional)

1 Thaw fish fillets, if frozen. Rinse fish; pat dry with paper towels. Sprinkle with salt and pepper. Measure thickness of fish; set aside.

2 Preheat broiler. In a small saucepan combine orange juice, red onion, balsamic vinegar, tarragon, oil, garlic, and hot pepper sauce. Bring to boiling; reduce heat. Simmer, uncovered, for 5 to 6 minutes or until reduced to about ⅓ cup. Remove from heat. Remove 2 tablespoons of the orange juice mixture; set both mixtures aside.

3 Coat the unheated rack of a broiler pan with nonstick cooking spray. Place fish fillets on rack. Brush both sides of each fish fillet with reserved 2 tablespoons orange juice mixture. Turn under any thin portions of fish to make uniform thickness. Broil 4 inches from heat for 4 to 6 minutes per ½-inch thickness of fish or until fish flakes easily when tested with a fork.

4 Meanwhile, for tangerine relish, separate tangerines into segments. Remove seeds and cut up segments. In a small bowl combine chopped tangerines, remaining orange juice mixture, and parsley.

5 To serve, divide greens, if using, among serving plates; top greens with fish. Spoon tangerine relish over fish. Makes 6 servings.

Broiled Fillets with Tangerine Relish

PREP: 25 minutes
BROIL: 4 minutes per ½-inch thickness

NUTRITION FACTS per serving:

CALORIES 175
TOTAL FAT 4 g (1 g sat. fat)
CHOLESTEROL 36 mg
PROTEIN 24 g
CARBOHYDRATE 11 g
FIBER 1 g
SODIUM 161 mg

EXCHANGES 0.5 Fruit, 3.5 Very Lean Meat, 0.5 Fat

NUTRITION NOTE

Red onions impart good flavor and bright color while supplying vitamin C, chromium, and flavonoids—which act as antioxidants.

Broiled Halibut with Balsamic Glaze

PREP: 15 minutes

MARINATE: 30 minutes to 1½ hours

BROIL: 8 minutes

NUTRITION FACTS per serving:

CALORIES 243
TOTAL FAT 9 g (1 g sat. fat)
CHOLESTEROL 36 mg
PROTEIN 24 g
CARBOHYDRATE 14 g
FIBER 0 g
SODIUM 569 mg

EXCHANGES 1 Other Carbohydrates,
3.5 Very Lean Meat, 1.5 Fat

4	4- to 6-ounce fresh or frozen halibut fillets, about 1 inch thick
½	cup balsamic vinegar
2	tablespoons soy sauce
2	tablespoons olive oil
2	tablespoons honey
2	cloves garlic, minced
1	teaspoon snipped fresh basil or ½ teaspoon dried basil, crushed
	Fresh basil sprigs (optional)

1 Thaw halibut, if frozen. Rinse fish; pat dry with paper towels. Set aside.

2 For marinade, in a shallow dish combine balsamic vinegar, soy sauce, oil, honey, garlic, and snipped or dried basil. Add halibut to dish; turn to coat with marinade. Cover and marinate in the refrigerator for 30 minutes to 1½ hours, turning fish occasionally.

3 Preheat broiler. Drain fish, reserving marinade. Place fish on the greased unheated rack of a broiler pan. Broil 4 inches from heat for 8 to 12 minutes or until fish flakes easily when tested with a fork, turning once halfway through broiling.

4 Meanwhile, for glaze, pour reserved marinade into a small saucepan. Bring to boiling; reduce heat. Simmer, uncovered, for 5 to 10 minutes or until reduced to ⅓ cup. Serve glaze over fish fillets. If desired, garnish with fresh basil sprigs. Makes 4 servings.

4   4- to 5-ounce fresh or frozen halibut or salmon steaks, cut 1 inch thick

¼   cup lemon juice

2   tablespoons olive oil

3   cloves garlic, minced

2   medium yellow summer squash and/or zucchini, halved lengthwise

¼   teaspoon salt

⅛   teaspoon black pepper

2   tablespoons snipped fresh basil or 2 teaspoons dried basil, crushed

1   tablespoon snipped fresh mint

Fresh mint leaves (optional)

1 Thaw fish, if frozen. Rinse fish; pat dry with paper towels. In a small bowl whisk together lemon juice, oil, and garlic. Set aside 3 tablespoons of the lemon juice mixture. Brush remaining lemon juice mixture on fish and on cut sides of the squash. Sprinkle fish and squash with salt and pepper.

2 For a charcoal grill, place fish on the lightly greased rack of an uncovered grill directly over medium coals. Grill for 8 to 12 minutes or until fish flakes easily when tested with a fork, turning once halfway through grilling. Add squash to grill for the last 5 to 6 minutes of grilling; grill just until tender, turning once halfway through grilling. (For a gas grill, preheat grill. Reduce heat to medium. Place fish, and later squash, on grill rack over heat. Cover and grill as above.)

3 Meanwhile, stir basil and snipped mint into the reserved 3 tablespoons lemon juice mixture.

4 Transfer squash to a cutting board; cool slightly. Cut squash into ⅛- to ¼-inch-thick slices. Place squash on a serving platter; drizzle with some of the basil mixture. Top with fish; drizzle with remaining basil mixture. If desired, garnish with mint leaves. Makes 4 servings.

Minty Halibut with Squash

PREP: 15 minutes

GRILL: 8 minutes

NUTRITION FACTS per serving:

CALORIES 203
TOTAL FAT 9 g (1 g sat. fat)
CHOLESTEROL 36 mg
PROTEIN 24 g
CARBOHYDRATE 4 g
FIBER 1 g
SODIUM 209 mg

EXCHANGES 3 Very Lean Meat, 1 Vegetable, 1.5 Fat

COOK'S TIP

To store fresh mint, place stems down in a glass of water with a plastic bag over the leaves. Refrigerate for up to one week, changing water every two days.

Lemon-Parsley Fish

PREP: 15 minutes

MARINATE: 30 minutes to 2 hours

BROIL: 8 minutes

NUTRITION FACTS per serving:

CALORIES 190
TOTAL FAT 9 g (1 g sat. fat)
CHOLESTEROL 36 mg
PROTEIN 24 g
CARBOHYDRATE 2 g
FIBER 0 g
SODIUM 208 mg
EXCHANGES 3.5 Very Lean Meat, 1.5 Fat

NUTRITION NOTE

Parsley, a dark leafy green, is an excellent source of vitamins A and C. Choose parsley that is bright green and shows no signs of wilting.

1 pound fresh or frozen halibut, swordfish, or salmon steaks, cut 1 inch thick

1 teaspoon finely shredded lemon peel

3 tablespoons lemon juice

2 tablespoons snipped fresh flat-leaf parsley

2 tablespoons olive oil

2 cloves garlic, minced

Salt

Black pepper

Hot cooked whole wheat couscous (optional)

Lemon slices (optional)

Fresh parsley sprigs (optional)

1 Thaw fish, if frozen. Preheat broiler. Rinse fish; pat dry with paper towels. Cut fish into four serving-size pieces. Place fish in a resealable plastic bag set in a shallow bowl. For marinade, in a small bowl combine lemon peel, lemon juice, snipped parsley, oil, and garlic. Pour marinade over fish. Seal bag; turn to coat fish. Marinate in the refrigerator for 30 minutes to 2 hours, turning bag occasionally.

2 Drain fish, reserving marinade. Place fish on the greased unheated rack of a broiler pan. Sprinkle fish with salt and pepper. Broil 4 inches from heat for 5 minutes. Using a wide spatula, carefully turn fish over. Brush with reserved marinade. Discard any remaining marinade. Broil for 3 to 7 minutes more or until fish flakes easily when tested with a fork. If desired, serve with couscous and lemon slices. If desired, garnish with fresh parsley sprigs. Makes 4 servings.

- 6 4-ounce fresh or frozen swordfish or halibut steaks, cut 1 inch thick
- 1 medium red sweet pepper, seeded and cut up
- 2 canned chipotle chile peppers in adobo sauce
- 1 tablespoon adobo sauce from canned chipotle chile peppers in adobo sauce
- 2 tablespoons lime juice
- 2 cloves garlic, halved
- 1 teaspoon dried oregano
- ¼ teaspoon salt

1 Thaw fish, if frozen. Rinse fish; pat dry with paper towels. Set aside.

2 For marinade, in a blender or food processor combine sweet pepper, chile peppers, adobo sauce, lime juice, garlic, oregano, and ⅛ teaspoon salt. Cover and blend until pureed. Set aside half of the marinade to serve with fish.

3 Place fish in a shallow glass dish. Spoon remaining marinade on the fish, spreading evenly. Turn fish once to coat with marinade. Cover and marinate in the refrigerator for 30 minutes.

4 Season fish with remaining ⅛ teaspoon salt. For a charcoal grill, place fish on the greased rack of an uncovered grill directly over medium coals. Grill for 8 to 12 minutes or until fish flakes easily when tested with a fork, gently turning once halfway through grilling. (For a gas grill, preheat grill. Reduce heat to medium. Place fish on greased grill rack over heat. Cover and grill as above.) Serve fish with reserved marinade. Makes 6 servings.

Spicy Smoked Pepper Swordfish

PREP: 15 minutes **MARINATE:** 30 minutes
GRILL: 8 minutes

NUTRITION FACTS per serving:

CALORIES 148
TOTAL FAT 5 g (1 g sat. fat)
CHOLESTEROL 44 mg
PROTEIN 23 g
CARBOHYDRATE 2 g
FIBER 1 g
SODIUM 213 mg

EXCHANGES 3.5 Very Lean Meat, 0.5 Fat

Seared Tilapia with Lemon-Tarragon Sauce

START TO FINISH: 35 minutes

NUTRITION FACTS per serving:

CALORIES 294
TOTAL FAT 7 g (1 g sat. fat)
CHOLESTEROL 57 mg
PROTEIN 28 g
CARBOHYDRATE 28 g
FIBER 7 g
SODIUM 448 mg

EXCHANGES 1.5 Starch, 3 Very Lean Meat, 1 Vegetable, 1 Fat

1½ pounds fresh or frozen tilapia fillets or other lean whitefish fillets
1 teaspoon seasoned salt
1 tablespoon olive oil
¼ cup dry white wine or reduced-sodium chicken broth
1 tablespoon lemon juice
1 teaspoon Dijon-style mustard
1 teaspoon snipped fresh tarragon or ¼ teaspoon dried tarragon, crushed
1 recipe Spinach Orzo
Paprika (optional)

1 Thaw fish, if frozen. Rinse fish; pat dry with paper towels. Sprinkle all sides of the fish with seasoned salt. In a very large skillet heat oil over medium heat. Add fish in a single layer; cook for 2 minutes. Using a wide spatula, carefully turn fish over; cook about 2 minutes more or until fish flakes easily when tested with a fork. Transfer fish to a serving platter. Cover and keep warm.

2 For sauce, add wine and lemon juice to skillet. Using a whisk, scrape up any crusty bits in the skillet. Whisk in mustard and tarragon; heat through.

3 Serve fish with Spinach Orzo. If desired, sprinkle fish with paprika. Pour sauce over fish. Makes 6 servings.

Spinach Orzo: Prepare 8 ounces dried whole wheat orzo pasta according to package directions; drain. Return to hot pan; immediately toss orzo with one 5- or 6-ounce package baby spinach, 1 tablespoon olive oil, 2 teaspoons finely shredded lemon or orange peel, and ¼ teaspoon salt. Season to taste with freshly ground black pepper.

COOK'S TIP

If fish hasn't been popular with the whole family, tilapia may be the one to win them over. Its flavor is mildly sweet, and its texture is suitable for baking, broiling, steaming, and grilling.

- 4   5- to 6-ounce fresh or frozen skinless mahi mahi or grouper fillets
- ½   cup reduced-sodium soy sauce
- 2   tablespoons honey
- 2   teaspoons toasted sesame oil or olive oil
- 1   teaspoon grated fresh ginger or ¼ teaspoon ground ginger
- 1   cup chopped, peeled mango
- 1   large firm, ripe banana, chopped (1 cup), or 1 cup sliced star fruit (carambola), quartered
- ⅓   cup chopped macadamia nuts
- 2   tablespoons lime juice
- 2   tablespoons coconut, toasted

1 Thaw fish, if frozen. Rinse fish; pat dry with paper towels. Place fish in a shallow dish.

2 In a small bowl combine soy sauce, honey, oil, and ginger. Pour over fish; turn fish to coat. Cover; marinate in the refrigerator for 30 minutes, turning fish occasionally.

3 For salsa, in a medium bowl stir together mango, banana, macadamia nuts, and lime juice. Cover and chill until ready to serve.

4 Drain fish, discarding marinade. Lightly grease a grill basket or lightly coat with nonstick cooking spray. Place fish in greased grill basket, tucking under any thin edges. For a charcoal grill, place fish in grill basket on the rack of an uncovered grill directly over medium coals. Grill for 4 to 6 minutes per ½-inch thickness of fish or until fish flakes easily when tested with a fork, turning basket once halfway through grilling. (For a gas grill, preheat grill. Reduce heat to medium. Place fish in grill basket on grill rack over heat. Cover and grill as above.)

5 Serve fish with salsa. Sprinkle individual servings with coconut. Makes 4 servings.

Mahi Mahi with Tropical Fruit Salsa

PREP: 25 minutes   **MARINATE:** 30 minutes
GRILL: 4 minutes per ½-inch thickness

NUTRITION FACTS per serving:

CALORIES 345
TOTAL FAT 13 g (3 g sat. fat)
CHOLESTEROL 103 mg
PROTEIN 30 g
CARBOHYDRATE 30 g
FIBER 3 g
SODIUM 1,328 mg

EXCHANGES 1.5 Other Carbohydrates, 0.5 Fruit, 4 Very Lean Meat, 2 Fat

NUTRITION NOTE

Mahi mahi offers a low-calorie and low-fat source of protein. As with all fish, it should be cooked until opaque but still moist on the inside.

1 pound fresh or frozen skinless fish fillets (sea bass, halibut, salmon, swordfish, or tuna), about 1 inch thick

3 tablespoons maple syrup

1 tablespoon balsamic vinegar

1 to 2 teaspoons Dijon-style mustard

1 recipe Spinach Sauté

Maple-Balsamic Glazed Fish with Spinach Saute

PREP: 15 minutes

BROIL: 8 minutes

NUTRITION FACTS per serving:

CALORIES 250
TOTAL FAT 10 g (1 g sat. fat)
CHOLESTEROL 46 mg
PROTEIN 25 g
CARBOHYDRATE 17 g
FIBER 3 g
SODIUM 386 mg

EXCHANGES 0.5 Other Carbohydrates, 3 Very Lean Meat, 2 Vegetable, 1.5 Fat

1 Thaw fish, if frozen. Preheat broiler. Rinse fish; pat dry with paper towels. If necessary, cut fish into four serving-size pieces. For glaze, in a small bowl whisk together syrup, balsamic vinegar, and mustard.

2 Place fish on the greased unheated rack of a broiler pan. Broil 4 inches from the heat for 8 to 12 minutes or until fish flakes easily when tested with a fork. Carefully turn once halfway through broiling and brush with glaze during the last 2 to 3 minutes of broiling.

3 Meanwhile, prepare Spinach Saute. Serve with fish. Makes 4 servings.

Spinach Saute: In a Dutch oven heat 1 tablespoon olive oil over medium-high heat. Add 1 pound fresh spinach; cook and stir for 1 to 2 minutes or just until spinach is wilted. Remove from heat. Stir in 3 tablespoons chopped toasted walnuts; 1 tablespoon Worcestershire sauce; ¼ teaspoon salt; and ⅛ teaspoon black pepper.

- 1 pound fresh or frozen grouper fillets, ½ to ¾ inch thick
- ½ teaspoon salt
- ¼ teaspoon black pepper
- 2 tablespoons lemon juice
- 2 tablespoons olive oil
- 1 large zucchini, halved lengthwise and thinly sliced
- 1 large yellow sweet pepper, seeded and cut into bite-size strips
- 2 cloves garlic, minced
- 4 teaspoons snipped fresh marjoram or basil or 1 teaspoon dried marjoram or basil, crushed

1 Thaw fish, if frozen. Preheat oven to 450°F. Cut fish into four serving-size pieces. Rinse fish; pat dry with paper towels. Place fish in a 2-quart rectangular baking dish; sprinkle with ¼ teaspoon salt and ⅛ teaspoon black pepper. Set aside.

2 In a small bowl stir together lemon juice and 1 tablespoon oil. Drizzle over fish. Bake, uncovered, for 4 to 6 minutes per ½-inch thickness of fish or until fish flakes easily when tested with a fork.

3 Meanwhile, in a large skillet cook zucchini, sweet pepper, and garlic in remaining 1 tablespoon oil until crisp-tender. Stir in half of the marjoram, remaining ¼ teaspoon salt, and remaining ⅛ teaspoon black pepper. Sprinkle fish with remaining marjoram. Serve fish with vegetables. Makes 4 servings.

Grouper with Summer Vegetables

PREP: 20 minutes

BAKE: 4 minutes per ½-inch thickness

OVEN: 450°F

NUTRITION FACTS per serving:

CALORIES 195
TOTAL FAT 8 g (1 g sat. fat)
CHOLESTEROL 42 mg
PROTEIN 23 g
CARBOHYDRATE 7 g
FIBER 1 g
SODIUM 359 mg

EXCHANGES 3 Very Lean Meat, 1 Vegetable, 1.5 Fat

NUTRITION NOTE

Grouper is a lean fish that is low in calories and fat and delivers plenty of protein. Prepare it using cooking methods from baking and broiling to poaching or grilling.

Fish with Tomato and Cannellini Relish

START TO FINISH: 30 minutes

NUTRITION FACTS per serving:

CALORIES 255
TOTAL FAT 8 g (1 g sat. fat)
CHOLESTEROL 48 mg
PROTEIN 32 g
CARBOHYDRATE 24 g
FIBER 8 g
SODIUM 492 mg

EXCHANGES 1.5 Starch, 3.5 Very Lean Meat, 1 Vegetable, 0.5 Fat

1 pound fresh or frozen skinless fish fillets (cod, flounder, catfish, or trout)
¼ teaspoon salt
⅛ teaspoon black pepper
3 tablespoons lemon juice
4 medium plum tomatoes
Olive oil
1 19-ounce can cannellini beans (white kidney beans), rinsed and drained
1 tablespoon olive oil
1 clove garlic, minced
1 teaspoon snipped fresh rosemary or ¼ teaspoon dried rosemary, crushed
⅛ teaspoon salt
Lemon wedges
Fresh rosemary sprigs (optional)

1 Thaw fish, if frozen. Rinse fish; pat dry with paper towels. Measure thickness of fish. Sprinkle fish with ¼ teaspoon salt and pepper; drizzle with 1 tablespoon lemon juice. Set aside.

2 Heat a nonstick or well-seasoned grill pan or skillet over medium heat until hot. Meanwhile, cut tomatoes in half lengthwise. Brush tomatoes lightly with oil. Add tomato halves, cut sides down, to grill pan or skillet. Cook for 6 to 8 minutes or until tomatoes are very tender, turning once. Remove tomatoes from pan; set aside to cool slightly.

3 Place fish fillets on grill pan. Cook for 4 to 6 minutes per ½-inch thickness of fish or until fish flakes easily when tested with a fork, turning once halfway through cooking.

4 Coarsely chop grilled tomatoes. In a medium serving bowl gently toss together tomatoes, remaining 2 tablespoons lemon juice, beans, 1 tablespoon oil, garlic, snipped or dried rosemary, and ⅛ teaspoon salt. Divide bean mixture among four dinner plates. Place fish on bean mixture. Serve with lemon wedges. If desired, garnish with fresh rosemary sprigs. Makes 4 servings.

- 1¼ pounds fresh or frozen cod or haddock fillets, ¾ to 1 inch thick
- ¼ teaspoon salt
- ⅛ teaspoon black pepper
- ¼ cup snipped fresh cilantro
- 1 tablespoon olive oil or canola oil
- 1 teaspoon shredded lime peel
- 1 tablespoon lime juice

1 Thaw fish, if frozen. Rinse fish; pat dry with paper towels. Cut fish into four serving-size pieces if necessary. Sprinkle with salt and pepper.

2 Place fish in a well-greased grill basket. Tuck under any thin edges. For a charcoal grill, place fish in grill basket on the rack of an uncovered grill directly over medium coals. Grill for 4 to 6 minutes per ½-inch thickness of fish or until fish flakes easily when tested with a fork, turning basket once. (For a gas grill, preheat grill. Reduce heat to medium. Place fish in grill basket on grill rack over heat. Cover and grill as above.)

3 Meanwhile, in a small bowl stir together cilantro, oil, lime peel, and lime juice. Spoon cilantro mixture over fish. Makes 4 servings.

COOK'S TIP

Grilled fish takes on tremendous flavor, but some fish, such as cod and haddock, are too delicate to cook directly on the grill. For these fish varieties use grill baskets to turn without tearing or flaking it and to keep the fillets safely out of the fire.

Cilantro-Lime Grilled Fish

PREP: 10 minutes

GRILL: 4 minutes per ½-inch thickness

NUTRITION FACTS per serving:

CALORIES 148
TOTAL FAT 4 g (1 g sat. fat)
CHOLESTEROL 60 mg
PROTEIN 25 g
CARBOHYDRATE 1 g
FIBER 0 g
SODIUM 225 mg

EXCHANGES 3.5 Very Lean Meat, 0.5 Fat

Catfish with Black Bean and Avocado Relish

PREP: 20 minutes

GRILL: 4 minutes

NUTRITION FACTS per serving:

CALORIES 273
TOTAL FAT 15 g (3 g sat. fat)
CHOLESTEROL 53 mg
PROTEIN 23 g
CARBOHYDRATE 14 g
FIBER 6 g
SODIUM 337 mg

EXCHANGES 0.5 Starch, 3 Very Lean Meat, 0.5 Vegetable, 2.5 Fat

6	4-ounce fresh or frozen catfish fillets, about ½ inch thick
1	teaspoon finely shredded lime peel
3	tablespoons lime juice
2	tablespoons snipped fresh cilantro
2	tablespoons snipped fresh oregano
2	tablespoons finely chopped green onion
1	tablespoon olive oil
¼	teaspoon salt
¼	teaspoon cayenne pepper
1	15-ounce can black beans, rinsed and drained
1	medium avocado, halved, seeded, peeled, and diced
1	medium tomato, chopped
	Lime wedges

1 Thaw fish, if frozen. Rinse fish; pat dry with paper towels. Set aside.

2 For relish, in a small bowl combine lime peel, lime juice, cilantro, oregano, green onion, oil, salt, and cayenne pepper. In a medium bowl combine beans, avocado, and tomato; stir in half of the cilantro mixture. Cover and chill until serving time.

3 For a charcoal grill, place fish on the greased rack of an uncovered grill directly over medium coals. Grill for 4 to 6 minutes or until fish flakes easily when tested with a fork, turning and brushing once with remaining cilantro mixture halfway through grilling. Discard any remaining cilantro mixture. (For a gas grill, preheat grill. Reduce heat to medium. Place fish on greased grill rack over heat. Cover and grill as above.) Serve fish with relish and lime wedges. Makes 6 servings.

- 1 pound fresh or frozen tuna or salmon steaks, bones and skin removed
- ½ cup bottled teriyaki sauce or other Asian marinade sauce
- 2 tablespoons chopped green onion
- 1½ to 2 teaspoons wasabi powder
- 2 cups water
- 1 cup brown rice
- 1 medium red sweet pepper, seeded and cut into thin strips
- ½ cup thinly sliced carrot
- ¼ teaspoon salt
- 1 cup broccoli florets

1 Thaw fish, if frozen. Rinse fish; pat dry with paper towels. Cut fish into strips about ¼ inch thick. For marinade, in a small bowl combine teriyaki sauce, green onion, and wasabi powder. Set aside half of the marinade to stir into rice later. Place fish in a shallow glass dish. Pour remaining marinade over fish; stir to coat fish. Cover and marinate in the refrigerator for 30 minutes.

2 Meanwhile, in a medium saucepan combine water, uncooked brown rice, sweet pepper, carrot, and salt. Bring to boiling; reduce heat. Cover and simmer for 40 minutes. Stir in broccoli. Cover and cook about 5 minutes more or until rice is tender. Remove from heat. Let stand, covered, for 5 minutes.

3 Preheat broiler. On eight 8-inch skewers,* thread tuna strips accordion-style. Discard any remaining marinade. Place skewers on the unheated rack of a broiler pan. Broil 4 to 5 inches from heat for 5 to 7 minutes or until fish flakes easily when tested with a fork, turning skewers once halfway through broiling.

4 Stir the reserved marinade mixture into cooked rice mixture. Serve skewers with rice mixture. Makes 4 servings.

*If using wooden skewers, soak in enough water to cover for 30 minutes; drain before using.

Tuna Skewers with Vegetable Rice

PREP: 20 minutes   **MARINATE:** 30 minutes
COOK: 45 minutes   **BROIL:** 5 minutes

NUTRITION FACTS per serving:

CALORIES 194
TOTAL FAT 4 g (1 g sat. fat)
CHOLESTEROL 22 mg
PROTEIN 17 g
CARBOHYDRATE 23 g
FIBER 2 g
SODIUM 805 mg

EXCHANGES 1 Starch, 2 Very Lean Meat, 1 Vegetable, 0.5 Fat

NUTRITION NOTE

Whenever possible opt for brown or wild rice instead of white for a nuttier flavor and more healthful nutrients. Brown rice is a source of protein, carbohydrates, and fiber all in one.

Italian Tuna Steak

START TO FINISH: 45 minutes

NUTRITION FACTS per serving:

CALORIES 237
TOTAL FAT 6 g (1 g sat. fat)
CHOLESTEROL 51 mg
PROTEIN 29 g
CARBOHYDRATE 13 g
FIBER 3 g
SODIUM 402 mg

EXCHANGES 3.5 Very Lean Meat, 2 Vegetable, 1 Fat

4	fresh or frozen tuna steaks, cut 1 inch thick (about 1 pound total)
1	tablespoon olive oil
1	small onion, chopped
2	cloves garlic, minced
2	pounds plum tomatoes, seeded and chopped, or one 28-ounce can diced tomatoes, drained
½	cup dry white wine
¼	to ½ teaspoon crushed red pepper
¼	cup pitted ripe olives, coarsely chopped
2	tablespoons capers, rinsed and drained
2	tablespoons snipped fresh basil or 2 teaspoons dried basil, crushed
1	tablespoon snipped fresh mint or 1 teaspoon dried mint, crushed
¼	teaspoon salt
⅛	teaspoon black pepper
	Lemon wedges

1 Thaw tuna, if frozen. Rinse tuna; pat dry with paper towels. Set aside.

2 In a very large skillet heat oil over medium heat. Add onion and garlic; cook until onion is tender. Stir in chopped tomatoes, wine, and crushed red pepper. Bring to boiling; reduce heat. Simmer, uncovered, for 7 minutes. Stir in olives, capers, and basil and mint; cook for 3 minutes more.

3 Sprinkle tuna with salt and black pepper. Add tuna to skillet on top of tomato mixture. Cover and cook over medium heat for 5 minutes. Uncover and cook for 10 to 15 minutes more or until tuna flakes easily when tested with a fork and is slightly pink in the center.

4 Transfer tuna to four serving plates. Spoon tomato mixture over tuna. Serve with lemon wedges. Makes 4 servings.

- 2 5- to 6-ounce fresh or frozen tuna or halibut steaks, cut 1 inch thick
- ¼ cup lime juice
- 2 tablespoons snipped fresh cilantro or parsley
- 1 tablespoon olive oil
- 2 cloves garlic, minced
- ¼ teaspoon coarsely ground black pepper
- ⅛ teaspoon cayenne pepper
- 8 6-inch corn tortillas
  Nonstick cooking spray
- 2 medium red and/or yellow sweet peppers, quartered and stems and membranes removed
- 1 cup purchased tomato salsa or tomatillo salsa

Broiled Tuna Fajitas

PREP: 20 minutes **MARINATE:** 30 minutes
BROIL: 8 minutes

NUTRITION FACTS per serving:

CALORIES 285
TOTAL FAT 9 g (2 g sat. fat)
CHOLESTEROL 27 mg
PROTEIN 21 g
CARBOHYDRATE 33 g
FIBER 6 g
SODIUM 440 mg

EXCHANGES 2 Starch, 2 Very Lean Meat, 1 Vegetable, 1 Fat

1 Thaw fish, if frozen. Rinse fish; pat dry with paper towels. Place fish in a large resealable plastic bag set in a shallow dish.

2 For marinade, in a small bowl stir together lime juice, cilantro, oil, garlic, black pepper, and cayenne pepper. Pour marinade over fish in bag. Seal bag; turn to coat fish. Marinate in the refrigerator for 30 minutes, turning bag occasionally.

3 Wrap tortillas tightly in foil. Drain fish, reserving marinade. Lightly coat the unheated rack of a broiler pan with nonstick cooking spray. Place fish on prepared broiler pan. Place sweet pepper quarters beside fish. Place wrapped tortillas alongside the broiler pan. Broil 4 to 5 inches from heat for 8 to 12 minutes or just until fish flakes easily when tested with a fork. Brush once with reserved marinade after 3 minutes of broiling and turn once halfway through broiling. Discard any remaining marinade. Broil sweet peppers about 8 minutes or until tender, turning occasionally. Broil tortillas about 8 minutes or until heated through, turning foil package once.

4 Using a fork, break fish into large chunks. Cut sweet peppers into ½-inch-wide strips. Immediately fill warm tortillas with fish and sweet pepper strips. Serve with salsa. Makes 4 servings.

Tuna with Rosemary

START TO FINISH: 20 minutes

NUTRITION FACTS per serving:

CALORIES 145
TOTAL FAT 3 g (1 g sat. fat)
CHOLESTEROL 51 mg
PROTEIN 27 g
CARBOHYDRATE 1 g
FIBER 0 g
SODIUM 166 mg

EXCHANGES 4 Very Lean Meat

4	4-ounce fresh or frozen tuna or salmon steaks, cut ½ to 1 inch thick
2	teaspoons olive oil
2	teaspoons lemon juice
⅛	teaspoon salt
⅛	teaspoon black pepper
2	teaspoons snipped fresh rosemary or tarragon or 1 teaspoon dried rosemary or tarragon, crushed
2	cloves garlic, minced
1	tablespoon capers, rinsed and drained

1 Thaw fish, if frozen. Preheat broiler. Rinse fish; pat dry with paper towels. Measure thickness of fish. Brush fish with oil and lemon juice; sprinkle with salt and pepper. Sprinkle rosemary and garlic on fish; rub in with your fingers.

2 Place fish on the greased rack of an unheated broiler pan. Broil 4 inches from heat for 4 to 6 minutes per ½-inch thickness of fish or until fish flakes easily when tested with a fork, turning once if fish is 1 inch thick or more. To serve, top fish with capers. Makes 4 servings.

- 12 fresh or frozen sea scallops (1¼ to 1½ pounds total)
- ½ teaspoon ancho chili powder or regular chili powder
- ⅛ teaspoon salt
  Nonstick cooking spray
- 1 tablespoon lime juice
- 1 recipe Gingered Tropical Fruit Salsa

1 Thaw scallops, if frozen. Rinse scallops; pat dry with paper towels. In a small bowl combine chili powder and salt. Sprinkle chili powder mixture evenly over scallops; rub in with your fingers.

2 Lightly coat an unheated large nonstick skillet with nonstick cooking spray. Preheat over medium-high heat. Add scallops to hot skillet; cook for 4 to 6 minutes or until opaque, turning once. Transfer scallops to a serving plate. Drizzle with lime juice; cover to keep warm.

3 Add Gingered Tropical Fruit Salsa to skillet; cook and stir about 1 minute or until heated through, scraping up the browned bits from bottom of skillet. Serve warmed salsa with the scallops. Makes 4 servings.

Gingered Tropical Fruit Salsa: In a medium bowl combine 1 tablespoon snipped fresh mint, 2 teaspoons seasoned rice vinegar, 2 teaspoons lime juice, ½ to 1 teaspoon grated fresh ginger, and, if desired, ⅛ teaspoon crushed red pepper. Add ½ cup chopped fresh pineapple, ½ cup chopped mango or peach, ½ cup chopped peeled kiwifruit, and one 5-ounce container mandarin orange sections, drained (½ cup); toss gently to coat. Serve immediately or cover and chill for up to 24 hours. Makes 2 cups.

COOK'S TIP
Choose fresh scallops that smell sweet and have a moist sheen. Refrigerate scallops immediately and use them within two days.

Ancho and Lime Seared Scallops

START TO FINISH: 25 minutes

NUTRITION FACTS per serving:

CALORIES 188
TOTAL FAT 1 g (0 g sat. fat)
CHOLESTEROL 47 mg
PROTEIN 25 g
CARBOHYDRATE 19 g
FIBER 2 g
SODIUM 333 mg

EXCHANGES 1 Fruit, 3.5 Very Lean Meat

Scallops with Anise-Orange Tapenade

START TO FINISH: 20 minutes

NUTRITION FACTS per serving:

CALORIES 145
TOTAL FAT 3 g (0 g sat. fat)
CHOLESTEROL 47 mg
PROTEIN 24 g
CARBOHYDRATE 5 g
FIBER 1 g
SODIUM 353 mg

EXCHANGES 3.5 Very Lean Meat, 0.5 Fat

12   fresh or frozen sea scallops
      (about 1¼ pounds total)
⅓   cup pitted kalamata olives,
      coarsely chopped
1   green onion, sliced
½   teaspoon finely shredded
      orange peel
2   teaspoons orange juice
¼   teaspoon anise seeds, crushed
⅛   teaspoon cayenne pepper
      Nonstick cooking spray
      Finely shredded orange peel
      (optional)

1 Thaw scallops, if frozen. Rinse scallops; pat dry with paper towels. Set aside.

2 For tapenade, in a small bowl combine olives, green onion, ½ teaspoon orange peel, orange juice, anise seeds, and cayenne pepper.

3 Coat an unheated large nonstick skillet with nonstick cooking spray. Preheat over medium-high heat. Add scallops to skillet; cook for 3 to 6 minutes or until scallops are opaque, turning once.

4 Serve scallops with tapenade. If desired, sprinkle with additional orange peel. Makes 4 servings.

12	fresh or frozen sea scallops (about 1¼ pound total)
8	fresh or frozen jumbo shrimp (about 8 ounces total)
4	teaspoons olive oil
2	cups thin bite-size strips zucchini or sweet peppers
1½	cups thin bite-size strips carrot
1	cup sliced leek
¼	cup Dijon-style mustard
2	tablespoons dry white wine or water
2	teaspoons snipped fresh thyme or ½ teaspoon dried thyme, crushed
⅛	teaspoon black pepper
	Lemon wedges

1 Thaw scallops and shrimp, if frozen. Peel and devein shrimp. Rinse scallops and shrimp; pat dry with paper towels. In a very large nonstick skillet heat 2 teaspoons oil over medium-high heat. Add scallops and shrimp; cook for 2 to 4 minutes or until shrimp and scallops are opaque. Remove from skillet and set aside.

2 Add remaining 2 teaspoons oil to skillet; add zucchini, carrot, and leek to skillet. Cook and stir for 3 to 5 minutes or until vegetables are crisp-tender. Reduce heat to medium-low. Add mustard, wine, thyme, and black pepper. Stir to coat vegetables.

3 Spoon vegetable mixture onto a serving platter. Top with shrimp and scallops. Serve with lemon wedges. Makes 4 servings.

COOK'S TIP

To store fresh uncooked shrimp, rinse and drain them thoroughly, then tightly cover and refrigerate for no more than two days.

Sauteed Shrimp and Scallops

START TO FINISH: 30 minutes

NUTRITION FACTS per serving:

CALORIES 265
TOTAL FAT 7 g (1 g sat. fat)
CHOLESTEROL 124 mg
PROTEIN 32 g
CARBOHYDRATE 14 g
FIBER 3 g
SODIUM 669 mg

EXCHANGES 0.5 Starch, 4 Very Lean Meat, 1 Vegetable, 0.5 Fat

Spicy Shrimp Tabbouleh

PREP: 25 minutes

COOK: 15 minutes

NUTRITION FACTS per serving:

CALORIES 201
TOTAL FAT 1 g (0 g sat. fat)
CHOLESTEROL 111 mg
PROTEIN 16 g
CARBOHYDRATE 32 g
FIBER 6 g
SODIUM 495 mg

EXCHANGES 2 Starch, 1.5 Very Lean Meat, 0.5 Vegetable

8	ounces fresh or frozen peeled and deveined cooked shrimp with tails, halved lengthwise
1⅓	cups water
⅔	cup bulgur
1	cup fresh pea pods, halved crosswise
½	cup chopped radishes or daikon
½	cup snipped fresh cilantro
¼	cup bias-sliced green onion
½	cup bottled fat-free ranch salad dressing
½	teaspoon finely shredded lime peel
2	tablespoons lime juice
¼	teaspoon crushed red pepper
	Lettuce leaves (optional)

1 Thaw shrimp, if frozen; set aside. In a medium saucepan combine water and bulgur. Bring to boiling; reduce heat. Cover and simmer about 15 minutes or until most of the water is absorbed and bulgur is tender. Stir in pea pods. Transfer to a large bowl. Stir in radishes or daikon, cilantro, and green onion.

2 In a small bowl combine salad dressing, lime peel, lime juice, and crushed red pepper; stir into bulgur mixture. Stir in shrimp. Serve immediately or cover and chill for up to 8 hours.

3 To serve, if desired, line serving bowl with lettuce leaves; spoon in tabbouleh. Makes 4 servings.

COOK'S TIP

Reduce the pungency of radishes by salting and washing them to remove some of the peppery flavor. To increase crispness of radishes, soak them in ice water for several hours before serving.

1	8-ounce carton fat-free or light dairy sour cream
½	cup snipped fresh basil
3	tablespoons snipped fresh chives
½	teaspoon salt
⅛	teaspoon black pepper
1¼	pounds fresh or frozen large shrimp
2	medium zucchini, halved lengthwise and cut into 1-inch-thick slices (about 1 pound total)
2	tablespoons olive oil
½	teaspoon finely shredded orange peel or lime peel
1	tablespoon orange juice or lime juice
¼	teaspoon cayenne pepper
5	cups torn fresh spinach, arugula, and/or romaine

1 For sauce, in a food processor or blender combine sour cream, basil, chives, ¼ teaspoon salt, and black pepper. Cover and process or blend until nearly smooth. Cover and chill until ready to serve.

2 Thaw shrimp, if frozen. Peel and devein shrimp, leaving tails intact if desired. Rinse shrimp; pat dry with paper towels. On long skewers,* alternately thread shrimp and zucchini, leaving a ¼-inch space between pieces. In a small bowl combine oil, orange or lime peel, orange or lime juice, cayenne pepper, and remaining ¼ teaspoon salt; brush evenly on shrimp and zucchini. Discard any remaining oil-juice mixture.

3 For a charcoal grill, place kabobs on the greased rack of an uncovered grill directly over medium coals. Grill about 10 minutes or until shrimp are opaque, turning once halfway through grilling. (For a gas grill, preheat grill. Reduce heat to medium. Place kabobs on greased grill rack over heat. Cover and grill as above.)

4 Serve kabobs with greens and sauce. Makes 6 servings.

*If using wooden skewers, soak in enough water to cover for 30 minutes; drain before using.

Shrimp-Zucchini Kabobs with Basil Cream Sauce

PREP: 40 minutes

GRILL: 10 minutes

NUTRITION FACTS per serving:

CALORIES 171
TOTAL FAT 6 g (1 g sat. fat)
CHOLESTEROL 108 mg
PROTEIN 19 g
CARBOHYDRATE 10 g
FIBER 2 g
SODIUM 447 mg

EXCHANGES 2 Very Lean Meat, 2 Vegetable, 1 Fat

Mexican-Style Shrimp Pizza

PREP: 25 minutes   **BAKE:** 16 minutes
OVEN: 400°F

NUTRITION FACTS per serving:

CALORIES 288
TOTAL FAT 11 g (4 g sat. fat)
CHOLESTEROL 125 mg
PROTEIN 26 g
CARBOHYDRATE 22 g
FIBER 12 g
SODIUM 673 mg

EXCHANGES 1 Starch, 3 Lean Meat, 1 Vegetable, 0.5 Fat

4   8-inch whole wheat flour tortillas
2   teaspoons olive oil
     Nonstick cooking spray
2   large red and/or yellow sweet peppers, seeded and cut into bite-size strips
⅔   cup thinly sliced green onion
1   medium fresh jalapeño chile pepper, seeded and thinly sliced* (optional)
2   tablespoons water
¼   to ⅓ cup purchased green salsa
8   ounces peeled and deveined cooked medium shrimp
⅔   cup shredded reduced-fat or regular Monterey Jack cheese
2   tablespoons snipped fresh cilantro

1 Preheat oven to 400°F. Brush both sides of each tortilla with oil; place tortillas in a single layer on two ungreased baking sheets. Place sheets on separate oven racks; bake about 10 minutes or until crisp, turning tortillas and rotating baking sheets halfway through baking.

2 Meanwhile, coat an unheated large nonstick skillet with nonstick cooking spray. Preheat skillet over medium heat. Add sweet pepper, green onion, and, if desired, chile pepper. Cook about 5 minutes or until nearly crisp-tender, stirring occasionally. Add water; cover and cook for 2 minutes more.

3 Spread each tortilla with about 1 tablespoon of the green salsa. Top with cooked vegetable mixture and shrimp. Sprinkle with cheese. Bake, one baking sheet at a time, about 3 minutes or until cheese is melted and shrimp is heated through. Sprinkle with cilantro. Makes 4 servings.

*Because chile peppers contain volatile oils that can burn your skin and eyes, avoid direct contact with them as much as possible. When working with chile peppers, wear plastic or rubber gloves. If your bare hands do touch the peppers, wash your hands and nails well with soap and warm water.

1½ pounds fresh or frozen large shrimp

1½ cups water

1 cup whole wheat couscous

2 teaspoons olive oil

1 cup chopped onion

1 medium red sweet pepper, seeded and cut into bite-size strips

1 tablespoon grated fresh ginger

½ teaspoon curry powder

½ teaspoon ground cumin

¼ teaspoon cayenne pepper

6 ounces fresh pea pods, trimmed and halved lengthwise

¼ cup orange juice

3 tablespoons unsweetened light coconut milk

¼ teaspoon salt

½ cup snipped fresh cilantro

Curried Shrimp with Couscous

PREP: 40 minutes
STAND: 5 minutes

NUTRITION FACTS per serving:

CALORIES 315
TOTAL FAT 5 g (1 g sat. fat)
CHOLESTEROL 172 mg
PROTEIN 30 g
CARBOHYDRATE 39 g
FIBER 7 g
SODIUM 273 mg

EXCHANGES 2 Starch, 3 Very Lean Meat, 1 Vegetable, 0.5 Fat

1 Thaw shrimp, if frozen. Peel and devein shrimp. Rinse shrimp; pat dry with paper towels. Set aside. To prepare couscous, in a medium saucepan bring water to boiling; add couscous. Remove from heat and let stand for 5 minutes.

2 Meanwhile, in a very large nonstick skillet heat oil over medium heat. Add onion and sweet pepper; cook and stir about 5 minutes or just until tender. Add ginger, curry powder, cumin, and cayenne pepper; cook and stir for 1 minute. Add shrimp and pea pods, stirring to coat with spices. Cook and stir about 3 minutes or until shrimp are opaque. Stir in orange juice, coconut milk, and salt; heat through.

3 Serve shrimp mixture with couscous. Top individual servings with cilantro. Makes 6 servings.

Cajun Shrimp with Mango-Edamame Salsa

START TO FINISH: 30 minutes

NUTRITION FACTS per serving:

CALORIES 317
TOTAL FAT 12 g (2 g sat. fat)
CHOLESTEROL 129 mg
PROTEIN 27 g
CARBOHYDRATE 29 g
FIBER 6 g
SODIUM 287 mg

EXCHANGES 1 Starch, 0.5 Fruit, 3.5 Very
Lean Meat, 0.5 Vegetable, 1.5 Fat

1   pound fresh or frozen large shrimp
2   teaspoons purchased salt-free
    Cajun seasoning or Homemade
    Cajun Seasoning
1   tablespoon canola oil
1   recipe Mango-Edamame Salsa
    Belgian endive leaves (optional)

1 Thaw shrimp, if frozen. Peel and devein shrimp, leaving tails intact if desired. Rinse shrimp; pat dry with paper towels. Set aside.

2 In a large bowl toss shrimp with Cajun seasoning. In a heavy large skillet heat oil over medium-high heat. Add shrimp; cook and stir about 5 minutes or until shrimp are opaque.

3 Serve shrimp with Mango-Edamame Salsa and, if desired, Belgian endive leaves. Makes 4 servings.

Homemade Cajun Seasoning: In a small bowl stir together ½ teaspoon onion powder, ½ teaspoon paprika, ¼ teaspoon white pepper, ¼ teaspoon garlic powder, ¼ teaspoon cayenne pepper, and ¼ teaspoon black pepper.

Mango-Edamame Salsa: In a medium bowl combine 2 seeded, peeled, and chopped mangoes; 1 cup fresh or frozen shelled sweet soybeans (edamame), cooked and cooled; 1 red sweet pepper, seeded and chopped; ½ cup finely chopped green onion; ¼ cup snipped fresh cilantro; 2 tablespoons lime juice; 2 teaspoons canola oil; and ¼ teaspoon salt. Toss gently to mix. Cover and chill until serving time or for up to 2 hours. Makes 3 cups.

9 dried whole grain lasagna noodles

Nonstick cooking spray

1 medium onion, chopped

4 cloves garlic, minced

1 cup vegetable broth

1 tablespoon snipped fresh rosemary or 1 teaspoon dried rosemary, crushed

1 14-ounce package frozen broccoli florets

2 10-ounce packages frozen chopped spinach, thawed and well drained

1 26- to 28-ounce jar meatless tomato pasta sauce

2 cups shredded part-skim mozzarella cheese (8 ounces)

Fresh rosemary sprigs (optional)

Broccoli-Spinach Lasagna

PREP: 35 minutes   **BAKE:** 55 minutes
STAND: 10 minutes   **OVEN:** 375°F

NUTRITION FACTS per serving:

CALORIES 249
TOTAL FAT 6 g (3 g sat. fat)
CHOLESTEROL 18 mg
PROTEIN 16 g
CARBOHYDRATE 33 g
FIBER 9 g
SODIUM 696 mg

EXCHANGES 1.5 Starch, 1 Lean Meat, 2 Vegetable

1 Preheat oven to 375°F. Cook lasagna noodles according to package directions. Drain noodles; rinse with cold water and drain well. Set aside.

2 Meanwhile, lightly coat an unheated large skillet with nonstick cooking spray. Add onion and garlic; cook over medium heat for 3 minutes, stirring occasionally. Stir in vegetable broth and snipped or dried rosemary; bring to boiling. Stir in broccoli. Return to boiling; reduce heat. Cover and simmer for 1 minute. Uncover and stir in spinach; remove from heat.

3 Lightly coat a 3-quart rectangular baking dish with nonstick cooking spray. Spread ½ cup pasta sauce evenly in bottom of dish. Arrange 3 lasagna noodles on the sauce. Layer with half of the spinach mixture; sprinkle with ½ cup mozzarella cheese. Spoon ¾ cup pasta sauce on the cheese. Top with 3 more noodles, the remaining spinach mixture, ½ cup mozzarella cheese, and ¾ cup pasta sauce. Top with remaining 3 noodles. Spoon remaining pasta sauce on the noodles. Sprinkle with remaining 1 cup mozzarella cheese.

4 Cover and bake for 40 minutes. Uncover and bake about 15 minutes more or until hot in the center. Let stand for 10 minutes before serving. If desired, garnish with rosemary sprigs. Makes 8 servings.

Make-Ahead Directions: Prepare lasagna as at left through step 3. Cover with plastic wrap, then foil and refrigerate for up to 24 hours. To serve, preheat oven to 375°F. Remove plastic wrap. Bake, covered with foil, for 50 minutes. Uncover and bake about 15 minutes more or until hot in the center. Let stand for 10 minutes before serving.

Pasta with Mushrooms and Spinach

START TO FINISH: 25 minutes

NUTRITION FACTS per serving:

- -

CALORIES 303
TOTAL FAT 7 g (2 g sat. fat)
CHOLESTEROL 5 mg
PROTEIN 16 g
CARBOHYDRATE 47 g
FIBER 6 g
SODIUM 189 mg

EXCHANGES 2.5 Starch, 0.5 Lean Meat,
2 Vegetable, 0.5 Fat

8	ounces dried multigrain or whole grain penne, rotini, or bow tie pasta
1	tablespoon olive oil
2	cups sliced portobello or other fresh mushrooms
1	large onion, chopped
4	cloves garlic, minced
2	teaspoons snipped fresh thyme or ½ teaspoon dried thyme, crushed
8	cups thinly sliced fresh spinach
⅓	cup shredded Parmesan cheese

1 Cook pasta according to package directions. Drain well.

2 Meanwhile, in a very large skillet heat oil over medium heat. Add mushrooms, onion, and garlic; cook for 2 to 3 minutes or until mushrooms are nearly tender, stirring occasionally. Stir in thyme. Gradually add spinach, cooking and tossing about 1 minute or until heated through and spinach is slightly wilted.

3 Stir cooked pasta into spinach mixture; toss gently to combine. Sprinkle with cheese to serve. Makes 4 (1¾-cup) servings.

2 14½-ounce cans no-salt-added diced tomatoes, undrained

1 15-ounce can garbanzo beans (chickpeas), rinsed and drained

1 15-ounce can red kidney beans, rinsed and drained

1 8-ounce can tomato sauce

1 cup finely chopped onion

1 cup chopped green or yellow sweet pepper

2 to 3 teaspoons chili powder

2 cloves garlic, minced

½ teaspoon dried oregano, crushed

⅛ teaspoon cayenne pepper

8 ounces dried whole wheat wagon wheel pasta and/or vegetable wagon wheel pasta (2 cups)

½ cup shredded reduced-fat cheddar cheese (2 ounces)

Chili-Style Vegetable Pasta

PREP: 20 minutes

COOK: 5 to 6 hours (low) or 2½ to 3 hours (high)

1 In a 3½- or 4-quart slow cooker combine undrained tomatoes, garbanzo beans, kidney beans, tomato sauce, onion, sweet pepper, chili powder, garlic, oregano, and cayenne pepper. Cover; cook on low-heat setting for 5 to 6 hours or on high-heat setting for 2½ to 3 hours.

2 To serve, cook pasta according to package directions; drain. Serve bean mixture over hot cooked pasta. Sprinkle with cheese. Makes 6 servings.

NUTRITION FACTS per serving:

CALORIES 327
TOTAL FAT 4 g (1 g sat. fat)
CHOLESTEROL 7 mg
PROTEIN 18 g
CARBOHYDRATE 63 g
FIBER 12 g
SODIUM 693 mg

EXCHANGES 3.5 Starch, 0.5 Very Lean Meat, 1.5 Vegetable

NUTRITION NOTE

Red beans, such as kidney beans, are sources of minerals such as iron, potassium, copper, and phosphorus. They are also low-fat, low-calorie sources of protein and fiber.

4 ounces dried whole grain bow tie or mostaccioli pasta

6 ounces fresh Swiss chard or spinach

1½ teaspoons olive oil

2 cloves garlic, minced

⅓ cup light ricotta cheese

2 tablespoons fat-free milk

2 tablespoons snipped fresh basil or 1 teaspoon dried basil, crushed

⅛ teaspoon salt

⅛ teaspoon black pepper

Dash ground nutmeg

1 medium tomato, seeded and chopped

2 tablespoons shredded Parmesan cheese

Pasta with Swiss Chard

START TO FINISH: 35 minutes

NUTRITION FACTS per serving:

CALORIES 307
TOTAL FAT 8 g (2 g sat. fat)
CHOLESTEROL 14 mg
PROTEIN 14 g
CARBOHYDRATE 51 g
FIBER 8 g
SODIUM 435 mg

EXCHANGES 3 Starch, 0.5 Lean Meat, 1 Vegetable, 1 Fat

1 Cook pasta according to package directions, except omit any oil or salt. Drain well. Return pasta to hot saucepan. Cover and keep warm.

2 Meanwhile, cut out and discard center ribs from Swiss chard or remove stems from spinach. Coarsely chop greens; set aside. In a large nonstick skillet heat oil over medium heat. Add garlic; cook for 15 seconds. Add Swiss chard or spinach. Cook over medium-low heat about 3 minutes or until greens are wilted and tender, stirring frequently. Stir in ricotta cheese, milk, basil, salt, pepper, and nutmeg. Cook and stir for 3 to 5 minutes more or until heated through.

3 Add ricotta mixture and tomato to cooked pasta; toss gently to combine. Sprinkle individual servings with Parmesan cheese. Makes 2 servings.

- 9 dried whole grain lasagna noodles
- 1 tablespoon olive oil
- 2 8- or 9-ounce packages frozen artichoke hearts, thawed and well drained
- ¼ cup pine nuts
- 4 cloves garlic, minced
- 1 15-ounce carton light ricotta cheese
- 1½ cups reduced-fat shredded Italian blend cheese or part-skim mozzarella cheese (6 ounces)
- 1 cup snipped fresh basil or 4 teaspoons dried basil, crushed
- 1 egg
- ¼ teaspoon salt
- 1 cup reduced-sodium chicken broth
- ¼ cup all-purpose flour
- 2 cups fat-free milk
   Chopped fresh tomato (optional)
   Snipped fresh parsley (optional)

Artichoke-Basil Lasagna

PREP: 45 minutes **BAKE:** 40 minutes
STAND: 15 minutes **OVEN:** 350°F

NUTRITION FACTS per serving:

CALORIES 330
TOTAL FAT 12 g (5 g sat. fat)
CHOLESTEROL 52 mg
PROTEIN 21 g
CARBOHYDRATE 35 g
FIBER 8 g
SODIUM 431 mg

EXCHANGES 2 Starch, 2 Lean Meat, 1 Vegetable, 1 Fat

1 Preheat oven to 350°F. Cook lasagna noodles according to package directions. Drain noodles; rinse with cold water and drain well. Set aside.

2 In a large skillet heat oil over medium heat. Add artichokes, pine nuts, and garlic; cook about 5 minutes or until artichokes, nuts, and garlic start to brown, stirring frequently. Transfer to a large bowl. Stir in ricotta cheese, ½ cup Italian blend cheese, ½ cup fresh basil or 1 tablespoon dried basil, egg, and salt.

3 For sauce, in a medium saucepan whisk together chicken broth and flour until smooth. Stir in milk. Cook and stir over medium heat until sauce is slightly thickened and bubbly. Remove from heat. Stir in remaining ½ cup fresh basil or 1 teaspoon dried basil.

4 Pour 1 cup sauce into a 3-quart rectangular baking dish. Top with 3 cooked lasagna noodles. Dollop with one-third of the ricotta mixture (about 1⅓ cups); carefully spread evenly over noodles. Top with one-third of the remaining sauce (about ⅔ cup). Sprinkle with ⅓ cup of the remaining Italian blend cheese. Repeat layers twice more, beginning with lasagna noodles and ending with the Italian blend cheese.

5 Bake, uncovered, about 40 minutes or until heated through and top is lightly browned. Let stand for 15 minutes before serving. If desired, top with tomato and parsley. Makes 8 servings.

1 9-ounce package refrigerated whole wheat linguine

1 pound fresh asparagus, trimmed and cut into 2-inch-long pieces

1 cup evaporated fat-free milk

2 ounces reduced-fat cream cheese (Neufchâtel), cubed

2 ounces Gorgonzola or other blue cheese, crumbled (½ cup)

¼ teaspoon salt

2 tablespoons chopped walnuts, toasted

Linguine with Gorgonzola Sauce

START TO FINISH: 25 minutes

NUTRITION FACTS per serving:

CALORIES 361
TOTAL FAT 13 g (6 g sat. fat)
CHOLESTEROL 42 mg
PROTEIN 19 g
CARBOHYDRATE 44 g
FIBER 7 g
SODIUM 476 mg

EXCHANGES 2 Starch, 0.5 Milk, 1 High-Fat Meat, 1 Vegetable, 0.5 Fat

NUTRITION NOTE

Whole wheat pasta requires slightly longer cooking time than traditional pasta, but the added fiber and protein make whole wheat worth the wait.

1 Cook pasta and asparagus according to package directions for the pasta; drain well. Return pasta and asparagus to pan. Cover and keep warm.

2 Meanwhile, for sauce, in a medium saucepan combine milk, cream cheese, half of the Gorgonzola cheese, and salt. Bring to boiling over medium heat, whisking constantly; reduce heat. Simmer, uncovered, for 2 minutes, stirring frequently (sauce may appear slightly curdled).

3 Pour sauce over pasta mixture; toss gently to coat. Transfer to four shallow bowls. Sprinkle individual servings with remaining Gorgonzola cheese and walnuts. Serve immediately (sauce will thicken upon standing). Makes 4 servings.

1 medium eggplant, cut into
1-inch cubes

1 28-ounce can Italian-style whole
peeled tomatoes in puree,
undrained, cut up

1 6-ounce can no-salt-added
tomato paste

1 4-ounce can or jar (drained
weight) sliced mushrooms,
drained

½ cup chopped onion

¼ cup dry red wine or water

¼ cup water

1½ teaspoons dried oregano, crushed

2 cloves garlic, minced

½ cup pitted kalamata olives or
pitted ripe olives

Salt

Black pepper

8 ounces dried multigrain or
whole grain rotini or penne
pasta, cooked according to
package directions

⅓ cup grated reduced-fat
Parmesan cheese

2 tablespoons snipped fresh parsley

2 tablespoons pine nuts, toasted
(optional)

Pasta with Eggplant Sauce

PREP: 25 minutes

COOK: 7 to 8 hours (low) or 3½ to 4 hours (high)

NUTRITION FACTS per serving:

CALORIES 265
TOTAL FAT 5 g (1 g sat. fat)
CHOLESTEROL 4 mg
PROTEIN 13 g
CARBOHYDRATE 43 g
FIBER 10 g
SODIUM 634 mg

EXCHANGES 1.5 Starch, 1 Other
Carbohydrates, 1 Lean Meat, 1 Vegetable

1 In a 4- to 5-quart slow cooker combine
eggplant, undrained tomatoes, tomato paste,
mushrooms, onion, dry red wine, water, oregano,
and garlic.

2 Cover and cook on low-heat setting for
7 to 8 hours or on high-heat setting for
3½ to 4 hours.

3 Stir in olives. Season to taste with salt and
pepper. Serve over hot cooked pasta. Top
with Parmesan cheese, parsley, and, if desired,
toasted pine nuts. Makes 6 servings.

Range-top Directions: In a 4 quart Dutch oven
combine eggplant, undrained tomatoes, tomato
paste, mushrooms, onion, dry red wine, water,
oregano, and garlic. Bring to boiling; reduce heat.
Cover and simmer 15 minutes or until eggplant
and onion are tender. Simmer, uncovered,
about 10 minutes more or until sauce is desired
consistency. Stir in olives. Season to taste with salt
and pepper. Serve as above.

1 9-ounce package refrigerated whole wheat four-cheese ravioli

1 tablespoon olive oil

2 medium red and/or green sweet peppers, seeded and cut into thin strips

2 medium carrots, thinly sliced

1 medium onion, chopped

2 cloves garlic, minced

1 14½-ounce can diced tomatoes, undrained

3 tablespoons snipped fresh basil or 2 teaspoons dried basil, crushed

Black pepper

Snipped fresh basil and/or small basil leaves (optional)

Ravioli with Sweet Peppers

START TO FINISH: 25 minutes

NUTRITION FACTS per serving:
- -

CALORIES 287
TOTAL FAT 10 g (4 g sat. fat)
CHOLESTEROL 43 mg
PROTEIN 11 g
CARBOHYDRATE 38 g
FIBER 6 g
SODIUM 617 mg

EXCHANGES 2 Starch, 0.5 Medium-Fat Meat, 1.5 Vegetable, 1 Fat

1 Cook pasta according to package directions, except omit any oil or salt. Drain. Return pasta to hot saucepan. Cover and keep warm.

2 Meanwhile, in a large nonstick skillet heat oil over medium-high heat. Add sweet pepper, carrot, onion, and garlic; cook and stir about 5 minutes or until vegetables are tender. Stir in undrained tomatoes and 3 tablespoons snipped or dried basil. Cook and stir about 2 minutes more or until heated through. Season to taste with black pepper.

3 Add vegetable mixture to the cooked pasta; toss gently to combine. If desired, sprinkle with additional snipped basil and/or small basil leaves. Makes 4 servings.

- 1 medium spaghetti squash (2¼ pounds)
- ¼ cup water
- 1 tablespoon olive oil
- 2 cups sliced fresh mushrooms
- 1 medium red or green sweet pepper, seeded and chopped
- 1 medium onion, chopped
- 3 cloves garlic, minced
-    Nonstick cooking spray
- ½ teaspoon dried Italian seasoning, crushed
- ⅛ teaspoon black pepper
- 1½ cups purchased tomato-based pasta sauce
- 1 cup shredded part-skim mozzarella cheese (4 ounces)
- 2 tablespoons snipped fresh flat-leaf parsley

1 Halve squash crosswise; remove seeds. Place squash, cut sides down, in a microwave-safe 2-quart rectangular baking dish. Add water. Cover with vented plastic wrap. Microwave on 100% power (high) for 13 to 15 minutes or until squash is tender when pierced with fork, rearranging once for even cooking. Drain. Set aside until cool enough to handle.

2 In a large skillet heat oil over medium heat. Add mushrooms, sweet pepper, onion, and garlic; cook and stir about 5 minutes or until vegetables are tender.

3 Preheat oven to 350°F. Using two forks, shred and separate the squash pulp into strands (you should have about 3 cups). Wipe out baking dish; coat with nonstick cooking spray. Spread half of the squash in the prepared baking dish. Add half of the mushroom mixture. Sprinkle with Italian seasoning and black pepper. Top with half of the pasta sauce and half of the cheese. Top with remaining squash, mushroom mixture, and sauce.

4 Bake, uncovered, for 30 minutes. Sprinkle with remaining cheese. Bake about 5 minutes more or until cheese is melted. Let stand for 10 minutes before serving. Sprinkle with parsley. Makes 6 servings.

Cheesy Spaghetti Squash

PREP: 30 minutes   **BAKE:** 35 minutes
MICROWAVE: 13 minutes
STAND: 10 minutes **OVEN:** 350°F

NUTRITION FACTS per serving:

CALORIES 170
TOTAL FAT 7 g (3 g sat. fat)
CHOLESTEROL 12 mg
PROTEIN 8 g
CARBOHYDRATE 21 g
FIBER 2 g
SODIUM 350 mg

EXCHANGES 1 Other Carbohydrates, 0.5 Lean Meat, 2 Vegetable, 1 Fat

COOK'S TIP

Spaghetti squash is a winter squash, but it is available year-round. Store it uncut at room temperature for up to three weeks.

Mushroom-Vegetable Fajitas

PREP: 25 minutes

GRILL: 15 minutes

NUTRITION FACTS per serving:

CALORIES 233
TOTAL FAT 10 g (2 g sat. fat)
CHOLESTEROL 0 mg
PROTEIN 11 g
CARBOHYDRATE 26 g
FIBER 15 g
SODIUM 475 mg
EXCHANGES 1.5 Starch, 1.5 Vegetable, 1.5 Fat

1 small avocado, halved, seeded, and peeled
1 tablespoon lime juice
1 clove garlic, minced
½ teaspoon ground cumin
½ teaspoon dried oregano, crushed
¼ teaspoon salt
⅛ teaspoon black pepper
3 small fresh portobello mushrooms, stems and gills removed
2 medium red, yellow and/or green sweet peppers, halved, stemmed, and seeded
½ of a medium red onion, cut into ½-inch-thick slices
   Nonstick cooking spray
4 7- to 8-inch whole wheat flour tortillas
   Lime wedges (optional)

1 Place avocado halves in a small bowl. With a potato masher or fork, mash avocado until nearly smooth. Stir in lime juice and garlic. Cover the surface of the avocado mixture with plastic wrap and chill until ready to serve.

2 In a small bowl combine cumin, oregano, salt, and black pepper. Coat mushrooms, sweet pepper halves, and red onion slices with nonstick cooking spray. Sprinkle cumin mixture on vegetables.

3 For a charcoal grill, place mushrooms, sweet pepper halves, and onion slices on rack of an uncovered grill directly over medium coals. Grill until vegetables are crisp-tender, turning once halfway through grilling and removing vegetables when they are done. Allow 8 to 10 minutes for the sweet peppers, 10 to 15 minutes for the mushrooms, and 15 to 20 minutes for the onion slices. (For a gas grill, preheat grill. Reduce heat to medium. Place vegetables on grill rack directly over heat. Cover and grill as above.)

4 Place tortillas on grill rack directly over medium coals. Grill for 20 to 30 seconds or until warm, turning once. Remove from grill and cover to keep warm. Thinly slice mushrooms and sweet peppers. Coarsely chop onion slices.

5 Spread avocado mixture on warm tortillas. Divide vegetables among tortillas. Fold over. If desired, serve with lime wedges. Makes 4 servings.

1   12-inch (10-ounce) whole wheat
    Italian bread shell (such as
    Boboli brand)
    Nonstick cooking spray
1   cup sliced fresh shiitake or
    button mushrooms
⅔   cup fresh pea pods cut into
    thin strips
¼   cup coarsely shredded carrot
¼   cup sliced green onion
¼   to ⅓ cup bottled peanut sauce
2   tablespoons chopped peanuts
2   tablespoons fresh cilantro leaves

1 Preheat oven to 450°F. Place bread shell
on an ungreased baking sheet. Bake for 6 to
8 minutes or until lightly browned and crisp.

2 Meanwhile, lightly coat an unheated large
nonstick skillet with nonstick cooking spray.
Preheat over medium heat. Add mushrooms,
pea pods, and carrot to hot skillet; cook about
2 minutes or just until tender. Stir in green
onion. Remove from heat.

3 Carefully spread hot bread shell with peanut
sauce. Top with hot vegetable mixture;
sprinkle with peanuts and cilantro leaves.
Makes 4 servings.

COOK'S TIP

Check for freshness in pea pods such as
sugar snap or snow peas by snapping one
in half. If it sounds crisp when snapped,
it's fresh and ready to eat.

Thai-Style Veggie Pizza

PREP: 20 minutes   **BAKE:** 6 minutes
COOK: 2 minutes   **OVEN:** 450°F

NUTRITION FACTS per serving:

CALORIES 286
TOTAL FAT 8 g (2 g sat. fat)
CHOLESTEROL 0 mg
PROTEIN 12 g
CARBOHYDRATE 46 g
FIBER 8 g
SODIUM 598 mg

EXCHANGES 3 Starch, 0.5 Vegetable, 1 Fat

1 tablespoon olive oil

½ of a medium red onion, thinly sliced (½ cup)

2 cloves garlic, minced

8 ounces fresh portobello mushrooms, coarsely chopped

1 9-ounce package fresh spinach (8 to 10 cups)

½ cup grated reduced-fat Parmesan cheese

½ cup shredded part-skim mozzarella cheese (2 ounces)

2 tablespoons snipped fresh basil or 2 teaspoons dried basil, crushed

4 7- or 8-inch whole wheat flour tortillas

Olive oil nonstick cooking spray

Spinach-Mushroom Quesadillas

PREP: 25 minutes

COOK: 2 minutes per batch

OVEN: 300°F

NUTRITION FACTS per serving:

CALORIES 293

TOTAL FAT 12 g (4 g sat. fat)

CHOLESTEROL 21 mg

PROTEIN 18 g

CARBOHYDRATE 29 g

FIBER 13 g

SODIUM 701 mg

EXCHANGES 1 Starch, 1.5 Lean Meat, 2.5 Vegetable, 1 Fat

1 Preheat oven to 300°F. In a large skillet heat oil over medium heat. Add onion and garlic; cook for 5 minutes, stirring occasionally. Add mushrooms; cook about 5 minutes more or until almost tender, stirring occasionally. Add spinach in batches; cook and stir just until spinach is wilted before adding more. When all spinach is just wilted, remove from heat. Stir in Parmesan cheese, mozzarella cheese, and basil. Remove spinach mixture from skillet. Set skillet aside to cool.

2 Divide spinach mixture among tortillas, spooning it on half of each tortilla. Fold each tortilla over spinach mixture, pressing gently. Lightly coat both sides of each quesadilla with nonstick cooking spray. Rinse and dry the skillet.

3 Heat skillet over medium heat. Place two quesadillas in hot skillet; cook for 2 to 3 minutes or until lightly browned, turning once. Remove quesadillas from skillet; place on baking sheet. Keep warm in oven. Repeat with remaining two quesadillas. Cut quesadillas in half to serve. Makes 4 servings.

COOK'S TIP

Spinach is available in a few varieties. For mild, sweet flavor, choose baby spinach. Look for leaves with bright color and no discoloration or wilting.

1 tablespoon olive oil

1 cup coarsely chopped zucchini

⅔ cup chopped onion

½ cup shredded carrot

2 cloves garlic, minced

1 14½-ounce can diced tomatoes, undrained

1 8-ounce can tomato sauce

2 tablespoons tomato paste

2 teaspoons dried Italian seasoning, crushed

⅛ teaspoon black pepper

4 cups cooked spaghetti squash*

¼ cup shredded Parmesan cheese (2 ounces)

Small fresh basil leaves (optional)

Spaghetti Squash with Chunky Tomato Sauce

PREP: 25 minutes

COOK: 15 minutes

NUTRITION FACTS per serving:

CALORIES 154
TOTAL FAT 6 g (1 g sat. fat)
CHOLESTEROL 4 mg
PROTEIN 5 g
CARBOHYDRATE 23 g
FIBER 3 g
SODIUM 610 mg

EXCHANGES 1 Other Carbohydrates, 2 Vegetable, 1 Fat

1 For chunky tomato sauce, in a large saucepan heat oil over medium heat. Add zucchini, onion, carrot, and garlic; cook until tender, stirring occasionally. Add undrained diced tomatoes, tomato sauce, tomato paste, Italian seasoning, and pepper. Bring to boiling; reduce heat. Simmer, uncovered, for 15 minutes, stirring occasionally.

2 Serve chunky tomato sauce over spaghetti squash. Sprinkle with Parmesan cheese. If desired, garnish with basil leaves. Makes 4 servings.

*To cook spaghetti squash, cut a 3-pound spaghetti squash in half lengthwise; remove seeds and strings. Place one half, cut side down, in a microwave-safe baking dish. Using a fork, prick the skin all over. Microwave on 100% power (high) for 6 to 7 minutes or until tender when pierced with a fork; carefully remove from baking dish. Repeat with the other half. (Or preheat oven to 350°F. Place both halves, cut sides down, in a shallow baking pan and bake for 30 to 40 minutes or until tender.) Cool slightly; using two forks, shred and separate the squash pulp into strands. Makes about 4 cups.

1   14-ounce can reduced-sodium chicken broth

¼   cup water

1½   cups fresh green beans, trimmed and cut into 2-inch-long pieces

⅔   cup quick-cooking barley

2   tablespoons lemon juice

1   tablespoon olive oil

⅛   teaspoon salt

⅛   teaspoon black pepper

½   cup whole wheat couscous

4   cups coarsely shredded fresh spinach

¼   cup sliced green onion

1½   teaspoons snipped fresh thyme or ½ teaspoon dried thyme, crushed

     Lemon wedges (optional)

Grain-Vegetable Medley

PREP: 20 minutes   **COOK:** 10 minutes
STAND: 5 minutes

NUTRITION FACTS per serving:

CALORIES 274
TOTAL FAT 5 g (1 g sat. fat)
CHOLESTEROL 0 mg
PROTEIN 11 g
CARBOHYDRATE 51 g
FIBER 11 g
SODIUM 340 mg

EXCHANGES 2.5 Starch, 2 Vegetable, 0.5 Fat

1 In a large saucepan bring chicken broth and water to boiling; stir in green beans and uncooked barley. Return to boiling; reduce heat. Cover and simmer for 10 to 12 minutes or until barley is tender.

2 Meanwhile, in a small bowl whisk together lemon juice, oil, salt, and pepper.

3 Stir uncooked couscous into barley mixture. Stir in lemon juice mixture, spinach, green onion, and thyme. Remove from heat. Cover and let stand for 5 minutes. To serve, fluff with a fork. If desired, serve with lemon wedges. Makes 4 (about 1-cup) servings.

- 6 ounces dried soba (buckwheat noodles) or multigrain spaghetti
- 1 tablespoon toasted sesame oil
- 5 cups broccoli florets
- 3 medium yellow and/or red sweet peppers, seeded and cut into thin strips
- 6 medium green onions, bias-sliced into 1-inch-long pieces
- ¼ cup bottled plum sauce
- 1 tablespoon rice vinegar
- 1 tablespoon soy sauce
- ½ teaspoon crushed red pepper
- 2 tablespoons sliced almonds, toasted

  Sliced green onion (optional)

1 Cook soba according to package directions; drain. Return to hot saucepan. Cover and keep warm.

2 Meanwhile, pour toasted sesame oil into a wok or very large skillet. Preheat over medium-high heat. Stir-fry broccoli and sweet pepper in hot oil for 3 minutes. Add green onions. Stir-fry for 1 to 2 minutes more or until vegetables are crisp-tender. Add plum sauce, rice vinegar, soy sauce, and crushed red pepper; stir to coat vegetables with sauce. Heat through. Serve immediately with soba. Sprinkle with sliced almonds and, if desired, additional sliced green onion. Makes 4 servings.

COOK'S TIP

Green onions, also called scallions, require refrigeration because they spoil more quickly than other onion varieties. Store them in the refrigerator, unwashed in plastic bags, for up to seven days.

Soba-Vegetable Toss

START TO FINISH: 35 minutes

NUTRITION FACTS per serving:

CALORIES 313
TOTAL FAT 6 g (1 g sat. fat)
CHOLESTEROL 0 mg
PROTEIN 12 g
CARBOHYDRATE 59 g
FIBER 7 g
SODIUM 737 mg

EXCHANGES 3 Starch, 2.5 Vegetable, 0.5 Fat

Brown Rice-Spinach Custards

PREP: 25 minutes   **BAKE:** 25 minutes
OVEN: 350°F

NUTRITION FACTS per serving:

CALORIES 213
TOTAL FAT 8 g (3 g sat. fat)
CHOLESTEROL 146 mg
PROTEIN 14 g
CARBOHYDRATE 20 g
FIBER 4 g
SODIUM 648 mg

EXCHANGES 1 Starch, 1.5 Lean Meat, 1 Vegetable, 0.5 Fat

1	tablespoon olive oil
1	medium onion, chopped
4	eggs
½	cup low-fat cottage cheese
3	ounces reduced-fat feta cheese, crumbled
1	tablespoon snipped fresh dill or ½ teaspoon dried dill
½	teaspoon salt
2	10-ounce packages frozen chopped spinach, thawed and well drained
2	cups cooked brown rice
1	tablespoon lemon juice
	Fresh lemon peel strips (optional)

1 Preheat oven to 350°F. In a small skillet heat oil over medium heat. Add onion; cook until tender, stirring occasionally. Cool slightly.

2 In a large bowl beat eggs with a fork. Stir in cottage cheese, feta cheese, dill, salt, and cooked onion. Add spinach, cooked brown rice, and lemon juice, stirring until well mixed. Place six 8- to 10-ounce ramekins or custard cups in a 15×10×1-inch baking pan. Divide rice mixture among the dishes. Bake for 25 to 30 minutes or until a knife inserted near the center of each custard comes out clean. If desired, garnish with lemon peel. Makes 6 servings.

COOK'S TIP

Cottage cheese is more perishable than other cheeses. A good sign that it's past its prime is when the cheese mixture separates and becomes watery. Store cottage cheese in the coldest part of the refrigerator for up to 10 days beyond the date stamped on the container.

- 4 medium green, red, and/or yellow sweet peppers
- 1 cup cooked brown rice
- 1 15-ounce can spicy chili beans or mild chili beans
- 1 cup shredded reduced-fat Monterey Jack cheese (4 ounces)
- 1 4½-ounce can stewed tomatoes, undrained, cut up

1 Remove tops from sweet peppers; set tops aside. Remove membranes and seeds from sweet peppers. In a medium bowl stir together cooked brown rice, undrained beans, and cheese; spoon into sweet peppers. Pour stewed tomatoes into the bottom of a 5- to 6-quart slow cooker. Place sweet peppers, filled sides up, in cooker on tomatoes. Replace sweet pepper tops.

2 Cover and cook on low-heat setting for 6 to 6½ hours or on high-heat setting for 3 to 3½ hours. Makes 4 servings.

Spicy Bean- and Rice-Stuffed Peppers

PREP: 15 minutes
COOK: 6 to 6½ hours (low) or 3 to 3½ hours (high)

NUTRITION FACTS per serving:

CALORIES 290
TOTAL FAT 8 g (4 g sat. fat)
CHOLESTEROL 20 mg
PROTEIN 15 g
CARBOHYDRATE 42 g
FIBER 9 g
SODIUM 848 mg

EXCHANGES 2 Starch, 1 Lean Meat, 2 Vegetable, 0.5 Fat

Greek Garbanzo Salad

PREP: 25 minutes

CHILL: 4 to 24 hours

NUTRITION FACTS per serving:

CALORIES 200
TOTAL FAT 10 g (3 g sat. fat)
CHOLESTEROL 5 mg
PROTEIN 11 g
CARBOHYDRATE 25 g
FIBER 7 g
SODIUM 694 mg

EXCHANGES 1 Starch, 0.5 Lean Meat, 2 Vegetable, 1.5 Fat

1	15-ounce can garbanzo beans (chickpeas), rinsed and drained
2	medium tomatoes, cut into chunks
1	large cucumber, seeded and chopped (about 2 cups)
1	cup coarsely chopped green sweet pepper
½	cup thinly sliced red onion
2	tablespoons olive oil
2	tablespoons red wine vinegar
1	tablespoon snipped fresh mint
1	tablespoon lemon juice
2	cloves garlic, minced
½	cup crumbled reduced-fat feta cheese (2 ounces)
	Salt
	Black pepper
2	cups packaged mixed salad greens

1 In a large bowl combine garbanzo beans, tomato, cucumber, sweet pepper, and red onion.

2 In a small bowl whisk together oil, red wine vinegar, mint, lemon juice, and garlic. Pour over garbanzo bean mixture; toss to coat. Cover and chill for 4 to 24 hours.

3 Stir in feta cheese. Season to taste with salt and black pepper. Serve over mixed greens. Makes 4 (1⅔-cup) servings.

COOK'S TIP

To seed a cucumber, cut it in half lengthwise and run a spoon end to end to scoop out the seeds.

1   15- to 16-ounce can cannellini beans (white kidney beans), rinsed and drained
¾   cup soft whole wheat bread crumbs (1 slice)
½   cup chopped onion
¼   cup walnut pieces, toasted if desired
2   tablespoons coarsely chopped fresh basil or 1 teaspoon dried basil, crushed
2   cloves garlic, quartered
1   tablespoon olive oil
4   whole grain hamburger buns, split and toasted
2   tablespoons bottled light ranch salad dressing
2   cups fresh spinach leaves
½   of a medium tomato, sliced

1 In a food processor combine cannellini beans, ¼ cup bread crumbs, onion, walnuts, basil, and garlic. Cover and process until mixture is coarsely chopped and holds together.

2 Shape bean mixture into four ½-inch-thick patties. Place remaining ½ cup bread crumbs in a shallow dish. Carefully brush both sides of each patty with oil. Dip patties into bread crumbs, turning to coat.

3 Preheat a grill pan or large skillet over medium heat. Add patties to pan or skillet. Cook for 10 to 12 minutes or until heated through, turning patties once. (Reduce heat to medium-low if patties brown too quickly.)

4 Spread cut sides of bun bottoms with salad dressing. Top with patties, spinach, tomato slices, and bun tops. Makes 4 servings.

Cannellini Bean Burgers

PREP: 25 minutes
COOK: 10 minutes

NUTRITION FACTS per serving:

CALORIES 299
TOTAL FAT 11 g (1 g sat. fat)
CHOLESTEROL 2 mg
PROTEIN 13 g
CARBOHYDRATE 44 g
FIBER 9 g
SODIUM 497 mg

EXCHANGES 2.5 Starch, 0.5 Very Lean Meat, 1 Vegetable, 1.5 Fat

Lentil- and Rice-Stuffed Peppers

PREP: 30 minutes

COOK: 3 to 3½ hours (high); plus 30 minutes

NUTRITION FACTS per serving:

CALORIES 206
TOTAL FAT 1 g (0 g sat. fat)
CHOLESTEROL 0 mg
PROTEIN 9 g
CARBOHYDRATE 40 g
FIBER 10 g
SODIUM 848 mg

EXCHANGES 2 Starch, 1.5 Vegetable

1½ cups chopped carrot

1½ cups chopped celery

1 cup dry brown lentils, rinsed and drained

⅔ cup brown rice

2 tablespoons packed brown sugar

2 tablespoons yellow mustard

½ teaspoon salt

2 14-ounce cans vegetable broth

½ cup water

1 15-ounce can tomato sauce with garlic and onion

2 tablespoons cider vinegar

4 green and/or red sweet peppers
Snipped fresh flat-leaf parsley (optional)

1 In a 3½- or 4-quart slow cooker combine carrot, celery, lentils, uncooked brown rice, brown sugar, mustard, and salt. Stir in vegetable broth and water.

2 Cover and cook on high-heat setting for 3 to 3½ hours. Stir in tomato sauce and vinegar. Cover and cook for 30 minutes more.

3 Halve sweet peppers lengthwise; remove seeds and membranes.* To serve, spoon lentil mixture in and around pepper halves. If desired, sprinkle with parsley. Makes 8 servings.

*If desired, in a Dutch oven cook sweet pepper halves in a large amount of boiling water about 3 minutes or until crisp-tender. Drain well.

Nonstick cooking spray

1 medium red sweet pepper, seeded and finely chopped

2 cloves garlic, minced

1 15-ounce can black beans, rinsed and drained

1½ cups cooked brown rice

1 egg, lightly beaten

2 tablespoons snipped fresh cilantro

1 canned chipotle chile pepper in adobo sauce, finely chopped*

1 teaspoon adobo sauce from canned chipotle chile peppers in adobo sauce (optional)

½ teaspoon ground cumin

4 teaspoons olive oil

¼ cup light dairy sour cream

Snipped fresh cilantro (optional)

Spicy Rice and Bean Cakes

PREP: 30 minutes

COOK: 8 minutes per batch

NUTRITION FACTS per serving:

CALORIES 236
TOTAL FAT 8 g (2 g sat. fat)
CHOLESTEROL 57 mg
PROTEIN 11 g
CARBOHYDRATE 35 g
FIBER 7 g
SODIUM 307 mg

EXCHANGES 2 Starch, 1 Very Lean Meat, 1 Fat

1 Coat an unheated large nonstick skillet with nonstick cooking spray. Preheat over medium-high heat. Add sweet pepper and garlic; cook and stir until crisp-tender. Transfer to a large bowl and cool slightly.

2 Place black beans in a food processor;** cover and process until smooth. Transfer to bowl with sweet pepper mixture. Stir in cooked brown rice, egg, 2 tablespoons cilantro, chipotle pepper, adobo sauce (if using), and cumin; mix well. With wet hands, shape mixture evenly into eight patties, each about ½ inch thick.

3 In the same skillet heat 2 teaspoons olive oil over medium heat. Add half of the bean patties. Cook for 8 to 10 minutes or until browned and heated through, carefully turning once halfway through cooking. Remove from skillet and keep warm. Repeat with remaining 2 teaspoons oil and remaining bean patties. Serve bean patties with sour cream. If desired, garnish with additional snipped cilantro. Makes 4 servings.

*Because chile peppers contain volatile oils that can burn your skin and eyes, avoid direct contact with them as much as possible. When working with chile peppers, wear plastic or rubber gloves. If your bare hands do touch the peppers, wash your hands and nails well with soap and warm water.

**If you do not have a food processor, use a potato masher to mash the beans into a nearly smooth paste.

Triple-Pepper Nachos

PREP: 25 minutes   **BAKE:** 13 minutes
OVEN: 425°F

NUTRITION FACTS per serving:

CALORIES 201
TOTAL FAT 7 g (3 g sat. fat)
CHOLESTEROL 13 mg
PROTEIN 15 g
CARBOHYDRATE 24 g
FIBER 11 g
SODIUM 838 mg

EXCHANGES 1.5 Starch, 1.5 Lean Meat,
0.5 Vegetable

5   7- to 8-inch whole wheat flour
    tortillas or 4 ounces baked
    tortilla chips (about 5 cups)
    Nonstick cooking spray (optional)

1   15-ounce can black beans, rinsed
    and drained

¾   cup purchased chunky salsa

1   cup shredded reduced-fat colby
    and Monterey Jack cheese
    (4 ounces)

¾   cup bottled roasted red sweet
    peppers, drained and cut
    into strips

1   bottled pepperoncini salad pepper,
    seeded and cut into strips

2   to 4 tablespoons bottled
    sliced pickled jalapeño chile
    peppers, chopped*
    Thinly sliced green onion
    Light dairy sour cream (optional)
    Purchased chunky salsa (optional)

1 Preheat oven to 425°F. If using whole wheat flour tortillas, lightly coat both sides of each tortilla with nonstick cooking spray. Cut each tortilla into six wedges. Place wedges in a single layer on a very large ungreased baking sheet. Bake for 8 to 10 minutes or until lightly browned and crisp, turning once halfway through baking. Tortilla wedges will continue to crisp as they cool.

2 Meanwhile, in a medium saucepan combine black beans and ¾ cup salsa; cook and stir over medium heat just until heated through.

3 On a very large ovenproof platter arrange tortilla chips one to two layers deep, overlapping slightly. Spoon bean mixture on chips. Sprinkle cheese, roasted red peppers, pepperoncini pepper, and jalapeño peppers over bean mixture on chips.

4 Bake about 5 minutes or until cheese is melted. Sprinkle with green onion. If desired, serve with sour cream and additional salsa. Makes 6 servings.

*See chile pepper handling note, page 333.

- ½ cup whole wheat couscous
- 2 tablespoons whole wheat flour
- ¼ teaspoon baking soda
- ⅛ teaspoon salt
- 1 egg
- ¾ cup buttermilk or sour fat-free milk*
- 1 tablespoon canola oil
- 1 recipe Black Bean Salsa
  Nonstick cooking spray

1 In a medium bowl combine uncooked couscous, whole wheat flour, baking soda, and salt. In a small bowl beat egg with a fork. Stir in buttermilk and oil. Stir buttermilk mixture into couscous mixture. Let stand for 20 minutes (batter will thicken as it stands).

2 Meanwhile, prepare Black Bean Salsa; set aside. Preheat oven to 200°F.

3 Lightly coat an unheated griddle or large nonstick skillet with nonstick cooking spray. Preheat over medium heat. For each cake, spoon 2 slightly rounded tablespoons of the batter onto the hot griddle or skillet; quickly spread to 3½-inch rounds. Cook about 2 minutes per side or until browned, turning when bottoms are lightly browned and edges are slightly dry. Keep warm in oven while cooking remaining cakes.

4 To serve, spoon Black Bean Salsa over cakes. Makes 4 servings.

Black Bean Salsa: In a medium bowl stir together ¾ cup loose-pack frozen whole kernel corn, thawed; ½ of a 15-ounce can black beans (¾ cup), rinsed and drained; ¾ cup purchased fresh salsa;** ½ cup chopped, peeled jicama; 1 tablespoon snipped fresh cilantro; 1 tablespoon lime juice; and ½ teaspoon ground cumin. Makes 2 cups.

*To make ¾ cup sour fat-free milk, place 2 teaspoons lemon juice or vinegar in a glass measuring cup. Add enough fat-free milk to make ¾ cup total liquid; stir. Let stand for 5 minutes before using.

**Look for fresh salsa in the deli or produce section of your supermarket.

Couscous Cakes with Salsa

PREP: 20 minutes   **STAND:** 20 minutes
COOK: 4 minutes per batch   **OVEN:** 200°F

NUTRITION FACTS per serving:

CALORIES 270
TOTAL FAT 6 g (1 g sat. fat)
CHOLESTEROL 55 mg
PROTEIN 13 g
CARBOHYDRATE 46 g
FIBER 8 g
SODIUM 639 mg

EXCHANGES 3 Starch, 0.5 Very Lean Meat, 0.5 Fat

COOK'S TIP

Couscous is widely available in grocery stores, but the whole wheat variety may be hard to find. If you do not see it with rice or pasta, try a health food store or specialty market.

Southwest Quinoa Pilaf

START TO FINISH: 40 minutes

NUTRITION FACTS per serving:

CALORIES 261
TOTAL FAT 5 g (1 g sat. fat)
CHOLESTEROL 0 mg
PROTEIN 12 g
CARBOHYDRATE 48 g
FIBER 7 g
SODIUM 443 mg

EXCHANGES 3 Starch, 0.5 Vegetable, 0.5 Fat

COOK'S TIP

When you've cut into a jicama and find more than you need for one recipe, wrap the excess tightly and store it in the refrigerator for up to one week. Look for tasty ways to add it to recipes—salads, stir-fries, dippers, and crudités.

1   tablespoon olive oil
1½ cups chopped onion
6   cloves garlic, minced
1¼ cups quinoa*
½   teaspoon ground cumin
1   14-ounce can reduced-sodium chicken broth or vegetable broth
1¼ cups water
1   recipe Black Bean, Corn, and Jicama Salsa
2   tablespoons snipped fresh cilantro
    Fresh cilantro sprigs (optional)

1 In a 4-quart Dutch oven heat oil over medium heat. Add onion and garlic; cook about 5 minutes or until onion is tender, stirring occasionally. Rinse and drain quinoa. Add quinoa and cumin to onion and garlic in Dutch oven; cook and stir about 3 minutes or until quinoa is lightly browned.

2 Add chicken broth and water to quinoa mixture. Bring to boiling; reduce heat. Cover and simmer for 15 to 20 minutes or until all of the liquid is absorbed and quinoa is tender. Divide quinoa mixture among six serving plates. Top quinoa with Black Bean, Corn, and Jicama Salsa. Sprinkle with snipped cilantro. If desired, garnish with cilantro sprigs. Makes 6 servings.

Black Bean, Corn, and Jicama Salsa: In a large bowl toss together one 15-ounce can black beans, rinsed and drained; 1 cup loose-pack frozen whole kernel corn, thawed; 1 large tomato, chopped; ½ cup peeled, chopped jicama; 2 green onions, thinly sliced; 1 fresh jalapeño chile pepper, halved, seeded, and finely chopped;** 2 tablespoons lime juice; and ¼ teaspoon salt. Makes 4 cups.

*Look for quinoa (pronounced KEEN-wa) at health food stores or in the grains section of large supermarkets.

**Because chile peppers contain volatile oils that can burn your skin and eyes, avoid direct contact with them as much as possible. When working with chile peppers, wear plastic or rubber gloves. If your bare hands do touch the peppers, wash your hands and nails well with soap and warm water.

1 18.8- to 19-ounce can ready-to-serve lentil soup

1 15-ounce can black beans, rinsed and drained

1 cup small fresh mushrooms, sliced

1 cup sliced carrot

1 cup loose-pack frozen whole kernel corn

½ cup regular barley

⅓ cup bulgur

¼ cup chopped onion

½ teaspoon black pepper

¼ teaspoon salt

¾ cup water

½ cup shredded reduced-fat cheddar cheese (2 ounces)

1 Preheat oven to 350°F. In an ungreased 2-quart casserole combine lentil soup, black beans, mushrooms, carrot, corn, uncooked barley, uncooked bulgur, onion, pepper, and salt; stir in the water.

2 Cover and bake about 1¼ hours or until barley and bulgur are tender, stirring twice. Stir again; sprinkle with cheese. Cover; let stand about 5 minutes or until cheese is melted. Makes 5 servings.

Vegetable Two-Grain Casserole

PREP: 20 minutes **BAKE:** 1¼ hours
STAND: 5 minutes **OVEN:** 350°F

NUTRITION FACTS per serving:

CALORIES 292
TOTAL FAT 4 g (2 g sat. fat)
CHOLESTEROL 10 mg
PROTEIN 17 g
CARBOHYDRATE 55 g
FIBER 13 g
SODIUM 828 mg

EXCHANGES 3.5 Starch, 1 Very Lean Meat, 0.5 Vegetable

8 ounces dried udon or whole wheat linguine

2 6- to 8-ounce packages smoked teriyaki-flavored or plain firm tofu (fresh bean curd), cut into ½-inch pieces

1½ cups chopped cucumber

1 large carrot, cut into bite-size pieces

½ cup sliced green onion

1 recipe Ginger-Soy Vinaigrette

1 Cook pasta according to package directions; drain well. Cool pasta slightly.

2 Meanwhile, in a large bowl combine tofu, cucumber, carrot, and green onion. Add drained pasta; toss gently to combine.

3 Drizzle Ginger-Soy Vinaigrette on cooked pasta mixture. Toss salad gently to coat. Makes 6 (about 1¼ cup) servings.

Ginger-Soy Vinaigrette: In a small bowl whisk together 2 tablespoons rice vinegar or cider vinegar; 1 tablespoon toasted sesame oil; 2 teaspoons reduced-sodium soy sauce; 4 cloves garlic, minced; 1 teaspoon grated fresh ginger; and ¼ teaspoon crushed red pepper. Makes ¼ cup.

Make-Ahead Directions: Prepare as above. Cover and chill for up to 6 hours.

Udon with Tofu

START TO FINISH: 25 minutes

NUTRITION FACTS per serving:

- -

CALORIES 231
TOTAL FAT 4 g (0 g sat. fat)
CHOLESTEROL 0 mg
PROTEIN 7 g
CARBOHYDRATE 39 g
FIBER 3 g
SODIUM 571 mg

EXCHANGES 2 Starch, 0.5 Medium-Fat Meat, 0.5 Vegetable, 0.5 Fat

COOK'S TIP

Udon noodles, popular in Japanese cuisine, resemble spaghetti but are usually made from wheat. If udon is not available in the Asian section of the grocery store, try a health food store or Asian market.

2 teaspoons canola oil

¾ teaspoon grated fresh ginger

2 cloves garlic, minced

1 8-ounce package tempeh (fermented soybean cake), cut into ½-inch pieces

4 cups sliced bok choy

1 cup packaged julienned carrots

1 6-ounce package frozen pea pods or sugar snap peas, thawed

¼ cup orange juice

3 tablespoons hoisin sauce

1½ cups hot cooked brown rice

1 In a large wok or very large skillet heat oil over medium-high heat. Add ginger and garlic; cook and stir about 30 seconds or until fragrant. Stir in tempeh, bok choy, and carrots. Cook and stir for 4 to 5 minutes or until vegetables are crisp-tender. Stir in pea pods, orange juice, and hoisin sauce. Heat through.

2 Serve mixture over hot cooked brown rice. Makes 4 servings.

Hoisin Tempeh with Stir-Fry Vegetables

START TO FINISH: 25 minutes

NUTRITION FACTS per serving:

CALORIES 285
TOTAL FAT 10 g (2 g sat. fat)
CHOLESTEROL 0 mg
PROTEIN 15 g
CARBOHYDRATE 38 g
FIBER 4 g
SODIUM 273 mg

EXCHANGES 1.5 Starch, 1 Medium-Fat Meat, 2 Vegetable, 0.5 Fat

NUTRITION NOTE

Tempeh is an excellent meat substitute that can be used in place of ground beef or chicken in a variety of recipes. It provides plenty of protein with very little cholesterol and fat.

Tofu and Eggplant

START TO FINISH: 30 minutes

NUTRITION FACTS per serving:

CALORIES 272
TOTAL FAT 8 g (1 g sat. fat)
CHOLESTEROL 0 mg
PROTEIN 11 g
CARBOHYDRATE 38 g
FIBER 7 g
SODIUM 334 mg

EXCHANGES 2 Starch, 0.5 Very Lean Meat,
1 Vegetable, 1 Fat

¾ cup cold water

3 tablespoons dry sherry or water

2 tablespoons reduced-sodium
soy sauce

2 teaspoons cornstarch

1 to 2 teaspoons Asian chili sauce

1 teaspoon sugar

1 tablespoon cooking oil

2 Japanese eggplants, halved
lengthwise and cut into ¼-inch-
thick slices

2 medium red sweet peppers,
seeded and cut into strips

1 tablespoon grated fresh ginger

2 to 3 cloves garlic, minced

12 to 16 ounces firm tofu (fresh bean
curd), cut into ½-inch cubes

2 cups hot cooked brown rice

Fresh cilantro or basil leaves
(optional)

1 For sauce, in a small bowl stir together water,
dry sherry, soy sauce, cornstarch, chili sauce,
and sugar; set aside.

2 In a large nonstick skillet or wok heat oil
over medium-high heat. Add eggplant slices
and sweet pepper. Cook for 3 to 4 minutes or just
until eggplant is tender, stirring often. Remove
eggplant mixture from skillet. Add ginger and
garlic to skillet; cook for 1 minute. Stir sauce and
add to skillet. Cook and stir until thickened and
bubbly. Cook and stir for 1 minute more. Add
eggplant mixture and tofu to skillet; gently stir to
combine. Heat through. Serve over hot cooked
rice. If desired, garnish with cilantro or basil
leaves. Makes 4 servings.

2½ cups water

1¼ cups bulgur

¼ cup lemon juice

3 tablespoons purchased basil pesto

2 cups fresh or thawed frozen shelled sweet soybeans (edamame)

2 cups cherry tomatoes, cut up

⅓ cup crumbled, reduced-fat feta cheese

⅓ cup thinly sliced green onion

2 tablespoons snipped fresh parsley

¼ teaspoon black pepper

Fresh parsley sprigs (optional)

1 In a medium saucepan bring water to boiling; add uncooked bulgur. Return to boiling; reduce heat. Cover and simmer about 15 minutes or until most of the liquid is absorbed. Transfer to a large bowl.

2 In a small bowl whisk together lemon juice and pesto. Add lemon juice mixture to cooked bulgur along with soybeans, cherry tomatoes, feta cheese, green onion, snipped parsley, and pepper. Toss gently to combine. If desired, garnish with parsley sprigs. Makes 6 servings.

Make-Ahead Directions: Prepare as above. Cover and chill for up to 4 hours.

Tabbouleh with Edamame and Feta

PREP: 25 minutes

COOK: 15 minutes

NUTRITION FACTS per serving:

CALORIES 313

TOTAL FAT 12 g total fat (1 g sat. fat)

CHOLESTEROL 3 mg

PROTEIN 18 g

CARBOHYDRATE 37 g

FIBER 10 g

SODIUM 187 mg

EXCHANGES 2 Starch, 1.5 Very Lean Meat, 0.5 Vegetable, 2 Fat

NUTRITION NOTE

Soybeans are great for health. Feel confident including more soybeans in your diet to provide protein, iron, calcium, and vitamin C. Add them to soups, salads, and pasta dishes.

Sesame-Orange Tofu

START TO FINISH: 30 minutes

NUTRITION FACTS per serving:

CALORIES 330
TOTAL FAT 12 g (2 g sat. fat)
CHOLESTEROL 1 mg
PROTEIN 16 g
CARBOHYDRATE 41 g
FIBER 6 g
SODIUM 854 mg

EXCHANGES 2.5 Starch, 1 Very Lean Meat, 1 Vegetable, 2 Fat

NUTRITION NOTE

Soy protein products such as tofu can be substituted for animal protein. Soy protein is a complete protein that has all essential amino acids and often contains less fat, especially saturated fat, than animal proteins.

¼ cup finely chopped peanuts
1 tablespoon sesame seeds
1 teaspoon grated fresh ginger or ½ teaspoon ground ginger
⅛ teaspoon crushed red pepper
1 12-ounce package firm or extra-firm tub-style tofu (fresh bean curd), drained and cut into ½-inch cubes
1 tablespoon olive oil
3 cups loose-pack frozen stir-fry vegetables (any combination), thawed
½ cup bottled stir-fry sauce
2 cups hot cooked brown rice
2 green onions, thinly sliced
1 medium orange, cut into 8 wedges

1 In a large bowl combine 1 tablespoon peanuts, sesame seeds, ginger, and crushed red pepper. Add tofu; gently toss to coat.

2 In a large skillet heat oil over medium heat. (If necessary, add more oil during cooking.) Add tofu mixture to skillet. Cook, stirring gently, until sesame seeds are toasted and tofu begins to brown.

3 Push tofu mixture to side of skillet. Add vegetables; cook and stir until heated through. Add stir-fry sauce; cook and stir gently until mixture is bubbly. Serve over hot cooked brown rice. Sprinkle individual servings with remaining 3 tablespoons peanuts and green onion. Serve with orange wedges. Makes 4 servings.

On the divider: Roasted Potatoes and Tomatoes (see recipe, page 366)

VEGETABLE SALADS

CLASSIC SALADS

GRAINS & BEANS

POTATOES

VEGETABLES

- 4 cups fresh baby spinach
- 1 medium green-skinned apple (such as Granny Smith), cored and sliced
- ¼ cup thin wedges red onion
- 2 tablespoons snipped dried tart red cherries
- ¼ cup Thyme-Dijon Vinaigrette
- ½ cup crumbled reduced-fat feta cheese or crumbled blue cheese (2 ounces) (optional)

1 In a large bowl toss together spinach, apple, red onion, and dried cherries. Drizzle with Thyme-Dijon Vinaigrette. Toss gently to coat. If desired, top individual servings with cheese. Makes 4 (about 1-cup) servings.

Thyme-Dijon Vinaigrette: In a screw-top jar combine ¼ cup olive oil; ¼ cup white balsamic vinegar or regular balsamic vinegar; 2 teaspoons snipped fresh thyme or ½ teaspoon dried thyme, crushed; 1 teaspoon Dijon-style mustard; and ¼ teaspoon salt. Cover; shake well to mix. Chill for up to 1 week. Shake before serving. Makes ⅔ cup.

Apple-Spinach Salad with Thyme-Dijon Vinaigrette

START TO FINISH: 25 minutes

NUTRITION FACTS per serving:

CALORIES 91
TOTAL FAT 5 g (1 g sat. fat)
CHOLESTEROL 0 mg
PROTEIN 1 g
CARBOHYDRATE 11 g
FIBER 2 g
SODIUM 91 mg

EXCHANGES 0.5 Fruit, 1 Vegetable, 1 Fat

3 cups torn mixed salad greens
1 cup fresh spinach
1 medium cucumber, seeded and chopped
1 cup cherry tomatoes, halved
¼ cup sliced pitted ripe olives
2 tablespoons dried cranberries
3 tablespoons olive oil
2 tablespoons lemon juice
2 tablespoons water
1¼ teaspoons Homemade Spice Mix
Cracked black pepper (optional)

Cranberry-Cucumber Salad

START TO FINISH: 25 minutes

NUTRITION FACTS per serving:

CALORIES 89
TOTAL FAT 8 g (1 g sat. fat)
CHOLESTEROL 0 mg
PROTEIN 1 g
CARBOHYDRATE 6 g
FIBER 1 g
SODIUM 85 mg

EXCHANGES 1 Vegetable, 1.5 Fat

1 In a large bowl combine mixed greens, spinach, cucumber, cherry tomatoes, olives, and dried cranberries. Set aside.

2 For dressing, in a small screw-top jar combine oil, lemon juice, water, and Homemade Spice Mix; shake well. Pour over greens mixture; toss to coat. If desired, sprinkle with black pepper. Makes 6 (about 1-cup) servings.

Homemade Spice Mix: In a small bowl combine ½ teaspoon paprika, ½ teaspoon ground coriander, ½ teaspoon ground cumin, ¼ teaspoon garlic powder, ¼ teaspoon ground turmeric, ⅛ teaspoon salt, and ⅛ teaspoon cayenne pepper. Store any leftover mix in an airtight container at room temperature for up to 6 months. Makes about 2¼ teaspoons.

- 8 cups mixed baby salad greens
- ½ cup bottled reduced-fat or fat-free balsamic vinaigrette salad dressing
- 4 small cooked beets or two 8¼-ounce cans whole beets, chilled
- 2 tablespoons snipped fresh basil or flat-leaf parsley
- ¼ teaspoon black pepper
- ¼ cup coarsely chopped walnuts, toasted
- 2 ounces semisoft goat cheese (chèvre), crumbled

1 In a bowl drizzle salad greens with ¼ cup salad dressing. Set aside.

2 If using canned beets, drain beets. Cut beets into bite-size pieces. In a medium bowl combine beets, basil or parsley, and pepper. Drizzle with remaining ¼ cup salad dressing; toss to coat. Toss beet mixture with salad greens. Transfer to a serving platter. Sprinkle with walnuts and goat cheese. Makes 4 servings.

Beet Salad with Goat Cheese and Walnuts

START TO FINISH: 15 minutes

NUTRITION FACTS per serving:

CALORIES 147
TOTAL FAT 10 g (3 g sat. fat)
CHOLESTEROL 7 mg
PROTEIN 6 g
CARBOHYDRATE 11 g
FIBER 3 g
SODIUM 571 mg

EXCHANGES 0.5 Medium-Fat Meat, 2.5 Vegetable, 1.5 Fat

NUTRITION NOTE

Read labels when buying bottled salad dressings. Even those low in calories and fat may have high amounts of sodium or sugar.

1 pound fresh asparagus

2 medium oranges, peeled and sliced crosswise

¼ cup orange juice

4 teaspoons olive oil

1 teaspoon Dijon-style mustard

¼ teaspoon salt

⅛ teaspoon black pepper

1 Snap off and discard woody bases from asparagus. If desired, scrape off scales. Cut stems into 2-inch-long pieces. In a covered medium saucepan cook asparagus in a small amount of boiling water for 1 minute; drain. Cool immediately in a bowl of ice water. Drain on paper towels. Cut orange slices into 2-section pieces.

2 For dressing, in a medium bowl whisk together orange juice, oil, mustard, salt, and pepper. Add asparagus and orange pieces; stir gently to coat. Makes 4 (about ¾-cup) servings.

Make-Ahead Directions: Prepare as above. Cover and chill for up to 6 hours.

Orange-Asparagus Salad

START TO FINISH: 25 minutes

NUTRITION FACTS per serving:
- -

CALORIES 74
TOTAL FAT 5 g (1 g sat. fat)
CHOLESTEROL 0 mg
PROTEIN 2 g
CARBOHYDRATE 8 g
FIBER 2 g
SODIUM 177 mg

EXCHANGES 1 Vegetable, 1 Fat

8   ears fresh corn on the cob

12   ounces fresh green beans, trimmed and cut into bite-size pieces

3   tablespoons cider vinegar

½   teaspoon salt

½   teaspoon black pepper

3   tablespoons olive oil

⅓   cup finely chopped red onion

2   tablespoons snipped fresh parsley

1 Husk and silk corn. In a covered 4-quart Dutch oven cook corn in enough lightly salted boiling water to cover for 5 to 7 minutes or until tender; drain. When cool enough to handle, cut kernels from cobs (to make about 4 cups corn kernels).

2 Meanwhile, in a covered medium saucepan cook beans in a small amount of lightly salted boiling water for 3 to 5 minutes or until crisp-tender. Drain; rinse under cold water. Drain again.

3 In a large bowl combine cider vinegar, salt, and pepper; whisk in oil. Add corn kernels, green beans, red onion, and parsley; toss to coat. Cover and chill for 2 to 4 hours. Makes 8 (about ¾-cup) servings.

Corn and Green Bean Salad

PREP: 25 minutes

CHILL: 2 to 4 hours

NUTRITION FACTS per serving:

CALORIES 139
TOTAL FAT 6 g (1 g sat. fat)
CHOLESTEROL 0 mg
PROTEIN 4 g
CARBOHYDRATE 21 g
FIBER 4 g
SODIUM 198 mg

EXCHANGES 1 Starch, 1 Vegetable, 1 Fat

2 cups chopped tomato

1 cup chopped cucumber

½ cup chopped yellow, red, and/or green sweet pepper

¼ cup chopped red onion

1½ teaspoons snipped fresh thyme or ½ teaspoon dried thyme, crushed

1 teaspoon snipped fresh oregano or ¼ teaspoon dried oregano, crushed

2 tablespoons white balsamic vinegar or regular balsamic vinegar

2 tablespoons olive oil

Leaf lettuce (optional)

½ cup crumbled reduced-fat feta cheese (2 ounces)

Greek Vegetable Salad

START TO FINISH: 30 minutes

NUTRITION FACTS per serving:

CALORIES 65
TOTAL FAT 5 g (1 g sat. fat)
CHOLESTEROL 3 mg
PROTEIN 2 g
CARBOHYDRATE 4 g
FIBER 1 g
SODIUM 120 mg

EXCHANGES 0.5 Vegetable, 1 Fat

1 In a large bowl combine tomato, cucumber, sweet pepper, red onion, thyme, and oregano. For dressing, in a small bowl whisk together balsamic vinegar and oil. Pour dressing over vegetable mixture. Toss gently to coat.

2 If desired, line a serving bowl with lettuce; spoon in vegetable mixture. Sprinkle with feta cheese. Makes 8 (½-cup) servings.

COOK'S TIP

To select firm cucumbers, look first at the ends, which are first to soften.

5   radishes, sliced
1   large tomato, chopped
⅓   cup sliced green onion
½   of a 15-ounce can garbanzo beans
    (chickpeas), rinsed and drained
1   tablespoon olive oil
2   teaspoons white wine vinegar
½   teaspoon Homemade Spice Mix
4   cups torn mixed salad greens
    Cracked black pepper (optional)

1 In a large bowl combine radishes, tomato, and green onion. Stir in garbanzo beans.

2 For dressing, in a small bowl whisk together oil, vinegar, and Homemade Spice Mix. Pour dressing over bean mixture; toss gently to coat. Cover and chill for 1 to 24 hours.

3 To serve, toss salad greens with bean mixture. If desired, sprinkle with black pepper. Makes 4 (about 1½-cup) servings.

Homemade Spice Mix: In a small bowl combine ½ teaspoon paprika, ½ teaspoon ground coriander, ½ teaspoon ground cumin, ¼ teaspoon garlic powder, ¼ teaspoon ground turmeric, ⅛ teaspoon salt, and ⅛ teaspoon cayenne pepper. Store any leftover mix in an airtight container at room temperature for up to 6 months. Makes about 2¼ teaspoons.

Radish and Tomato Salad

PREP: 25 minutes

CHILL: 1 to 24 hours

NUTRITION FACTS per serving:

CALORIES 111
TOTAL FAT 4 g (1 g sat. fat)
CHOLESTEROL 0 mg
PROTEIN 4 g
CARBOHYDRATE 15 g
FIBER 4 g
SODIUM 187 mg

EXCHANGES 0.5 Starch, 1.5 Vegetable, 0.5 Fat

2 medium red and/or yellow tomatoes or 4 plum tomatoes, cut into wedges

1 medium green sweet pepper, seeded and chopped

1 small zucchini or yellow summer squash, thinly sliced (about 1 cup)

½ of a small red onion, thinly sliced

2 tablespoons snipped fresh parsley

2 tablespoons olive oil

2 tablespoons balsamic vinegar or wine vinegar

2 tablespoons water

1 tablespoon snipped fresh thyme or basil or 1 teaspoon dried thyme or basil, crushed

1 clove garlic, minced

Toasted pine nuts (optional)

Marinated Vegetable Salad

PREP: 25 minutes

STAND: 30 to 60 minutes

NUTRITION FACTS per serving:

CALORIES 64
TOTAL FAT 5 g (1 g sat. fat)
CHOLESTEROL 0 mg
PROTEIN 1 g
CARBOHYDRATE 5 g
FIBER 1 g
SODIUM 7 mg

EXCHANGES 1 Vegetable, 1 Fat

1 In a medium bowl combine tomato wedges, sweet pepper, zucchini, red onion, and parsley; set aside.

2 For dressing, in a screw-top jar combine oil, vinegar, water, thyme, and garlic. Cover; shake well. Pour over vegetable mixture. Toss lightly to coat.

3 Let salad stand at room temperature for 30 to 60 minutes, stirring occasionally. If desired, garnish with pine nuts. Serve with a slotted spoon. Makes 6 (⅔-cup) servings.

Make-Ahead Directions: Prepare as above through step 2. Cover and chill for 4 to 24 hours, stirring once or twice. Let stand at room temperature about 30 minutes before serving. If desired, garnish with pine nuts. Serve with a slotted spoon.

COOK'S TIP

To peel garlic cloves easily, set a clove on a cutting board. Holding a knife with a broad blade (such as a chef's knife) horizontally above the clove, press down firmly or gently strike with the knife to separate the clove from its skin. When using several cloves, strike the cloves with the bottom of a skillet.

3 large yellow sweet peppers, seeded and thinly sliced into rings (about 3 cups)

4 cups fresh watercress or baby spinach

3 or 4 medium tomatoes (about 1 pound), cut into wedges

1 recipe Herb-Dijon Vinaigrette

¼ cup crumbled Gorgonzola or blue cheese (1 ounce)

1 In a covered Dutch oven cook sweet pepper rings in a large amount of boiling water for 1 to 2 minutes or just until crisp-tender. Drain and rinse with cold water to cool. Drain well.

2 Arrange watercress on a platter. Top with sweet pepper rings and tomato wedges. Shake dressing; drizzle over salad. Sprinkle with cheese. Makes 8 servings.

Herb-Dijon Vinaigrette: In a screw-top jar combine 2 tablespoons olive oil, 2 tablespoons white wine vinegar or balsamic vinegar, 1 tablespoon snipped fresh chives, 2 teaspoons snipped fresh basil, ½ teaspoon sugar, ½ teaspoon Dijon-style mustard, and ⅛ teaspoon black pepper. Cover and shake well to combine; use immediately or cover and chill for up to 3 days. Shake before serving. Makes ¼ cup.

Tomato and Sweet Pepper Salad

START TO FINISH: 25 minutes

NUTRITION FACTS per serving:

- - - - - - - - - - - - - - - - - - -

CALORIES 85
TOTAL FAT 5 g (1 g sat. fat)
CHOLESTEROL 3 mg
PROTEIN 3 g
CARBOHYDRATE 9 g
FIBER 2 g
SODIUM 78 mg

EXCHANGES 1.5 Vegetable, 1 Fat

1 pound tiny new potatoes
½ cup light mayonnaise or
  salad dressing
1 stalk celery, chopped
⅓ cup chopped red onion
2 tablespoons chopped sweet
  pickles or dill pickles
¼ teaspoon salt
⅛ teaspoon coarsely ground
  black pepper
1 hard-cooked egg, chopped
2 to 3 teaspoons fat-free milk
  Coarsely ground black pepper

New Potato Salad

PREP: 40 minutes

CHILL: 6 to 24 hours

NUTRITION FACTS per serving:

CALORIES 111
TOTAL FAT 6 g (1 g sat. fat)
CHOLESTEROL 32 mg
PROTEIN 2 g
CARBOHYDRATE 13 g
FIBER 1 g
SODIUM 233 mg

EXCHANGES 1 Starch, 1 Fat

1 In a large saucepan combine potatoes and enough water to cover potatoes. Bring to boiling; reduce heat. Cover and simmer for 15 to 20 minutes or just until tender. Drain well; cool potatoes. Cut potatoes into quarters.

2 In a large bowl combine mayonnaise, celery, red onion, pickles, salt, and ⅛ teaspoon pepper. Add potatoes and egg, gently tossing to coat. Cover and chill for 6 to 24 hours.

3 To serve, stir enough milk into salad to reach desired consistency. Season to taste with additional pepper. Makes 8 (about ½-cup) servings.

1½ pounds round red potatoes, cut into ½-inch cubes

1 cup fresh green beans cut into 2-inch-long pieces

2 cups broccoli and/or cauliflower florets

½ cup coarsely shredded carrot

½ cup bottled reduced-calorie ranch salad dressing

¼ teaspoon black pepper

1 to 2 tablespoons fat-free milk (optional)

1 Place cubed potatoes in a large saucepan; add enough lightly salted water to cover. Bring to boiling; reduce heat. Cover and simmer for 5 to 7 minutes or just until tender. Drain well; cool.

2 In a small saucepan bring a small amount of lightly salted water to boiling. Add green beans; return to boiling. Cover and cook about 3 minutes or until crisp-tender. Drain; rinse with cold water.

3 In a very large bowl combine cooked potatoes, green beans, broccoli and/or cauliflower, and carrot. Add salad dressing and pepper; toss to coat. Cover and chill for 4 to 24 hours. If necessary, stir in enough milk to reach desired consistency. Makes 8 (1-cup) servings.

Confetti Potato Salad

PREP: 30 minutes

CHILL: 4 to 24 hours

NUTRITION FACTS per serving:

CALORIES 108
TOTAL FAT 3 g (0 g sat. fat)
CHOLESTEROL 5 mg
PROTEIN 3 g
CARBOHYDRATE 18 g
FIBER 3 g
SODIUM 179 mg

EXCHANGES 1 Starch, 0.5 Vegetable, 0.5 Fat

NUTRITION NOTE

Ranch salad dressings without reduced fat contain as much as 20 grams of fat in just two tablespoons! Always opt for reduced-fat ranch with about 7 grams of fat in two tablespoons. Enjoy the rich creaminess of the dressing with less than half the fat.

- ¼ cup cider vinegar or rice vinegar
- 2 tablespoons canola oil
- 1 teaspoon sugar
- ½ teaspoon dry mustard
- ¼ teaspoon onion powder
- ⅛ teaspoon salt
- ⅛ teaspoon white pepper or black pepper
- 2½ cups packaged shredded broccoli (broccoli slaw mix)
- 2 tablespoons crumbled blue cheese

1 For dressing, in a screw-top jar combine vinegar, oil, sugar, dry mustard, onion powder, salt, and pepper. Cover and shake well. Chill until serving time.

2 To serve, in a large bowl combine broccoli and blue cheese. Shake dressing; drizzle over cabbage mixture, gently tossing to coat. Makes 4 (about ½-cup) servings.

Make-Ahead Hints: The dressing may be chilled for up to 1 week. The dressed salad may be covered and chilled for up to 24 hours before serving.

Blue Cheese Coleslaw

START TO FINISH: 15 minutes

NUTRITION FACTS per serving:

CALORIES 100
TOTAL FAT 8 g (1 g sat. fat)
CHOLESTEROL 3 mg
PROTEIN 2 g
CARBOHYDRATE 5 g
FIBER 1 g
SODIUM 148 mg

EXCHANGES 0.5 Vegetable, 1.5 Fat

- 4 ounces dried whole wheat rotini, penne, or bow tie pasta (about 1½ cups)
- 1 cup fresh sugar snap peas (4 ounces), trimmed
- ½ cup chopped red sweet pepper
- ¼ cup shredded fresh basil*
- 2 tablespoons pitted kalamata or niçoise olives, quartered
- 2 tablespoons red wine vinegar
- 2 tablespoons olive oil
- 1 clove garlic, minced
- ⅛ teaspoon salt

  Dash black pepper

1 Cook pasta according to package directions, adding sugar snap peas for the last 1 minute of cooking. Drain well. Rinse with cold water; drain again. In a large bowl combine pasta mixture, sweet pepper, basil, and olives. Set aside.

2 For dressing, in a screw-top jar combine red wine vinegar, oil, garlic, salt, and black pepper. Cover and shake well. Pour dressing over pasta and vegetables; toss gently to coat. Makes 6 (½-cup) servings.

*To shred (chiffonade) fresh basil, stack several leaves and roll up the leaves. Starting at one end, use a sharp knife to cut crosswise into thin slices.

Italian Pasta Salad

START TO FINISH: 25 minutes

NUTRITION FACTS per serving:

CALORIES 123
TOTAL FAT 5 g (1 g sat. fat)
CHOLESTEROL 0 mg
PROTEIN 3 g
CARBOHYDRATE 16 g
FIBER 2 g
SODIUM 81 mg

EXCHANGES 1 Starch, 1 Fat

2½ cups water
¼ teaspoon salt
½ cup brown rice
½ cup wild rice, rinsed and drained
1 medium apple, cored and coarsely chopped
¼ cup orange juice or apple juice
1 tablespoon cider vinegar
¾ cup seedless red grapes, halved
2 tablespoons snipped fresh cilantro or parsley
1 tablespoon olive oil
⅛ teaspoon black pepper
2 tablespoons chopped pecans, toasted (optional)

Apple-Wild Rice Salad

PREP: 20 minutes   **COOK:** 40 minutes
STAND: 5 minutes   **CHILL:** 2 to 12 hours

NUTRITION FACTS per serving:

CALORIES 116
TOTAL FAT 2 g (0 g sat. fat)
CHOLESTEROL 0 mg
PROTEIN 3 g
CARBOHYDRATE 22 g
FIBER 2 g
SODIUM 78 mg

EXCHANGES 1 Starch, 0.5 Fruit

1 In a large saucepan combine water and salt; bring to boiling. Add uncooked brown rice and wild rice. Return to boiling; reduce heat. Cover and simmer for 40 to 45 minutes or until rice is tender and most of the liquid is absorbed. Remove from heat; let stand, covered, for 5 minutes. Drain if necessary.

2 Meanwhile, in a large bowl toss chopped apple with orange juice and vinegar. Add grapes, cilantro, oil, and pepper. Stir in cooked rice. Cover and chill for 2 to 12 hours.

3 If desired, stir in pecans before serving. Makes 8 (about ¾-cup) servings.

Nonstick cooking spray

- 2 tablespoons finely chopped shallot
- 2½ cups reduced-sodium chicken broth
- 1 cup bulgur
- 1 cup chopped, seeded cucumber
- ¼ cup dried cranberries
- ¼ cup snipped fresh cilantro
- ½ teaspoon finely shredded lime peel
- 2 tablespoons lime juice
- ⅛ teaspoon black pepper

1 Coat an unheated large nonstick saucepan with nonstick cooking spray. Preheat saucepan over medium heat. Add shallot to hot saucepan; cook and stir about 3 minutes or just until tender. Add chicken broth; bring to boiling. Stir in uncooked bulgur. Return to boiling; reduce heat. Cover and simmer about 15 minutes or until tender. Remove from heat; cool slightly. Transfer cooked bulgur to a large bowl. Cover and chill about 3 hours or until completely cool.

2 Add cucumber, dried cranberries, cilantro, lime peel, lime juice, and pepper to cooled bulgur; mix well. Makes 6 (¾-cup) servings.

Make-Ahead Directions: Prepare as above. Cover and chill for up to 24 hours.

COOK'S TIP

No zester for the lime peel? No problem. Use an ordinary vegetable peeler to remove the outermost skin of the lime (leaving behind the white part). Finely chop the peel.

Cilantro Tabbouleh with Cranberries

PREP: 25 minutes   **CHILL:** 3 hours
COOK: 15 minutes

NUTRITION FACTS per serving:

CALORIES 109
TOTAL FAT 0 g (0 g sat. fat)
CHOLESTEROL 0 mg
PROTEIN 4 g
CARBOHYDRATE 24 g
FIBER 5 g
SODIUM 293 mg

EXCHANGES 1 Starch, 0.5 Other Carbohydrates

2 cups water
½ cup wild rice, rinsed and drained
¼ cup barley
1 cup fresh pea pods, cut into thirds
⅓ cup golden raisins
3 green onions, sliced
1 teaspoon finely shredded orange peel
⅓ cup orange juice
1 tablespoon olive oil
¼ teaspoon salt
⅛ teaspoon black pepper
2 tablespoons snipped fresh mint
Shredded orange peel (optional)

Minted Wild Rice and Barley Salad

PREP: 30 minutes   **CHILL:** 4 to 6 hours
COOK: 40 minutes

NUTRITION FACTS per serving:

CALORIES 136
TOTAL FAT 3 g (0 g sat. fat)
CHOLESTEROL 0 mg
PROTEIN 4 g
CARBOHYDRATE 26 g
FIBER 3 g
SODIUM 103 mg

EXCHANGES 1 Starch, 0.5 Fruit, 0.5 Fat

1 In a medium saucepan bring water to boiling; stir in uncooked wild rice and barley. Return to boiling; reduce heat. Cover and simmer about 40 minutes or until wild rice and barley are tender. Drain off liquid. Transfer wild rice and barley to a large bowl.

2 Stir in pea pods, golden raisins, green onion, orange peel, orange juice, oil, salt, and pepper. Cover and chill for 4 to 6 hours.

3 Stir in mint. If desired, garnish with additional orange peel. Makes 6 (about ⅔-cup) servings.

1 tablespoon olive oil

1 cup quartered fresh mushrooms

1½ cups water

¾ cup quinoa*

1 cup canned red beans, rinsed and drained

1 cup chopped zucchini

1 cup cherry tomatoes, halved if desired

1 tablespoon snipped fresh basil or 1 teaspoon dried basil, crushed

1 tablespoon red wine vinegar

6 cloves garlic, minced

¼ teaspoon salt

¼ teaspoon black pepper

Snipped fresh basil (optional)

1 In a very large skillet heat olive oil over medium heat. Add mushrooms; cook about 5 minutes or until golden brown, stirring occasionally. Add water; bring to boiling. Add quinoa. Return to boiling; reduce heat. Cover and simmer about 15 minutes or until liquid is nearly absorbed.

2 Stir beans, zucchini, cherry tomatoes, the 1 tablespoon snipped basil, the vinegar, garlic, salt, and pepper into quinoa mixture. Heat through. Remove from heat; let stand, covered, for 5 minutes before serving. If desired, sprinkle with additional snipped basil. Makes 6 (1-cup) servings.

*Look for quinoa at a health food store or in the grains section of a large supermarket.

Hearty Grain Medley

PREP: 20 minutes   **COOK:** 15 minutes
STAND: 5 minutes

NUTRITION FACTS per serving:

CALORIES 149
TOTAL FAT 4 (0 g sat. fat)
CHOLESTEROL 0 mg
PROTEIN 6 g
CARBOHYDRATE 24 g
FIBER 4 g
SODIUM 264 mg

EXCHANGES 1.5 Starch, 0.5 Vegetable, 0.5 Fat

NUTRITION NOTE

Quinoa is not only high in protein, but it is also a complete protein, which means that it includes all the essential amino acids.

Rice Primavera with Basil

PREP: 25 minutes

COOK: 40 minutes

NUTRITION FACTS per serving:

CALORIES 148
TOTAL FAT 5 g (1 g sat. fat)
CHOLESTEROL 0 mg
PROTEIN 5 g
CARBOHYDRATE 23 g
FIBER 2 g
SODIUM 162 mg

EXCHANGES 1.5 Starch, 0.5 Vegetable, 0.5 Fat

1	14-ounce can reduced-sodium chicken broth
¾	cup regular brown rice
1	tablespoon olive oil
3	cups assorted fresh vegetables (such as sugar snap peas; asparagus, cut into 1-inch-long pieces; red, green, or yellow sweet pepper, cut into 1-inch pieces; and/or cherry tomatoes, quartered)
¼	cup finely chopped red onion
⅓	cup cold water
½	teaspoon cornstarch
1	teaspoon finely shredded lemon peel
¼	teaspoon black pepper
¼	cup small fresh basil leaves
2	tablespoons pine nuts, toasted

1 In a large saucepan combine chicken broth and brown rice. Bring to boiling; reduce heat. Cover and simmer for 40 to 45 minutes or until most of the liquid is absorbed and brown rice is tender.

2 Meanwhile, in a large skillet heat oil over medium heat. Add assorted vegetables (except cherry tomatoes, if using) and red onion; cook for 3 to 4 minutes or until vegetables are crisp-tender, stirring occasionally. In a small bowl combine cold water and cornstarch; stir until smooth. Add to vegetables in skillet along with lemon peel and black pepper. Cook and stir until thickened and bubbly. Cook and stir for 2 minutes more (reduce heat to medium-low, if necessary). Stir in basil and cherry tomatoes (if using).

3 Add vegetable mixture to cooked brown rice. Toss to combine. Serve immediately. Top individual servings with pine nuts. Makes 6 (about ⅔-cup) servings.

COOK'S TIP

Pine nuts, which are harvested by hand, are expensive. Fortunately recipes call for only a few at a time. To prolong their shelf life after opening, store them in the refrigerator for up to one month or in the freezer for up to 3 months.

1   cup chicken broth
⅛   teaspoon black pepper
⅔   cup whole wheat couscous
2   green onions, chopped
1   teaspoon finely shredded
      orange peel
1   medium orange, peeled,
      sectioned, and coarsely
      chopped

1 In a medium saucepan combine chicken
broth and pepper; bring to boiling. Stir in
couscous and green onion; remove from heat.
Cover and let stand for 5 minutes. Fluff couscous
with a fork; gently stir in orange peel and
chopped orange. Serve immediately. Makes
4 (about ⅔-cup) servings.

Couscous with Orange

PREP: 15 minutes
STAND: 5 minutes

NUTRITION FACTS per serving:

CALORIES 162
TOTAL FAT 1 g (0 g sat. fat)
CHOLESTEROL 1 mg
PROTEIN 6 g
CARBOHYDRATE 35 g
FIBER 6 g
SODIUM 241 mg

EXCHANGES 2 Starch

½   cup chopped onion

¼   cup shredded carrot

2   tablespoons snipped dried
     tomatoes (not oil pack)

½   teaspoon dried thyme, crushed

⅛   teaspoon black pepper

1   tablespoon olive oil

1   cup coarsely chopped fresh
     cremini, stemmed shiitake,
     and/or button mushrooms

⅔   cup quick-cooking barley

1   14-ounce can reduced-sodium
     chicken broth

⅓   cup water

2   tablespoons shredded
     Parmesan cheese

Thyme-Barley Risotto

START TO FINISH: 35 minutes

NUTRITION FACTS per serving:

CALORIES 169
TOTAL FAT 4 g (1 g sat. fat)
CHOLESTEROL 2 mg
PROTEIN 6 g
CARBOHYDRATE 28 g
FIBER 4 g
SODIUM 317 mg

EXCHANGES 1.5 Starch, 0.5 Vegetable, 0.5 Fat

NUTRITION NOTE

Mushrooms are 80 to 90 percent water, have little sodium and fat, and 8 to 10 percent of their dry weight is pure fiber, making them an ideal health food.

1 In a large saucepan cook onion, carrot, dried tomatoes, thyme, and pepper in hot oil about 5 minutes or just until vegetables are tender, stirring occasionally. Stir in mushrooms and uncooked barley.

2 Meanwhile, in a small saucepan bring chicken broth and water to boiling. Reduce heat to low; cover to keep warm. Add 1 cup broth mixture to barley mixture, stirring constantly. Continue to cook and stir over medium heat until liquid is absorbed. Add remaining broth mixture, about ½ cup at a time, cooking and stirring constantly until liquid is absorbed before adding more liquid. Cook until barley is tender. (This should take 10 to 15 minutes total.)

3 Sprinkle with Parmesan cheese. Makes 4 (⅔-cup) servings.

1 tablespoon canola oil

2 small yellow summer squash, thinly sliced (about 2 cups)

1 to 2 fresh jalapeño chile peppers, seeded (if desired) and chopped*

2 cloves garlic, minced

½ teaspoon cumin seeds, crushed

1 15-ounce can black-eyed peas, rinsed and drained

2 tablespoons sliced green onion

1 tablespoon snipped fresh cilantro or parsley

⅛ teaspoon salt

2 medium tomatoes, cut into thin wedges

1 In a large skillet heat oil over medium heat. Add squash, chile peppe, garlic, and cumin seeds; cook for 5 to 6 minutes or until squash is crisp-tender, stirring occasionally. Remove from heat; cool.

2 In a large bowl combine squash mixture, black-eyed peas, green onion, cilantro, and salt. Cover and chill for 4 to 24 hours.

3 To serve, gently toss black-eyed pea mixture with tomato wedges. Makes 4 (about 1-cup) servings.

*Because chile peppers contain volatile oils that can burn your skin and eyes, avoid direct contact with them as much as possible. When working with chile peppers, wear plastic or rubber gloves. If your bare hands do touch the peppers, wash your hands and nails well with soap and warm water.

Southern Black-Eyed Pea Salad

PREP: 20 minutes
CHILL: 4 to 24 hours

NUTRITION FACTS per serving:

CALORIES 158
TOTAL FAT 5 g (0 g sat. fat)
CHOLESTEROL 0 mg
PROTEIN 7 g
CARBOHYDRATE 23 g
FIBER 7 g
SODIUM 375 mg
EXCHANGES 1 Starch, 1 Vegetable, 1 Fat

NUTRITION NOTE

One cup of cooked black-eyed peas provides more than 20 percent of your daily recommended calcium, folate, and vitamin A.

Roasted Potatoes and Tomatoes

PREP: 15 minutes   **BAKE:** 25 minutes
OVEN: 450°F

NUTRITION FACTS per serving:

CALORIES 102
TOTAL FAT 5 g (1 g sat. fat)
CHOLESTEROL 2 mg
PROTEIN 3 g
CARBOHYDRATE 11 g
FIBER 2 g
SODIUM 208 mg

EXCHANGES 1 Starch, 1 Fat

1 pound tiny new potatoes (10 to 12), scrubbed and quartered
2 tablespoons olive oil
2 teaspoons snipped fresh oregano or ½ teaspoon dried oregano, crushed
¼ teaspoon salt
¼ teaspoon black pepper
4 plum tomatoes, quartered lengthwise
½ cup pitted kalamata olives
3 cloves garlic, minced
¼ cup grated Parmesan cheese

1 Preheat oven to 450°F. Lightly grease a 15×10×1-inch baking pan; place potatoes in pan. In a small bowl combine oil, oregano, salt, and pepper; drizzle over potatoes, tossing to coat.

2 Bake for 20 minutes, stirring once. Add tomatoes, olives, and garlic; toss to combine. Bake for 5 to 10 minutes more or until potatoes are tender and brown on the edges and tomatoes are soft. Transfer to a serving dish. Sprinkle with Parmesan cheese. Makes 8 (½-cup) servings.

1 pound round red, Yukon gold, or round white potatoes, scrubbed and quartered

1 teaspoon bottled minced roasted garlic

¼ cup light dairy sour cream

2 to 4 tablespoons fat-free milk

1 teaspoon snipped fresh thyme or ½ teaspoon dried thyme, crushed

¼ teaspoon salt

⅛ teaspoon black pepper

Snipped fresh thyme (optional)

1 In a covered large saucepan cook potatoes in enough boiling water to cover for 20 to 25 minutes or until tender. Drain well and return to saucepan.

2 Add garlic to potatoes. Mash with a potato masher or an electric mixer on low speed. Add sour cream, 2 tablespoons milk, snipped thyme, salt, and pepper. Beat until light and fluffy, adding remaining 2 tablespoons milk if necessary. If desired, sprinkle with additional snipped thyme. Makes 4 (about ⅔-cup) servings.

COOK'S TIP

If you prefer roasting the garlic yourself, it's supereasy. Scatter unpeeled garlic cloves on a baking sheet, drizzle with olive oil, and bake at 375°F for 30 minutes. Squeeze the garlic out of the skins to use it for any roasted garlic called for in recipes.

Roasted Garlic Mashed Potatoes

PREP: 15 minutes

COOK: 20 minutes

NUTRITION FACTS per serving:

CALORIES 106

TOTAL FAT 1 g (1 g sat. fat)

CHOLESTEROL 5 mg

PROTEIN 4 g

CARBOHYDRATE 19 g

FIBER 2 g

SODIUM 162 mg

EXCHANGES 1.5 Starch

3 cups fresh green beans (about 10 ounces), trimmed if desired
¼ cup sliced almonds, toasted
1 tablespoon olive oil
½ teaspoon Homemade Spice Mix

1 In a covered large saucepan cook beans in a small amount of boiling water for 8 to 10 minutes or until crisp-tender. Drain well. Return to hot pan. Stir in almonds, oil, and Homemade Spice Mix. Heat through. Makes 6 (about ½-cup) servings.

Homemade Spice Mix: In a small bowl combine ½ teaspoon paprika, ½ teaspoon ground coriander, ½ teaspoon ground cumin, ¼ teaspoon garlic powder, ¼ teaspoon ground turmeric, ⅛ teaspoon salt, and ⅛ teaspoon cayenne pepper. Store any leftover mix in an airtight container at room temperature for up to 6 months. Makes about 2¼ teaspoons.

Green Beans with Toasted Almonds

START TO FINISH: 20 minutes

NUTRITION FACTS per serving:
- -

CALORIES 59
TOTAL FAT 4 g (0 g sat. fat)
CHOLESTEROL 0 mg
PROTEIN 2 g
CARBOHYDRATE 5 g
FIBER 2 g
SODIUM 14 mg

EXCHANGES 1 Vegetable, 0.5 Fat

1½ pounds broccoli rabe or 3½ cups broccoli florets

1 tablespoon olive oil

3 cloves garlic, minced

2 tablespoons reduced-sodium chicken broth

¼ teaspoon black pepper

⅛ teaspoon salt

1 If using broccoli rabe, remove large leaves and, if necessary, cut stems to 6- to 8-inch-long pieces. In a 4-quart Dutch oven cook broccoli rabe or broccoli, half at a time if necessary, in a large amount of boiling water for 3 minutes if using broccoli rabe or 6 minutes if using broccoli florets. Drain well; gently squeeze vegetable if necessary to get it really dry.

2 In the same Dutch oven heat oil over medium heat. Add garlic; cook and stir for 30 seconds. Carefully add drained broccoli rabe or broccoli florets (oil will spatter if the vegetable is not drained well); cook and stir for 1 minute. Add chicken broth. Cook, uncovered, until all of the broth has evaporated, stirring frequently. Stir in pepper and salt. Serve immediately. Makes 6 (½-cup) servings.

COOK'S TIP

Americans rarely eat the greens of broccoli rabe because of their bitter taste, yet they are packed with the same nutrients in cabbage and turnips. Italian cuisine often combines garlic with broccoli rabe, cutting the bitterness with garlic's mellow taste.

Broccoli Rabe with Garlic

START TO FINISH: 20 minutes

NUTRITION FACTS per serving:

CALORIES 48
TOTAL FAT 3 g (0 g sat. fat)
CHOLESTEROL 0 mg
PROTEIN 4 g
CARBOHYDRATE 4 g
FIBER 3 g
SODIUM 98 mg

EXCHANGES 1 Vegetable, 0.5 Fat

4 medium yellow summer squash or zucchini

½ of an 8-ounce package reduced-fat cream cheese (Neufchâtel), softened

½ cup shredded carrot

⅓ cup crumbled blue cheese

⅓ cup thinly sliced green onion

⅓ cup fine dry bread crumbs

¼ cup fat-free or light dairy sour cream

⅛ teaspoon black pepper

2 tablespoons chopped walnuts

Snipped fresh parsley (optional)

Blue Cheese-Stuffed Summer Squash

PREP: 25 minutes   **BAKE:** 20 minutes
OVEN: 400°F

NUTRITION FACTS per serving:

CALORIES 107
TOTAL FAT 6 g (3 g sat. fat)
CHOLESTEROL 15 mg
PROTEIN 5 g
CARBOHYDRATE 8 g
FIBER 1 g
SODIUM 179 mg

EXCHANGES 0.5 Medium-Fat Meat, 1 Vegetable, 1 Fat

1 Preheat oven to 400°F. Grease a 3-quart rectangular baking dish; set aside.

2 Halve the squash lengthwise. Remove seeds from each squash half with a spoon, leaving a shell about ¼ inch thick. Place squash halves, cut sides down, in prepared baking dish. Bake, uncovered, for 10 minutes. Turn squash halves cut sides up.

3 Meanwhile, in a medium bowl stir together cream cheese, shredded carrot, blue cheese, green onion, ¼ cup bread crumbs, sour cream, and pepper. (Mixture will be stiff.)

4 Spoon cream cheese mixture evenly into squash halves. Sprinkle with walnuts and remaining bread crumbs. Bake, uncovered, about 10 minutes or until squash is tender and filling is heated through. If desired, sprinkle with parsley. Makes 8 servings.

COOK'S TIP

Summer squash is perishable and should be refrigerated tightly covered in a bag for no more than 4 days.

Chapter 13

Snacks

On the divider: Guacamole-Stuffed Tomatoes *(see recipe, page 384)*

2 tablespoons tub-style light cream cheese spread with garden vegetables

2 tablespoons light mayonnaise or salad dressing

1 teaspoon apple cider vinegar

¼ teaspoon black pepper

1 9-ounce package refrigerated cooked chicken breast strips, cut into bite-size pieces

½ cup chopped celery

¼ cup dried cranberries

3 medium apples, cored and thinly sliced

1 For chicken salad, in a medium bowl combine cream cheese, mayonnaise, vinegar, and pepper. Stir in chicken breast, celery, and dried cranberries. Serve with apple slices. Makes 6 servings.

Make-Ahead Directions: Prepare as above in step 1. Cover and chill for up to 24 hours. Serve as above.

Chicken Salad with Apple Slices

START TO FINISH: 15 minutes

NUTRITION FACTS per serving:

- -

CALORIES 125
TOTAL FAT 3 g (1 g sat. fat)
CHOLESTEROL 27 mg
PROTEIN 12
CARBOHYDRATE 15 g
FIBER 2 g
SODIUM 201 mg

EXCHANGES 1 Fruit, 1.5 Very Lean Meat, 0.5 Fat

Inside-Out Tuna Salad Snack

START TO FINISH: 15 minutes

NUTRITION FACTS per serving:

CALORIES 76
TOTAL FAT 3 g (1 g sat. fat)
CHOLESTEROL 12 mg
PROTEIN 6 g
CARBOHYDRATE 6 g
FIBER 1 g
SODIUM 237 mg

EXCHANGES 0.5 Very Lean Meat, 0.5 Vegetable, 0.5 Fat

1	3-ounce can chunk white tuna (waterpack), drained and broken into chunks
½	cup seedless red grapes, halved
¼	cup finely chopped red onion
2	tablespoons light mayonnaise or salad dressing
2	cloves garlic, minced
¼	teaspoon black pepper
⅛	teaspoon salt
3	large celery stalks, ends trimmed

1 In a medium bowl combine tuna, grapes, red onion, mayonnaise, garlic, pepper, and salt.

2 To serve, cut each celery stalk crosswise into four pieces. Serve tuna mixture with celery pieces. Makes 4 (3-piece) servings.

Make-Ahead Directions: Prepare as above in step 1. Cover and chill for up to 24 hours. Serve as above.

COOK'S TIP
For the equivalent of two cloves of fresh garlic minced, use a teaspoon of prepared minced garlic.

4 slices reduced-sodium bacon

¼ cup light dairy sour cream

2 tablespoons light mayonnaise or salad dressing

1½ teaspoons white vinegar

1 teaspoon sugar

⅛ teaspoon salt

⅛ teaspoon black pepper

1 medium tomato, seeded and chopped

8 leaves butterhead (Boston or Bibb) lettuce (about 1 small head)

1 Line a microwave-safe plate with a microwave-safe paper towel. Arrange bacon on the paper towel. Cover bacon with another microwave-safe paper towel. Microwave on 100% power (high) for 3 to 4 minutes or until bacon is crisp. Cool bacon; crumble and set aside.

2 In a small bowl combine sour cream, mayonnaise, vinegar, sugar, salt, and pepper. Gently stir in tomato and crumbled bacon.

3 To serve, spoon a scant 2 tablespoons bacon mixture on each lettuce leaf; roll up. Makes 4 (2-wrap) servings.

Make-Ahead Directions: Prepare as above through step 2. Cover and chill for up to 6 hours. Serve as above.

Bacon-Tomato Lettuce Wraps

START TO FINISH: 15 minutes

NUTRITION FACTS per serving:

CALORIES 88
TOTAL FAT 7 g (2 g sat. fat)
CHOLESTEROL 12 mg
PROTEIN 4 g
CARBOHYDRATE 4 g
FIBER 1 g
SODIUM 228 mg

EXCHANGES 1 Vegetable, 1.5 Fat

4 medium tomatoes
   (about 6 ounces each)
1 ripe avocado, halved, seeded,
   peeled, and chopped
1 tablespoon finely chopped onion
2 teaspoons snipped fresh cilantro
2 teaspoons lemon juice
1 clove garlic, minced
⅛ teaspoon salt
   Fresh cilantro leaves (optional)
2 ounces multigrain tortilla chips

Guacamole-
Stuffed Tomatoes

START TO FINISH: 20 minutes

NUTRITION FACTS per serving:

- -

CALORIES 164
TOTAL FAT 10 g (1 g sat. fat)
CHOLESTEROL 0 mg
PROTEIN 7 g
CARBOHYDRATE 19 g
FIBER 5 g
SODIUM 152 mg

EXCHANGES 1 Starch, 1 Vegetable, 2 Fat

1 Cut a ¼-inch-thick slice from the stem end of each tomato. Using a spoon, carefully scoop out the tomato pulp, leaving a ¼- to ½-inch-thick shell. Discard seeds. Set tomatoes, cut sides down, on paper towels until ready to stuff. Chop enough tomato pulp to measure ⅓ cup; discard remaining pulp.

2 In a medium bowl mash avocado slightly; stir in chopped tomato pulp, onion, snipped cilantro, lemon juice, garlic, and salt. Stuff avocado mixture evenly into tomato shells. If desired, garnish with fresh cilantro leaves. Serve with tortilla chips. Makes 4 servings.

COOK'S TIP

To get juice flowing from a lemon, press on the fruit and roll it a few times on a hard surface. Getting the juice you need should be simple. If the lemon is still stubborn, warm it in the microwave for 15 seconds.

- 2 cloves garlic
- 2 tablespoons fresh parsley leaves
- 4 teaspoons fresh oregano leaves or ½ teaspoon dried oregano, crushed
- 1 15-ounce can garbanzo beans (chickpeas) or cannellini beans (white kidney beans), rinsed and drained
- 2 tablespoons light dairy sour cream
- 1 tablespoon lemon juice
- ¼ teaspoon ground black pepper
- ¼ teaspoon bottled hot pepper sauce
- 18 slices whole wheat baguette, toasted

1 In a food processor combine garlic, parsley, and oregano; cover and process with several on/off turns until finely chopped. Add garbanzo beans, sour cream, lemon juice, black pepper, and hot pepper sauce. Cover and process until blended. Transfer to serving bowl.

2 Serve with toasted baguette slices. Makes 6 servings (about 3 tablespoons spread and 3 baguette slices per serving).

Make-Ahead Directions: Prepare as above in step 1. Cover and chill for up to 24 hours. Serve as above.

Herby Garbanzo Bean Spread on Toast

START TO FINISH: 15 minutes

NUTRITION FACTS per serving:

CALORIES 187
TOTAL FAT 3 g (1 g sat. fat)
CHOLESTEROL 1 mg
PROTEIN 9 g
CARBOHYDRATE 33 g
FIBER 6 g
SODIUM 394 mg

EXCHANGES 2 Starch, 0.5 Fat

Very Veggie Dip

START TO FINISH: 20 minutes

NUTRITION FACTS per serving dip:

CALORIES 39
TOTAL FAT 3 g (2 g sat. fat)
CHOLESTEROL 10 mg
PROTEIN 1 g
CARBOHYDRATE 2 g
FIBER 0 g
SODIUM 76 mg

EXCHANGES 1 Fat

1 8-ounce carton light dairy sour cream
½ of an 8-ounce package reduced-fat cream cheese (Neufchâtel)
1 tablespoon fat-free milk
¼ cup finely chopped red or yellow sweet pepper
¼ cup finely chopped zucchini
2 tablespoons shredded carrot
1 tablespoon snipped fresh chives or green onion tops
¼ teaspoon salt
¼ teaspoon black pepper
   Fresh vegetable dippers, whole grain crackers, and/or multigrain tortilla chips

1 In a medium bowl combine sour cream, cream cheese, and milk; beat with an electric mixer on low to medium speed until smooth. Stir in sweet pepper, zucchini, carrot, and chives. Stir in salt and pepper.

2 To serve, stir dip. Serve with vegetables, crackers, and/or tortilla chips. Makes 16 servings (2 tablespoons dip per serving).

Italian Veggie Dip: Prepare as above, except omit sweet pepper, carrot, and chives. Stir in ¼ cup seeded and finely chopped tomato and 1 clove garlic, minced. Stir in 1 tablespoon snipped fresh basil, oregano, and/or thyme or 1 teaspoon dried Italian seasoning, crushed. Makes 16 servings (2 tablespoons dip per serving).

Nutrition Facts per serving dip: 39 cal., 3 g total fat (2 g sat. fat), 10 mg chol., 75 mg sodium, 2 g carbo., 0 g fiber, 1 g pro. Exchanges: 1 Fat

South-of-the-Border Veggie Dip: Prepare as above, except omit sweet pepper, zucchini carrot, and chives. Stir in ⅔ cup purchased salsa. Makes 16 servings (2 tablespoons dip per serving).

Nutrition Facts per serving: 41 cal., 3 g total fat (2 g sat. fat), 10 mg chol., 139 mg sodium, 2 g carbo., 0 g fiber, 1 g pro. Exchanges: 1 Fat

Make-Ahead Directions: Prepare as above in step 1. Cover and chill for up to 3 days. Serve as above.

- 1 8-ounce carton light dairy sour cream
- ¼ cup chopped bottled roasted red sweet peppers
- 2 tablespoons sliced green onion
- 1 tablespoon snipped fresh basil or ½ teaspoon dried basil, crushed
- 1 clove garlic, minced
- ¼ teaspoon salt

   Baked tortilla chips, baked potato chips, baked pita chips, or assorted vegetable dippers

1 In a small bowl stir together sour cream, roasted red peppers, green onion, basil, garlic, and salt. Cover and chill for 4 to 24 hours to allow flavors to blend.

2 Stir before serving. Serve with baked chips or vegetable dippers. Makes 10 servings (2 tablespoons dip per serving).

COOK'S TIP

Serve roasted red peppers with everything from salads and sandwiches to pastas and quesadillas. Once opened, a jar will keep in the fridge for up to 6 months.

Roasted Red Pepper Dip

PREP: 15 minutes

CHILL: 4 to 24 hours

NUTRITION FACTS per serving dip:

CALORIES 33
TOTAL FAT 2 g (1 g sat. fat)
CHOLESTEROL 8 mg
PROTEIN 1 g
CARBOHYDRATE 2 g
FIBER 0 g
SODIUM 75 mg

EXCHANGES 0.5 Fat

1 ripe avocado, halved, seeded, and peeled

1 tablespoon lemon juice or lime juice

½ cup light dairy sour cream

1 clove garlic, minced

⅛ teaspoon salt

4 medium sweet peppers, seeded and cut into strips

1 In a medium bowl use a fork to mash avocado with lemon juice. Stir in sour cream, garlic, and salt. Serve with sweet pepper strips. Makes 8 servings (2 tablespoons dip and ½ of a sweet pepper per serving).

Make-Ahead Directions: Prepare as above in step 1. Cover the surface of the dip with plastic wrap and chill for up to 4 hours. Serve as above.

Lemony Avocado Dip

START TO FINISH: 15 minutes

NUTRITION FACTS per serving:

CALORIES 61
TOTAL FAT 4 g (1 g sat. fat)
CHOLESTEROL 4 mg
PROTEIN 1 g
CARBOHYDRATE 6 g
FIBER 2 g
SODIUM 49 mg

EXCHANGES 1 Vegetable, 1 Fat

NUTRITION NOTE

An avocado spread makes a great substitute for mayo-based spreads on sandwiches and wraps. The avocado spread adds moistness, flavor, and heart-healthy monounsaturated fat.

1 cup round toasted oat cereal with nuts and honey

¾ cup bite-size whole grain fish-shape cheddar cheese crackers

½ cup honey wheat braided pretzel twists, broken into bite-size pieces

½ cup semisweet or dark chocolate pieces

1 In a large bowl combine cereal, crackers, pretzels, and chocolate pieces. Makes 6 (½-cup) servings.

Sweet 'n' Salty Snack Mix

START TO FINISH: 5 minutes

NUTRITION FACTS per serving:

CALORIES 129
TOTAL FAT 6 g (3 g sat. fat)
CHOLESTEROL 2 mg
PROTEIN 2 g
CARBOHYDRATE 20 g
FIBER 1 g
SODIUM 146 mg

EXCHANGES 1 Starch, 1 Fat

4 cups sweetened or brown sugar-flavored oat square cereal

½ cup sliced almonds

2 tablespoons butter, melted

½ teaspoon apple pie spice
   Dash kosher salt

1 cup dried cherries and/or golden raisins

Cherry-Almond Snack Mix

PREP: 10 minutes   **BAKE:** 30 minutes
COOL: 20 minutes   **OVEN:** 300°F

1 Preheat oven to 300°F. In a 15×10×1-inch baking pan combine cereal and almonds. In a small bowl stir together melted butter, apple pie spice, and salt. Drizzle butter mixture over cereal mixture; toss to evenly coat cereal and almonds.

2 Bake 30 to 35 minutes or until almonds are toasted, stirring once during baking. Cool snack mix in pan on a wire rack for 20 minutes.

3 Stir in dried cherries. Cool completely. Store tightly covered at room temperature for up to 1 week. Makes 20 (¼-cup) servings.

NUTRITION FACTS per serving:

CALORIES 79
TOTAL FAT 3 g (1 g sat. fat)
CHOLESTEROL 3 mg
PROTEIN 1 g
CARBOHYDRATE 12 g
FIBER 1 g
SODIUM 60 mg

EXCHANGES 1 Starch, 0.5 Fat

NUTRITION NOTE

Almonds are bursting with fiber, riboflavin, magnesium, and iron. They have more calcium than any other nut, and they are one of the best plant sources of protein.

⅓ cup cornflakes, coarsely crushed

2 tablespoons flaked coconut

2 tablespoons vanilla fat-free yogurt

2 tablespoons peanut butter

2 small bananas (each about 5 ounces or about 6 inches long)

1 In a small skillet combine crushed cornflakes and coconut; cook and stir over medium heat for 2 to 3 minutes or until coconut is starting to brown. Remove from heat; set aside. In a small bowl stir together yogurt and peanut butter. If desired, sprinkle with a little of the cornflake mixture.

2 Slice each banana in half crosswise and then lengthwise to make eight pieces total. Place each piece, cut side up, on a small plate. Spread peanut butter mixture on banana pieces. Sprinkle evenly with cornflake mixture. Makes 8 servings.

Crunch-Topped Bananas

START TO FINISH: 20 minutes

NUTRITION FACTS per serving:
- -

CALORIES 55
TOTAL FAT 2 g (1 g sat. fat)
CHOLESTEROL 0 mg
PROTEIN 2 g
CARBOHYDRATE 8 g
FIBER 1 g
SODIUM 32 mg

EXCHANGES 0.5 Fruit, 0.5 Fat

1 cup canned mandarin orange sections; cubed fresh pineapple; sliced, peeled fresh peaches; or fresh strawberries

1 8-ounce carton light dairy sour cream

1 8-ounce package reduced-fat cream cheese (Neufchâtel)

1 teaspoon vanilla

½ teaspoon finely shredded orange peel

Assorted fresh fruit dippers

Creamy Fruit Dip

START TO FINISH: 15 minutes

NUTRITION FACTS per serving dip:

CALORIES 60
TOTAL FAT 4 g (3 g sat. fat)
CHOLESTEROL 14 mg
PROTEIN 2 g
CARBOHYDRATE 3 g
FIBER 0 g
SODIUM 60 mg

EXCHANGES 1 Fat

1 Place fruit in a blender or food processor. Cover and blend or process until smooth. Add sour cream, cream cheese, vanilla, and orange peel. Cover and blend or process until smooth.

2 Serve with assorted fruit dippers. Makes 18 servings (2 tablespoons dip per serving).

Apple-Cinnamon Dip: Prepare as above, except omit 1 cup fruit and orange peel. Add ½ cup unsweetened applesauce and ¼ to ½ teaspoon apple pie spice or ground cinnamon with the vanilla. Makes 16 servings (2 tablespoons dip per serving).

Nutrition Facts per serving: 60 cal., 5 g total fat (3 g sat. fat), 16 mg chol., 67 mg sodium, 2 g carbo., 0 g fiber, 2 g pro. Exchanges: 1 Fat

Peanut Butter Dip: Prepare as above, except omit the 1 cup fruit and the orange peel. Add ½ cup creamy peanut butter with the sour cream. Stir in 2 to 4 tablespoons fat-free milk to reach desired consistency. Makes about 18 servings (2 tablespoons dip per serving).

Nutrition Facts per serving: 93 cal., 8 g total fat (3 g sat. fat), 14 mg chol., 93 mg sodium, 3 g carbo., 0 g fiber, 4 g pro. Exchanges: 1 Fat, 0.5 High-Fat Meat

Make-Ahead Directions: Prepare as above in step 1. Cover and chill for up to 24 hours. If dip is too thick after chilling, stir in enough fat-free milk, 1 tablespoon at a time, to reach desired consistency. Serve as above.

COOK'S TIP

To make this dip a special dessert, serve it with grilled fruit such as peaches or nectarines, or spread over reduced-fat graham crackers.

¼	cup plain fat-free yogurt
2	tablespoons peanut butter
4	6-inch whole wheat flour tortillas
¾	cup fresh raspberries and/or chopped fresh strawberries

1 In a small bowl stir together yogurt and peanut butter. Spread yogurt mixture on one side of each tortilla. Top with fruit; roll up.

2 To serve, use a serrated knife to cut each wrap crosswise into 1-inch-wide slices. Makes 4 servings.

Make-Ahead Directions: Prepare as above in step 1. Wrap each tortilla roll-up in plastic wrap. Chill for up to 3 hours. Serve as above.

PB & B Pinwheels

START TO FINISH: 15 minutes

NUTRITION FACTS per serving:

CALORIES 118
TOTAL FAT 6 g (1 g sat. fat)
CHOLESTEROL 0 mg
PROTEIN 8 g
CARBOHYDRATE 16 g
FIBER 10 g
SODIUM 229 mg

EXCHANGES 1 Starch, 0.5 High-Fat Meat

Nonstick cooking spray

2 cups regular rolled oats

¾ cup coarsely chopped walnuts
and/or almonds

¼ cup packed brown sugar

2 tablespoons canola oil

⅛ teaspoon salt

8 cups plain fat-free yogurt

1 Preheat oven to 325°F. Coat a 15×10×1-inch baking pan with nonstick cooking spray; set aside.

2 In a large bowl combine rolled oats, nuts, brown sugar, oil, and salt. Spread in an even layer in prepared baking pan. Bake about 25 minutes or until golden brown, stirring twice.

3 Spread on a large piece of foil to cool. For each serving, spoon ½ cup yogurt into a parfait glass or dessert dish; sprinkle with 2 tablespoons oat mixture. Store oat mixture in an airtight container at room temperature for up to 3 weeks or freeze for up to 3 months. Makes 16 servings (½ cup yogurt and 2 tablespoons oat mixture per serving).

Sweet 'n' Crunchy Yogurt Topping

PREP: 15 minutes **BAKE:** 25 minutes
OVEN: 325°F

NUTRITION FACTS per serving:

CALORIES 170
TOTAL FAT 6 g (1 g sat. fat)
CHOLESTEROL 2 mg
PROTEIN 9 g
CARBOHYDRATE 20 g carbo
FIBER 1 g
SODIUM 114 mg

EXCHANGES 1 Starch, 0.5 Milk, 1 Fat

- ¼ cup light ricotta cheese
- 1 tablespoon honey
- ½ teaspoon finely shredded lemon peel
- ¾ cup fresh blueberries, coarsely chopped
- 4 slices low-calorie whole grain bread, toasted
- ¼ cup sliced almonds, toasted

1 In a small bowl combine ricotta cheese, honey, and lemon peel. Stir in coarsely chopped blueberries. Cut bread slices diagonally into four pieces.

2 Divide blueberry mixture among bread pieces. Sprinkle with toasted almonds. Makes 4 servings.

Sweet Blueberry Crostini

START TO FINISH: 15 minutes

NUTRITION FACTS per serving:

CALORIES 124
TOTAL FAT 4 g (1 g sat. fat)
CHOLESTEROL 4 mg
PROTEIN 5 g
CARBOHYDRATE 19 g
FIBER 3 g
SODIUM 134 mg

EXCHANGES 1 Starch, 1 Fat

2   cups fat-free milk

1   medium banana, sliced and frozen*

3   tablespoons unsweetened cocoa powder

2   tablespoons honey

1   teaspoon vanilla

1 In a blender combine milk, frozen banana, cocoa powder, honey, and vanilla. Cover and blend until smooth and frothy. Makes 4 (about 8-ounce) servings.

*Peel and slice banana. Place banana slices in a single layer on a baking sheet lined with plastic wrap. Freeze about 1 hour or until firm.

Chocolate-Banana Sipper

START TO FINISH: 5 minutes

NUTRITION FACTS per serving:

CALORIES 120
TOTAL FAT 1 g (0 g sat. fat)
CHOLESTEROL 2 mg
PROTEIN 5 g
CARBOHYDRATE 23 g
FIBER 1 g
SODIUM 52 mg

EXCHANGES 0.5 Other Carbohydrates, 0.5 Fruit, 0.5 Milk

- 1 2-quart-size envelope low-calorie lemonade-flavor soft drink mix
- 5 cups water
- 8 medium fresh strawberries, hulled and quartered
- 1 2-quart-size envelope low-calorie cherry- or raspberry-flavor soft drink mix
- 1 1-liter bottle club soda, chilled
     Ice cubes

1 In a 2-quart pitcher stir together lemonade drink mix and water. Place one strawberry quarter in each of 32 compartments of ice cube trays; fill trays with 3 cups of lemonade mixture. Freeze about 4 hours or until solid.

2 Stir cherry or raspberry drink mix into remaining lemonade mixture in pitcher. Cover and chill until serving time.

3 To serve, slowly pour club soda into lemonade mixture in pitcher. Put four ice cubes in each of eight glasses. Pour lemonade mixture into glasses. Makes 8 (6-ounce) servings.

Sparkling Berry Lemonade

PREP: 15 minutes

FREEZE: 4 hours

NUTRITION FACTS per serving:

CALORIES 4
TOTAL FAT 0 g (0 g sat. fat)
CHOLESTEROL 0 mg
PROTEIN 0 g
CARBOHYDRATE 1 g
FIBER 0 g
SODIUM 31 mg

EXCHANGES Free

1¼ cups rolled oats

1 cup all-purpose flour

½ teaspoon baking powder

½ teaspoon baking soda

4 ounces soft silken-style tofu (fresh bean curd)

2 tablespoons butter, softened

½ cup granulated sugar

½ cup packed brown sugar

¼ cup canola oil

½ teaspoon vanilla

4 ounces dark chocolate chunks or bittersweet chocolate pieces

1 Preheat oven to 375°F. Place oats in a food processor or blender. Cover and process or blend until oats resemble coarse flour. In a medium bowl stir together oats, flour, baking powder, and baking soda. Set aside. Place tofu in food processor or blender. Cover and process or blend until smooth. Set aside.

2 In a large bowl beat butter with an electric mixer on medium to high speed for 30 seconds. Add tofu; beat until combined, scraping side of bowl occasionally. Add granulated sugar and brown sugar; beat until combined. Beat in oil and vanilla. Beat in as much of the flour mixture as you can with the mixer. Using a wooden spoon, stir in any remaining flour mixture. Stir in chocolate.

3 Drop dough by rounded teaspoons 2 inches apart onto an ungreased cookie sheet. Bake for 8 to 10 minutes or until edges are golden brown. Transfer cookies to a wire rack; cool. Makes about 24 cookies.

COOK'S TIP

Adding tofu to cookies may seem odd. With its bland flavor, versatile tofu takes on the flavors of the other ingredients in a recipe. It can add nutrition to beverages, baked goods, dressings, soups, spreads, and casseroles.

Chocolate Chunk Cookies

PREP: 30 minutes

BAKE: 8 minutes per batch

OVEN: 375°F

NUTRITION FACTS per cookie:

CALORIES 125
TOTAL FAT 5 g (1 g sat. fat)
CHOLESTEROL 3 mg
PROTEIN 1 g
CARBOHYDRATE 18 g
FIBER 1 g
SODIUM 40 mg

EXCHANGES 1 Other Carbohydrates, 1 Fat

Chocolate-Drizzled Graham Cookies

PREP: 30 minutes   **BAKE:** 8 minutes per batch
STAND: 30 minutes   **OVEN:** 375°F

NUTRITION FACTS per cookie:

CALORIES 68
TOTAL FAT 3 g (2 g sat. fat)
CHOLESTEROL 14 mg
PROTEIN 1 g
CARBOHYDRATE 9 g
FIBER 1 g
SODIUM 41 mg

EXCHANGES 0.5 Other Carbohydrates, 0.5 Fat

COOK'S TIP

Honey will crystallize and harden when refrigerated and when exposed to air. Store it, tightly sealed, in a cool, dry area. If honey crystallizes, place it in warm water or microwave it for only a few seconds until it turns to liquid.

½	cup butter, softened
¼	cup packed brown sugar
1	teaspoon baking powder
¼	teaspoon baking soda
¼	teaspoon salt
¼	teaspoon ground cinnamon
2	eggs, lightly beaten
¼	cup honey
½	teaspoon vanilla
1¼	cups all-purpose flour
1	cup white whole wheat flour or whole wheat flour
½	cup miniature semisweet chocolate pieces
3	ounces bittersweet chocolate or ½ cup miniature semisweet chocolate pieces
½	teaspoon shortening

1 Preheat oven to 375°F. In a large bowl beat butter with an electric mixer on medium to high speed for 30 seconds. Add brown sugar, baking powder, baking soda, salt, and cinnamon. Beat until light and fluffy, scraping side of bowl occasionally.

2 Beat in eggs, honey, and vanilla until combined. Beat in as much of the all-purpose flour and the whole wheat flour as you can with the mixer. Using a wooden spoon, stir in any remaining flour. Stir in ½ cup semisweet chocolate pieces.

3 Shape dough into 1-inch balls. Place balls 1 inch apart on an ungreased cookie sheet. Flatten slightly. Bake for 8 to 9 minutes or until bottoms are lightly browned. Transfer cookies to a wire rack; cool.

4 In a small saucepan combine bittersweet chocolate and shortening; heat over low heat until melted and smooth, stirring often. Cool slightly. Transfer melted chocolate mixture to a small resealable plastic bag; seal bag. Snip a small hole in one corner of the bag; pipe chocolate on tops of cookies. Let stand about 30 minutes or until set. Makes about 48 cookies.

Chocolate Chocolate-Drizzled Graham Cookies: Prepare as above, except add ¼ cup unsweetened cocoa powder with the all-purpose flour.

Nutrition Facts per cookie: 70 cal., 3 g total fat (2 g sat. fat), 14 mg chol., 41 mg sodium, 9 g carbo., 1 g fiber, 1 g pro.
Exchanges: 0.5 Other Carbohydrates, 0.5 Fat

- ¼ cup butter, softened
- ½ cup packed brown sugar
- ½ teaspoon baking powder
- ¼ teaspoon ground cinnamon or ground cardamom
- ⅛ teaspoon baking soda
- 2 egg whites
- ½ teaspoon vanilla
- ½ cup all-purpose flour
- ¼ cup white whole wheat flour or whole wheat flour
- 1 cup quick-cooking rolled oats
- 1 egg white
- ¾ cup finely chopped walnuts and/or pecans
- ¼ cup low-sugar strawberry, apricot, and/or red raspberry preserves

1 In a large bowl beat butter with an electric mixer on medium to high speed for 30 seconds. Add brown sugar, baking powder, cinnamon, and baking soda. Beat until combined, scraping side of bowl occasionally. Beat in 2 egg whites and vanilla until combined. Beat in as much of the all-purpose flour and whole wheat flour as you can with the mixer. Using a wooden spoon, stir in any remaining flour and oats. Cover and chill dough about 2 hours or until easy to handle.

2 Preheat oven to 375°F. Lightly grease two large cookie sheets or line with parchment paper. Shape dough into ¾-inch balls. In a small bowl lightly beat 1 egg white; roll dough balls in egg white. Roll in nuts to coat. Place on prepared cookie sheets. Using your thumb, make an indentation in the center of each cookie.

3 Bake for 7 to 8 minutes or until edges are golden brown. If indentations puff during baking, gently press the back of a measuring teaspoon into indentations when cookies are removed from oven. Cool cookies on cookie sheet for 1 minute. Transfer to a wire rack; cool.

4 Just before serving, spoon preserves into indentations in cookies. Makes about 36 cookies.

Walnut-Crusted Oatmeal-Raspberry Thumbprints

PREP: 30 minutes   **CHILL:** 2 hours

BAKE: 7 minutes per batch   **COOL:** 1 minute

OVEN: 375°F

NUTRITION FACTS per cookie:

CALORIES 61
TOTAL FAT 3 g (1 g sat. fat)
CHOLESTEROL 3 mg
PROTEIN 1 g
CARBOHYDRATE 8 g
FIBER 1 g
SODIUM 23 mg

EXCHANGES 0.5 Other Carbohydrates, 0.5 Fat

Nonstick cooking spray
¾ cup all-purpose flour
¼ cup granulated sugar
Dash salt
¼ cup butter
2 eggs, beaten
¾ cup granulated sugar
2 tablespoons all-purpose flour
1 teaspoon finely shredded lemon peel
⅓ cup lemon juice
⅓ cup fat-free half-and-half
Powdered sugar (optional)

Lemon Bars

PREP: 30 minutes   **BAKE:** 40 minutes
OVEN: 350°F

NUTRITION FACTS per bar:

CALORIES 113
TOTAL FAT 4 g (2 g sat. fat)
CHOLESTEROL 34 mg
PROTEIN 1 g
CARBOHYDRATE 19 g
FIBER 0 g
SODIUM 44 mg

EXCHANGES 1 Other Carbohydrates, 1 Fat

1 Preheat oven to 350°F. Coat an 8×8×2-inch baking pan with nonstick cooking spray; set aside. In a small bowl combine ¾ cup flour, ¼ cup granulated sugar, and salt. Using a pastry blender, cut in butter until crumbly. Using the back of a large spoon, pat mixture into prepared baking pan. Bake for 15 minutes.

2 Meanwhile, for filling, in a medium bowl stir together eggs, ¾ cup granulated sugar, and 2 tablespoons flour. Stir in lemon peel, lemon juice, and half-and-half. Pour filling over hot crust. Bake about 25 minutes more or until surface is set. Cool in pan on a wire rack.

3 If desired, sift powdered sugar over cooled recipe. Cut into bars. Cover and store in the refrigerator. Makes 16 bars.

Nonstick cooking spray

- ¾ cup all-purpose flour
- ¼ cup whole wheat flour
- ½ cup sugar or sugar substitute* equivalent to ½ cup sugar
- 1½ teaspoons pumpkin pie spice
- 1 teaspoon baking powder
- ⅛ teaspoon salt
- 1 cup finely shredded carrot
- ¾ cup chopped walnuts or pecans, toasted
- 1 egg, lightly beaten
- ¼ cup cooking oil
- ¼ cup fat-free milk
- 1 recipe Fluffy Cream Cheese Frosting

Nutty Carrot Cake Cheesecake Bars

PREP: 25 minutes   **BAKE:** 15 minutes
OVEN: 350°F

NUTRITION FACTS per bar:

CALORIES 123
TOTAL FAT 8 g (2 g sat. fat)
CHOLESTEROL 15 mg
PROTEIN 3 g
CARBOHYDRATE 12 g
FIBER 1 g
SODIUM 60 mg

EXCHANGES 1 Other Carbohydrates, 1 Fat

1 Preheat oven to 350°F. Line a 9×9×2-inch baking pan with foil, extending foil over the edges of the pan. Lightly coat foil with nonstick cooking spray. Set aside.

2 In a medium bowl combine all-purpose flour, whole wheat flour, sugar, pumpkin pie spice, baking powder, and salt. Add carrot, ½ cup nuts, egg, oil, and milk. Stir just until combined. Spread mixture evenly in the prepared pan.

3 Bake for 15 to 18 minutes or until a toothpick inserted near center comes out clean. Cool bars in pan on a wire rack.

4 Using the edges of the foil, lift uncut bars out of the pan. Spread top evenly with Fluffy Cream Cheese Frosting. Sprinkle with remaining ¼ cup nuts. Cut into 20 bars. Makes 20 bars.

*Sugar Substitute: Choose Sweet'N Low bulk or packets. Follow package directions to use product amount equivalent to ½ cup sugar.

Per serving with substitute: same as above, except 102 cal., 7 g carbo.
Exchanges: 0.5 Other Carbohydrates

Fluffy Cream Cheese Frosting: Thaw ½ cup frozen light whipped topping. In a medium bowl beat half of an 8-ounce package reduced-fat cream cheese (Neufchâtel), softened, with an electric mixer on medium speed until smooth. Beat in ¼ cup vanilla low-fat yogurt until smooth. Fold whipped topping into cream cheese mixture.

Pear-Rhubarb Crisp

PREP: 25 minutes **BAKE:** 40 minutes
COOL: 30 minutes **OVEN:** 375°F

NUTRITION FACTS per serving:

CALORIES 169
TOTAL FAT 5 g (2 g sat. fat)
CHOLESTEROL 7 mg
PROTEIN 2 g
CARBOHYDRATE 32 g
FIBER 4 g
SODIUM 55 mg

EXCHANGES 0.5 Starch, 0.5 Other
Carbohydrates, 1 Fruit, 1 Fat

4	medium Bartlett pears or cooking apples (such as Rome, Braeburn, or Jonathan), cored and thinly sliced
2	cups sliced fresh rhubarb or frozen unsweetened sliced rhubarb*
¼	cup all-purpose flour
½	teaspoon ground nutmeg
¼	cup honey
2	tablespoons apple juice or apple cider
1	cup oat square cereal, crushed
¼	cup whole bran cereal, crushed
¼	cup chopped almonds or pecans
2	tablespoons butter, melted
1	tablespoon honey
	Honey (optional)

1 Preheat oven to 375°F. In a large bowl combine pear or apple slices, rhubarb, flour, and nutmeg. Add ¼ cup honey and apple juice; toss gently to coat. Transfer fruit mixture to a 2-quart square baking dish. Cover and bake for 30 to 40 minutes or just until pear or apple slices are tender.

2 Meanwhile, for topping, in a medium bowl combine crushed cereals and nuts. Add butter and 1 tablespoon honey; toss to coat. Sprinkle over partially baked fruit mixture. Bake, uncovered, about 10 minutes more or until fruit is very tender and topping is lightly browned.

3 Cool on a wire rack for 30 minutes. Serve warm. If desired, drizzle with additional honey. Makes 9 servings.

*If using frozen rhubarb, measure while still frozen. Allow rhubarb to thaw in a large bowl 1 hour or until the fruit is partially thawed but still icy; do not drain rhubarb. Continue as above.

- ⅓ cup sugar or sugar substitute* equivalent to ⅓ cup sugar
- 2 tablespoons cornstarch
- ½ teaspoon ground cinnamon
- 10 cups sliced, pitted, peeled fresh peaches (3½ to 4 pounds) or 10 cups frozen unsweetened peach slices, thawed
- ½ cup water
- 1¼ cups whole wheat flour
- 2 tablespoons sugar or sugar substitute* equivalent to 2 tablespoons sugar
- ¾ teaspoon baking powder
- ¼ teaspoon baking soda
- ¼ teaspoon salt
- ¼ cup butter
- ½ cup buttermilk
- 4 cups vanilla frozen yogurt (optional)

Old-Fashioned Peach Cobbler

PREP: 30 minutes   **BAKE:** 25 minutes
COOL: 30 minutes   **OVEN:** 400°F

NUTRITION FACTS per serving:

CALORIES 175
TOTAL FAT 4 g (3 g sat. fat)
CHOLESTEROL 11 mg
PROTEIN 3 g
CARBOHYDRATE 34 g
FIBER 4 g
SODIUM 129 mg

EXCHANGES 1 Other Carbohydrates, 1 Fruit, 1 Fat

1 Preheat oven to 400°F. For filling, in a very large bowl stir together ⅓ cup sugar, cornstarch, and cinnamon; add peaches and toss gently to mix. Gently stir in water. Spread fruit mixture evenly in a 3-quart rectangular baking dish. Set aside.

2 For topping, in a medium bowl stir together whole wheat flour, 2 tablespoons sugar, baking powder, baking soda, and salt. Using a pastry blender, cut in butter until mixture resembles coarse crumbs. Make a well in the center of the flour mixture. Add buttermilk all at once. Using a fork, stir just until moistened. Knead mixture gently to shape into a ball.

3 On a lightly floured surface, roll dough to ½-inch thickness. Using a 2- to 2½-inch star cookie cutter, cut out 12 stars, rerolling dough as needed. Arrange stars on fruit mixture.

4 Bake for 25 to 30 minutes or until stars are lightly browned and fruit mixture is bubbly in the center. Cool on a wire rack for 30 minutes. Serve warm. If desired, serve with frozen yogurt. Makes 12 servings.

*Sugar Substitutes: Choose from Splenda granular or Sweet'N Low bulk or packets. Follow package directions to use product amounts equivalent to ⅓ cup and 2 tablespoons sugar.

Per serving with substitute: same as above, except 147 cal., 28 carbo.
Exchanges: 0.5 Other Carbohydrates

COOK'S TIP

An easy way to peel a peach is to blanch it in boiling water for 30 seconds, then plunge it into ice water. Drain off the water, then pull off the skins, using a paring knife if necessary.

Apple-Mango Crisp

PREP: 25 minutes   **BAKE:** 40 minutes

OVEN: 375°F

NUTRITION FACTS per serving:

CALORIES 169
TOTAL FAT 6 g (1 g sat. fat)
CHOLESTEROL 0 mg
PROTEIN 4 g
CARBOHYDRATE 28 g
FIBER 3 g
SODIUM 4 mg

EXCHANGES 1 Other Carbohydrates,
1 Fruit, 1 Fat

NUTRITION NOTE

Apples contain pectin, a soluble fiber
that slows the digestion of complex
carbohydrates. It helps you feel full longer.

Nonstick cooking spray
¾ cup all-purpose flour
¾ cup rolled oats
½ cup toasted wheat germ
½ cup packed brown sugar or
   brown sugar substitute*
1½ teaspoons ground cinnamon
¼ cup canola oil
4 Granny Smith apples
2 red sweet apples (such as Gala,
   Fuji, or Rome Beauty)
3 tablespoons lime juice
2 medium mangoes, seeded, peeled,
   and chopped
⅓ cup chopped pecans
Frozen light whipped dessert
   topping, thawed, or low-fat
   vanilla frozen yogurt (optional)

1 Preheat oven to 375°F. Coat two 1½- or
2-quart baking dishes or a 3-quart rectangular
baking dish with nonstick cooking spray.

2 In a medium bowl stir together ½ cup
flour, oats, wheat germ, brown sugar, and
cinnamon. Stir in oil; set aside.

3 Core apples; chop apples and place in a
very large bowl. Sprinkle chopped apples
with lime juice; stir. Stir in remaining ¼ cup flour.
Fold in chopped mangoes.

4 Place apple-mango mixture in the prepared
baking dish(es). Evenly sprinkle flour-oat
mixture over fruit. Bake, uncovered, for
30 minutes. Sprinkle with pecans; bake for 10 to
15 minutes more or until apples are tender. Cool
slightly. Serve warm. If desired, top individual
servings with whipped topping.
Makes 16 servings.

*Sugar Substitutes: Choose from Sweet'N Low
Brown or Sugar Twin Granulated Brown. Follow
package directions to use product amount
equivalent to ½ cup brown sugar.

Per serving with substitute: same as above, except
158 cal., 25 g carbo., 2 mg sodium
Exchanges: 0.5 Other Carbohydrates

Nonstick cooking spray

1 cup all-purpose flour

2 tablespoons packed brown sugar or brown sugar substitute* equivalent to 2 tablespoons brown sugar

1½ teaspoons finely snipped crystallized ginger or ½ teaspoon ground ginger

1 teaspoon baking powder

⅛ teaspoon baking soda

2 tablespoons butter

½ cup buttermilk or sour fat-free milk**

¾ cup frozen fat-free whipped dessert topping, thawed

¼ cup fat-free dairy sour cream

¼ teaspoon ground ginger

1 cup chopped fresh strawberries and/or small fresh blueberries

Finely snipped crystallized ginger (optional)

Gingered Shortcake Bites

PREP: 25 minutes   **BAKE:** 8 minutes
OVEN: 450°F

NUTRITION FACTS per bite:

CALORIES 83
TOTAL FAT 2 g (1 g sat. fat)
CHOLESTEROL 6 mg
PROTEIN 2 g
CARBOHYDRATE 14 g
FIBER 1 g
SODIUM 65 mg

EXCHANGES 0.5 Starch, 0.5 Other Carbohydrates, 0.5 Fat

1 Preheat oven to 450°F. Lightly coat a baking sheet with nonstick cooking spray; set aside. In a medium bowl combine flour, brown sugar, 1½ teaspoons crystallized ginger or ½ teaspoon ground ginger, baking powder, and baking soda. Using a pastry blender, cut in butter until mixture resembles coarse crumbs. Make a well in the center of flour mixture. Add buttermilk all at once. Using a fork, stir just until moistened.

2 Drop dough by slightly rounded tablespoons into 12 mounds on the prepared baking sheet. Bake for 8 to 10 minutes or until lightly golden and a toothpick inserted into centers comes out clean. Cool on a wire rack.

3 In a medium bowl combine whipped topping, sour cream, and ¼ teaspoon ground ginger. Set aside ⅓ cup of the topping mixture. Fold the berries into remaining topping mixture.

4 Split shortcakes in half horizontally. Spoon berry mixture onto bottom halves of shortcakes. Add tops; dollop with reserved topping mixture. If desired, garnish with additional snipped crystallized ginger. Makes 12 bites.

***Sugar Substitutes:** Choose from Sweet'N Low Brown or Sugar Twin Granulated Brown. Follow package directions to use product amount equivalent to 2 tablespoons brown sugar.

Per serving with substitute: same as above, except 75 cal., 11 g carbo., 64 mg sodium

****To make ½ cup sour fat-free milk, place 1½ teaspoons lemon juice or vinegar in a glass measuring cup. Add enough fat-free milk to make ½ cup total liquid; stir. Let stand for 5 minutes before using.

Piled-High Shortcake

PREP: 25 minutes **BAKE:** 7 minutes
OVEN: 425°F

NUTRITION FACTS per serving:

CALORIES 212
TOTAL FAT 10 g (6 g sat. fat)
CHOLESTEROL 62 mg
PROTEIN 6 g
CARBOHYDRATE 25 g
FIBER 1 g
SODIUM 232 mg
EXCHANGES 1.5 Other Carbohydrates,
2 Fat

NUTRITION NOTE

The deep color of blackberries is telling of its antioxidant content. Generally the darker the fruits or veggies, the more antioxidants. Color isn't the only way to measure antioxidant content, but it is a simple guide.

¾ cup all-purpose flour
2 teaspoons sugar
1 teaspoon baking powder
⅛ teaspoon baking soda
   Dash salt
2 tablespoons butter
¼ cup buttermilk
1 egg yolk, lightly beaten
   Nonstick cooking spray
½ of an 8-ounce package reduced-fat cream cheese (Neufchâtel), softened
1 cup plain low-fat yogurt
3 tablespoons low-sugar strawberry preserves
1½ cups fresh raspberries, blueberries, blackberries, cut-up nectarine, and/or peeled and cut-up kiwifruit

1 Preheat oven to 425°F. For shortcakes, in a medium bowl stir together flour, sugar, baking powder, baking soda, and salt. Using a pastry blender, cut in butter until mixture resembles coarse crumbs. Make a well in center of flour mixture. In a small bowl combine buttermilk and egg yolk. Add to flour mixture all at once, stirring just until moistened.

2 Lightly coat a baking sheet with nonstick cooking spray; set aside. On a lightly floured surface, pat or roll dough to ½-inch thickness. Using a floured 1½- to 2-inch cookie cutter, cut dough into desired shapes, rerolling scraps as necessary. Place on prepared baking sheet. Bake for 7 to 8 minutes or until golden. Cool on a wire rack.

3 In a medium bowl beat cream cheese with an electric mixer on medium speed for 30 seconds. Gradually beat in yogurt and preserves until smooth.

4 Split shortcakes in half horizontally. Divide shortcake bottoms among six dessert plates; top each with some of the fresh fruit and yogurt mixture. Add shortcake tops. Serve immediately. Makes 6 servings.

Nonstick cooking spray

- ½ cup yellow cornmeal
- ⅓ cup whole wheat flour
- 2 tablespoons sugar or sugar substitute* equivalent to 2 tablespoons sugar
- 1½ teaspoons finely shredded lemon peel
- 1 teaspoon baking powder
- ⅛ teaspoon baking soda
- ⅛ teaspoon salt
- ⅔ cup buttermilk
- ⅔ cup shredded, cored red cooking apple (such as Gala or Jonathan)
- 2 egg whites, lightly beaten
- 3 tablespoons finely chopped dried figs (about 5 figs)
- 1 small red cooking apple (such as Gala or Jonathan)
- ½ cup apple juice or apple cider
- ½ teaspoon cornstarch

1 Preheat oven to 400°F. Lightly coat six 3¼- to 3½-inch muffin cups with nonstick cooking spray. Set aside.

2 In a large bowl combine cornmeal, whole wheat flour, sugar, lemon peel, baking powder, baking soda, and salt; set aside. In a medium bowl combine buttermilk, shredded apple, egg whites, and figs. Add apple mixture to cornmeal mixture. Stir just until moistened.

3 Core whole apple. Cut whole apple horizontally into six rings, each about ¼ inch thick. Place one ring in each muffin cup, cutting slices to fit if necessary. Spoon cornmeal batter evenly into muffin cups on top of apple slices, filling each about half full.

4 Bake for 15 to 20 minutes or until tops are golden brown and a toothpick inserted into cakes comes out clean.

5 Meanwhile, in a small saucepan whisk together apple juice and cornstarch. Cook and stir until slightly thickened and bubbly; cook and stir 2 minutes more.

6 Let cakes cool in muffin cups on a wire rack for 10 minutes. Run a thin metal spatula around edges of cakes to loosen from sides of muffin cups. Invert pan onto a baking sheet;

Upside-Down Apple-Corn Cakes

PREP: 25 minutes **BAKE:** 15 minutes
COOL: 10 minutes **OVEN:** 400°F

NUTRITION FACTS per serving:
- -

CALORIES 133
TOTAL FAT 1 g (0 g sat. fat)
CHOLESTEROL 1 mg
PROTEIN 5 g
CARBOHYDRATE 29 g
FIBER 3 g
SODIUM 167 mg

EXCHANGES 1 Starch, 1 Fruit

remove pan. Transfer cakes to a serving platter. While hot, slowly drizzle cakes with hot apple juice mixture. Serve warm. Makes 6 servings.

***Sugar Substitutes:** Choose from Splenda granular, Equal Spoonful or packets, or Sweet'N Low bulk or packets. Follow package directions to use product amount equivalent to 2 tablespoons sugar.

Per serving with substitute: same as above, except 119 cal., 25 g carbo. Exchanges: 0.5 Starch

Coffee-Chocolate Marble Cake

PREP: 25 minutes **BAKE:** 30 minutes
COOL: 15 minutes **OVEN:** 350°F

NUTRITION FACTS per serving:

CALORIES 231
TOTAL FAT 8 g (1 g sat. fat)
CHOLESTEROL 27 mg
PROTEIN 4 g
CARBOHYDRATE 36 g
FIBER 0 g
SODIUM 128 mg

EXCHANGES 2.5 Other Carbohydrates, 1.5 Fat

*Sugar Substitutes: Choose from Equal Sugar Lite or Splenda Sugar Blend for Baking. Follow package directions to use product amount equivalent to 1¼ cups for cake and 1 tablespoon for Coffee Drizzle.
Per serving with substitute: same as above, except 198 cal., 27 carbo. Exchanges: 2 Other Carbohydrates

Coffee Drizzle: In a small bowl combine ½ cup boiling water, 1 tablespoon sugar or sugar substitute blend* equivalent to 1 tablespoon sugar, and 2 teaspoons instant espresso coffee powder or instant coffee crystals. Stir until sugar and espresso powder are dissolved.

2½   cups sifted cake flour or 2¼ cups all-purpose flour
1½   teaspoons baking powder
½   teaspoon baking soda
¼   teaspoon salt
1¼   cups buttermilk
1¼   cups granulated sugar or sugar substitute blend* equivalent to 1¼ cups sugar
½   cup canola oil or cooking oil
2   eggs
2   teaspoons vanilla
⅓   cup unsweetened cocoa powder
2   tablespoons instant espresso coffee powder or instant coffee crystals
1   recipe Coffee Drizzle
2   teaspoons powdered sugar and/or unsweetened cocoa powder

1 Preheat oven to 350°F. Grease and lightly flour a 10-inch fluted tube pan; set aside. Set aside ½ cup flour. In a large bowl combine remaining 2 cups cake flour or 1¾ cups all-purpose flour, baking powder, baking soda, and salt.

2 In another large bowl whisk together buttermilk, granulated sugar, oil, eggs, and vanilla. Add buttermilk mixture to flour mixture. Whisk just until combined. In a medium bowl combine cocoa powder and espresso powder. Add half of the buttermilk-flour mixture (about 1¾ cups) to cocoa mixture, stirring until smooth. Add reserved ½ cup flour to remaining buttermilk-flour mixture, whisking just until combined.

3 Evenly spoon half of the white batter into prepared pan. Carefully spoon half of the cocoa batter onto the white batter in pan in an even layer. Repeat layers.

4 Bake for 30 minutes or until a toothpick inserted near center of cake comes out clean. Cool in pan on a wire rack for 15 minutes. Remove cake from pan. Place cake on a wire rack set over a sheet of waxed paper. Using a long wooden skewer, poke cake all the way through to bottom of cake in several places. Slowly pour Coffee Drizzle evenly over cake. Cool completely. Sprinkle with powdered sugar and/or additional cocoa powder. Makes 16 servings.

- ⅔ cup quick-cooking rolled oats
- ½ cup white whole wheat flour or whole wheat flour
- ¼ cup pecans, toasted and ground
- 1 8-ounce package reduced-fat cream cheese (Neufchâtel), softened
- 2 tablespoons butter, softened
- 2 tablespoons packed brown sugar
- ¼ teaspoon baking soda
- ⅛ teaspoon salt
- Nonstick cooking spray
- ⅓ cup fat-free vanilla yogurt
- 1 tablespoon honey
- 2½ cups assorted fresh fruit (such as blueberries, sliced strawberries, sliced kiwifruit, raspberries, and/or sliced, pitted, peeled peaches)

Fruit Pizza

PREP: 40 minutes
CHILL: 30 minutes to 4 hours
BAKE: 13 minutes   **OVEN:** 400°F

NUTRITION FACTS per serving:

CALORIES 145
TOTAL FAT 8 g (4 g sat. fat)
CHOLESTEROL 20 mg
PROTEIN 4 g
CARBOHYDRATE 15 g
FIBER 2 g
SODIUM 145 mg

EXCHANGES 1 Starch, 1.5 Fat

1 For tart dough, in a small bowl combine oats, whole wheat flour, and ground pecans; set aside. In a large bowl combine half of the cream cheese and butter; beat with an electric mixer on medium to high speed for 30 seconds. Add brown sugar, baking soda, and salt; beat until well mixed. Beat in as much of the oat mixture as you can with the mixer. Using a wooden spoon, stir in any remaining oat mixture. If necessary, cover and chill for 30 to 60 minutes or until easy to handle.

2 Preheat oven to 400°F. Pat dough evenly on the bottom and up the side of a lightly greased 9-inch tart pan with a removable bottom. Coat a double thickness of foil with nonstick cooking spray. Line the pastry with foil, coated side down. Bake for 6 minutes. Remove foil. Bake for 7 to 8 minutes more or until crust is golden brown. Cool completely on a wire rack.

3 Meanwhile, in a medium bowl beat remaining cream cheese with an electric mixer on medium speed until smooth. Beat in yogurt and honey; cover and chill for 30 minutes to 4 hours.

4 Spread cream cheese mixture on the crust. Top with fruit. Serve immediately or cover and chill for up to 4 hours. Makes 12 servings.

Berry Pie with Creamy Filling

PREP: 20 minutes   **CHILL:** 3 to 6 hours
COOL: 1 hour

NUTRITION FACTS per serving:

CALORIES 216
TOTAL FAT 8 g (4 g sat. fat)
CHOLESTEROL 14 mg
PROTEIN 4 g
CARBOHYDRATE 32 g
FIBER 5 g
SODIUM 164 mg

EXCHANGES 1 Starch, 1 Fruit, 2 Fat

¾   cup low-calorie cranberry-
     raspberry drink
1   tablespoon cornstarch
½   of an 8-ounce package reduced-
     fat cream cheese (Neufchâtel),
     softened
⅓   cup light dairy sour cream
3   tablespoons powdered sugar
1   purchased reduced-fat graham
     cracker crumb pie shell
6   cups fresh raspberries,
     blueberries, quartered
     strawberries, and/or
     blackberries
1   recipe Lemon Cream (optional)
     Fresh mint leaves (optional)

1 For glaze, in a small saucepan stir together cranberry-raspberry drink and cornstarch. Cook and stir over medium heat until thickened and bubbly; cook and stir for 2 minutes more. Remove from heat. Transfer to a small bowl. Cover surface with plastic wrap; let stand at room temperature about 1 hour or until cooled.

2 Meanwhile, in a medium bowl beat cream cheese with an electric mixer on medium speed for 30 seconds. Add sour cream and powdered sugar. Beat until smooth. Spread cream cheese mixture evenly in pie shell. Set aside.

3 In a large bowl gently toss berries and cooled glaze. Spoon over cream cheese mixture. Cover and chill for 3 to 6 hours before serving. If desired, serve with Lemon Cream and/or garnish with fresh mint. Makes 8 servings.

Lemon Cream: In a small bowl stir together 1½ cups frozen light whipped dessert topping, thawed, and ¾ teaspoon finely shredded lemon peel.

- 1 cup pineapple-orange juice
- 1 tablespoon cornstarch
- 2 cups seeded, peeled mango cut into 1-inch pieces
- 2 cups seeded, peeled papaya cut into 1-inch pieces
- 1½ cups peeled kiwifruit half-slices
- 1 purchased reduced-fat graham cracker crumb pie shell
  Frozen light whipped dessert topping, thawed (optional)

1 In a small saucepan combine juice and cornstarch; cook and stir over medium heat until thickened and bubbly. Cook and stir for 2 minutes more. Transfer to a large bowl. Cover surface of juice mixture with plastic wrap; cool for 30 minutes. Divide mixture among three small bowls.

2 Fold a different fruit into each of the bowls of fruit juice mixture. Spoon fruit into pie shell, arranging as desired. Cover and chill for 3 to 4 hours. If desired, serve with whipped dessert topping. Makes 10 servings.

Glazed Tropical Fruit Pie

PREP: 25 minutes **CHILL:** 3 to 4 hours
COOL: 30 minutes

NUTRITION FACTS per serving:

CALORIES 144
TOTAL FAT 3 g (1 g sat. fat)
CHOLESTEROL 0 mg
PROTEIN 2 g
CARBOHYDRATE 28 g
FIBER 2 g
SODIUM 83 mg

EXCHANGES 1.5 Other Carbohydrates, 0.5 Fruit, 0.5 Fat

NUTRITION NOTE

Papaya will fuel your body with vitamin C, fiber, and folate. Papaya seeds are edible, although their peppery flavor doesn't fit with this recipe. They make a tasty addition to salads and dressings.

Chocolate Cream Cheese Pie

PREP: 20 minutes

CHILL: 4 hours

NUTRITION FACTS per serving:

CALORIES 180
TOTAL FAT 8 g (4 g sat. fat)
CHOLESTEROL 9 mg
PROTEIN 4 g
CARBOHYDRATE 22 g
FIBER 1 g
SODIUM 285 mg
EXCHANGES 1.5 Other Carbohydrates,
1.5 Fat

1	4-serving-size package fat-free, sugar-free instant chocolate pudding mix
1¾	cups fat-free milk
1	teaspoon vanilla
½	of an 8-ounce package reduced-fat cream cheese (Neufchâtel), softened
½	of an 8-ounce container frozen light whipped dessert topping, thawed
1	6-ounce chocolate-flavor crumb pie shell
1	cup fresh raspberries
1	tablespoon grated semisweet chocolate

1 In a medium bowl prepare pudding mix according to package directions using the 1¾ cups milk. Stir in vanilla; set aside.

2 Place cream cheese in a large microwave-safe bowl. Microwave, uncovered, on 100% power (high) for 15 seconds; stir. Microwave on 100% power (high) for 15 seconds more. Beat cream cheese with an electric mixer on medium speed for 15 seconds. Add half of the pudding mixture; beat until smooth. Add remaining pudding mixture; beat until smooth. Fold in half of the whipped topping. Spread mixture in pie shell. Chill about 4 hours or until set.

3 Top individual servings with remaining whipped topping, raspberries, and grated chocolate. Makes 10 servings.

Make-Ahead Directions: Prepare as above through step 2. Cover and chill for up to 24 hours. Serve as above in step 3.

2   eggs, lightly beaten

2   cups fat-free milk

3   tablespoons packed brown sugar

1   teaspoon vanilla

½   teaspoon pumpkin pie spice or
     ground cinnamon

5   cups dry oatmeal bread cubes*

2   medium bananas, halved
     lengthwise and sliced

½   cup chopped walnuts or pecans,
     toasted (optional)

1 Preheat oven to 350°F. In a medium bowl whisk together eggs, milk, brown sugar, vanilla, and pumpkin pie spice; set aside. In an ungreased 2-quart square baking dish toss together bread cubes, banana slices, and, if desired, nuts. Pour egg mixture evenly over bread mixture. Toss until bread is moistened.

2 Bake for 35 to 40 minutes or until a knife inserted near the center comes out clean. Cool slightly before serving. Makes 9 servings.

*For 5 cups dry bread cubes, preheat oven to 350°F. Spread 8½ cups bread cubes (11 slices) in a shallow baking pan. Bake for 10 to 15 minutes or until bread cubes are dry, stirring twice; cool.

Oatmeal-Banana Bread Pudding

PREP: 25 minutes   **BAKE:** 35 minutes
OVEN: 350°F

NUTRITION FACTS per serving:

CALORIES 167
TOTAL FAT 3 g (1 g sat. fat)
CHOLESTEROL 48 mg
PROTEIN 6 g
CARBOHYDRATE 30 g
FIBER 2 g
SODIUM 239 mg

EXCHANGES 1 Starch, 0.5 Other Carbohydrates, 0.5 Fruit, 0.5 Fat

NUTRITION NOTE

Bananas, a good source of fiber, vitamin C, and potassium, should be stored uncovered at room temperature. Hanging them on a banana hanger prevents resting bruises.

Nonstick cooking spray

2 cups firm-textured whole grain
bread cubes (about 3 ounces)

3 tablespoons snipped dried
tart red cherries

1 tablespoon toasted wheat germ

⅔ cup fat-free milk

¼ cup semisweet chocolate pieces

1 egg

1 egg white

1 teaspoon finely shredded
orange peel

½ teaspoon vanilla

Frozen light whipped dessert
topping, thawed (optional)

Unsweetened cocoa powder
(optional)

Cherry Chocolate Bread Puddings

PREP: 20 minutes   **BAKE:** 15 minutes
OVEN: 350°F

NUTRITION FACTS per serving:

CALORIES 168
TOTAL FAT 5 g (2 g sat. fat)
CHOLESTEROL 54 mg
PROTEIN 7 g
CARBOHYDRATE 27 g
FIBER 3 g
SODIUM 148 mg

EXCHANGES 1 Starch, 1 Other
Carbohydrates, 0.5 Fat

1 Preheat oven to 350°F. Coat four 6-ounce individual soufflé dishes or custard cups with nonstick cooking spray. Divide bread cubes, dried cherries, and wheat germ among the dishes.

2 In a small saucepan combine milk and chocolate pieces. Cook and stir over low heat until the chocolate melts; remove from heat. If necessary, beat smooth with a wire whisk.

3 In a small bowl beat together egg and egg white with a fork or wire whisk. Gradually stir chocolate mixture into eggs. Stir in orange peel and vanilla. Pour chocolate mixture over bread cubes in dishes. Press lightly with the back of a spoon to thoroughly moisten bread.

4 Bake for 15 to 20 minutes or until pudding tops appear firm and a knife inserted near the centers comes out clean. Serve warm. If desired, serve with whipped topping and sprinkle with cocoa powder. Makes 4 servings.

Make-Ahead Directions: Prepare as above through step 3. Cover and chill for up to 2 hours. Preheat oven to 350°F. Continue with step 4.

- 4 egg yolks, lightly beaten
- 1 cup fat-free milk
- 2 tablespoons sugar
- 1 teaspoon vanilla
- ½ cup finely crushed graham crackers
- ¼ cup chopped toasted sliced almonds
- ⅛ teaspoon ground cinnamon
- 1½ cups fresh raspberries and/or sliced strawberries
- 1½ cups fresh blueberries
  Toasted sliced almonds (optional)

Custard Towers

PREP: 25 minutes

CHILL: 2 to 24 hours

NUTRITION FACTS per serving:

- -

CALORIES 157
TOTAL FAT 6 g (1 g sat. fat)
CHOLESTEROL 137 mg
PROTEIN 5 g
CARBOHYDRATE 19 g
FIBER 5 g
SODIUM 62 mg

EXCHANGES 1 Other Carbohydrates, 0.5 Fruit, 0.5 Medium Fat Meat, 0.5 Fat

1 For custard, in a heavy small saucepan stir together egg yolks, milk, and sugar. Cook and stir over medium heat until mixture is thickened and coats the back of a metal spoon (do not boil).

2 Remove saucepan from heat. Quickly cool milk mixture by placing saucepan in a large bowl of ice water for 1 to 2 minutes, stirring constantly. Stir in vanilla. Pour mixture into a small bowl. Cover surface with plastic wrap to prevent a skin from forming. Chill for 2 to 24 hours before serving. Do not stir. (Custard will be thickened but will not be set.)

3 In a small bowl combine finely crushed graham crackers, ¼ cup almonds, and cinnamon.

4 Divide one-third of the graham cracker mixture among six tall 8-ounce glasses, small parfait glasses, or small dessert dishes. Divide half of the raspberries and one-third of the chilled custard among the glasses. Layer another one-third of the graham cracker mixture in the glasses. Top with half of the blueberries and another one-third of the custard. Divide remaining raspberries, graham cracker mixture, and blueberries among the glasses. Top each with some of the remaining custard. If desired, garnish with additional almonds. Serve immediately. Makes 6 servings.

COOK'S TIP

Toasting nuts intensifies their flavor and adds crunch. To toast nuts, place a single layer of them in a skillet over medium-high heat. Stir or shake the nuts continually until they turn golden.

Citrus Trifle with Orange Custard

PREP: 45 minutes

CHILL: 2 hours

NUTRITION FACTS per serving:

CALORIES 112
TOTAL FAT 3 g (2 g sat. fat)
CHOLESTEROL 10 mg
PROTEIN 4 g
CARBOHYDRATE 18 g
FIBER 1 g
SODIUM 283 mg

EXCHANGES 0.5 Other Carbohydrates, 0.5 Fruit, 0.5 Fat

2   cups fat-free milk

1   4-serving-size package fat-free sugar-free reduced-calorie vanilla instant pudding mix

2   teaspoons finely shredded orange peel

¼   cup orange juice

½   of an 8-ounce package reduced-fat cream cheese (Neufchâtel), softened

3   cups assorted citrus fruit sections (such as blood oranges, tangelos, grapefruit, and/or navel oranges)

½   of an 8-ounce angel food cake, cut into 1-inch cubes (about 4 cups)

Finely shredded orange peel (optional)

1 In a medium bowl combine milk and pudding mix; beat with an electric mixer on low speed for 2 minutes. Beat in 2 teaspoons orange peel and 2 tablespoons orange juice. Set aside. In a large bowl beat cream cheese with an electric mixer on medium to high speed for 30 seconds. Gradually add pudding mixture, beating until combined.

2 Divide half of the fruit among ten 6-ounce dessert glasses or dishes. (Or arrange half of the fruit in a 1½-quart glass bowl.) Arrange half of the cake cubes on the fruit. Drizzle with 1 tablespoon remaining orange juice. Spoon half of the pudding mixture over cake. Repeat layers. Cover and chill for 2 hours before serving. If desired, garnish individual servings with additional orange peel. Makes 10 servings.

Make-Ahead Directions: Prepare as above, except cover and chill for up to 6 hours before serving.

- ½ of a 3-ounce package ladyfingers (12 halves), cubed
- ¼ cup strong brewed Kona or other coffee
- ¼ of an 8-ounce package reduced-fat cream cheese (Neufchâtel), softened
- ⅓ cup light dairy sour cream
- 3 tablespoons sugar or sugar substitute* equivalent to 3 tablespoons sugar
- 1 teaspoon vanilla
- 2 to 3 teaspoons fat-free milk
  Instant espresso powder (optional)
- 4 chocolate-covered coffee beans (optional)

1 Place ladyfinger cubes on a piece of foil. Drizzle cubes with coffee. Set aside.

2 In a small bowl stir together cream cheese, sour cream, sugar, and vanilla. Whisk until smooth. Stir in enough milk to make desired consistency.

3 In four dessert glasses or dessert dishes layer ladyfinger cubes with cream cheese mixture. Cover and chill for 1 hour before serving. If desired, garnish with espresso powder and chocolate-covered coffee beans. Makes 4 servings.

*Sugar Substitutes: Choose from Equal Spoonful or packets or Sweet'N Low bulk or packets. Follow package directions to use product amount equivalent to 3 tablespoons sugar.

Per serving with substitute: same as above, except 106 cal., 8 g carbo.
Exchanges: 0.5 Other Carbohydrates

Make-Ahead Directions: Prepare as above, except chill for up to 24 hours.

Kona Trifle Cups

PREP: 20 minutes

CHILL: 1 hour

NUTRITION FACTS per serving:

CALORIES 141
TOTAL FAT 6 g (3 g sat. fat)
CHOLESTEROL 56 mg
PROTEIN 4 g
CARBOHYDRATE 17 g
FIBER 0 g
SODIUM 87 mg

EXCHANGES 1 Other Carbohydrates, 1.5 Fat

Nonstick cooking spray

6 tablespoons granulated sugar
   or sugar substitute blend*
   equivalent to
   6 tablespoons sugar

¼ cup all-purpose flour

2 teaspoons finely shredded
   lemon peel

¼ cup lemon juice

1 tablespoon butter, melted

2 egg yolks

1 cup fat-free milk

3 egg whites

Sifted powdered sugar

Lemon Soufflé Dessert

PREP: 25 minutes   **BAKE:** 40 minutes
COOL: 5 minutes   **OVEN:** 350°F

NUTRITION FACTS per serving:

CALORIES 190
TOTAL FAT 5 g (3 g sat. fat)
CHOLESTEROL 111 mg
PROTEIN 7 g
CARBOHYDRATE 29 g
FIBER 0 g
SODIUM 92 mg

EXCHANGES 2 Other Carbohydrates,
0.5 Medium-Fat Meat, 0.5 Fat

1 Preheat oven to 350°F. Lightly coat a 1-quart soufflé dish with nonstick cooking spray; set aside. In a large bowl combine 2 tablespoons granulated sugar (or equivalent amount of sugar substitute blend) and flour. Whisk in lemon peel, lemon juice, and melted butter until smooth. In a small bowl whisk together egg yolks and milk. Whisk into flour mixture just until combined. Set aside.

2 In a medium bowl beat egg whites with an electric mixer on medium speed until soft peaks form (tips curl). Gradually add remaining 4 tablespoons granulated sugar (or equivalent amount of sugar substitute blend), beating on high speed until stiff peaks form (tips stand straight). Fold a small amount of egg white mixture into lemon juice mixture. Fold in remaining egg white mixture (batter will be thin).

3 Transfer mixture to prepared soufflé dish. Place soufflé dish in a 13×9×2-inch baking pan. Place baking pan on oven rack. Pour boiling water into the baking pan to a depth of 1 inch. Bake about 40 minutes or until top springs back when lightly touched. Carefully remove soufflé dish from baking pan. Cool on a wire rack for 5 minutes. Sprinkle with powdered sugar. Serve warm. Makes 4 servings.

*Sugar Substitutes: Choose from Splenda Sugar Blend for Baking or Equal Sugar Lite. Follow package directions to use product amount equivalent to 6 tablespoons granulated sugar. Dessert will brown more on top when using sugar substitute blend.

Per serving with substitute: same as above, except 156 cal., 20 g carbo.
Exchanges: 1.5 Other Carbohydrates

1 cup light ricotta cheese

2 tablespoons orange liqueur or orange juice

½ teaspoon finely shredded orange peel

½ cup sliced fresh strawberries

½ cup fresh blueberries

½ cup fresh raspberries

½ cup fresh blackberries

1 teaspoon lemon juice

2 teaspoons honey

Fresh mint leaves (optional)

Orange peel strips (optional)

1 In a small bowl whisk together ricotta cheese, 1 tablespoon orange liqueur, and orange peel. Cover and chill for 1 to 24 hours.

2 In a medium bowl combine berries, lemon juice, and remaining 1 tablespoon liqueur. Cover and let stand at room temperature for 15 minutes to develop flavors.

3 To serve, divide berry mixture among four dessert dishes, spooning any juices over fruit in dishes. Top with ricotta mixture. Drizzle individual servings with honey. If desired, garnish with fresh mint and orange peel. Makes 4 servings.

Ricotta Mousse with Berries

PREP: 15 minutes   **CHILL:** 1 to 24 hours

STAND: 15 minutes

NUTRITION FACTS per serving:

CALORIES 123

TOTAL FAT 3 g (2 g sat. fat)

CHOLESTEROL 15 mg

PROTEIN 6 g

CARBOHYDRATE 16 g

FIBER 3 g

SODIUM 56 mg

EXCHANGES .5 Other Carbohydrates, 0.5 Fruit, 1 Lean Meat

NUTRITION NOTE

Strawberries pack a nutritional punch with vitamin C, folic acid, and fiber. The peak season for the popular juicy berries is from April to June.

½   of an 8-ounce package fat-free
    cream cheese, softened
¼   cup low-sugar orange marmalade
¼   teaspoon almond extract
16 pieces fresh fruit (such as large
    strawberries, kiwifruit, and/or
    fresh figs)*
    Grated orange or lemon peel
    (optional)

1 In a medium bowl beat cream cheese with an
electric mixer on medium speed until fluffy;
beat in orange marmalade and almond extract.
If desired, place cream cheese mixture in a pastry
bag fitted with a large star tip.

2 If using strawberries, slice off a small
portion of the stem ends; set aside. If using
kiwifruit, peel and quarter each one; set aside.
If using figs, halve each one; set aside. Pipe or
spoon cream cheese mixture into or on top of
fruit. If desired, garnish with orange peel.

3 Serve immediately or cover and chill for up
to 1 hour before serving. Makes 4 servings.

*If necessary, cut small slices from rounded sides
or bottoms of fruit to prevent them from rolling
around on the serving plate.

Creamy Fruit Morsels

START TO FINISH: 20 minutes

NUTRITION FACTS per serving:

CALORIES 68
TOTAL FAT 0 g (0 g sat. fat)
CHOLESTEROL 5 mg
PROTEIN 4 g
CARBOHYDRATE 12 g
FIBER 1 g
SODIUM 6 mg

EXCHANGES 1 Fruit

COOK'S TIP

Fresh figs are available June through
October. They should be used shortly after
purchasing because they are perishable.
Store them in the refrigerator for two to
three days.

2	6-ounce cartons plain low-fat yogurt
1	teaspoon vanilla
2	fresh plums or apricots, pitted and sliced
2	medium nectarines, pitted and sliced
2	tablespoons coarsely chopped walnuts, toasted
4	teaspoons honey

1 Line a strainer with 100%-cotton cheesecloth or a paper coffee filter. Set the strainer over a small bowl. Spoon yogurt into lined strainer. Cover and refrigerate for 8 to 24 hours. (Yogurt will thicken to form a soft cheese.)

2 Discard liquid in bowl. In another small bowl gently stir together thickened yogurt and vanilla. Divide fruit among four small dessert dishes. Top each serving with some of the yogurt mixture and sprinkle with walnuts. Drizzle individual servings with honey. Makes 4 servings.

Fresh Fruit with Yogurt and Honey

PREP: 15 minutes
CHILL: 8 to 24 hours

NUTRITION FACTS per serving:

CALORIES 147
TOTAL FAT 4 g (1 g sat. fat)
CHOLESTEROL 5 mg
PROTEIN 6 g
CARBOHYDRATE 23 g
FIBER 2 g
SODIUM 60 mg

EXCHANGES 0.5 Other Carbohydrates, 1 Fruit, 0.5 Milk, 0.5 Fat

2 6-ounce cartons peach fat-free yogurt with artificial sweetener

1 8-ounce package fat-free cream cheese, softened

½ of an 8-ounce container frozen light whipped dessert topping, thawed

1 cup chopped, pitted, peeled fresh peach; frozen unsweetened peach slices, thawed, drained, and chopped; or one 8¼-ounce can peach slices (juice pack), drained and chopped

1 cup fresh or frozen unsweetened blueberries, raspberries, and/or strawberries, thawed and drained if frozen

Fresh mint leaves (optional)

Fresh berries (optional)

Peach-Berry Frozen Dessert

PREP: 20 minutes **FREEZE:** 8 hours
STAND: 45 minutes

NUTRITION FACTS per serving:

CALORIES 89
TOTAL FAT 2 g (2 g sat. fat)
CHOLESTEROL 3 mg
PROTEIN 6 g
CARBOHYDRATE 12 g
FIBER 1 g
SODIUM 159 mg

EXCHANGES 1 Other Carbohydrates, 1 Very Lean Meat

1 In a medium bowl combine yogurt and cream cheese. Beat with an electric mixer on medium speed until smooth. Fold in whipped topping, peach, and 1 cup berries.

2 Spoon into a 2-quart square baking dish; spread evenly. Cover and freeze about 8 hours or until firm.

3 To serve, let stand at room temperature about 45 minutes to thaw slightly. Cut into squares. If desired, garnish with mint leaves and additional berries. Makes 9 servings.

COOK'S TIP

Fresh peaches are available from May through October. To ripen peaches, place them in a brown paper bag that has been pierced several times and let sit at room temperature for a couple of days.

2   cups fresh blueberries
2   cups fresh raspberries
½   cup cold water
¼   cup frozen pineapple-orange-
    banana juice concentrate or
    citrus beverage concentrate
    Fresh mint sprigs (optional)

1 Place berries in a single layer on a baking
sheet lined with waxed paper. Freeze for 1 to
2 hours or until solid.

2 In a large bowl combine frozen berries,
water, and frozen concentrate. Place half
of the berry mixture in a food processor. Cover
and process until almost smooth. Spoon into
serving dishes. Repeat with remaining berry
mixture. If desired, garnish with fresh mint. Serve
immediately. Makes 6 to 8 servings.

Make-Ahead Directions: Prepare as above.
Transfer berry mixture to a baking dish. Cover
and freeze about 4 hours or until firm. Use
within 2 days. If desired, scoop frozen mixture
into sugar cones.

Easy-Freezy Sorbet

PREP: 10 minutes

FREEZE: 1 to 2 hours

NUTRITION FACTS per serving:

CALORIES 66
TOTAL FAT 0 g (0 g sat. fat)
CHOLESTEROL 0 mg
PROTEIN 1 g
CARBOHYDRATE 15 g
FIBER 3 g
SODIUM 4 mg

EXCHANGES 1 Fruit

NUTRITION NOTE

Sorbets are a healthy alternative to ice
cream because they are lower in calories
and usually fat-free. The next time you're
standing at an ice cream shop, look for a
sorbet. You'll still enjoy a dessert that's
sweet and cold without the fat.

Choose-a-Fruit Tropical Sherbet

PREP: 20 minutes   **CHILL:** 4 hours

FREEZE: per manufacturer's directions

RIPEN: 4 hours (optional)

NUTRITION FACTS per serving:

CALORIES 90
TOTAL FAT 0 g (0 g sat. fat)
CHOLESTEROL 1 mg
PROTEIN 2 g
CARBOHYDRATE 21 g
FIBER 0 g
SODIUM 20 mg

EXCHANGES 1 Other Carbohydrates,
0.5 Fruit

1   cup sugar or sugar substitute* equivalent to
    1 cup sugar

1   envelope unflavored gelatin

2   cups unsweetened pineapple juice or
    orange juice

2   cups chopped, peeled mango, kiwifruit, or
    strawberry papaya

1   cup buttermilk

1   teaspoon finely shredded lime peel or
    lemon peel

¼   cup lime juice or lemon juice

3   drops yellow, green, red, or orange food
    coloring (optional)

    Mango, kiwifruit, or strawberry papaya
    (optional)

1 In a medium saucepan combine sugar and unflavored gelatin. Stir in pineapple juice. Cook and stir until sugar and gelatin dissolve. Remove from heat.

2 Place chopped mango, kiwifruit, or papaya in a blender or food processor; cover and blend or process until pureed.

3 In a large bowl stir together pureed fruit, gelatin mixture, buttermilk, lime peel, and lime juice. If desired, add food coloring to tint desired color (green for kiwifruit, yellow for mango, or pink or orange for papaya). Cover and chill mixture about 4 hours or until completely chilled.

4 Transfer mixture to a 4- to 5-quart ice cream freezer; freeze according to manufacturer's directions. If desired, ripen for 4 hours.** If desired, garnish with additional mango, kiwifruit, or strawberry papaya. Makes 16 (about ½-cup) servings.

*Sugar Substitutes: Choose from Splenda granular, Equal Spoonful or packets, or Sweet'N Low bulk or packets. Follow package directions to use product amount equivalent to 1 cup sugar.

Per serving with substitute: same as above, except 44 cal., 10 g carbo. Exchanges: 0.5 Fruit

**Ripening or hardening homemade sherbet isn't essential, but it improves the texture and prevents the sherbet from melting too quickly when served.
    To ripen in a traditional-style ice cream freezer, after churning remove the lid and dasher and cover the top of the freezer can with waxed paper or foil. Plug the hole in the lid with a small piece of cloth; replace the lid. Pack the outer freezer bucket with enough ice and rock salt to cover the top of the freezer can (use 1 cup salt for each 4 cups ice). Ripen about 4 hours.
    When using an ice cream freezer with an insulated freezer bowl, transfer the ice cream to a covered freezer container and ripen by freezing in your regular freezer about 4 hours (or follow the manufacturer's recommendations).

Freezer Directions: Prepare as above through step 3. Transfer mixture to a 2-quart rectangular baking dish or freezer container. Cover; freeze for 4½ to 5 hours or until almost firm. Break mixture into small chunks; transfer to a large chilled bowl. Beat with an electric mixer on medium speed about 2 minutes or until smooth but not melted. Return to dish or container. Cover and freeze about 4 hours more or until firm.

Shortcut Meals

2 teaspoons olive oil

12 ounces packaged beef
stir-fry strips

1 16-ounce package frozen (yellow,
green, and red) peppers and
onion stir-fry vegetables

1 15-ounce can cannellini beans
(white kidney beans), rinsed
and drained

1½ cups purchased roasted garlic
and herb pasta sauce or your
favorite tomato-based
pasta sauce

½ cup water

¼ teaspoon coarsely ground
black pepper

2 cups packaged fresh baby spinach

Coarsely ground black pepper
(optional)

1 In a large skillet heat oil over medium-high
heat. Add beef strips; cook for 3 to
4 minutes or until desired doneness. Stir in
stir-fry vegetables, cannellini beans, pasta
sauce, water, and black pepper; heat through.
Stir in spinach. If desired, garnish individual
servings with additional pepper. Makes
4 (about 1½-cup) servings.

Seasoned Steak Ragout

START TO FINISH: 20 minutes

NUTRITION FACTS per serving:

CALORIES 273
TOTAL FAT 7 g (2 g sat. fat)
CHOLESTEROL 52 mg
PROTEIN 27 g
CARBOHYDRATE 30 g
FIBER 7 g
SODIUM 601 mg

EXCHANGES 1 Starch, 2.5 Lean Meat,
3 Vegetable

Hot Pepper Pork Sandwiches

PREP: 15 minutes
COOK: 8 to 10 hours (low) or 4 to 5 hours (high)

NUTRITION FACTS per serving:

CALORIES 343
TOTAL FAT 11 g (3 g sat. fat)
CHOLESTEROL 92 mg
PROTEIN 33 g
CARBOHYDRATE 26 g
FIBER 3 g
SODIUM 559 mg
EXCHANGES 2 Starch, 3.5 Lean Meat

1 2½- to 3-pound boneless pork shoulder roast
2 teaspoons fajita seasoning
2 10-ounce cans enchilada sauce
2 fresh jalapeño chile peppers, seeded, if desired, and finely chopped,* or 1 large green or red sweet pepper, seeded and chopped
8 whole grain hamburger buns or kaiser rolls, split (and toasted, if desired)

1 Trim fat from roast. If necessary, cut roast to fit into a 3½- or 4-quart slow cooker. Place roast in the cooker. Sprinkle roast with fajita seasoning. Add enchilada sauce and chopped chile pepper or sweet pepper.

2 Cover and cook on low-heat setting for 8 to 10 hours or on high-heat setting for 4 to 5 hours.

3 Transfer roast to a cutting board. Using two forks, shred meat, discarding fat. Transfer shredded meat to a large bowl. Stir in 1 cup cooking liquid. Stir in enough additional cooking liquid to make desired moistness. Spoon mixture into buns. Makes 8 servings.

*Because chile peppers contain volatile oils that can burn your skin and eyes, avoid direct contact with them as much as possible. When working with chile peppers, wear plastic or rubber gloves. If your bare hands do touch the peppers, wash your hands and nails well with soap and warm water.

- 1 8-ounce can pizza sauce
- 1 12-inch whole wheat thin Italian bread shell (such as Boboli brand)
- 1 large green sweet pepper, seeded and thinly sliced
- ½ cup thinly sliced quartered red onion
- 1 8-ounce can crushed pineapple, well drained
- ½ of a 3½-ounce package pizza-style Canadian-style bacon
- ¾ cup shredded part-skim mozzarella cheese (3 ounces)

1 Preheat oven to 450°F. Spread pizza sauce on bread shell. Top with sweet pepper, red onion, pineapple, and Canadian-style bacon. Sprinkle with mozzarella cheese. Place pizza on a large baking pan.

2 Bake for 8 to 10 minutes or until cheese is melted and pizza is heated through. Makes 4 servings.

Hearty Pineapple Pizza

PREP: 15 minutes   **BAKE:** 8 minutes
OVEN: 450°F

NUTRITION FACTS per serving:

CALORIES 357
TOTAL FAT 9 g (3 g sat. fat)
CHOLESTEROL 20 mg
PROTEIN 18 g
CARBOHYDRATE 49 g
FIBER 6 g
SODIUM 876 mg

EXCHANGES 3 Starch, 0.5 Fruit, 1.5 Lean Meat

NUTRITION NOTE

A single cup of pineapple provides 73 percent of the daily recommendation for manganese, a mineral needed to build and maintain healthy bones and tissues.

1   12-inch whole wheat thin Italian bread shell (such as Boboli brand)

1   9-ounce package frozen chopped cooked chicken, thawed

½   cup bottled barbecue sauce

2   cups packaged fresh baby spinach

1   cup shredded reduced-fat Monterey Jack cheese or part-skim mozzarella cheese (4 ounces)

2   tablespoons snipped fresh cilantro

1 Preheat oven to 450°F. Place bread shell on a large baking sheet. In a medium bowl combine chicken and barbecue sauce. Evenly spread chicken mixture on bread shell. Sprinkle with spinach. Top with cheese.

2 Bake for 10 to 12 minutes or until cheese is melted and pizza is heated through. Sprinkle with cilantro. Makes 4 servings.

Spinach Barbecue Chicken Pizza

PREP: 15 minutes   **BAKE:** 10 minutes
OVEN: 450°F

NUTRITION FACTS per serving:

CALORIES 385
TOTAL FAT 13 g (5 g sat. fat)
CHOLESTEROL 65 mg
PROTEIN 33 g
CARBOHYDRATE 40 g
FIBER 6 g
SODIUM 1,258 mg

EXCHANGES 2 Starch, 0.5 Other Carbohydrates, 4 Lean Meat

NUTRITION NOTE

Spinach provides more than 20 percent daily recommended value of more than 11 vitamins and minerals, including vitamin K, vitamin A, folate, magnesium, iron, vitamin C, calcium, and potassium.

8   7- or 8-inch whole wheat flour tortillas

    Nonstick cooking spray

1   15-ounce can hot or mild chili beans in chili gravy

1   9-ounce package frozen grilled chicken breast strips, thawed

1   cup purchased chunky salsa

1   cup shredded reduced-fat colby and Monterey Jack cheese (4 ounces)

1   8-ounce can no-salt-added tomato sauce

1 Preheat oven to 350°F. Wrap tortillas tightly in foil. Bake for 10 minutes to soften. Lightly coat a 3-quart rectangular baking dish with nonstick cooking spray; set aside.

2 For filling, in a medium bowl stir together undrained chili beans, chicken breast strips, ½ cup salsa, and ½ cup cheese. Divide chicken mixture evenly among warm tortillas; roll up tortillas. Arrange filled tortillas, seam sides down, in prepared baking dish.

3 In a small bowl stir together remaining ½ cup salsa and tomato sauce. Spoon sauce down center of filled tortillas.

4 Bake, covered, about 30 minutes or until heated through. Top with remaining ½ cup cheese. Bake, uncovered, about 5 minutes more or until cheese is melted. Makes 8 servings.

Saucy Chicken Enchiladas

PREP: 15 minutes   **BAKE:** 35 minutes
OVEN: 350°F

NUTRITION FACTS per serving:

CALORIES 282
TOTAL FAT 8 g (3 g sat. fat)
CHOLESTEROL 33 mg
PROTEIN 23 g
CARBOHYDRATE 28 g
FIBER 14 g
SODIUM 889 mg

EXCHANGES 2 Starch, 2.5 Very Lean Meat, 0.5 Fat

Santa Fe Rice and Beans

START TO FINISH: 20 minutes

NUTRITION FACTS per serving:

CALORIES 245
TOTAL FAT 8 g (2 g sat. fat)
CHOLESTEROL 38 mg
PROTEIN 16 g
CARBOHYDRATE 29 g
FIBER 8 g
SODIUM 890 mg

EXCHANGES 1.5 Starch, 1.5 Lean Meat, 1.5 Vegetable, 0.5 Fat

NUTRITION NOTE

Boost your fiber intake with black beans to help you meet the daily fiber recommendation of at least 25 grams. With high fiber and protein, black beans keep you feeling full longer.

1   tablespoon olive oil
1   12-ounce package fresh green beans and carrots*
12 ounces smoked turkey sausage, halved lengthwise and sliced
1   14½-ounce can no-salt-added diced tomatoes, undrained
1   15-ounce can black beans, rinsed and drained
1   8.5-ounce pouch cooked whole grain Santa Fe rice medley

1 In a very large skillet heat oil over medium heat. Add green beans and carrots; cook for 5 to 6 minutes or until crisp-tender, stirring occasionally. Add sausage and undrained tomatoes to skillet; bring to boiling. Add black beans and rice; heat through. Makes 6 (about 1-cup) servings.

*Note: If you can't find the packaged green beans and carrots, use 4 cups fresh green beans, trimmed, and 1 cup purchased shredded carrots.

4   small skinless, boneless chicken breast halves (1 to 1¼ pounds total)

¼   cup bottled olive oil and vinegar salad dressing

4   teaspoons reduced-sodium soy sauce

1   tablespoon bottled hoisin sauce

¼   teaspoon ground ginger

1 Place chicken breast halves in a resealable plastic bag set in a deep bowl. For marinade, in a small bowl combine salad dressing, soy sauce, hoisin sauce, and ginger. Pour marinade over chicken. Seal bag; turn to coat chicken. Marinate in the refrigerator for 2 to 24 hours, turning bag occasionally.

2 Drain chicken, discarding marinade. For a charcoal grill, place chicken on the rack of an uncovered grill directly over medium coals. Grill for 12 to 15 minutes or until chicken is no longer pink (170°F). (For a gas grill, preheat grill. Reduce heat to medium. Place chicken on grill rack over heat. Cover and grill as above.) Makes 4 servings.

Easy Marinated Chicken Breasts

PREP: 10 minutes   **MARINATE:** 2 to 24 hours
GRILL: 12 minutes

NUTRITION FACTS per serving:

CALORIES 147
TOTAL FAT 3 g (1 g sat. fat)
CHOLESTEROL 66 mg
PROTEIN 26 g
CARBOHYDRATE 1 g
FIBER 0 g
SODIUM 147 mg

EXCHANGES 3.5 Very Lean Meat, 0.5 Fat

Pesto Chicken Pilaf

START TO FINISH: 35 minutes

NUTRITION FACTS per serving:

CALORIES 363
TOTAL FAT 9 g (3 g sat. fat)
CHOLESTEROL 75 mg
PROTEIN 36 g
CARBOHYDRATE 32 g
FIBER 6 g
SODIUM 472 mg

EXCHANGES 2 Starch, 4 Very Lean Meat,
1.5 Fat

NUTRITION NOTE

For the most cheese flavor and the fewest
calories, choose hard sharp cheeses such as
Parmesan and Asiago. Small amounts satisfy
taste buds without the excessive calories
and fat of other cheeses.

1 14-ounce can reduced-sodium
   chicken broth
¼ cup water
1 6½-ounce package seven
   whole grain pilaf mix
¼ cup snipped fresh basil
   Nonstick cooking spray
4 small skinless, boneless
   chicken breast halves
   (1 to 1¼ pounds total)
2 tablespoons purchased reduced-
   fat or regular basil pesto
1 ounce Asiago or Parmesan cheese,
   finely shredded (¼ cup)

1 In a medium saucepan combine chicken
broth and water. Bring to boiling. Stir in
pilaf mix. Return to boiling; reduce heat. Cover
and simmer about 25 minutes or until liquid is
absorbed. Stir in fresh basil.

2 Meanwhile, lightly coat an unheated large
skillet with nonstick cooking spray. Preheat
skillet over medium heat. Add chicken to hot
skillet; cook for 12 to 15 minutes or until chicken
is no longer pink (170°F), turning once halfway
through cooking. Transfer to four serving plates.

3 Spread pesto over chicken; cut chicken into
bite-size pieces. Sprinkle individual servings
with cheese. Serve with cooked pilaf. Makes
4 servings.

6   10-inch whole grain flour tortillas

1   15¼-ounce can whole kernel corn, drained

1   15-ounce can black beans, rinsed and drained

2   6-ounce packages refrigerated chopped cooked chicken breast

1   cup purchased lime and garlic salsa

2   tablespoons snipped, fresh cilantro

4   cups packaged mixed salad greens with carrots, red cabbage, radishes, and snow peas, or other mixed greens

    Purchased lime and garlic salsa (optional)

1 Preheat oven to 350°F. Stack tortillas and wrap tightly in foil. Heat in oven for 10 minutes to soften.

2 Meanwhile, in a medium saucepan combine corn, black beans, chicken, salsa, and cilantro. Cook over medium heat about 5 minutes or until heated through.

3 Divide salad greens among tortillas. Top with corn mixture. Roll up tortillas. If desired, serve with additional salsa. Makes 6 servings.

Cilantro-Lime Chicken Wraps

START TO FINISH: 25 minutes

OVEN: 350°F

NUTRITION FACTS per serving:

- -

CALORIES 326
TOTAL FAT 4 g (1 g sat. fat)
CHOLESTEROL 40 mg
PROTEIN 22 g
CARBOHYDRATE 53 g
FIBER 8 g
SODIUM 1,606 mg

EXCHANGES 3.5 Starch, 2 Very Lean Meat, 0.5 Vegetable

Chicken Penne Alfredo

START TO FINISH: 25 minutes

NUTRITION FACTS per serving:

CALORIES 354
TOTAL FAT 8 g (4 g sat. fat)
CHOLESTEROL 59 mg
PROTEIN 30 g
CARBOHYDRATE 43 g
FIBER 7 g
SODIUM 627 mg

EXCHANGES 2.5 Starch, 3 Very Lean Meat, 1 Vegetable, 0.5 Fat

6　ounces dried multigrain or whole wheat penne pasta

2　cups packaged peeled baby carrots

3　cups broccoli florets

1　9-ounce package frozen grilled chicken breast strips, thawed

½　of an 8-ounce tub light cream cheese spread with garden vegetables

½　to 1 cup fat-free milk

½　teaspoon cracked black pepper
　　Cracked black pepper (optional)

1 In a 4-quart Dutch oven cook pasta and carrots according to pasta package directions; add broccoli for the last 6 minutes of cooking time. Drain pasta and vegetables; return to Dutch oven.

2 Stir chicken strips, cream cheese spread, ½ cup milk, and pepper into pasta mixture. Cook and stir over low heat until cream cheese is melted. If necessary, stir in enough of the remaining ½ cup milk to make sauce desired consistency. If desired, sprinkle individual servings with additional pepper. Makes 4 (2-cup) servings.

1 7-ounce container hummus
1 cup bottled roasted red
   sweet peppers, drained
½ teaspoon ground cumin
1 tablespoon olive oil or canola oil
1 medium zucchini, sliced
1 medium yellow
   summer squash, sliced
1 9-ounce package refrigerated
   or frozen Southwestern-style
   cooked chicken breast strips,
   thawed if frozen
   Toasted pita wedges*

1 In a blender or food processor combine
hummus, roasted red peppers, and cumin.
Cover and blend or process until smooth;
set aside.

2 In a large skillet heat oil over medium-
high heat. Add zucchini and yellow squash;
cook for 3 to 4 minutes or until tender, stirring
occasionally. Add chicken; heat through. Divide
mixture among four serving plates. Serve with
hummus mixture and toasted pita wedges.
Makes 4 servings.

*To toast pita wedges, preheat oven to 375°F.
Split two whole wheat pita bread rounds in half
horizontally. Cut each half into eight wedges.
Arrange wedges in a single layer on a baking
sheet. Bake for 8 to 10 minutes or until toasted.
Makes 32 wedges.

Chicken and Vegetables with Red Pepper Hummus

START TO FINISH: 30 minutes

OVEN: 375°F

NUTRITION FACTS per serving:

CALORIES 309
TOTAL FAT 11 g (2 g sat. fat)
CHOLESTEROL 41 mg
PROTEIN 21 g
CARBOHYDRATE 34 g
FIBER 6 g
SODIUM 875 mg

EXCHANGES 1.5 Starch, 2 Very Lean Meat,
2 Vegetable, 1.5 Fat

NUTRITION NOTE

Tahini, or sesame seed paste, is an
important ingredient in hummus—
it provides essential fatty acids.

1 12-inch whole wheat Italian bread shell (such as Boboli brand)

½ cup shredded reduced-fat mozzarella cheese (2 ounces)

2 cups packaged European mixed salad greens

2 cups grilled chicken breast, cut into thin strips

2 medium plum tomatoes, chopped

¼ cup thinly sliced quartered red onion

2 tablespoons halved pitted kalamata olives

3 tablespoons bottled light Caesar salad dressing

2 tablespoons crumbled reduced-fat feta cheese

Chicken Caesar Salad Pizza

START TO FINISH: 20 minutes

OVEN: 450°F

NUTRITION FACTS per serving:

CALORIES 388
TOTAL FAT 11 g (3 g sat. fat)
CHOLESTEROL 70 mg
PROTEIN 35 g
CARBOHYDRATE 39 g
FIBER 6 g
SODIUM 830 mg

EXCHANGES 2 Starch, 4 Very Lean Meat, 1 Vegetable, 1.5 Fat

1 Preheat oven to 450°F. Sprinkle bread shell with mozzarella cheese. Place shell directly on middle oven rack. Bake about 5 minutes or until cheese is melted.

2 Meanwhile, in a large bowl toss together salad greens, chicken, tomato, onion, and olives. Add salad dressing; toss to coat. Remove bread shell from oven; immediately top with salad greens mixture. Sprinkle with feta cheese. Cut into wedges. Serve immediately. Makes 4 servings.

1   16-ounce package frozen (yellow, green, and red) peppers and onion stir-fry vegetables

1   14½-ounce can diced tomatoes, undrained

12 ounces smoked turkey sausage, sliced

1   teaspoon Cajun seasoning

1   8.8-ounce pouch cooked brown rice

1 In a large skillet combine stir-fry vegetables, undrained tomatoes, sausage, and Cajun seasoning. Bring to boiling; reduce heat. Cover and simmer about 5 minutes or just until vegetables are tender. Stir in cooked rice; heat through. Makes 6 (1-cup) servings.

COOK'S TIP

Chicken and turkey sausages are becoming more readily available in supermarkets. They are often located near meat alternatives such as tofu and organic poultry.

Jambalaya-Style Sausage and Rice

START TO FINISH: 20 minutes

NUTRITION FACTS per serving:

CALORIES 189
TOTAL FAT 6 g (1 g sat. fat)
CHOLESTEROL 38 mg
PROTEIN 12 g
CARBOHYDRATE 22 g
FIBER 2 g
SODIUM 671 mg

EXCHANGES 1 Starch, 1 Medium-Fat Meat, 2 Vegetable

Shrimp and Peanut Stir-Fry

START TO FINISH: 20 minutes

NUTRITION FACTS per serving:

CALORIES 323
TOTAL FAT 10 g (1 g sat. fat)
CHOLESTEROL 147 mg
PROTEIN 23 g
CARBOHYDRATE 34 g
FIBER 4 g
SODIUM 546 mg

EXCHANGES 2 Starch, 2 Very Lean Meat, 1 Vegetable, 1.5 Fat

NUTRITION NOTE

Asian dishes are often high in sodium. To cut it down, use reduced-sodium soy sauce. One tablespoon of reduced-sodium soy sauce has less than half the sodium of the full-sodium version.

⅓ cup bottled light Catalina salad dressing

2 tablespoons crunchy peanut butter

1 tablespoon reduced-sodium soy sauce

1 tablespoon canola oil

1 16-ounce package frozen broccoli stir-fry vegetable blend

16 ounces fresh or frozen peeled and deveined cooked shrimp* (tails intact if desired)

3 cups hot cooked brown rice

¼ cup chopped peanuts

1 In a small bowl whisk together salad dressing, peanut butter, and soy sauce; set aside.

2 In a wok or very large skillet heat oil over medium-high heat. Add frozen vegetables; cook and stir for 5 to 7 minutes or until vegetables are crisp-tender. Stir in salad dressing mixture and shrimp; heat through.

3 Serve over hot cooked brown rice. Sprinkle individual servings with peanuts. Makes 6 servings (¾ cup shrimp mixture and ½ cup rice per serving).

*Thaw and drain shrimp, if frozen.

1 14½-ounce can diced tomatoes
   and green chile peppers,
   undrained

1 medium red sweet pepper, seeded
   and cut into bite-size strips

¼ teaspoon salt

¼ teaspoon ground saffron
   or turmeric

¼ teaspoon bottled
   hot pepper sauce

12 ounces peeled and deveined
   cooked shrimp* (tails intact
   if desired)

1 8.8-ounce pouch cooked
   whole grain brown rice

1 cup loose-pack frozen peas
   Snipped fresh parsley (optional)

1 In a large saucepan combine undrained
tomatoes, sweet pepper, salt, saffron, and
hot pepper sauce. Bring to boiling; reduce heat.
Simmer, uncovered, for 5 minutes. Stir in shrimp,
cooked rice, and peas. Cook for 1 to 2 minutes
or until heated through, stirring occasionally. If
desired, sprinkle individual servings with parsley.
Makes 4 (1¼-cup) servings.

*Thaw and drain shrimp, if frozen.

COOK'S TIP

By weight, saffron threads are the most
expensive spice in the world, selling for
about $40 an ounce. Most supermarkets
carry powdered saffron in tiny packets in
the spice aisle. Although still expensive, it is
a perfect substitute for threads.

Shrimp Paella

START TO FINISH: 20 minutes

NUTRITION FACTS per serving:

CALORIES 241
TOTAL FAT 3 g (0 g sat. fat)
CHOLESTEROL 166 mg
PROTEIN 23 g
CARBOHYDRATE 30 g
FIBER 3 g
SODIUM 827 mg

EXCHANGES 1.5 Starch, 2.5 Very Lean
Meat, 1 Vegetable

Seasoned Fish with Potato Wedges

PREP: 15 minutes   **BAKE:** 9 minutes
OVEN: 450°F

NUTRITION FACTS per serving:

CALORIES 290
TOTAL FAT 15 g (3 g sat. fat)
CHOLESTEROL 53 mg
PROTEIN 21 g
CARBOHYDRATE 17 g
FIBER 3 g
SODIUM 285 mg

EXCHANGES 1 Starch, 3 Very Lean Meat, 2 Fat

4 4-ounce fresh or frozen catfish fillets, ½ to ¾ inch thick
   Nonstick cooking spray
½ of a 20-ounce package refrigerated red potato wedges (about 30 wedges)
2 teaspoons olive oil
¼ teaspoon garlic powder
¾ cup herb-seasoned stuffing mix
1 tablespoon olive oil
   Fresh parsley sprigs (optional)

1 Thaw fish, if frozen. Rinse fish; pat dry with paper towels. Set aside.

2 Preheat oven to 450°F. Line a 15×10×1-inch baking pan with foil. Coat foil with nonstick cooking spray. Arrange potato wedges in a single layer in half of the baking pan. Brush potatoes with 2 teaspoons oil; sprinkle with garlic powder. Set aside.

3 In a small bowl stir together stuffing mix and the 1 tablespoon oil. Place fish in baking pan next to potatoes. Sprinkle stuffing mixture on fish, pressing lightly. Bake for 9 to 12 minutes or until fish flakes easily when tested with a fork and potatoes are hot and beginning to brown. If desired, garnish individual servings with parsley. Makes 4 servings (1 piece of fish and 7 or 8 potato wedges per serving).

1   pound fresh or frozen skinless halibut fillets, ½ to ¾ inch thick

Olive oil nonstick cooking spray

1   teaspoon ancho chili powder or chili powder

¼   cup light dairy sour cream

¼   cup desired flavor purchased fruit salsa (such as pineapple, peach, or mango-peach)

2   cups packaged shredded cabbage with carrot (coleslaw mix)

4   8-inch whole grain flour tortillas

Packaged shredded cabbage with carrot (coleslaw mix) (optional)

Lime wedges (optional)

Desired flavor purchased fruit salsa (optional)

1 Thaw fish, if frozen. Preheat broiler. Rinse fish; pat dry with paper towels. Lightly coat the unheated rack of a broiler pan with nonstick cooking spray. Place fish on rack. Sprinkle with chili powder. Broil 4 to 5 inches from heat for 4 to 6 minutes per ½-inch thickness or until fish flakes easily when tested with a fork. Cool fish slightly. Using a fork, flake fish into bite-size chunks.

2 Meanwhile, in a medium bowl stir together sour cream and salsa. Add cabbage; toss to coat. Divide cabbage mixture among tortillas. Top with fish. Roll up tortillas. If desired, serve with additional cabbage and lime wedges. If desired, pass additional salsa. Makes 4 servings.

Fish Taco Wraps

START TO FINISH: 20 minutes

NUTRITION FACTS per serving:

- -

CALORIES 294
TOTAL FAT 7 g (2 g sat. fat)
CHOLESTEROL 40 mg
PROTEIN 32 g
CARBOHYDRATE 21 g
FIBER 11 g
SODIUM 450 mg

EXCHANGES 1 Starch, 0.5 Other Carbohydrates, 4 Very Lean Meat, 0.5 Fat

NUTRITION NOTE

Halibut, a low-fat fish, has primarily monounsaturated and polyunsaturated fat. Halibut also contains plenty of protein, magnesium, potassium, phosphorous, and several B vitamins.

2   cups packaged shredded broccoli (broccoli slaw mix)

2   5-ounce pouches zesty lemon-pepper marinated chunk light tuna

½   cup bottled light Caesar salad dressing

1   12-ounce package mixed salad greens with carrots, red cabbage, radishes, and snow peas, or other mixed greens

Cracked black pepper

1 In a medium bowl stir together broccoli, tuna, and salad dressing; toss to coat. Serve tuna mixture with mixed greens. Sprinkle individual servings with cracked black pepper. Makes 4 servings.

Black Pepper-Tuna Salad

START TO FINISH: 10 minutes

NUTRITION FACTS per serving:

- -

CALORIES 166
TOTAL FAT 2 g (0 g sat. fat)
CHOLESTEROL 32 mg
PROTEIN 25 g
CARBOHYDRATE 12 g
FIBER 2 g
SODIUM 583 mg

EXCHANGES 3 Very Lean Meat, 2 Vegetable

6   refrigerated or frozen plain or flavored meatless burger patties

6   whole wheat hamburger buns, toasted

1   recipe Ultra Ketchup Topper, Smoky Berry Topper, or Double Pepper Topper

1 Heat burgers according to package directions. Place heated burgers on bun bottoms. Top burgers with desired topper. Top with bun tops. Makes 6 burgers.

Ultra Ketchup Topper: In a small bowl combine ½ cup ketchup; 3 tablespoons chopped, drained oil-pack dried tomatoes; 2 teaspoons red wine vinegar; 2 teaspoons packed brown sugar; dash salt; and dash black pepper. Try with roasted onion-flavor burger and top with sliced tomatoes. Makes about ¾ cup topper.

Smoky Berry Topper: In a small bowl mash ¾ cup blueberries and/or raspberries with a potato masher or fork. Add 2 tablespoons cider vinegar and 2 slices crisp-cooked and crumbled bacon (stir in bacon just before serving). Try with roasted garlic-flavor burger and top with fresh watercress. Makes about ¾ cup topper.

Nutrition Facts per burger with 2 tablespoons Smoky Berry Topper: 204 cal., 3 g total fat (0 g sat. fat), 5 mg chol., 603 mg sodium, 30 g carbo., 6 g fiber, 18 g pro.
Exchanges: 2 Starch, 1.5 Very Lean Meat

Double Pepper Topper: In a small bowl combine ¾ cup chopped, drained bottled roasted red sweet peppers; 1 tablespoon adobo sauce from canned chipotle peppers in adobo sauce; 1 tablespoon sherry vinegar; and 1 teaspoon sugar. Try with grilled vegetable-flavor burger and top with shredded yellow summer squash. Makes about ¾ cup topper.

Nutrition Facts per burger with 2 tablespoons Double Pepper Topper: 194 cal., 2 g total fat (0 g sat. fat), 0 mg chol., 503 mg sodium, 30 g carbo., 7 g fiber, 17 g pro.
Exchanges: 2 Starch, 1.5 Very Lean Meat

You Choose Veggie Burgers

START TO FINISH: 20 minutes

NUTRITION FACTS per burger with 2 tablespoons Ultra Ketchup Topper:

CALORIES 220
TOTAL FAT 3 g (0 g sat. fat)
CHOLESTEROL 0 mg
PROTEIN 18 g
CARBOHYDRATE 36 g
FIBER 7 g
SODIUM 798 mg

EXCHANGES 2.5 Starch, 1.5 Very Lean Meat

4   8-inch whole wheat flour tortillas
     Olive oil nonstick cooking spray
1½   cups canned fat-free spicy
     refried beans, warmed
1½   cups shredded leaf lettuce
¾   cup purchased fresh deli salsa
½   cup shredded reduced-fat
     Mexican blend cheese
     (2 ounces)

1 Preheat oven to 425°F. Lightly coat both sides of each tortilla with nonstick cooking spray. Place tortillas on a very large baking sheet. Bake for 10 to 12 minutes or until lightly browned and crisp, turning once. Cool tortillas on a wire rack.

2 Evenly spread warm refried beans on tortillas. Top with lettuce, salsa, and cheese. Makes 4 servings.

Spicy Bean Tostadas

PREP: 15 minutes   **BAKE:** 10 minutes
OVEN: 425°F

NUTRITION FACTS per serving:

CALORIES 255
TOTAL FAT 6 g (3 g sat. fat)
CHOLESTEROL 5 mg
PROTEIN 17 g
CARBOHYDRATE 32 g
FIBER 15 g
SODIUM 1,252 mg

EXCHANGES 2 Starch, 2 Lean Meat

1 14½-ounce can Italian-style stewed tomatoes, undrained

½ cup water

2 medium zucchini and/or yellow summer squash, halved lengthwise and cut into ½-inch-thick slices

1 9-ounce package refrigerated whole wheat four-cheese ravioli

1 15- or 16-ounce can cannellini beans (white kidney beans) or navy beans, rinsed and drained

2 tablespoons snipped fresh basil or parsley

2 tablespoons finely shredded or grated Parmesan cheese

1 In a very large skillet combine undrained tomatoes and water; bring to boiling. Add zucchini and/or yellow summer squash and ravioli. Return to boiling; reduce heat. Cover and boil gently for 6 to 7 minutes or until ravioli is tender, stirring gently once or twice.

2 Stir beans into ravioli mixture; heat through. Sprinkle individual servings with basil and Parmesan cheese. Makes 4 (1⅔-cup) servings.

Ravioli Skillet

START TO FINISH: 20 minutes

NUTRITION FACTS per serving:

CALORIES 305
TOTAL FAT 8 g (4 g sat. fat)
CHOLESTEROL 44 mg
PROTEIN 18 g
CARBOHYDRATE 49 g
FIBER 11 g
SODIUM 986 mg

EXCHANGES 2.5 Starch, 1 Lean Meat, 1.5 Vegetable

Kung Pao Mock Chicken

START TO FINISH: 20 minutes

NUTRITION FACTS per serving:

CALORIES 266
TOTAL FAT 8 g (1 g sat. fat)
CHOLESTEROL 0 mg
PROTEIN 15 g
CARBOHYDRATE 32 g
FIBER 5 g
SODIUM 964 mg

EXCHANGES 1.5 Starch, 1 Very Lean Meat, 2 Vegetable, 1 Fat

1 10-ounce package frozen cooked, breaded meatless chicken-style nuggets
¼ cup light teriyaki sauce
¼ cup pineapple juice
1 tablespoon Szechwan seasoning
2 teaspoons cornstarch
   Nonstick cooking spray
1 16-ounce package frozen green bean stir-fry vegetable blend
½ of a 16-ounce package frozen (yellow, green, and red) peppers and onion stir-fry vegetables (2 cups)
2 tablespoons sliced almonds or coarsely chopped peanuts (toasted if desired)

1 Prepare nuggets according to package directions. Meanwhile, in a small bowl combine teriyaki sauce, pineapple juice, Szechwan seasoning, and cornstarch. Set aside.

2 Coat an unheated large wok or very large nonstick skillet with nonstick cooking spray. Preheat over medium-high heat. Add all stir-fry vegetables; stir-fry for 3 to 4 minutes or just until tender. Push vegetables from center of wok.

3 Stir teriyaki sauce mixture. Add to center of wok with vegetables. Cook and stir sauce until thickened and bubbly; cook and stir for 2 minutes more, stirring to coat vegetables. Divide vegetable mixture among four serving plates. Halve each chicken-style nugget crosswise; place halved nuggets on vegetables. Sprinkle with almonds. Makes 4 servings (3 nuggets and ¾ cup vegetable mixture per serving).

1	12-ounce package frozen cooked and crumbled ground meat substitute (soy protein)
1½	cups low-sodium tomato juice
1	15-ounce can pinto beans, rinsed and drained
1	15-ounce can black beans, rinsed and drained
1	14½-ounce can diced tomatoes and green chile peppers, undrained
2	tablespoons tomato paste
1	tablespoon chili powder
¼	cup light dairy sour cream (optional)
½	cup shredded reduced-fat cheddar cheese (2 ounces) (optional)

1 In a large saucepan combine ground meat substitute, tomato juice, pinto beans, black beans, undrained tomatoes, tomato paste, and chili powder. Bring to boiling; reduce heat. Simmer, uncovered, for 5 minutes. If desired, top individual servings with sour cream and cheddar cheese. Makes 4 (1½-cup) servings.

Copycat Chili

START TO FINISH: 20 minutes

NUTRITION FACTS per serving:
- -

CALORIES 321
TOTAL FAT 2 g (0 g sat. fat)
CHOLESTEROL 0 mg
PROTEIN 32 g
CARBOHYDRATE 54 g
FIBER 19 g
SODIUM 1,468 mg

EXCHANGES 3 Starch, 3 Very Lean Meat, 1 Vegetable

1   9-ounce package refrigerated whole wheat four-cheese ravioli

1   16-ounce package frozen broccoli stir-fry vegetable blend

¾   cup bottled roasted red sweet peppers, drained

⅓   cup bottled light ranch salad dressing

¼   cup packed fresh basil leaves

1 In a 4-quart Dutch oven cook ravioli according to package directions; add stir-fry vegetables for the last 5 minutes of cooking time. Drain ravioli and vegetables; return to Dutch oven.

2 Meanwhile, for sauce, in a blender or food processor combine roasted red peppers, salad dressing, and basil. Cover and blend or process until smooth. Serve with hot pasta mixture. Makes 4 (1-cup) servings.

Hot Tossed Vegetable Ravioli

START TO FINISH: 20 minutes

NUTRITION FACTS per serving:

- -

CALORIES 278
TOTAL FAT 11 g (4 g sat. fat)
CHOLESTEROL 49 mg
PROTEIN 12 g
CARBOHYDRATE 34 g
FIBER 6 g
SODIUM 673 mg

EXCHANGES 1.5 Starch, 0.5 Medium-Fat Meat, 2 Vegetable, 1.5 Fat

Chapter 16

Restaurant Meals

On the divider: Spicy Stir-Fried Chicken with Cashews *(see recipe, page 490)*

2 teaspoons olive oil

1 large sweet onion (such as Vidalia, Maui, or Walla Walla), halved and thinly sliced

1 pound extra-lean ground beef or uncooked ground turkey breast

2 teaspoons snipped fresh thyme or ½ teaspoon dried thyme, crushed

¼ teaspoon salt

¼ teaspoon black pepper

1 cup torn arugula

4 whole wheat hamburger buns, split and toasted

½ cup bottled roasted red sweet peppers, drained and cut into strips

¼ cup crumbled blue cheese (1 ounce)

Blue Cheese-Topped Burgers with Caramelized Onions

PREP: 15 minutes **COOK:** 20 minutes
GRILL: 14 minutes

NUTRITION FACTS per serving:

CALORIES 397
TOTAL FAT 17 g (6 g sat. fat)
CHOLESTEROL 79 mg
PROTEIN 29 g
CARBOHYDRATE 31 g
FIBER 4 g
SODIUM 540 mg

EXCHANGES 2 Starch, 3 Medium-Fat Meat, 0.5 Vegetable

1 In a large skillet heat oil over medium heat. Add onion; cover and cook for 15 minutes, stirring occasionally. Uncover and cook for 5 to 10 minutes more or until onion is very tender and golden brown, stirring frequently.

2 Meanwhile, in a large bowl combine ground beef, thyme, salt, and black pepper; mix well. Form into four ¾-inch-thick patties.

3 For a charcoal grill, place patties on the rack of an uncovered grill directly over medium coals. Grill for 14 to 18 minutes or until done (160°F for beef or 165°F for turkey),* turning once halfway through grilling. (For a gas grill, preheat grill. Reduce heat to medium. Place patties on grill rack over heat. Cover and grill as above.)

4 To serve, place arugula and patties on bun bottoms. Top patties with onion, roasted red peppers, blue cheese, and bun tops. Makes 4 servings.

COOK'S TIP

Can't decide which sweet onion variety to choose? The Maui variety is easy to find because it's available year-round. Vidalia and Walla Walla are widely available in the summer months.

*The internal color of a burger is not a reliable doneness indicator. A beef patty cooked to 160°F or a turkey patty cooked to 165°F is safe, regardless of color. To measure the doneness of a patty, insert an instant-read thermometer through the side of the patty to a depth of 2 to 3 inches.

Nonstick cooking spray

1¼ ounces reduced-fat shredded wheat crackers, broken (½ cup)

1 ounce honey wheat pretzel rods, broken (½ cup)

¼ teaspoon cayenne pepper

2 eggs

¼ cup fat-free milk

1½ pounds chicken breast tenderloins

⅓ cup light mayonnaise or salad dressing

¼ cup crumbled blue cheese (1 ounce)

1 clove garlic, minced

½ cup Buffalo Sauce

Buffalo Chicken Tenders

PREP: 30 minutes **BAKE:** 10 minutes
OVEN: 425°F

NUTRITION FACTS per serving:

CALORIES 265
TOTAL FAT 10 g (2 g sat. fat)
CHOLESTEROL 145 mg
PROTEIN 31 g
CARBOHYDRATE 12 g
FIBER 1 g
SODIUM 444 mg

EXCHANGES 1 Starch, 4 Very Lean Meat, 1 Fat

1 Preheat oven to 425°F. Line a 15×10×1-inch baking pan with foil; coat with nonstick cooking spray. Set pan aside. Place crackers in a food processor; cover and process until coarsely ground. Add pretzels to food processor; cover and process until pretzels are coarsely ground. Transfer cracker mixture to a shallow dish; stir in cayenne pepper. In another shallow dish whisk together eggs and 2 tablespoons milk.

2 Dip chicken tenderloins into egg mixture, allowing excess to drip off. Dip tenderloins into crumb mixture, turning to coat. Arrange tenderloins in prepared pan. Lightly coat breaded tenderloins with nonstick cooking spray. Bake chicken for 10 to 15 minutes or until no longer pink (170°F).

3 Meanwhile, for blue cheese dip, in a small bowl stir together mayonnaise, blue cheese, remaining 2 tablespoons milk, and garlic. Serve chicken tenderloins with blue cheese dip and Buffalo Sauce. Makes 6 servings.

Buffalo Sauce: In a small saucepan stir together one 8-ounce can tomato sauce, ¼ cup cider vinegar, 2 tablespoons water, 2 teaspoons packed brown sugar, 1½ teaspoons bottled hot pepper sauce, ½ teaspoon dry mustard, ¼ teaspoon celery seeds, and ⅛ teaspoon salt. Bring to boiling; reduce heat. Simmer, uncovered, for 8 to 10 minutes or until mixture is reduced to 1 cup, stirring occasionally. Use immediately or cool, cover, and store in the refrigerator for up to 1 week. Makes 1 cup.

2/3   cup crushed cornflakes

1   teaspoon paprika

1/2   teaspoon garlic powder

1/2   teaspoon dried oregano, crushed

1/8   teaspoon cayenne pepper
      (optional)

1   egg white

1   pound skinless, boneless chicken
      breast, cut into 1-inch pieces

1 Preheat oven to 450°F. In a plastic bag combine crushed cornflakes, paprika, garlic powder, oregano, and, if desired, cayenne pepper. In a small bowl beat egg white with a fork.

2 Dip chicken pieces into egg white, allowing excess to drain off. Add chicken pieces, a few at a time, to cornflake mixture; shake to coat well.

3 Place chicken pieces in a single layer in an ungreased shallow baking pan. Bake for 7 to 9 minutes or until chicken is no longer pink. Makes 4 servings.

Chicken Nuggets

PREP: 20 minutes   **BAKE:** 7 minutes
OVEN: 450°F

NUTRITION FACTS per serving:

CALORIES 191
TOTAL FAT 2 g (0 g sat. fat)
CHOLESTEROL 66 mg
PROTEIN 29 g
CARBOHYDRATE 13 g
FIBER 0 g
SODIUM 228 mg

EXCHANGES 1 Starch, 3.5 Very Lean Meat

NUTRITION NOTE

Breading chicken in cornflakes and baking it is a healthier alternative than battering in bread crumbs, which contain fat on their own, and frying it, which is how they are commonly prepared at restaurants.

Classic French Dips

PREP: 20 minutes

COOK: 9 to 10 hours (low) or 4½ to 5 hours (high)

NUTRITION FACTS per serving:

CALORIES 339
TOTAL FAT 7 g (2 g sat. fat)
CHOLESTEROL 45 mg
PROTEIN 33 g
CARBOHYDRATE 39 g
FIBER 9 g
SODIUM 453 mg
EXCHANGES 2.5 Starch, 3.5 Lean Meat

NUTRITION NOTE

When you have a choice between a flat cut and point cut of beef brisket, select the flat cut, which is lower in fat. Always cook brisket using a long, slow method.

1 large sweet onion (such as Vidalia, Maui, or Walla Walla), cut into ½-inch-thick slices and separated into rings (1 cup)

1 2- to 2½-pound fresh beef brisket or boneless beef bottom round roast

2 cloves garlic, minced

1 teaspoon dried thyme, marjoram, or oregano, crushed

½ teaspoon black pepper

1 14-ounce can lower-sodium beef broth

2 tablespoons Worcestershire sauce

1 16-ounce loaf whole grain baguette-style bread, cut crosswise into 6 pieces and halved lengthwise, or 6 whole grain hoagie buns, split, and, if desired, toasted

1 Place onion in a 3½- to 5-quart slow cooker. Trim separable fat from beef. If necessary, cut beef to fit cooker. Place beef on top of onions. Sprinkle with garlic, thyme, and pepper. Pour beef broth and Worcestershire sauce over all.

2 Cover and cook on low-heat setting for 9 to 10 hours for brisket or 8 to 9 hours for bottom round, or on high-heat setting for 4½ to 5 hours for brisket or 4 to 4½ hours for bottom round.

3 Transfer meat to a cutting board; thinly slice across the grain, removing any visible fat as you slice. Using a slotted spoon, remove onions from cooker. Divide sliced brisket and onion slices among bread bottoms. Add bread tops. Skim fat from cooking juices in cooker; pass juices for dipping sandwiches. Makes 6 servings.

1   12-ounce boneless beef top sirloin steak, cut 1-inch thick

½   teaspoon garlic-pepper seasoning
    Nonstick cooking spray

2   medium red and/or green sweet peppers, seeded and cut into thin strips

1   large onion, thinly sliced and separated into rings

4   whole wheat frankfurter buns, split

½   cup shredded reduced-fat cheddar or reduced-fat Monterey Jack cheese (2 ounces)

1 Preheat broiler. Trim fat from steak. Sprinkle steak with garlic-pepper seasoning. Place seasoned steak on the unheated rack of a broiler pan. Broil 3 to 4 inches from heat until desired doneness. Allow 15 to 17 minutes for medium-rare doneness (145°F) or 20 to 22 minutes for medium doneness (160°F).

2 Meanwhile, coat an unheated very large nonstick skillet* with nonstick cooking spray. Preheat skillet over medium heat. Add sweet pepper and onion. Cover and cook for 5 minutes. Uncover and cook about 5 minutes more or just until tender, stirring occasionally.

3 Place split buns on a large baking sheet. Broil 4 to 5 inches from heat for 1 to 2 minutes or until lightly toasted. Remove bun tops from baking sheet; set aside. Slice steak into bite-size strips. Divide steak strips and sweet pepper mixture among bun bottoms. Sprinkle with cheese. Broil 4 to 5 inches from the heat for 1 to 2 minutes or until cheese is melted. Top with bun tops. Makes 4 servings.

*If you do not have a very large nonstick skillet, use a large nonstick skillet and cook sweet pepper and onion separately.

Philly Steak Sandwiches

PREP: 20 minutes

BROIL: 15 minutes (medium rare) or 20 minutes (medium)

NUTRITION FACTS per serving:

CALORIES 320
TOTAL FAT 12 g (5 g sat. fat)
CHOLESTEROL 52 mg
PROTEIN 25 g
CARBOHYDRATE 29 g
FIBER 4 g
SODIUM 414 mg

EXCHANGES 2 Starch, 2.5 Lean Meat, 0.5 Vegetable, 0.5 Fat

Herbed Steak with Portobello Mushroom Sauce

PREP: 25 minutes   **COOK:** 20 minutes
GRILL: 9 minutes (medium rare) or
11 minutes (medium)

NUTRITION FACTS per serving:
- -

CALORIES 270
TOTAL FAT 8 g (2 g sat. fat)
CHOLESTEROL 60 mg
PROTEIN 33 g
CARBOHYDRATE 10 g
FIBER 1 g
SODIUM 343 mg

EXCHANGES 4 Lean Meat, 1 Vegetable

4	5-ounce boneless beef top sirloin steaks, cut ¾-inch thick
1	teaspoon herbes de Provence
½	teaspoon cracked black pepper
¼	teaspoon salt
2	teaspoons olive oil
6	ounces portobello mushroom caps or other assorted mushrooms, tough stems removed and thinly sliced (about 2½ cups)
⅓	cup finely chopped shallot or onion
2	cloves garlic, minced
¼	cup port or dry red wine or beef broth
½	cup beef broth
1½	teaspoons cornstarch
2	tablespoons balsamic vinegar
1	recipe Roasted Garlic Mashed Potatoes (see page 367) (optional)
	Snipped fresh thyme (optional)

1 Trim fat from steaks. Sprinkle ½ teaspoon herbes de Provence, cracked pepper, and salt evenly on steaks; rub in with your fingers. For a charcoal grill, place steaks on the rack of an uncovered grill directly over medium coals. Grill until desired doneness, turning once halfway through grilling. Allow 9 to 11 minutes for medium-rare doneness (145°F) or 11 to 14 minutes for medium doneness (160°F). (For a gas grill, preheat grill. Reduce heat to medium. Place steaks on grill rack over heat. Cover and grill as above.)

2 Meanwhile, for sauce, in a large nonstick skillet heat oil over medium heat. Add mushrooms, shallot, and garlic; cook about 5 minutes or until mushrooms are tender, stirring frequently. Remove skillet from heat. Add port and remaining ½ teaspoon herbes de Provence to skillet. Return to heat; cook, uncovered, for 1 to 2 minutes or until most of the liquid has evaporated.

3 In a small bowl stir together beef broth and cornstarch. Add to skillet; cook and stir until thickened and bubbly. Cook and stir for 2 minutes more. Stir in balsamic vinegar. Serve sauce over steaks. If desired, serve with Roasted Garlic Mashed Potatoes. If desired, sprinkle with thyme. Makes 4 servings.

Broiler Directions: Preheat broiler. Place seasoned steaks on the unheated rack of a broiler pan. Broil 3 to 4 inches from the heat until desired doneness. Allow 11 to 13 minutes for medium-rare doneness (145°F) or 14 to 16 minutes for medium doneness (160°F).

2 large Yukon gold potatoes or
   russet potatoes
   (about 1 pound total)

Olive oil nonstick cooking spray

¼ teaspoon salt

⅛ teaspoon black pepper

1 tablespoon olive oil

2 cups broccoli florets

1½ cups sliced fresh mushrooms

2 cloves garlic, minced

1¼ cups fat-free milk

2 tablespoons all-purpose flour

1 teaspoon snipped fresh thyme or
   oregano or ½ teaspoon dried
   thyme or oregano, crushed

⅛ teaspoon black pepper

6 ounces cooked ham, chopped
   (about 1 cup)

¼ cup shredded Swiss cheese
   (1 ounce)

Broccoli- and Ham-Smothered Potatoes

START TO FINISH: 50 minutes **OVEN:** 400°F

NUTRITION FACTS per serving:

CALORIES 280
TOTAL FAT 10 g (3 g sat. fat)
CHOLESTEROL 32 mg
PROTEIN 17 g
CARBOHYDRATE 33 g
FIBER 5 g
SODIUM 771 mg

EXCHANGES 2 Starch, 1.5 Very Lean Meat, 1 Vegetable, 0.5 Fat

1 Preheat oven to 400°F. Scrub potatoes; quarter lengthwise and arrange in a 9×9×2-inch baking pan. Lightly coat potatoes with nonstick cooking spray; sprinkle with salt and ⅛ teaspoon pepper. Roast for 35 to 45 minutes or until potatoes are tender and lightly browned.

2 Meanwhile, in a large skillet heat oil over medium heat. Add broccoli, mushrooms, and garlic; cook for 4 to 5 minutes or until vegetables are crisp-tender. In a medium bowl whisk together milk, flour, thyme, and ⅛ teaspoon pepper; add all at once to broccoli mixture. Cook and stir until thickened and bubbly; cook and stir for 1 minute more. Add ham; heat through.

3 Arrange roasted potatoes on a serving platter. Top with ham mixture; sprinkle with cheese. Makes 4 servings.

Pecan-Crusted Fish with Peppers and Squash

PREP: 30 minutes   **BAKE:** 20 minutes
OVEN: 425°F

NUTRITION FACTS per serving:

CALORIES 471
TOTAL FAT 20 g (4 g sat. fat)
CHOLESTEROL 106 mg
PROTEIN 26 g
CARBOHYDRATE 7 g
FIBER 6 g
SODIUM 485 mg

EXCHANGES 3 Starch, 2 Lean Meat, 1 Vegetable, 2 Fat

NUTRITION NOTE

Catfish is a low-fat fish with mild flavor that's loaded with B vitamins and protein. Serve this recipe to help meet the minimum recommendation of two servings of fish a week.

1   pound fresh or frozen skinless catfish, white fish, or cod fillets, about ½ inch thick

2   small red and/or orange sweet peppers, seeded and cut into 1-inch-wide strips

2   medium zucchini and/or yellow summer squash, halved lengthwise and cut into ½-inch-thick diagonal slices

2   teaspoons cooking oil

½   teaspoon seasoned salt

½   cup yellow cornmeal

⅓   cup finely chopped pecans

½   teaspoon salt

¼   cup all-purpose flour

¼   teaspoon cayenne pepper

1   egg

1   tablespoon water
    Nonstick cooking spray

2   cups hot cooked brown rice

1 Preheat oven to 425°F. Thaw fish, if frozen. Rinse fish; pat dry with paper towels. Cut fish into 3- to 4-inch pieces; set aside. Line a 15x10x1-inch baking pan with foil. Lightly grease the foil; set aside.

2 In a large bowl combine sweet pepper and zucchini. Add oil and seasoned salt; toss to coat. Arrange vegetable mixture in prepared pan. Bake, uncovered, for 10 minutes.

3 Meanwhile, in a shallow dish stir together cornmeal, pecans, and salt. In another shallow dish stir together flour and cayenne pepper. In a third shallow dish whisk together egg and water. Dip one piece of fish in flour mixture to coat lightly, shaking off any excess. Dip fish in egg mixture, then in cornmeal mixture to coat. Repeat with remaining fish pieces. Lightly coat each fish piece with cooking spray.

4 Push vegetables to one side of the pan; place fish in a single layer in the baking pan next to the partially baked vegetables. Bake, uncovered, for 10 to 15 minutes or until fish flakes easily when tested with a fork and vegetables are crisp-tender. Serve with hot cooked brown rice. Makes 4 servings.

1   recipe Pizza Dough
½   cup purchased pizza sauce
½   of a 6-ounce package thinly sliced cooked turkey pepperoni or pizza-style Canadian-style bacon
1½   cups thinly sliced fresh mushrooms
½   of a small green sweet pepper, sliced into strips
¼   cup chopped onion
1   cup shredded reduced-fat 4-cheese Italian blend cheese or part-skim mozzarella cheese (4 ounces)
2   tablespoons snipped fresh flat-leaf parsley

1 Prepare Pizza Dough. Preheat oven to 425°F. Grease a 12-inch round pizza pan; set aside. Punch down dough; let rest for 10 minutes. On a lightly floured surface, roll dough to a 12-inch circle. Transfer to prepared pizza pan, building up edges slightly. Prick dough all over with a fork.

2 Bake crust about 10 minutes or until lightly browned. Spread pizza sauce on partially baked crust. Top with pepperoni or Canadian-style bacon, mushrooms, sweet pepper, and onion. Sprinkle with cheese.

3 Bake for 10 to 15 minutes more or until cheese is melted and edge of crust is browned. Sprinkle with parsley. Makes 8 servings.

Pizza Dough: In a small bowl combine 1 package active dry yeast and ⅔ cup warm water (105°F to 115°F). Let stand for 5 minutes. Stir in 1 tablespoon honey and 1 tablespoon olive oil.

In a large bowl combine ¾ cup white whole wheat flour, ¼ cup cornmeal, and ¼ teaspoon salt. Stir in yeast mixture. Stir in as much of ¾ to 1 cup all-purpose flour as you can with a wooden spoon.

Turn out dough onto a lightly floured surface. Knead in enough of the remaining all-purpose flour to make a moderately stiff dough that is smooth and elastic (6 to 8 minutes total). Shape dough into a ball. Cover and let rise in a warm place until nearly double in size (30 to 45 minutes). Makes enough for 1 pizza.

Whole Wheat Pizza with the Works

PREP: 20 minutes   **RISE:** 30 minutes
BAKE: 20 minutes   **OVEN:** 425°F

NUTRITION FACTS per serving:

CALORIES 215
TOTAL FAT 6 g (2 g sat. fat)
CHOLESTEROL 21 mg
PROTEIN 11 g
CARBOHYDRATE 29 g
FIBER 2 g
SODIUM 467 mg

EXCHANGES 1.5 Starch, 1 Medium-Fat Meat, 0.5 Vegetable

Buffalo Chicken Pizza

PREP: 45 minutes   **RISE:** 30 minutes
BAKE: 20 minutes   **OVEN:** 425°F

NUTRITION FACTS per serving:

CALORIES 431
TOTAL FAT 12 g (5 g sat. fat)
CHOLESTEROL 66 mg
PROTEIN 30 g
CARBOHYDRATE 51 g
FIBER 4 g
SODIUM 656 mg

EXCHANGES 3.5 Starch, 3 Lean Meat

1 recipe Pizza Dough (see page 471)
½ cup Buffalo Sauce (see page 464)
1½ cups chopped cooked chicken breast (about 8 ounces)
½ cup thinly sliced red onion
¼ cup thinly sliced celery
¾ cup shredded reduced-fat mozzarella cheese (3 ounces)
¼ cup crumbled blue cheese (1 ounce)
2 tablespoons snipped fresh parsley

1 Prepare Pizza Dough. Preheat oven to 425°F. Punch down dough; let rest for 10 minutes. On a lightly floured surface, roll dough to a 12-inch circle. Transfer to a greased 12-inch round pizza pan, building up edge slightly. Using a fork, prick dough all over.

2 Bake crust about 10 minutes or until lightly browned. Spread Buffalo Sauce over partially baked crust. Top with chicken, red onion, and celery. Sprinkle with mozzarella cheese and blue cheese.

3 Bake for 10 to 15 minutes more or until cheese is melted and edge of crust is browned. Sprinkle with parsley. Makes 4 servings.

- 1 recipe Pizza Dough (see page 471)
- 1 tablespoon olive oil
- 1 tablespoon snipped fresh oregano or 1 teaspoon dried oregano, crushed
- 2 medium plum tomatoes, thinly sliced
- ¾ cup bottled roasted red sweet peppers, drained and coarsely chopped
- ¼ cup pitted kalamata olives, chopped, or sliced pitted ripe olives
- ¼ cup crumbled, reduced-fat feta cheese (1 ounce)
- ¼ cup finely shredded Parmesan cheese (1 ounce)

Snipped fresh oregano (optional)

Cracked black pepper (optional)

1 Prepare Pizza Dough. Preheat oven to 425°F. Grease a large baking sheet; set aside. Punch down dough; let rest for 10 minutes. On a lightly floured surface, roll dough to a 14-inch oblong shape. Transfer to prepared baking sheet. Prick dough all over with a fork. Bake for 8 to 10 minutes or until lightly browned.

2 Brush partially baked crust with oil and sprinkle with snipped or dried oregano or 1 teaspoon dried oregano. Top with tomato, roasted red pepper, olives, feta cheese, and Parmesan cheese. Bake for 5 to 10 minutes more or until cheese is melted.

3 To serve, if desired, sprinkle with additional snipped fresh oregano and cracked black pepper. Makes 6 to 8 servings.

Greek-Style Pizza

PREP: 30 minutes   **RISE:** 30 minutes
BAKE: 13 minutes   **OVEN:** 425°F

NUTRITION FACTS per serving:

CALORIES 236
TOTAL FAT 8 g (2 g sat. fat)
CHOLESTEROL 5 mg
PROTEIN 8 g
CARBOHYDRATE 36 g
FIBER 3 g
SODIUM 322 mg

EXCHANGES 2 Starch, 0.5 Vegetable, 1.5 Fat

Taco Pizza

PREP: 30 minutes   **RISE:** 30 minutes
BAKE: 16 minutes   **OVEN:** 425°F

NUTRITION FACTS per serving:

CALORIES 284
TOTAL FAT 10 g (4 g sat. fat)
CHOLESTEROL 38 mg
PROTEIN 17 g
CARBOHYDRATE 33 g
FIBER 3 g
SODIUM 261 mg

EXCHANGES 2 Starch, 1.5 Medium-Fat Meat, 0.5 Vegetable

1   recipe Pizza Dough (see page 471)
1   cup shredded reduced-fat cheddar cheese (4 ounces)
12   ounces extra-lean ground beef
1   medium onion, chopped
⅔   cup Easy Fresh Salsa (see page 483) or purchased salsa
1½   cups chopped tomato
½   to 1 cup shredded lettuce and/or spinach
1   cup packaged baked tortilla chips, coarsely crushed
     Light dairy sour cream (optional)
     Easy Fresh Salsa (see page 483) or purchased salsa (optional)

1 Prepare Pizza Dough. Preheat oven to 425°F. Grease a 12-inch round pizza pan; set aside. Punch down dough; let rest for 10 minutes. On a lightly floured surface, roll dough to a 13-inch circle. Transfer to prepared pizza pan, allowing excess dough to extend over edge of pan. Sprinkle half of the cheese in a thin strip around the edge of the dough. Moisten edge of dough. Fold edge over cheese and seal tightly to enclose the cheese. Using a fork, prick crust inside the cheese edge all over. Bake about 10 minutes or until lightly browned.

2 Meanwhile, in a large skillet cook beef and onion until beef is brown and onion is tender. Drain off fat. Stir the ⅔ cup Easy Fresh Salsa into the beef mixture. Spoon beef mixture on crust. Bake for 5 minutes more. Sprinkle with tomatoes and remaining cheese. Bake for 1 to 2 minutes more or until cheese melts.

3 To serve, cut pizza into eight wedges. Top with lettuce and tortilla chips. If desired, serve with sour cream and additional Easy Fresh Salsa. Makes 8 servings.

- 1 pound fresh or frozen peeled, deveined large shrimp with tails
- ⅛ teaspoon salt
- ⅛ teaspoon black pepper
- 3 cups fresh spinach or arugula
- 1 tablespoon olive oil
- 6 red and/or yellow plum tomatoes, seeded and coarsely chopped (3 cups)
- 3 cloves garlic, minced
- 2 tablespoons white balsamic vinegar or regular balsamic vinegar
- 1 tablespoon snipped fresh basil
- ¼ cup thinly sliced green onion
- 1 ounce Parmesan cheese, shaved

Crusty whole wheat bread slices (optional)

1 Thaw shrimp, if frozen. Rinse shrimp; pat dry with paper towels. Season shrimp with salt and pepper. Chop 1 cup of the spinach; set spinach aside.

2 In a large skillet heat oil over medium-high heat. Add shrimp; cook for 2 to 3 minutes or until opaque, stirring occasionally. Remove shrimp from skillet; keep warm.

3 Add tomato and garlic to hot skillet; cook and stir for 2 minutes. Remove from heat. Stir in 1 cup chopped spinach, balsamic vinegar, and basil.

4 Divide remaining spinach and shrimp among four serving plates. Serve with tomato mixture, green onion, and Parmesan cheese. If desired, serve with bread. Makes 4 servings.

COOK'S TIP

Plum tomatoes are ideal for sauces and drying because of their thick flesh, few seeds, and low acidity. So while other tomato varieties will work, when making sauce, as in this recipe, it's best to use plum tomatoes.

Bruschetta-Style Shrimp

START TO FINISH: 25 minutes

NUTRITION FACTS per serving:

CALORIES 223
TOTAL FAT 8 g (2 g sat. fat)
CHOLESTEROL 177 mg
PROTEIN 28 g
CARBOHYDRATE 10 g
FIBER 2 g
SODIUM 382 mg

EXCHANGES 0.5 Other Carbohydrates, 3.5 Very Lean Meat, 1 Vegetable, 1 Fat

Chicken Parmesan

PREP: 20 minutes   **MARINATE:** 2 to 8 hours
BAKE: 20 minutes   **OVEN:** 400°F

NUTRITION FACTS per serving:

CALORIES 422
TOTAL FAT 8 g (4 g sat. fat)
CHOLESTEROL 76 mg
PROTEIN 39 g
CARBOHYDRATE 48 g
FIBER 9 g
SODIUM 742 mg

EXCHANGES 3 Starch, 4 Very Lean Meat,
0.5 Vegetable, 0.5 Fat

COOK'S TIP

Always wash fruits and vegetables even
when you plan to peel them. Prevent the
possibility of peel contamination getting on
your hands, cutting board, or knife.

4   skinless, boneless chicken breast
     halves (1 to 1¼ pounds total)

¾   cup buttermilk

1   cup soft whole wheat bread
     crumbs

½   cup grated Parmesan cheese

2   teaspoons dried Italian seasoning,
     crushed

     Olive oil nonstick cooking spray

4   ounces dried multigrain or whole
     grain spaghetti

1   medium zucchini, halved
     lengthwise and thinly sliced, or
     2 cups (1-inch pieces)
     peeled eggplant

2   cups purchased tomato-basil
     pasta sauce

     Grated Parmesan cheese
     (optional)

1 In a large resealable plastic bag combine chicken
and buttermilk. Seal bag; turn to coat chicken.
Marinate in the refrigerator for 2 to 8 hours,
turning bag occasionally.

2 Preheat oven to 400°F. Place crumbs in a
15×10×1-inch baking pan. Bake for 5 to
7 minutes or until dry and golden brown, stirring
once halfway through baking. Cool completely
on a wire rack. Transfer crumbs to a shallow
dish. Stir in ½ cup Parmesan cheese and Italian
seasoning. Line the 15×10×1-inch baking pan
with foil; coat foil with nonstick cooking spray.

3 Drain chicken, discarding excess buttermilk.
Dip chicken pieces, 1 at a time, in crumb
mixture, turning to coat evenly. Place in foil-lined
pan. Coat tops of chicken pieces with nonstick
cooking spray. Bake for 20 to 25 minutes or until
chicken is no longer pink (170°F).

4 Meanwhile, cook spaghetti according
to package directions; drain and keep
warm. Coat an unheated medium saucepan
with nonstick cooking spray. Preheat over
medium heat. Add zucchini; cook for 3 to
4 minutes or until tender (5 to 6 minutes for
eggplant), stirring occasionally. Add pasta
sauce; heat through.

5 Divide spaghetti among four serving plates.
Top with chicken and zucchini mixture.
If desired, sprinkle with additional Parmesan
cheese. Makes 4 servings.

1	tablespoon olive oil
6	small bone-in chicken breast halves, skinned (about 2½ pounds total)
8	ounces fresh mushrooms, sliced (about 3 cups)
1	medium onion, sliced
1	clove garlic, minced
1	14½-ounce can diced tomatoes, undrained
1	6-ounce can tomato paste
½	cup dry white wine or reduced-sodium chicken broth
1	teaspoon dried Italian seasoning, crushed
½	teaspoon salt
⅛	teaspoon black pepper
6	ounces dried multigrain or whole grain fettuccine or linguine, cooked according to package directions
2	tablespoons small fresh basil leaves

1 In a very large skillet heat oil over medium heat. Add chicken; brown chicken on all sides, turning to brown evenly. Remove chicken, reserving drippings in skillet. Set chicken aside.

2 Add mushrooms, onion, and garlic to drippings in skillet. Cook and stir about 5 minutes or just until vegetables are tender. Return chicken to skillet.

3 In a medium bowl combine undrained tomatoes, tomato paste, dry white wine, Italian seasoning, salt, and pepper. Pour over chicken in skillet. Bring to boiling; reduce heat. Cover and simmer for 30 to 35 minutes or until chicken is no longer pink (170°F), turning once during cooking. Serve over hot cooked pasta. Sprinkle with basil. Makes 6 servings.

Chicken Cacciatore

PREP: 30 minutes

COOK: 30 minutes

NUTRITION FACTS per serving:

CALORIES 311
TOTAL FAT 4 g (1 g sat. fat)
CHOLESTEROL 68 mg
PROTEIN 34 g
CARBOHYDRATE 33 g
FIBER 6 g
SODIUM 427 mg

EXCHANGES 2 Starch, 4 Very Lean Meat, 0.5 Vegetable

Chicken and Vegetable Fettuccine

START TO FINISH: 30 minutes

NUTRITION FACTS per serving:

CALORIES 286
TOTAL FAT 7 g (2 g sat. fat)
CHOLESTEROL 40 mg
PROTEIN 25 g
CARBOHYDRATE 35 g
FIBER 2 g
SODIUM 380 mg

EXCHANGES 2 Starch, 2.5 Very Lean Meat, 1 Vegetable, 0.5 Fat

8 ounces dried whole wheat or spinach fettuccine
2 cups zucchini and/or yellow summer squash, halved lengthwise and sliced
2 cups broccoli florets
¼ cup snipped dried tomatoes (not oil pack)
2 cups fresh baby spinach
3 tablespoons snipped fresh basil
¼ teaspoon salt
¼ teaspoon freshly cracked black pepper
¾ cup finely shredded Parmesan, Romano, or Asiago cheese (3 ounces)
¼ cup fat-free milk
1 tablespoon olive oil
12 ounces chicken breast tenderloins
2 cloves garlic, minced
Shredded Parmesan, Romano, or Asiago cheese (optional)

1 In a Dutch oven cook pasta according to package directions, except do not use salt; add zucchini and/or yellow squash, broccoli, and dried tomatoes for the last 3 minutes of cooking; drain. Return pasta mixture to hot Dutch oven. Add spinach, basil, salt, and pepper to pasta; toss gently. Add ¾ cup Parmesan cheese and milk; toss to coat.

2 Meanwhile, in a large skillet heat oil over medium heat. Add chicken and garlic; cook for 3 to 5 minutes or until chicken is no longer pink, stirring occasionally. Add cooked chicken to pasta mixture; toss gently. Divide among six serving plates. If desired, garnish with additional Parmesan cheese. Makes 6 servings.

COOK'S TIP

Look for zucchini and yellow summer squash with skins that are free of soft spots, nicks, and shriveling. Smaller, less mature squash have fewer seeds and a more delicate flavor than the large ones, which can become woody and bitter.

- 8 ounces uncooked bulk turkey sausage or extra-lean ground beef
- ¾ cup chopped onion
- 4 cloves garlic, minced
- 1 15-ounce can tomato sauce
- 1 cup bottled roasted red sweet peppers, drained and chopped
- 2 tablespoons snipped fresh basil or 2 teaspoons dried basil, crushed
- 1 tablespoon snipped fresh oregano or 1 teaspoon dried oregano, crushed
- ¼ teaspoon black pepper
- 6 dried whole grain lasagna noodles
- 1 15-ounce carton light ricotta cheese
- 1 10-ounce package frozen chopped spinach, thawed and well drained
- 1 egg white, lightly beaten
  Nonstick cooking spray
- 1 cup shredded reduced-fat mozzarella cheese (4 ounces)

Sausage and Spinach Lasagna

PREP: 45 minutes   **BAKE:** 30 minutes
STAND: 15 minutes **OVEN:** 375°F

NUTRITION FACTS per serving:

CALORIES 237
TOTAL FAT 7 g (3 g sat. fat)
CHOLESTEROL 42 mg
PROTEIN 18 g
CARBOHYDRATE 25 g
FIBER 5 g
SODIUM 613 mg

EXCHANGES 1.5 Starch, 2 Lean Meat, 1 Vegetable

1 Preheat oven to 375°F. For meat sauce, in a large skillet combine sausage, onion, and garlic; cook over medium heat until meat is brown and vegetables are tender, stirring to break up sausage. Drain off fat, if necessary.

2 Stir tomato sauce, roasted red peppers, dried basil (if using), dried oregano (if using), and black pepper into meat mixture in skillet. Bring to boiling; reduce heat. Cover and simmer for 10 minutes, stirring occasionally. Stir in fresh basil and fresh oregano, if using.

3 Meanwhile, cook lasagna noodles according to package directions, except omit the cooking oil and salt. Drain well. For ricotta mixture, in a medium bowl stir together ricotta cheese, spinach, and egg white.

4 Lightly coat a 2-quart rectangular baking dish with nonstick cooking spray. Place two cooked lasagna noodles in the prepared baking dish. Spread with one-third of the ricotta mixture. Top with one-third of the meat sauce and one-third of the mozzarella cheese. Repeat layers twice, except do not add the last layer of mozzarella cheese.

5 Bake, covered, for 25 to 30 minutes or until bubbly. Uncover and sprinkle with remaining mozzarella cheese. Bake about 5 minutes more or until cheese is melted. Let stand for 15 minutes before serving. Makes 8 servings.

8　dried manicotti shells
　　Nonstick cooking spray
1　cup chopped fresh mushrooms
¾　cup shredded carrot
3　or 4 cloves garlic, minced
1　cup light ricotta cheese or low-fat cream-style cottage cheese
¾　cup shredded reduced-fat mozzarella cheese (3 ounces)
2　eggs, lightly beaten
¼　cup grated Parmesan cheese
2　teaspoons dried Italian seasoning, crushed
1　14½-ounce can diced tomatoes with basil, garlic, and oregano, undrained
1　cup bottled roasted red sweet peppers, drained and chopped

Cheese Manicotti with Roasted Pepper Sauce

PREP: 30 minutes **BAKE:** 25 minutes
STAND: 10 minutes **OVEN:** 350°F

NUTRITION FACTS per serving:

CALORIES 378
TOTAL FAT 13 g (7 g sat. fat)
CHOLESTEROL 141 mg
PROTEIN 22 g
CARBOHYDRATE 43 g
FIBER 3 g
SODIUM 860 mg

EXCHANGES 2.5 Starch, 2 Lean Meat, 1 Vegetable, 1 Fat

1 Preheat oven to 350°F. Cook manicotti shells according to package directions; drain. Rinse with cold water and drain again. Set aside.

2 Meanwhile, for filling, coat an unheated large nonstick skillet with nonstick cooking spray. Preheat over medium heat. Add mushrooms, carrot, and garlic to hot skillet. Cook for 3 to 5 minutes or just until vegetables are tender, stirring occasionally. Remove from heat; cool slightly. Stir in ricotta cheese, ½ cup mozzarella cheese, eggs, Parmesan cheese, and Italian seasoning. Spoon filling into cooked manicotti shells.

3 For sauce, place undrained tomatoes in a blender or food processor. Cover and blend or process until smooth. Stir in roasted red peppers. Spread about ⅓ cup of the sauce into the bottom of four 12- to 16-ounce ungreased individual baking dishes or a 2-quart rectangular baking dish. Arrange stuffed manicotti shells in the individual baking dishes or on the large baking dish, overlapping shells slightly if necessary. Pour remaining sauce over manicotti.

4 Bake, covered, for 20 to 25 minutes for individual baking dishes, 35 to 40 minutes for large baking dish, or until heated through. Uncover and sprinkle with remaining ¼ cup mozzarella cheese. Bake for 5 minutes more. Let stand for 10 minutes before serving. Makes 4 servings.

COOK'S TIP

Mushrooms can be stored in the refrigerator up to one week. Keep them in the original packaging until ready to use. Once the package is opened, store mushrooms in a porous paper bag or other loosely closed bag: Mushrooms stored in airtight containers spoil quickly.

- 8 ounces dried multigrain or whole grain penne or mostaccioli
- 3 cups assorted fresh vegetables (such as red sweet pepper strips, trimmed sugar snap peas, 2-inch-long pieces trimmed asparagus, and/or quartered-lengthwise packaged peeled baby carrots)
- 1 cup halved cherry tomatoes
- ½ cup reduced-sodium chicken broth
- 3 tablespoons all-purpose flour
- ½ teaspoon salt
- 1¼ cups low-fat milk
- ¼ cup dry sherry or reduced-sodium chicken broth
- 3 ounces Parmesan or Asiago cheese, finely shredded (¾ cup)
- ½ cup lightly packed fresh basil, coarsely chopped
- 4 teaspoons snipped fresh thyme or oregano
- ⅓ cup sliced green onion (optional)

1 In a 4-quart Dutch oven cook pasta according to package directions; add 3 cups assorted vegetables for the last 2 minutes of cooking. Drain well. Return to hot Dutch oven. Add cherry tomatoes.

2 In a medium saucepan whisk together chicken broth, flour, and salt until smooth. Stir in milk and sherry. Cook and stir until thickened and bubbly; cook and stir for 2 minutes more. Remove from heat; stir in finely shredded Parmesan cheese, basil, and thyme.

3 Add herb sauce to pasta mixture; toss gently to coat. Divide among six serving plates. If desired, sprinkle with green onion. Makes 6 servings.

Fresh-Herb Pasta Primavera

START TO FINISH: 35 minutes

NUTRITION FACTS per serving:

CALORIES 253
TOTAL FAT 5 g (3 g sat. fat)
CHOLESTEROL 12 mg
PROTEIN 13 g
CARBOHYDRATE 41 g
FIBER 6 g
SODIUM 496 mg

EXCHANGES 2.5 Starch, 0.5 Medium-Fat Meat, 0.5 Vegetable

Chipotle Chicken Quesadillas

PREP: 30 minutes
COOK: 2 minutes per batch **OVEN:** 300°F

NUTRITION FACTS per serving:

CALORIES 262
TOTAL FAT 7 g (0 g sat. fat)
CHOLESTEROL 49 mg
PROTEIN 36 g
CARBOHYDRATE 30 g
FIBER 18 g
SODIUM 440 mg

EXCHANGES 2 Starch, 4 Very Lean Meat, 0.5 Vegetable, 0.5 Fat

*Because chile peppers contain oils that can burn your skin and eyes, avoid direct contact with them as much as possible. When working with chile peppers, wear plastic or rubber gloves. If your bare hands do touch the peppers, wash your hands and nails well with soap and warm water.

8   7-inch whole wheat tortillas
    Nonstick cooking spray
12 ounces skinless, boneless chicken breast halves, cut into thin bite-size strips
2   small red and/or green sweet peppers, seeded and chopped
2   cloves garlic, minced
¼   cup thinly sliced green onion
1   canned chipotle chile pepper in adobo sauce, drained and finely chopped*
2   tablespoons lime juice
3   ounces queso fresco, crumbled, or ¾ cup shredded reduced-fat Monterey Jack cheese (3 ounces)
¼   cup light dairy sour cream (optional)
1   teaspoon finely chopped canned chipotle chile pepper in adobo sauce* (optional)
4   cups shredded lettuce
    Purchased salsa and/or lime wedges (optional)

1 Preheat oven to 300°F. Lightly coat one side of each tortilla with nonstick cooking spray. Place tortillas, coated sides down, on a tray or clean work surface. Set aside.

2 Coat an unheated large nonstick skillet with nonstick cooking spray. Preheat skillet over medium-high heat. Add chicken, sweet pepper, and garlic to hot skillet. Cook for 4 to 6 minutes or until chicken is no longer pink, stirring occasionally. Remove from heat; stir in green onion, 1 chipotle pepper, and lime juice.

3 Divide chicken and pepper mixture among tortillas, placing the mixture on one half of each tortilla. Sprinkle chicken mixture with cheese. Fold tortillas over filling; press down lightly.

4 Heat a nonstick skillet or griddle over medium-high heat; reduce heat to medium. Cook quesadillas, 2 or 3 at a time, for 2 to 3 minutes or until tortilla is lightly browned, turning once halfway through cooking. Keep quesadillas warm in the oven while cooking the remaining quesadillas.

5 If desired, in a small bowl stir together sour cream and 1 teaspoon chipotle pepper. Cut each quesadilla into three wedges. Serve with lettuce. If desired, serve with sour cream mixture, salsa, and/or lime wedges. Makes 4 servings.

4   8-inch whole wheat, jalapeño chile
      pepper, basil, and/or tomato
      flour tortillas*
½   of a 16-ounce can fat-free refried
      beans (scant 1 cup)
¼   cup Easy Fresh Salsa
⅛   teaspoon ground cumin
½   cup shredded reduced-fat
      cheddar cheese (2 ounces)
¾   cup shredded lettuce
½   cup Easy Fresh Salsa
      Chopped avocado, light dairy sour
      cream, and/or snipped fresh
      cilantro (optional)
      Chili powder (optional)

1 Preheat oven to 375°F. Cut each tortilla into
      eight wedges; spread wedges on two large
baking sheets. Bake for 8 to 10 minutes or until
tortillas are dry and crisp. Cool on wire racks.

2 Meanwhile, in a medium saucepan
      combine refried beans, ¼ cup salsa, and
cumin. Cook and stir over medium-low heat
until heated through.

3 Spread cooled tortilla wedges into six
      small baking dishes or a 3-quart au gratin
or baking dish. Spoon bean mixture on tortilla
wedges.** Sprinkle with cheese. Bake, uncovered,
about 5 minutes or until cheese melts. Top with
lettuce and ½ cup salsa. If desired, top with
avocado, sour cream, and/or cilantro. If desired,
sprinkle with chili powder.
Makes 6 appetizer servings.

*You may substitute 2 ounces purchased baked
tortilla chips for the tortillas. Prepare as directed
above, starting with step 2.

**For a heartier dish, sprinkle 1 cup chopped
cooked chicken on top of the beans before
adding cheese. Continue as above.

Easy Fresh Salsa: In a medium bowl combine
2 medium tomatoes, seeded and chopped; ¼ cup
finely chopped red onion; ¼ cup chopped yellow
and/or green sweet pepper; 2 to 3 teaspoons
snipped fresh cilantro; 1 clove garlic, minced; and
dash black pepper. Season to taste with bottled
hot pepper sauce and salt. Serve immediately
or cover and chill for up to 3 days. Stir before
serving. Makes about 1⅔ cups.

Salsa, Beans, and More Nachos

START TO FINISH: 35 minutes
OVEN: 375°F

NUTRITION FACTS per serving:

CALORIES 154
TOTAL FAT 4 g (2 g sat. fat)
CHOLESTEROL 7 mg
PROTEIN 10 g
CARBOHYDRATE 18 g
FIBER 9 g
SODIUM 452 mg

EXCHANGES 1 Starch, 1 Lean Meat

Grilled Steak Fajitas

PREP: 25 minutes

GRILL: 20 minutes

NUTRITION FACTS per serving:

CALORIES 333
TOTAL FAT 12 g (3 g sat. fat)
CHOLESTEROL 69 mg
PROTEIN 33 g
CARBOHYDRATE 22 g
FIBER 12 g
SODIUM 454 mg
EXCHANGES 1 Starch, 4 Lean Meat, 1 Vegetable

3   green and/or red sweet peppers, sliced
1   medium onion, sliced
1   tablespoon olive oil
1½ teaspoons fajita seasoning
1   clove garlic, minced
1   pound boneless beef top sirloin steak, cut 1-inch thick
4   8-inch whole wheat tortillas
    Purchased salsa (optional)
    Dairy sour cream (optional)

1 Fold a 36×18-inch piece of heavy-duty foil in half crosswise. Place sweet pepper and onion slices in the center of the foil. Drizzle with oil; sprinkle with ½ teaspoon fajita seasoning and garlic. Bring up the opposite edges of the foil; seal with a double fold. Fold in remaining edges, leaving space for steam to build. Set aside.

2 Sprinkle remaining 1 teaspoon fajita seasoning on both sides of steak; rub in with your fingers. For a charcoal grill, place steak and vegetable packet on the rack of an uncovered grill directly over medium coals. Grill steak until desired doneness, turning once halfway through grilling. Allow 14 to 18 minutes for medium-rare doneness (145°F) or 18 to 22 minutes for medium doneness (160°F). Remove steak and keep warm. Grill vegetables about 20 minutes or until tender. (For a gas grill, preheat grill. Reduce heat to medium. Place steak and vegetable packet on grill rack over heat. Cover and grill as above.)

3 Meanwhile, wrap tortillas in foil. Place tortilla packet next to steak on grill rack; grill about 10 minutes or until tortillas are heated through. Slice meat into thin bite-size strips. Divide meat among tortillas; top with vegetables. Roll up. If desired, serve with salsa and sour cream. Makes 4 servings.

12 ounces boneless beef chuck steak, cut ½ to ¾ inch thick, or 12 ounces skinless, boneless chicken breast halves

Nonstick cooking spray

½ cup water

6 8-inch whole wheat or whole grain flour tortillas

2 teaspoons canola oil

1 medium red or green sweet pepper, seeded and chopped

1 medium onion, chopped

1 10-ounce package frozen chopped spinach, thawed and well drained

1 recipe Enchilada Sauce

½ cup shredded reduced-fat cheddar cheese (2 ounces)

Shredded lettuce, light dairy sour cream, and/or chopped fresh tomato (optional)

1 Trim fat from beef. Lightly coat an unheated large skillet with nonstick cooking spray. Preheat over medium heat. Add beef or chicken and brown on each side. Carefully add water. Bring to boiling; reduce heat. Cover and simmer beef 1 to 1¼ hours or until tender, or chicken 12 to 14 minutes or until no longer pink (170°F) (add additional water to skillet as necessary while cooking beef). Drain well; cool slightly. When cool enough to handle, use two forks to shred beef or chicken, discarding any fat.

2 Preheat oven to 350°F. Lightly coat six individual 12 to 16-ounce au gratin or baking dishes* or a 3-quart rectangular baking dish with nonstick cooking spray; set aside. Wrap tortillas tightly in foil. Heat in oven for 10 minutes. Meanwhile, carefully wipe out the large skillet used to cook the meat. Add oil to the skillet; heat over medium heat. Add sweet pepper and onion; cook about 5 minutes or until vegetables are tender, stirring occasionally. Remove skillet from heat. Stir in shredded beef or chicken, spinach, and 1 cup Enchilada Sauce.

3 Divide meat mixture evenly among warm tortillas; roll up tortillas. Arrange filled tortillas, seam sides down, in prepared individual baking dishes or large baking dish. Top with remaining Enchilada Sauce.

4 Cover and bake about 25 minutes for individual dishes, 25 to 30 minutes for large baking dish, or until heated through. Uncover and sprinkle with cheese. Let stand about 5 minutes or until cheese melts. If desired, serve with shredded lettuce, sour cream, and/or chopped tomato. Makes 6 servings.

*If using individual baking dishes, you may need to halve the filled enchiladas or tuck under the ends to fit the dishes.

Beef and Vegetable Enchiladas

PREP: 40 minutes

COOK: 1 hour (beef); 12 minutes (chicken)

BAKE: 25 minutes   **STAND:** 5 minutes

OVEN: 350°F

NUTRITION FACTS per serving:

CALORIES 323
TOTAL FAT 12 g (4 g sat. fat)
CHOLESTEROL 37 mg
PROTEIN 25 g
CARBOHYDRATE 28 g
FIBER 14 g
SODIUM 740 mg

EXCHANGES 1.5 Starch, 2.5 Lean Meat, 1 Vegetable, 0.5 Fat

Enchilada Sauce: In a blender or food processor combine one 14½-ounce can Mexican-style stewed tomatoes, undrained; ½ of a 6-ounce can tomato paste (⅓ cup); 2 cloves garlic, quartered; and, if desired, a few dashes bottled hot pepper sauce. Cover and blend or process until smooth. Transfer to a medium saucepan. Bring just to boiling; reduce heat. Cover and simmer for 5 minutes. Stir in one 4- to 4½-ounce can diced green chile peppers, undrained. Makes about 2 cups.

Nonstick cooking spray

- 1 cup chopped onion
- 1 clove garlic, minced
- 2 cups chopped cooked chicken (about 10 ounces)
- 1 8-ounce can tomato sauce
- 1 4-ounce can diced green chile peppers, drained
- ½ teaspoon chili powder (optional)
- ¼ teaspoon ground cumin (optional)
- 12 taco shells or twelve 6- to 8-inch corn or whole wheat flour tortillas, warmed*
- 2 cups shredded lettuce
- 1 medium tomato, seeded and chopped
- ½ cup finely shredded reduced-fat cheddar cheese and/or Monterey Jack cheese (2 ounces)

Chicken Tacos

START TO FINISH: 30 minutes

NUTRITION FACTS per serving:

CALORIES 276
TOTAL FAT 12 g (3 g sat. fat)
CHOLESTEROL 48 mg
PROTEIN 19 g
CARBOHYDRATE 23 g
FIBER 3 g
SODIUM 434 mg

EXCHANGES 1.5 Starch, 2 Lean Meat, 0.5 Vegetable, 1 Fat

1 Coat an unheated large skillet with nonstick cooking spray. Preheat skillet over medium heat. Add onion and garlic to hot skillet; cook about 5 minutes or until onion is tender, stirring occasionally.

2 Stir in chicken, tomato sauce, chile peppers, and, if desired, chili powder and ground cumin. Cook and stir until heated through.

3 Divide chicken mixture among taco shells or tortillas. Top with lettuce, tomato, and cheese. Roll up tortillas, if using. Makes 6 servings.

*To warm tortillas, preheat oven to 350°F. Wrap tortillas tightly in foil; bake for 5 to 8 minutes or until warm. (Or wrap tortillas in white microwave-safe paper towels; microwave on 100% power [high] for 20 to 30 seconds or until tortillas are softened.)

4   8-inch whole wheat flour tortillas
     Nonstick cooking spray

12   ounces beef sirloin steak

1   teaspoon fajita seasoning

1   large red or green sweet pepper,
     seeded and cut into thin strips

1   medium onion, cut into
     thin wedges

1   clove garlic, minced

3   cups shredded romaine or
     baby spinach

12   cherry tomatoes, quartered

¼   cup shredded reduced-fat
     cheddar cheese (1 ounce)

¼   cup light dairy sour cream
     (optional)

¼   cup Fresh Guacamole (optional)

1 For tortilla bowls, preheat oven to 350°F. Wrap tortillas in foil. Warm in the oven for 10 minutes. Coat four 10-ounce custard cups with nonstick cooking spray. Carefully press one tortilla into each custard cup. Bake for 10 to 15 minutes or until golden and crisp. Cool; remove from custard cups.

2 Meanwhile, sprinkle beef with fajita seasoning; rub in with your fingers. Cut beef across the grain into thin strips. Coat an unheated very large skillet with nonstick cooking spray. Preheat skillet over medium-high heat. Add beef, sweet pepper, onion, and garlic to hot skillet. Cook about 5 minutes or until beef is desired doneness, stirring occasionally.

3 Place tortilla bowls on four serving plates. Add romaine to bowls. Top with beef-pepper mixture, tomatoes, and cheese. If desired, serve with sour cream and/or Fresh Guacamole. Makes 4 servings.

Fresh Guacamole: Halve, pit, and peel 1 ripe avocado. Place avocado in a medium bowl. Mash lightly with a fork. Stir in ⅓ cup chopped tomato; 1 tablespoon finely chopped onion; 1 tablespoon snipped fresh cilantro; 2 teaspoons lemon juice; 1 small clove garlic, minced; and ⅛ teaspoon salt. Makes about 1 cup. Store any leftovers in an airtight container in the refrigerator for up to 24 hours.

Make-Ahead Tip: Prepare tortilla bowls. Place in large freezer container with paper towels between bowls and crumpled around sides to protect the bowls. Seal, label, and freeze for up to 1 month.

Fajita Taco Bowl Salads

START TO FINISH: 35 minutes   **OVEN:** 350°F

NUTRITION FACTS per serving:
- -

CALORIES 335
TOTAL FAT 12 g (4 g sat. fat)
CHOLESTEROL 47 mg
PROTEIN 24 g
CARBOHYDRATE 35 g
FIBER 5 g
SODIUM 544 mg

EXCHANGES 2 Starch, 2.5 Lean Meat, 1 Vegetable, 0.5 Fat

COOK'S TIP

Sweet or bell peppers change color as they mature from green, yellow, red, purple, and finally brown. Choose peppers by using their color as a flavor guide.

Baked Bean and Corn Chimichangas

PREP: 25 minutes   **BAKE:** 10 minutes
OVEN: 425°F

NUTRITION FACTS per serving:

CALORIES 315
TOTAL FAT 11 g (3 g sat. fat)
CHOLESTEROL 10 mg
PROTEIN 16 g
CARBOHYDRATE 47 g
FIBER 10 g
SODIUM 1147 mg

EXCHANGES 3 Starch, 1 Lean Meat, 1 Fat

Nonstick cooking spray

- 6 10-inch whole wheat flour tortillas
- ½ cup chopped onion
- 1 15-ounce can black beans, rinsed and drained
- 1 8¾-ounce can whole kernel corn, rinsed and drained
- 1 medium tomato, chopped
- 1 cup purchased green salsa or red salsa
- ¼ cup snipped fresh cilantro
- 3 ounces reduced-fat Monterey Jack cheese, shredded (¾ cup)

1 Preheat oven to 425°F. Coat a baking sheet with nonstick cooking spray; set aside. Wrap the tortillas in foil. Heat in the oven for 5 minutes.

2 Meanwhile, for the filling, coat an unheated large skillet with nonstick cooking spray. Preheat skillet over medium heat. Add onion; cook about 5 minutes or until tender, stirring occasionally. Add black beans. Using a fork or potato masher, mash beans slightly. Stir in corn, tomato, and ½ cup salsa. Heat through. Stir in cilantro.

3 To assemble, spoon about ½ cup filling onto each tortilla, just below the center. Fold bottom edge of each tortilla up and over filling. Fold opposite sides in and over filling. Roll up from the bottom. If necessary, secure rolled tortillas with wooden toothpicks. Place filled tortillas on prepared baking sheet, seam sides down. Coat top and sides of the filled tortillas with nonstick cooking spray.

4 Bake for 10 to 12 minutes or until tortillas are golden brown and crisp. To serve, sprinkle chimichangas with cheese and top with remaining ½ cup salsa. Makes 6 servings.

2 tablespoons bottled hoisin sauce

2 teaspoons creamy peanut butter

1 teaspoon water

½ teaspoon cider vinegar

⅛ teaspoon crushed red pepper (optional)

2 cups packaged shredded cabbage with carrot (coleslaw mix)

¼ cup unsalted peanuts, chopped

16 Belgian endive leaves or 4 butterhead lettuce (Boston or Bibb) leaves

Radishes (optional)

Green onion strips (optional)

1 In a medium bowl whisk together hoisin sauce, peanut butter, water, vinegar, and, if desired, crushed red pepper. Add coleslaw mix and peanuts; toss to coat. Spoon mixture into endive leaves or divide mixture among butterhead lettuce leaves; roll up lettuce leaves, if using. If desired, garnish with radishes and green onions. Makes 4 snacks.

COOK'S TIP

For milder flavor, choose whiter endive. Also look for crisp endive heads that are free of brown spots and wilting.

Peanut-Hoisin Snacks

START TO FINISH: 15 minutes

NUTRITION FACTS per serving:

CALORIES 100
TOTAL FAT 6 g (1 g sat. fat)
CHOLESTEROL mg
PROTEIN 4 g
CARBOHYDRATE 9 g
FIBER 2 g
SODIUM 158 mg

EXCHANGES 0.5 High-Fat Meat, 1 Vegetable, 0.5 Fat

Spicy Stir-Fried Chicken with Cashews

START TO FINISH: 30 minutes

NUTRITION FACTS per serving:

CALORIES 349
TOTAL FAT 10 g (2 g sat. fat)
CHOLESTEROL 49 mg
PROTEIN 26 g
CARBOHYDRATE 41 g
FIBER 4 g
SODIUM 443 mg

EXCHANGES 2.5 Starch, 2.5 Very Lean Meat, 1 Vegetable, 1 Fat

COOK'S TIP

Store bok choy in a perforated plastic bag up to five days in the refrigerator. Before shredding it, pull stalks apart and rinse them in cold water several times to remove any grit.

2 tablespoons bottled oyster sauce
1 tablespoon reduced-sodium soy sauce
1 tablespoon packed brown sugar
2 teaspoons cornstarch
⅓ cup water
1 tablespoon canola oil
2 medium red and/or green sweet peppers, seeded and cut into bite-size strips
1 medium onion, sliced
3 cups coarsely shredded bok choy or napa cabbage
2 to 4 fresh red hot chile peppers, seeded and finely chopped*
1 clove garlic, minced
12 ounces skinless, boneless chicken breast halves, cut into bite-size strips
2 cups hot cooked brown rice
¼ cup lightly salted roasted cashews, coarsely chopped

1 For sauce, in a small bowl stir together oyster sauce, soy sauce, brown sugar, and cornstarch. Stir in water. Set aside.

2 In a large wok or very large nonstick skillet heat oil over medium-high heat. Add sweet pepper and onion; stir-fry for 2 minutes. Add bok choy, chile pepper, and garlic; stir-fry for 1 to 2 minutes more or until peppers and onion are crisp-tender. Remove vegetable mixture from wok and set aside.

3 Add chicken to wok. Stir-fry for 3 to 4 minutes or until no longer pink. Push chicken to the side of wok. Stir sauce; add to wok. Cook and stir until thickened and bubbly. Return vegetable mixture to wok. Cook and stir for 1 minute more or until heated through. Serve over rice and sprinkle with cashews. Makes 4 servings.

*Because chile peppers contain volatile oils that can burn your skin and eyes, avoid direct contact with them as much as possible. When working with chile peppers, wear plastic or rubber gloves. If your bare hands do touch the peppers, wash your hands and nails well with soap and warm water.

- ¾ cup reduced-sodium chicken broth
- 3 tablespoons red wine vinegar
- 2 tablespoons reduced-sodium soy sauce
- 4 teaspoons sugar
- 1 tablespoon cornstarch
- 1 clove garlic, minced
- 4 teaspoons canola oil
- 3 medium carrots, thinly sliced
- 1 large red sweet pepper, seeded and cut into bite-size strips
- 2 cups fresh pea pods, tips and stems removed
- 12 ounces skinless, boneless chicken breast halves, cut into 1-inch pieces
- 1 8-ounce can pineapple chunks (juice-packed), drained
- 3 cups hot cooked brown rice

1 For sauce, in a small bowl stir together chicken broth, vinegar, soy sauce, sugar, cornstarch, and garlic; set aside.

2 In a large nonstick skillet heat 3 teaspoons oil over medium-high heat. Add carrot and sweet peppers\; cook for 3 minutes. Add pea pods. Cook and stir about 1 minute more or until vegetables are crisp-tender. Remove from skillet; set aside.

3 Add remaining 1 teaspoon oil to skillet. Add chicken to skillet. Cook and stir for 3 to 4 minutes or until chicken is no longer pink. Push chicken from center of skillet. Stir sauce; add to center of skillet. Cook and stir until thickened and bubbly. Add vegetable mixture and pineapple chunks to skillet; heat through. Serve with hot cooked brown rice. Makes 6 servings.

Sweet-and-Sour Chicken

START TO FINISH: 30 minutes

NUTRITION FACTS per serving:

CALORIES 270
TOTAL FAT 5 g (1 g sat. fat)
CHOLESTEROL 33 mg
PROTEIN 18 g
CARBOHYDRATE 39 g
FIBER 4 g
SODIUM 321 mg

EXCHANGES 2 Starch, 1.5 Very Lean Meat, 1 Vegetable, 0.5 Fat

12 ounces boneless pork loin

10 ounces dried multigrain spaghetti or angel hair pasta or soba (buckwheat noodles)

¼ cup bottled oyster sauce

¼ cup reduced-sodium teriyaki sauce

¼ cup dry sherry, Chinese rice wine, sake, or chicken broth

2 teaspoons canola oil

2 teaspoons toasted sesame oil

1 tablespoon finely chopped fresh ginger

1 medium red onion, halved lengthwise and thinly sliced (1 cup)

8 ounces fresh mushrooms, sliced

2 cups fresh sugar snap peas, halved

Pork Lo Mein

PREP: 35 minutes

FREEZE: 45 minutes

NUTRITION FACTS per serving:

- -

CALORIES 331

TOTAL FAT 7 g (1 g sat. fat)

CHOLESTEROL 31 mg

PROTEIN 24 g

CARBOHYDRATE 41 g

FIBER 5 g

SODIUM 634 mg

EXCHANGES 2.5 Starch, 2 Very Lean Meat, 1 Vegetable, 1 Fat

1 Trim fat from pork. Freeze pork about 45 minutes or until partially frozen. Thinly slice pork across the grain into bite-size strips. Set aside.

2 Cook pasta or noodles according to package directions. Drain well. Rinse with cold water. Drain well. Set aside.

3 For sauce, in a small bowl combine oyster sauce, teriyaki sauce, and dry sherry. Set aside.

4 In a wok or a 12-inch nonstick skillet combine canola oil and sesame oil; heat over medium-high heat. Stir-fry ginger in hot oil for 15 seconds. Add red onion; stir-fry for 2 minutes. Add mushrooms; stir-fry for 2 minutes. Add sugar snap peas; stir-fry for 1 minute more. Remove vegetables from wok. Keep warm.

5 Add pork to wok; stir-fry about 3 minutes or until juices run clear. Add cooked noodles, vegetables, and sauce. Using two spatulas or wooden spoons, lightly toss the mixture for 3 to 4 minutes or until heated through. Transfer to a serving platter. Serve immediately. Makes 6 servings.

COOK'S TIP

To make slicing meat easier, partially freeze it to make it firmer. Slices will be more even.

- ¼ cup very finely chopped green onion
- 1 tablespoon grated fresh ginger
- 6 cloves garlic, minced
- 4 teaspoons olive oil
- ¼ teaspoon salt
- 4 small skinless, boneless chicken breast halves (1 to 1¼ pounds total)
- 4 ounces dried rice noodles
- 2 cups broccoli florets
- 1 cup chopped carrot
- 1 teaspoon finely shredded lime peel
- 2 tablespoons lime juice
- 2 to 3 tablespoons snipped fresh cilantro
- 3 tablespoons coarsely chopped peanuts
  Snipped fresh cilantro (optional)

1 For rub, in a small bowl combine green onion, ginger, garlic, 2 teaspoons oil, and salt. Sprinkle evenly over chicken; rub in with your fingers.

2 For a charcoal grill, place chicken on the rack of an uncovered grill directly over medium coals. Grill for 12 to 15 minutes or until tender and no longer pink (170°F), turning once halfway through grilling. (For a gas grill, preheat grill. Reduce heat to medium. Place chicken on grill rack over heat. Cover and grill as above.) Thinly slice chicken diagonally; set aside.

3 Meanwhile, in a large saucepan cook rice noodles, broccoli, and carrot in a large amount of boiling water for 3 to 4 minutes or just until noodles are tender; drain. Rinse with cold water; drain again. Using kitchen scissors, snip noodles into short lengths. In a medium bowl stir together lime peel, lime juice, and remaining 2 teaspoons oil. Add noodle mixture and 2 to 3 tablespoons cilantro; toss gently to coat.

4 Divide noodle mixture among four serving bowls; add chicken slices. Sprinkle with peanuts and, if desired, additional cilantro. Serve immediately. Makes 4 servings.

Ginger Chicken with Rice Noodles

PREP: 20 minutes
GRILL: 12 minutes

NUTRITION FACTS per serving:

CALORIES 348
TOTAL FAT 10 g (2 g sat. fat)
CHOLESTEROL 66 mg
PROTEIN 31 g
CARBOHYDRATE 34 g
FIBER 3 g
SODIUM 311 mg

EXCHANGES 2 Starch, 3.5 Very Lean Meat, 1 Vegetable, 1 Fat

COOK'S TIP

Check the Asian foods section of a supermarket for rice noodles. If the supermarket doesn't carry them, try a local Asian food market. They're usually packaged in coiled nest shapes and wrapped in cellophane.

3 pounds turkey breast tenderloins

¼ teaspoon black pepper

⅛ teaspoon cayenne pepper

¼ cup reduced-sodium chicken broth

¼ cup soy sauce or reduced-sodium soy sauce

4 teaspoons grated fresh ginger

1 tablespoon lemon juice

1 tablespoon toasted sesame oil

2 cloves garlic, minced

2 tablespoons cornstarch

2 tablespoons cold water

2 tablespoons sliced green onion

1 tablespoon sesame seeds, toasted

Sesame Turkey

PREP: 20 minutes

COOK: 5 to 6 hours (low)

or 2½ to 3 hours (high)

NUTRITION FACTS per serving:

CALORIES 222

TOTAL FAT 3 g (1 g sat. fat)

CHOLESTEROL 112 mg

PROTEIN 42 g

CARBOHYDRATE 3 g

FIBER 0 g

SODIUM 373 mg

EXCHANGES 6 Very Lean Meat

1 Place turkey in a 3½- or 4-quart slow cooker. Sprinkle with black pepper and cayenne pepper. In a small bowl combine chicken broth, soy sauce, ginger, lemon juice, sesame oil, and garlic. Pour over turkey in cooker.

2 Cover and cook on low-heat setting for 5 to 6 hours or on high-heat setting for 2½ to 3 hours.

3 Transfer turkey to a serving platter, reserving cooking liquid. Cover turkey to keep warm.

4 For sauce, strain cooking liquid into a small saucepan. In a small bowl combine cornstarch and cold water. Stir into liquid in saucepan. Cook and stir over medium heat until thickened and bubbly. Cook and stir for 2 minutes more. If desired, slice turkey. Spoon sauce over turkey. Sprinkle with green onion and sesame seeds. Makes 8 servings.

COOK'S TIP

Sesame oil has a strong resistance to rancidity and when stored in a cool, dry place will keep for months.

Chapter 17

Holiday

On the divider: Herb Roast Turkey (see recipe, page 498)

- 1 12- to 14-pound turkey
- 1 tablespoon snipped fresh rosemary or 1 teaspoon dried rosemary, crushed
- 1 tablespoon snipped fresh thyme or 1 teaspoon dried thyme, crushed
- 1 tablespoon snipped fresh sage or 1 teaspoon dried sage, crushed
- ½ teaspoon salt
- ½ teaspoon black pepper
- 1 tablespoon olive oil
- Fresh rosemary sprigs, fresh thyme sprigs, fresh sage leaves, and/or pomegranate pieces (optional)

Traditional Roast Turkey

PREP: 20 minutes   **ROAST:** 3 hours
STAND: 15 minutes   **OVEN:** 425°F/325°F

NUTRITION FACTS per serving:

CALORIES 229
TOTAL FAT 7 g (2 g sat. fat)
CHOLESTEROL 137 mg
PROTEIN 38 g
CARBOHYDRATE 0 g
FIBER 0 g
SODIUM 123 mg

EXCHANGES 5 Very Lean Meat, 1 Fat

1 Preheat oven to 425°F. Remove neck and giblets from turkey. Rinse the inside of the turkey; pat dry with paper towels. In a small bowl stir together snipped or dried rosemary, snipped or dried thyme, snipped or dried sage, salt, and pepper. Season inside of body cavity with half of the herb mixture. Pull neck skin to the back; fasten with a skewer. Tuck ends of the drumsticks under the band of skin across the tail. If there is no band of skin, tie the drumsticks securely to the tail with 100%-cotton kitchen string. Twist wing tips under the back.

2 Place turkey, breast side up, on a rack in a shallow roasting pan. Brush turkey with oil. Sprinkle turkey with remaining herb mixture. Insert an oven-going meat thermometer into the center of an inside thigh muscle. The thermometer should not touch bone. Cover turkey loosely with foil.

3 Roast for 30 minutes. Reduce oven temperature to 325°F. Roast for 2½ to 3 hours more or until the thermometer registers 180°F. About 45 minutes before end of roasting, remove foil and cut band of skin or string between drumsticks so thighs cook evenly. When turkey is done, juices should run clear and drumsticks should move easily in their sockets.

4 Remove turkey from oven. Transfer turkey to a serving platter. Cover; let stand for 15 to 20 minutes before carving. If desired, garnish platter with rosemary sprigs, thyme sprigs, sage leaves, and/or pomegranate pieces. Makes 24 (about 4-ounce) servings.

COOK'S TIP

Garnishing this dish with pomegranate seeds lends brilliant ruby color and a new flavor combination. And yes, the entire seed is edible.

Herb Roast Turkey

PREP: 20 minutes   **ROAST:** 40 minutes
OVEN: 400°F/350°F

NUTRITION FACTS per serving:

CALORIES 170
TOTAL FAT 4 g (1 g sat. fat)
CHOLESTEROL 71 mg
PROTEIN 28 g
CARBOHYDRATE 2 g
FIBER 0 g
SODIUM 309 mg

EXCHANGES 4 Very Lean Meat, 1 Fat

COOK'S TIP

Use a clean instant-read thermometer to check the temperature of cooked meat. Insert the thermometer into the thickest part of the meat and as close to the center as possible. Don't let the thermometer touch the pan or bone; doing so will produce an inaccurate reading.

1	2-pound boneless turkey breast, skinned
½	teaspoon salt
½	teaspoon black pepper
2	teaspoons finely shredded lemon peel
3	tablespoons lemon juice
2	tablespoons olive oil
1	tablespoon snipped fresh flat-leaf parsley
1	tablespoon snipped fresh rosemary
1	tablespoon snipped fresh sage
1	tablespoon snipped fresh thyme
6	cloves garlic, minced
1	cup chicken broth
¼	cup dry white wine or chicken broth
1	recipe Onion and Mushroom Gravy (see page 499) (optional)
1	tablespoon snipped fresh flat-leaf parsley

1 Preheat oven to 400°F. Season turkey breast with salt and pepper. Place turkey in a shallow roasting pan. In a small bowl combine lemon peel, lemon juice, oil, 1 tablespoon parsley, rosemary, sage, thyme, and garlic. Sprinkle herb mixture evenly over turkey breast; rub in with your fingers.

2 Roast turkey for 15 minutes. Pour chicken broth and wine over turkey. Reduce oven temperature to 350°F. Roast turkey about 25 minutes more or until tender and no longer pink (170°F), spooning juices in pan over turkey every 10 minutes.

3 To serve, slice turkey. If desired, serve with Onion and Mushroom Gravy. Or spoon some of the cooking juices from the roasting pan over individual servings. Sprinkle with 1 tablespoon parsley. Makes 8 servings.

Nonstick cooking spray

4 ounces shallots, peeled and coarsely chopped (about 1 cup)

1½ cups sliced fresh mushrooms (such as stemmed shiitake, cremini, and/or button)

1 14-ounce can reduced-sodium chicken broth

¼ cup all-purpose flour

2 teaspoons balsamic vinegar

1 tablespoon snipped fresh oregano or marjoram or ½ teaspoon dried oregano or marjoram, crushed

Dash black pepper

1 Lightly coat an unheated medium nonstick saucepan with nonstick cooking spray. Preheat saucepan over medium heat. Add shallots to hot saucepan; cook and stir about 6 minutes or until shallots are tender and golden brown. Add mushrooms; cook for 4 to 6 minutes more or until tender. Stir together ½ cup chicken broth and flour; add to saucepan. Add remaining broth, balsamic vinegar, and dried herbs (if using). Cook and stir until thickened and bubbly; cook and stir for 1 minute more. Stir in fresh herbs, if using. Season with pepper. Serve with turkey and/or potatoes. Makes about 2¼ cups (10 servings).

Onion and Mushroom Gravy

START TO FINISH: 25 minutes

NUTRITION FACTS per serving:

- -

CALORIES 27
TOTAL FAT 0 g (0 g sat. fat)
CHOLESTEROL 0 mg
PROTEIN 1 g
CARBOHYDRATE 5 g
FIBER 0 g
SODIUM 97 mg

EXCHANGES Free

Turkey and Vegetable Bake

PREP: 35 minutes **BAKE:** 30 minutes
STAND: 15 minutes **OVEN:** 350°F

NUTRITION FACTS per serving:

CALORIES 302
TOTAL FAT 9 g (2 g sat. fat)
CHOLESTEROL 31 mg
PROTEIN 28 g
CARBOHYDRATE 34 g
FIBER 12 g
SODIUM 625 mg

EXCHANGES 2 Starch, 3 Very Lean Meat,
1 Vegetable, 0.5 Fat

2	tablespoons canola oil
2	cups sliced fresh mushrooms
¾	cup coarsely chopped red and/or yellow sweet pepper
½	cup chopped onion
2	cloves garlic, minced
¼	cup all-purpose flour
¾	teaspoon salt
1½	teaspoons snipped fresh thyme or ½ teaspoon dried thyme, crushed
¼	teaspoon black pepper
2	cups fat-free milk
1	10-ounce package frozen chopped spinach, thawed and well drained
2	cups cooked brown or white rice
2	cups chopped cooked turkey or chicken (about 10 ounces)
½	cup finely shredded Parmesan cheese (2 ounces)

1 Preheat oven to 350°F. In a 12-inch skillet heat oil over medium heat. Add mushrooms, sweet pepper, onion, and garlic; cook and stir until tender. Stir in flour, salt, thyme, and black pepper. Add milk all at once; cook and stir until thickened and bubbly. Stir in spinach, cooked rice, chopped cooked turkey, and ¼ cup Parmesan cheese.

2 Spoon mushroom mixture into a 2-quart rectangular baking dish. Sprinkle with remaining ¼ cup Parmesan cheese. Bake, covered, for 20 minutes. Uncover and bake about 10 minutes more or until heated through. Let stand for 15 minutes before serving. Makes 8 servings.

COOK'S TIP

Read labels on rice packages to determine how much dry rice will yield the amount of cooked rice needed. Usually for brown and wild rice, 1 cup dry will yield 3 to 4 cups cooked rice.

- 1 12-ounce package
   fresh cranberries
- 1 cup water
- ½ cup sugar
- 1 4-serving-size package sugar-
   free, low-calorie cranberry- or
   raspberry-flavored gelatin
- 1 15¼-ounce can crushed pineapple
   (juice pack), undrained
- ⅓ cup coarsely chopped pecans,
   toasted

1 In a large saucepan combine cranberries and water. Bring to boiling; reduce heat. Simmer, uncovered, about 3 minutes or until berries pop. Remove from heat.

2 Add sugar and gelatin to cranberries, stirring to dissolve. Stir in undrained pineapple. Transfer to a serving bowl. Cover and chill about 6 hours or until thickened.

3 To serve, sprinkle with pecans. Makes 10 servings.

Make-Ahead Directions: Prepare as above in step 2. Cover and chill for up to 1 week. Serve as above in step 3.

Cranberry-Pecan Salad

PREP: 15 minutes

CHILL: 6 hours

NUTRITION FACTS per serving:

CALORIES 106
TOTAL FAT 3 g (0 g sat. fat)
CHOLESTEROL 0 mg
PROTEIN 1 g
CARBOHYDRATE 20 g
FIBER 2 g
SODIUM 27 mg

EXCHANGES 1 Other Carbohydrates, 0.5 Fruit, 0.5 Fat

Wild Rice Stuffing

PREP: 15 minutes

COOK: 45 minutes

NUTRITION FACTS per serving:

CALORIES 97
TOTAL FAT 1 g (0 g sat. fat)
CHOLESTEROL 0 mg
PROTEIN 5 g
CARBOHYDRATE 19 g
FIBER 2 g
SODIUM 193 mg

EXCHANGES 1 Starch, 0.5 Vegetable

2½   cups reduced-sodium chicken broth

½   cup wild rice, rinsed

½   cup long grain brown rice

¼   teaspoon ground sage or dried thyme, crushed

3   cups sliced fresh mushrooms

1   cup chopped celery

6   green onions, sliced

½   cup slivered almonds, toasted (optional)

1 In a large saucepan combine chicken broth, wild rice, brown rice, and sage or thyme. Bring to boiling; reduce heat. Cover and simmer for 20 minutes.

2 Stir in mushrooms, celery, and green onions. Cover and cook over medium-low heat about 25 minutes or just until wild rice and vegetables are tender, stirring frequently. If desired, garnish with toasted almonds. Serve immediately. Makes 8 servings.

8 cups whole grain bread cubes (about 9 slices)

1 medium fennel bulb with tops

2 tablespoons olive oil

1 cup finely chopped carrots

1 cup chopped onion

2 cloves garlic, minced

1 teaspoon dried Italian seasoning, crushed

¼ teaspoon black pepper

⅛ teaspoon salt

1 to 1½ cups reduced-sodium chicken broth

1 Preheat oven to 300°F. Spread bread cubes in a large shallow roasting pan. Bake for 10 to 15 minutes or until bread cubes are dry, stirring twice. Cool. Increase oven temperature to 325°F.

2 Remove green leafy tops from fennel; snip enough of the tops to measure 1 to 2 tablespoons. Set aside. Cut off and discard upper stalks. Remove any wilted outer layers and cut a thin slice from the fennel base. Cut fennel bulb into wedges, removing the core. Coarsely chop fennel.

3 In a large skillet heat oil over medium heat. Add chopped fennel, carrot, onion, and garlic; cook until tender, stirring occasionally. Stir in snipped fennel tops, Italian seasoning, pepper, and salt. Place fennel mixture in a very large bowl. Stir in bread cubes. Drizzle with enough of the broth to moisten; toss gently to coat. Transfer mixture to a 2-quart casserole. Bake, covered, in 325°F oven for 20 minutes. Uncover; bake about 20 minutes more or until heated through. Makes 12 to 14 servings.

Fennel-Herb Bread Stuffing

PREP: 35 minutes   **BAKE:** 40 minutes
OVEN: 300°F/325°F

NUTRITION FACTS per serving:

CALORIES 98
TOTAL FAT 3 g (0 g sat. fat)
CHOLESTEROL 0 mg
PROTEIN 4 g
CARBOHYDRATE 17 g
FIBER 3 g
SODIUM 217 mg

EXCHANGES 1 Starch, 0.5 Fat

COOK'S TIP

Look for fennel bulbs that are clean and crisp with fresh green leaves and no browning. To store fennel, wrap it tightly in a plastic bag and refrigerate for up to five days.

1½ pounds fresh green beans, trimmed

3 tablespoons all-purpose flour

2 tablespoons canola oil

1 tablespoon dry ranch salad dressing mix

¼ teaspoon white pepper

1½ cups fat-free milk

Nonstick cooking spray

1 cup chopped onion

2 cloves garlic, minced

1½ cups sliced fresh mushrooms

1 cup soft whole wheat or white bread crumbs (1⅓ slices bread)

Fresh Green Bean and Mushroom Casserole

PREP: 30 minutes   **BAKE:** 25 minutes
OVEN: 375°F

NUTRITION FACTS per serving:

CALORIES 110
TOTAL FAT 3 g (0 g sat. fat)
CHOLESTEROL 1 mg
PROTEIN 4 g
CARBOHYDRATE 14 g
FIBER 3 g
SODIUM 130 mg

EXCHANGES 0.5 Starch, 1 Vegetable, 0.5 Fat

1 Preheat oven to 375°F. In a covered large saucepan cook green beans in a small amount of boiling water for 10 to 15 minutes or until crisp-tender; drain and set aside.

2 Meanwhile, for white sauce, in a medium saucepan combine flour, oil, dry dressing mix, and white pepper. Stir in milk. Cook and stir over medium heat until thickened and bubbly; remove from heat.

3 Coat an unheated medium nonstick skillet with nonstick cooking spray. Preheat over medium heat. Add onion and garlic; cook for 2 to 3 minutes or until tender. Remove half of the onion mixture; set aside.

4 Add mushrooms to remaining onion mixture in skillet; cook about 5 minutes or until tender. In a 1½-quart casserole combine mushroom mixture, beans, and white sauce.

5 In a small bowl stir together reserved onion mixture and bread crumbs. Sprinkle bread crumb mixture over bean mixture in casserole. Bake, uncovered, for 25 to 30 minutes or until heated through. Makes 10 servings.

NUTRITION NOTE

Sautéing veggies and other foods adds little or no fat. When sauteed foods will be added to a larger dish, such as casseroles, use nonstick cooking spray and avoid adding any fat at all.

- 3 cups low-calorie cranberry-raspberry drink
- 1 cup water
- 4 bags orange-spice-flavor tea
- ½ cup orange juice
- ¼ cup vodka or water
- 6 cinnamon sticks (optional)

1 In a medium saucepan combine cranberry-raspberry drink and water. Bring just to boiling. Add tea bags. Remove from heat; cover and let stand for 4 minutes. Remove tea bags and discard. Stir in orange juice; heat through. Stir in vodka. Serve warm.* If desired, garnish individual servings with cinnamon sticks. Makes 6 (about 6-ounce) servings.

* You can chill any leftover sipper. To reheat, place ¾ cup sipper in a microwave-safe tea cup. Microwave on 50% power (medium) about 3 minutes or until hot.

Cranberry-Orange Tea Sipper

START TO FINISH: 15 minutes

NUTRITION FACTS per serving:

CALORIES 51
TOTAL FAT 0 g (0 g sat. fat)
CHOLESTEROL 0 mg
PROTEIN 0 g
CARBOHYDRATE 7 g
FIBER 0 g
SODIUM 39 mg

EXCHANGES 0.5 Fruit

No-Bake Pumpkin Cheesecake

PREP: 35 minutes   **BAKE:** 5 minutes
CHILL: 4 to 24 hours   **OVEN:** 350°F

NUTRITION FACTS per serving:

CALORIES 150
TOTAL FAT 8 g (4 g sat. fat)
CHOLESTEROL 11 mg
PROTEIN 5 g
CARBOHYDRATE 14 g
FIBER 1 g
SODIUM 144 mg

EXCHANGES 1 Other Carbohydrates, 1.5 Fat

1 recipe Graham Cracker Crust
1 envelope unflavored gelatin
¼ cup water
1½ 8-ounce tubs light cream cheese
1 15-ounce can pumpkin
2 tablespoons sugar or sugar substitute* equivalent to 2 tablespoons sugar
1 teaspoon ground cinnamon
¾ of an 8-ounce container frozen light whipped dessert topping, thawed
    Chopped pecans (optional)

1 Prepare Graham Cracker Crust; set aside. In a small saucepan stir together gelatin and water; let stand for 5 minutes to soften. Cook and stir over low heat until gelatin dissolves; set aside to cool slightly.

2 In a large bowl beat cream cheese with an electric mixer on medium speed until smooth. Add pumpkin, sugar, cinnamon, and gelatin mixture; beat until well mixed. Fold in dessert topping. Spread mixture into crust in springform pan. Cover and chill for 4 to 24 hours or until set.

3 Using a thin metal spatula or table knife, loosen cheesecake from the side of the springform pan. If desired, use a wide spatula to remove cheesecake from bottom of pan and place on a serving plate. Cut into wedges to serve. If desired, garnish with pecans. Makes 14 servings.

*Sugar Substitutes: Choose from Splenda granular, Equal Spoonful or packets, or Sweet'N Low bulk or packets. Follow package directions to use product amount equivalent to 2 tablespoons sugar for both crust and filling.

Per serving with substitute: same as above, except 136 cal., 11 g carbo.

Graham Cracker Crust: Preheat oven to 350°F. In a small bowl combine ¾ cup finely crushed graham crackers, 3 tablespoons canola oil, and 2 tablespoons sugar or sugar substitute* equivalent to 2 tablespoons sugar. Mix well. Spread evenly in bottom of an 8- or 9-inch springform pan; press firmly onto bottom. Bake for 5 minutes. Cool on a wire rack.

- 5 cups thinly sliced, cored cooking apple
- 1 cup cranberries
- 2 tablespoons granulated sugar
- ½ teaspoon apple pie spice or ground cinnamon
- ½ cup quick-cooking rolled oats
- 3 tablespoons packed brown sugar
- 2 tablespoons all-purpose flour
- ½ teaspoon apple pie spice or ground cinnamon
- 2 tablespoons butter

1 Preheat oven to 375°F. In a 2-quart baking dish combine sliced apple and cranberries. Stir together granulated sugar and ½ teaspoon apple pie spice. Sprinkle over fruit mixture in baking dish; toss to coat.

2 In a small bowl combine oats, brown sugar, flour, and ½ teaspoon apple pie spice. Using a pastry blender, cut in butter until crumbly. Sprinkle oat mixture evenly over apple mixture.

3 Bake for 30 to 35 minutes or until apples are tender. Serve warm. Makes 6 servings.

COOK'S TIP

Choose apples such as Jonathan, Rome Beauty, Granny Smith, and Gala for baking. These types hold up while cooking and retain good apple flavor.

Apple-Cranberry Crisp

PREP: 20 minutes   **BAKE:** 30 minutes
OVEN: 375°F

NUTRITION FACTS per serving:

CALORIES 168
TOTAL FAT 4 g (3 g sat. fat)
CHOLESTEROL 10 mg
PROTEIN 3 g
CARBOHYDRATE 33 g
FIBER 4 g
SODIUM 31 mg

EXCHANGES 1 Other Carbohydrates, 1 Fruit, 1 Fat

Pumpkin-Gingerbread Coffee Cake

PREP: 25 minutes **BAKE:** 50 minutes
COOL: 40 minutes **OVEN:** 350°F

NUTRITION FACTS per serving:

CALORIES 244
TOTAL FAT 6 g (1 g sat. fat)
CHOLESTEROL 40 mg
PROTEIN 6 g
CARBOHYDRATE 44 g
FIBER 2 g
SODIUM 189 mg

EXCHANGES 2 Starch, 1 Other
Carbohydrates, 1 Fat

NUTRITION NOTE

Pumpkin is a good source of vitamin A, which promotes eye health, growth, bone development, and immunity.

2¼	cups all-purpose flour
1¼	cups white whole wheat flour or whole wheat flour
1½	teaspoons baking powder
1½	teaspoons pumpkin pie spice
½	teaspoon ground ginger
½	teaspoon baking soda
½	teaspoon salt
1¼	cups buttermilk or sour fat-free milk*
1	cup canned pumpkin
¾	cup packed brown sugar
⅔	cup mild-flavor molasses
⅓	cup canola oil
3	eggs, lightly beaten
	Powdered sugar

1 Preheat oven to 350°F. Grease and lightly flour a 10-inch fluted tube pan; set aside. In a large bowl combine all-purpose flour, white whole wheat flour, baking powder, pumpkin pie spice, ginger, baking soda, and salt; set aside.

2 In a medium bowl whisk together buttermilk, pumpkin, brown sugar, molasses, oil, and eggs. Add to flour mixture and stir just until moistened (mixture will be thick). Spoon mixture evenly into prepared pan.

3 Bake for 50 to 55 minutes or until top springs back when lightly touched and cake sides pull away from the sides of the pan. Cool in the pan on a wire rack for 10 minutes. Invert cake onto a wire rack. Cool about 30 minutes. Sift powdered sugar over cake before serving. Serve warm. Makes 16 servings.

*To make 1¼ cups sour fat-free milk, place 1 tablespoon lemon juice or vinegar in a glass measuring cup. Add enough fat-free milk to equal 1¼ cups total liquid; stir. Let stand for 5 minutes before using.

1   cup whole bran cereal
¾   cup all-purpose flour
½   cup white whole wheat flour
1   teaspoon baking powder
¼   teaspoon baking soda
¼   teaspoon salt
1   cup fat-free milk
½   cup packed brown sugar
1   egg, lightly beaten
2   tablespoons canola oil
½   teaspoon almond extract
½   cup coarsely chopped
     dried cranberries
½   cup chopped almonds, toasted

1 Preheat oven to 350°F. Grease the bottom and ½ inch up sides of an 8×4×2-inch loaf pan; set aside. In a large bowl stir together whole bran cereal, all-purpose flour, white whole wheat flour, baking powder, baking soda, and salt. Make a well in center of the flour mixture; set aside.

2 In a medium bowl combine milk, brown sugar, egg, oil, and almond extract. Add milk mixture all at once to flour mixture. Stir just until moistened (batter should be lumpy). Fold in dried cranberries and almonds. Spoon batter into prepared pan.

3 Bake for 45 to 50 minutes or until a wooden toothpick inserted near center comes out clean. Cool in pan on a wire rack for 10 minutes. Remove from pan. Cool completely on wire rack. Wrap and store overnight before slicing. Makes 12 servings.

Cranberry-Almond Bread

PREP: 25 minutes   **BAKE:** 45 minutes
COOL: 2 hours   **STAND:** overnight
OVEN: 350°F

NUTRITION FACTS per serving:

CALORIES 165
TOTAL FAT 5 g (0 g sat. fat)
CHOLESTEROL 18 mg
PROTEIN 4 g
CARBOHYDRATE 28 g
FIBER 3 g
SODIUM 137 mg

EXCHANGES 1 Starch, 1 Other Carbohydrates, 0.5 Fat

2 tablespoons coriander seeds, crushed

2 tablespoons finely shredded lemon peel

1 tablespoon olive oil

1 teaspoon cumin seeds, crushed

½ to 1 teaspoon crushed red pepper

¼ teaspoon salt

1 4- to 5-pound beef rib roast

8 cloves garlic, peeled and cut into slivers

1 In a small bowl stir together coriander seeds, lemon peel, oil, cumin seeds, crushed red pepper, and salt; set aside.

2 Cut ½-inch-deep slits randomly into top and sides of roast. Insert garlic slivers deep into slits. Using your fingers, rub lemon mixture into surface of roast. If desired, cover and chill roast for up to 24 hours.

3 Preheat oven to 350°F. Insert an oven-going meat thermometer into center of roast. The thermometer should not touch bone. Place roast, bone side down, in shallow roasting pan. Roast until desired doneness. Allow 1¾ to 2¼ hours for medium-rare doneness (135°F) or 2¼ to 2¾ hours for medium doneness (150°F).

4 Remove roast from oven. Cover with foil; let stand for 15 minutes before carving. The temperature of the meat after standing should be 145°F for medium-rare doneness or 160°F for medium doneness. Makes 12 servings.

Moroccan Rib Roast

PREP: 20 minutes **ROAST:** 1¾ hours
STAND: 15 minutes **OVEN:** 350°F

NUTRITION FACTS per serving:

CALORIES 163
TOTAL FAT 9 g (3 g sat. fat)
CHOLESTEROL 51 mg
PROTEIN 17 g
CARBOHYDRATE 1 g
FIBER 1 g
SODIUM 106 mg

EXCHANGES 2.5 Lean Meat, 0.5 Fat

1 cup fresh cranberries or ½ cup canned whole cranberry sauce

½ cup apple juice or apple cider

¼ cup snipped dried figs

2 tablespoons packed brown sugar or granulated sugar

1 teaspoon snipped fresh rosemary or ¼ teaspoon dried rosemary, crushed

¼ teaspoon salt

⅛ teaspoon black pepper

12 ounces pork tenderloin

¼ teaspoon salt-free herb seasoning

Nonstick cooking spray

Hot cooked brown or long-grain rice (optional)

Fresh rosemary sprigs (optional)

Pork Medallions with Cranberry Chutney

START TO FINISH: 20 minutes

NUTRITION FACTS per serving:

CALORIES 185
TOTAL FAT 3 g (1 g sat. fat)
CHOLESTEROL 55 mg
PROTEIN 18 g
CARBOHYDRATE 22 g
FIBER 3 g
SODIUM 335 mg

EXCHANGES 0.5 Other Carbohydrates, 1 Fruit, 2.5 Very Lean Meat

1 For chutney, in a heavy small saucepan stir together cranberries or cranberry sauce, apple juice, figs, sugar, snipped or dried rosemary, salt, and pepper. Bring to boiling; reduce heat. Simmer, uncovered, for 5 to 8 minutes or until chutney reaches desired consistency, stirring occasionally. Set aside.

2 Meanwhile, trim fat from pork. Cut pork crosswise into 12 pieces, each about 1 inch thick. Press each piece with the palm of your hand to an even thickness. Sprinkle herb seasoning evenly on pork. Coat an unheated large nonstick skillet with nonstick cooking spray. Preheat over medium-high heat. Cook pork in hot skillet for 2 to 3 minutes or until pork is slightly pink in center and juices run clear, turning once halfway through cooking.

3 If desired, serve pork medallions over hot cooked rice. Spoon some warm chutney over pork. If desired, garnish with rosemary sprigs. Pass remaining chutney.
Makes 4 servings.

COOK'S TIP

Cranberries are resilient little fruits. Unlike most berries that should be stored in the refrigerator for only 2 to 3 days, cranberries can be stored for up to 7 days in the refrigerator without diminishing in quality. They also tolerate freezing better than other berries.

Sweet Potatoes with Rosemary

PREP: 20 minutes

COOK: Microwave: 6 minutes

BROIL: 6 minutes

NUTRITION FACTS per serving:
- -
CALORIES 159

TOTAL FAT 3 g (0 g sat. fat)

CHOLESTEROL 0 mg

PROTEIN 2 g

CARBOHYDRATE 29 g

FIBER 4 g

SODIUM 249 mg

EXCHANGES 2 Starch, 0.5 Fat

1½   pounds sweet potatoes, peeled and cut lengthwise into ½-inch-thick wedges

1   cup water

2   tablespoons Dijon-style mustard

1   tablespoon olive oil

1   tablespoon honey

2   teaspoons snipped fresh rosemary or ½ teaspoon dried rosemary, crushed

⅛   teaspoon black pepper

1 Preheat broiler. Place sweet potato wedges and water in a 2-quart microwave-safe baking dish. Cover with plastic wrap; vent plastic wrap to allow steam to escape. Microwave on 100% power (high) for 6 to 8 minutes or until sweet potatoes are nearly tender, rearranging sweet potatoes once halfway through cooking. Drain well.

2 Meanwhile, in a small bowl combine mustard, oil, honey, rosemary, and pepper; set aside.

3 Place sweet potatoes on the greased unheated rack of a broiler pan. Broil 3 to 4 inches from the heat for 4 minutes, using a metal spatula to carefully turn once halfway through broiling. Brush with half of the mustard mixture. Broil for 2 to 3 minutes more or until tender, turning and brushing once with remaining mustard mixture halfway through broiling. Makes 4 servings.

1 12-ounce package fresh
   cranberries (3 cups)
2 medium tangerines or
   small oranges
¼ to ⅓ cup sugar or sugar substitute*
   equivalent to ¼ to ⅓ cup sugar

1 Rinse cranberries under running water and discard any soft or discolored berries; set aside. Slice each unpeeled tangerine in fifths; remove seeds. Place tangerine slices in a food processor; cover and process until coarsely chopped. Transfer to a medium bowl.

2 Add all but ½ cup cranberries to the food processor; cover and process until coarsely chopped. Add chopped cranberries to tangerine slices in bowl; stir in remaining ½ cup cranberries. Stir in enough sugar to sweeten to taste; cover and chill for 1 hour. Stir before serving. Makes 12 (¼-cup) servings.

*Sugar Substitutes: Choose from Splenda granular, Equal Spoonful or packets, or Sweet 'N Low bulk or packets. Follow package directions to use product amount equivalent to ¼ to ⅓ cup sugar.

Per serving with substitute: same as above, except 20 cal., 6 g carbo.

Make-Ahead Directions: Prepare as above. Cover and chill for up to 2 days. Stir before serving.

Tangerine-Cranberry Relish

PREP: 15 minutes

CHILL: 1 hour

NUTRITION FACTS per serving:

CALORIES 37
TOTAL FAT 0 g (0 g sat. fat)
CHOLESTEROL 0 mg
PROTEIN 0 g
CARBOHYDRATE 10 g
FIBER 2 g
SODIUM 1 mg

EXCHANGES 0.5 Other Carbohydrates

Hot Cranberry Toddy

START TO FINISH: 20 minutes

NUTRITION FACTS per serving:

CALORIES 38
TOTAL FAT 0 g (0 g sat. fat)
CHOLESTEROL 0 mg
PROTEIN 0 g
CARBOHYDRATE 6 g
FIBER 0 g
SODIUM 5 mg

EXCHANGES 0.5 Other Carbohydrates

1	48-ounce bottle (6 cups) low-calorie cranberry juice
2	cups water
3	1-inch-long strips lemon peel (set aside)
¼	cup lemon juice
3	inches stick cinnamon
½	teaspoon whole cloves
⅓	cup bourbon, rum, or orange juice
	Fresh lemon slices (optional)
	Stick cinnamon (optional)

1 In a 4-quart saucepan or Dutch oven combine cranberry juice, water, and lemon juice.

2 For spice bag, place lemon peel, stick cinnamon, and cloves in the center of a double-thick 6-inch square of 100%-cotton cheesecloth. Bring the corners together; tie with clean kitchen string. Add to juice mixture.

3 Bring just to boiling; reduce heat. Cover and simmer for 10 minutes. Discard spice bag. Stir bourbon into juice mixture. If desired, garnish individual servings with lemon slices. and additional stick cinnamon. Makes 12 (scant 6-ounce) servings.

COOK'S TIP

Cloves are a strong-flavored spice, so you need only a small amount. To ensure the best flavor, store whole cloves in a cool, dry place in an airtight container for up to one year.

- 1 750-milliliter bottle dry red wine
- 1 cup light orange juice
- ¼ cup brandy or cognac
- ¼ cup orange liqueur
- 2 tablespoons sugar
- 2 medium oranges, sliced
- 2 cups club soda, chilled
   Crushed ice and/or orange peel curls (optional)

1 In a large pitcher combine wine, orange juice, brandy, orange liqueur, and sugar. Add orange slices. Chill for at least 2 hours. Add club soda before serving. If desired, serve over crushed ice and/or with orange peel curls. Makes 12 servings.

Sangria Sparkler

PREP: 10 minutes

CHILL: 2 hours

NUTRITION FACTS per serving:

CALORIES 100
TOTAL FAT 0 g (0 g sat. fat)
CHOLESTEROL 0 mg
PROTEIN 0 g
CARBOHYDRATE 9 g
FIBER 0 g
SODIUM 9 mg

EXCHANGES 0.5 Other Carbohydrates

Lattice-Topped Apple Pie

PREP: 30 minutes   **BAKE:** 40 minutes
OVEN: 375°F

NUTRITION FACTS per serving:

CALORIES 152
TOTAL FAT 5 g (2 g sat. fat)
CHOLESTEROL 12 mg
PROTEIN 2 g
CARBOHYDRATE 26 g
FIBER 3 g
SODIUM 48 mg
EXCHANGES 1 Other Carbohydrates,
1 Fruit, 0.5 Fat

6   cups sliced, cored cooking apple (such as Jonathan or Rome Beauty) (about 2 pounds)
3   tablespoons sugar
1   teaspoon ground cinnamon
1   tablespoon cornstarch
1   recipe Whole Wheat Pastry
    Fat-free milk

1 In a 2-quart rectangular baking dish arrange apple slices; set aside. In a small bowl combine sugar and cinnamon; set aside 1 teaspoon of the mixture. Stir cornstarch into remaining sugar mixture. Sprinkle sugar-cornstarch mixture on apples; toss to combine.

2 Preheat oven to 375°F. On a lightly floured surface, flatten Whole Wheat Pastry dough. Roll dough from center to edges into a 10×5-inch rectangle. Cut pastry lengthwise into ten ½-inch-wide strips. Carefully place five pastry strips crosswise over apples. Fold alternate pastry strips back halfway. Place one of the remaining pastry strips in the center across the strips already in place. Unfold the folded strips; fold back remaining crosswise strips. Place another of the remaining pastry strips across the first set of strips parallel to the strip in the center. Repeat the weaving steps with remaining pastry strip. Trim pastry strips; tuck ends into dish. Brush pastry with milk; sprinkle with reserved sugar mixture.

3 Bake for 40 to 45 minutes or until apples are tender. Serve warm or cool. Makes 8 servings.

Whole Wheat Pastry: In a medium bowl stir together ½ cup all-purpose flour, ¼ cup whole wheat pastry flour or whole wheat flour, 2 tablespoons toasted wheat germ, and ⅛ teaspoon ground nutmeg. Using a pastry blender, cut in 3 tablespoons butter until mixture resembles coarse crumbs. Sprinkle 1 tablespoon cold water over part of the mixture; toss with a fork. Push moistened dough to side of bowl. Repeat, using 1 tablespoon cold water at a time, until moistened (2 to 3 tablespoons cold water total). Form dough into a ball.

- 1 recipe Oil Pastry
- 1 12.3-ounce package light firm silken-style tofu (fresh bean curd)
- 1 15-ounce can pumpkin
- ⅔ cup sugar or sugar substitute blend* equivalent to ⅔ cup sugar
- 1 teaspoon ground cinnamon
- ¼ teaspoon salt
- ¼ teaspoon ground ginger
- ⅛ teaspoon ground cloves
- Light frozen whipped dessert topping, thawed (optional)
- Ground cinnamon (optional)
- Chopped crystallized ginger (optional)

Light-Style Pumpkin Pie

PREP: 25 minutes **BAKE:** 55 minutes
OVEN: 375°F

NUTRITION FACTS per serving:

CALORIES 190
TOTAL FAT 6 g (1 g sat. fat)
CHOLESTEROL 0 mg
PROTEIN 3 g
CARBOHYDRATE 31 g
FIBER 2 g
SODIUM 151 mg

EXCHANGES 1 Starch, 1 Other Carbohydrates, 1 Fat

1 Preheat oven to 375°F. Prepare Oil Pastry. On a well-floured surface, use your hands to slightly flatten pastry dough. Roll dough from center to edge into a circle about 12 inches in diameter. To transfer pastry, wrap it around the rolling pin. Unroll pastry into a 9-inch pie plate. Ease pastry into pie plate, being careful not to stretch pastry. Trim pastry to ½ inch beyond edge of pie plate. Fold under extra pastry. Flute or crimp edge as desired. Do not prick.

2 Place tofu in a blender. Cover and blend until very smooth, stopping to scrape down side of container as necessary. Add pumpkin, sugar, 1 teaspoon cinnamon, salt, ginger, and cloves. Cover and blend until well mixed. Pour pumpkin mixture into pastry-lined pie plate, spreading to an even layer.

3 To prevent overbrowning, cover edge of the pie with foil. Bake for 25 minutes. Remove foil. Bake for 30 minutes more. Cool on a wire rack. Cover and refrigerate within 2 hours.

4 To serve, if desired, top with whipped topping, additional ground cinnamon, and crystallized ginger. Makes 10 servings.

*Sugar Substitute: Choose Equal Sugar Lite. Follow package directions to use product amount equivalent to ⅔ cup sugar.

Per serving with substitute: same as above, except 164 cal., 24 carbo.
Exchanges: 0.5 Other Carbohydrates.

Oil Pastry: In a medium bowl stir together 1⅓ cups all-purpose flour and ¼ teaspoon salt. Add ¼ cup cooking oil and ¼ cup fat-free milk all at once to flour mixture. Stir lightly with a fork until combined (dough will appear crumbly). Use your hands to gently work dough into a ball.

1⅓ cups all-purpose flour
½ teaspoon ground ginger
½ teaspoon apple pie spice
¼ teaspoon ground cloves
¼ teaspoon ground cardamom
⅛ teaspoon cayenne pepper
⅓ cup butter, softened
⅓ cup mild-flavor molasses
¼ cup packed dark brown sugar

1 In a medium bowl stir together flour, ginger, apple pie spice, cloves, cardamom, and cayenne pepper; set aside.

2 In a large bowl beat butter with an electric mixer on medium speed for 30 seconds. Add molasses and brown sugar. Beat until combined, scraping side of bowl occasionally. Beat in flour mixture just until combined. Divide dough in half. Cover and chill dough about 1 hour or until easy to handle.

3 Preheat oven to 375°F. On a lightly floured surface, roll dough, half at a time, to ⅛-inch thickness. Using a floured 2-inch scalloped round or round cookie cutter, cut out dough. Place cutouts 1 inch apart on an ungreased cookie sheet.

4 Bake for 5 to 6 minutes or until edges are lightly browned. Transfer cookies to a wire rack; cool. Makes about 60 cookies.

To store: Layer cookies between waxed paper in an airtight container. Cover; seal. Store at room temperature for up to 3 days or freeze for up to 3 months.

Gossamer Spice Cookies

PREP: 40 minutes   **CHILL:** 1 hour
BAKE: 5 minutes per batch **OVEN:** 375°F

NUTRITION FACTS per cookie:

CALORIES 28
TOTAL FAT 1 g (1 g sat. fat)
CHOLESTEROL 3 mg
PROTEIN 0 g
CARBOHYDRATE 4 g
FIBER 0 g
SODIUM 8 mg

EXCHANGES 0.5 Other Carbohydrates

- ¼ cup butter, softened
- ½ cup sugar or sugar substitute blend* equivalent to ½ cup sugar
- 1 teaspoon baking powder
- ¼ teaspoon salt
- ¼ cup canola oil
- 1 egg
- 1 teaspoon vanilla
- 2½ cups sifted cake flour

Coarse sugar, unsweetened cocoa powder, colored sugar, and/or small decorative candies (optional)

1 In a large bowl beat butter with an electric mixer on medium to high speed for 30 seconds. Add sugar, baking powder, and salt; beat until combined, scraping side of bowl occasionally. Add oil, egg, and vanilla; beat until combined. Beat in as much of the flour as you can with the mixer. Using a wooden spoon, stir in any remaining flour. Divide dough in half. Cover and chill for 1 to 2 hours or until easy to handle.

2 Preheat oven to 375°F. On a lightly floured surface, roll dough, half at a time, to ⅛-inch thickness. Using a 2½-inch cookie cutter, cut into desired shapes.** Place cutouts 1 inch apart on ungreased cookie sheets. Reroll scraps as necessary. If desired, decorate cookies with coarse sugar, unsweetened cocoa powder, colored sugar, and/or small decorative candies.

3 Bake for 6 to 8 minutes or until edges are firm and just starting to brown. Transfer to a wire rack; cool. Makes about 48 cookies.

***Sugar Substitutes:** Choose from Splenda Sugar Blend for Baking or Equal Sugar Lite. Follow package directions to use product amount equivalent to ½ cup sugar.

Per cookie with substitute: same as above, except 50 cal., 7 g carbo.

****To make holes in cookies for hanging, use a drinking straw to pierce cutouts before baking.

Sugar Cookie Cutouts

PREP: 30 minutes   **CHILL:** 1 to 2 hours
BAKE: 6 minutes per batch   **OVEN:** 375°F

NUTRITION FACTS per cookie:

CALORIES 54
TOTAL FAT 2 g (1 g sat. fat)
CHOLESTEROL 7 mg
PROTEIN 1 g
CARBOHYDRATE 8 g
FIBER 0 g
SODIUM 26 mg

EXCHANGES 0.5 Other Carbohydrates, 0.5 Fat

1 6- to 7-pound cooked ham, rump half
3 tablespoons spicy brown mustard
2 tablespoons packed brown sugar
½ cup peach nectar or apricot nectar

1 Preheat oven to 325°F. Score ham in a diamond pattern by making shallow diagonal cuts at 1-inch intervals. Place ham on a rack in a shallow roasting pan. Insert an oven-going meat thermometer into center of ham. The thermometer should not touch bone. Roast for 1½ to 2 hours or until thermometer registers 140°F.

2 Meanwhile, for glaze, in a small bowl combine mustard and brown sugar. Whisk in nectar until smooth. Occasionally brush ham with glaze during the last 20 minutes of baking. Makes 24 servings.

COOK'S TIP

Scoring meat serves several purposes. It decorates, tenderizes, aids flavor absorption of glazes and rubs, and allows fat to drain while roasting.

Peach-Mustard Glazed Ham

PREP: 15 minutes   **ROAST:** 1½ hours
OVEN: 325°F

NUTRITION FACTS per serving:

CALORIES 160
TOTAL FAT 7 g (2 g sat. fat)
CHOLESTEROL 81 mg
PROTEIN 20 g
CARBOHYDRATE 3 g
FIBER 0 g
SODIUM 1,403 mg

EXCHANGES 3 Lean Meat

1½ pounds fresh asparagus spears, trimmed

2 tablespoons snipped assorted fresh herbs or 2 teaspoons assorted dried herbs, crushed (optional)

¼ teaspoon salt

⅛ teaspoon black pepper

2 tablespoons olive oil

1 ounce Parmesan cheese, shaved

1 Preheat oven to 450°F. Arrange asparagus in a shallow roasting pan. Sprinkle with herbs (if desired), salt, and pepper. Drizzle with oil. Toss to coat.

2 Roast, uncovered, for 10 to 12 minutes or just until asparagus is tender, stirring once halfway through roasting.

3 Transfer asparagus to a serving platter. Top with Parmesan cheese. Makes 4 to 6 servings.

Roasted Fingerling Potatoes or New Potatoes:
Prepare as above, except substitute 1½ pounds fingerling potatoes or new potatoes for the asparagus. Cut fingerling potatoes in half lengthwise and new potatoes in half. Arrange in shallow roasting pan and toss with herbs (if desired), salt, pepper, and oil as in step 1. Roast as in step 2, except increase roasting time to 25 to 30 minutes and stir potatoes twice during roasting. Serve as above.

Nutrition Facts per serving: 221 cal., 9 g total fat (2 g sat. fat), 6 mg chol., 5 g pro., 30 g carbo., 4 fiber, 264 mg sodium. Exchanges: 2 Starch, 1.5 Fat

Roasted Carrots: Prepare as above, except substitute 1 pound carrots, peeled and cut into 1-inch pieces, for the asparagus. Arrange carrot pieces in shallow roasting pan and toss with herbs (if desired), salt, pepper, and oil as in step 1. Roast as in step 2, except increase roasting time to 35 to 40 minutes and stir carrots twice during roasting. Serve as above.

Nutrition Facts per serving: 137 cal., 9 g total fat (2 g sat. fat), 6 mg chol., 4 g pro., 11 g carbo., 3 fiber, 332 mg sodium.
Exchanges: 2 Vegetable, 2 Fat

Roasted Green Beans: Prepare as above, except substitute 1 pound fresh green beans, trimmed, for the asparagus. In a medium saucepan cook green beans in a small amount of boiling water for 2 minutes. Drain well and arrange in shallow roasting pan. Toss with herbs (if desired), salt, pepper, and oil as in step 1. Roast as in step 2, except decrease roasting time to 8 to 10 minutes. Serve as above.

Nutrition Facts per serving: 126 cal., 9 g total fat (2 g sat. fat), 6 mg chol., 5 g pro., 8 g carbo., 4 fiber, 261 mg sodium. Exchanges: 2 Vegetable, 2 Fat

Roasted Asparagus

PREP: 10 minutes   **ROAST:** 10 minutes
OVEN: 450°F

NUTRITION FACTS per serving:

CALORIES 113
TOTAL FAT 9 g (2 g sat. fat)
CHOLESTEROL 6 mg
PROTEIN 5 g
CARBOHYDRATE 4 g
FIBER 2 g
SODIUM 256 mg

EXCHANGES 1 Vegetable, 2 Fat

Olive Deviled Eggs

PREP: 40 minutes   **CHILL:** 1 hour
STAND: 15 minutes

NUTRITION FACTS per serving:

CALORIES 49
TOTAL FAT 4 g (1 g sat. fat)
CHOLESTEROL 107 mg
PROTEIN 3 g
CARBOHYDRATE 1 g
FIBER 0 g
SODIUM 83 mg

EXCHANGES 0.5 Very Lean Meat, 0.5 Fat

12   eggs
¼   cup chopped pimiento-stuffed
       green olives
¼   cup light mayonnaise or
       salad dressing
1   tablespoon Dijon-style mustard
⅛   to ¼ teaspoon black pepper
       Snipped fresh chives and/or
       cracked black pepper (optional)

1 Place eggs in a single layer in a Dutch oven (do not stack eggs). Add enough cold water to cover the eggs by 1 inch. Bring to a rapid boil over high heat (water will have large rapidly breaking bubbles). Remove from heat. Cover and let stand for 15 minutes; drain. Run cold water over the eggs or place them in ice water until cool enough to handle; drain.

2 Peel eggs; cut eggs in half lengthwise. Remove egg yolks. Place egg yolks in a medium bowl. Place egg white halves on a serving platter.

3 Use a fork to mash egg yolks. Stir in olives, mayonnaise, mustard, and ⅛ teaspoon black pepper.

4 Fill egg white halves with yolk mixture. Cover and chill for 1 hour before serving. If desired, garnish with chives and/or cracked black pepper. Makes 24 servings

Make-Ahead Directions: Prepare as above, except cover and chill for up to 24 hours before serving.

COOK'S TIP

Placing hard-cooked eggs in ice water makes them easier to handle and prevents eggs from getting an ugly green ring around the yolk.

⅓ cup bottled reduced-calorie raspberry vinaigrette salad dressing

1 teaspoon finely shredded orange peel

1 tablespoon orange juice

8 cups packaged fresh baby spinach or torn mixed salad greens

3 cups sliced fresh strawberries and/or whole blueberries

¼ cup coarsely chopped pecans, toasted

1 For dressing, in a small bowl stir together salad dressing, orange peel, and orange juice; set aside.

2 Divide spinach and berries among eight salad plates. Drizzle with dressing and sprinkle with pecans. Makes 8 servings.

Spinach-Berry Salad

START TO FINISH: 15 minutes

NUTRITION FACTS per serving:
- -

CALORIES 72
TOTAL FAT 4 g (0 g sat. fat)
CHOLESTEROL 0 mg
PROTEIN 2 g
CARBOHYDRATE 10 g
FIBER 2 g
SODIUM 34 mg

EXCHANGES 0.5 Fruit, 0.5 Vegetable, 1 Fat

1 pound spring greens mix (mesclun)
    (about 16 cups)
1 medium cucumber, cut into thin
    bite-size strips
4 plum tomatoes, cut into wedges
¾ cup pitted kalamata olives, halved
¼ cup snipped fresh chives
1 recipe Herbed Balsamic
    Vinaigrette

1 In a very large bowl toss together greens,
cucumber, plum tomatoes, olives, and chives.
Drizzle Herbed Balsamic Vinaigrette over; toss
gently to coat. Makes 14 servings.

Herbed Balsamic Vinaigrette: In a food
processor or blender combine ⅓ cup balsamic
vinegar, ⅓ cup olive oil, 2 tablespoons fresh
oregano leaves, and 2 cloves garlic, quartered.
Cover and process or blend until well mixed.
Season to taste with black pepper. Makes
about ⅔ cup.

COOK'S TIP
Spring greens are a mixture of sweet, spicy,
and bitter flavors that brings a variety of
textures to salads. Look for these greens
bagged in the fresh produce section.

Mixed Greens with Herbed Balsamic Vinaigrette

START TO FINISH: 25 minutes

NUTRITION FACTS per serving:

CALORIES 76
TOTAL FAT 6 g (1 g sat. fat)
CHOLESTEROL 0 mg
PROTEIN 1 g
CARBOHYDRATE 5 g
FIBER 1 g
SODIUM 86 mg

EXCHANGES 1 Vegetable, 1 Fat

- 1½ cups berry-flavored carbonated water (sweetened with aspartame), chilled
- 2 cups crushed ice
- 1 cup frozen unsweetened whole strawberries
- ½ cup chopped, peeled mango
- 2 tablespoons lime juice
- ½ cup vodka (optional)

1 In a blender combine carbonated water, crushed ice, strawberries, mango, and lime juice. Cover and blend until slushy. If desired, stir in vodka. Pour into chilled glasses. Serve immediately. Makes 6 to 8 (about 6-ounce) servings.

COOK'S TIP

Mangoes are in season May through September. When looking for a fresh ripe mango, choose one that is yellow with red blushing and that gives slightly to pressure.

Berry-Mango Slush

START TO FINISH: 10 minutes

NUTRITION FACTS per serving:
- -

CALORIES 20
TOTAL FAT 0 g (0 g sat. fat)
CHOLESTEROL 0 mg
PROTEIN 0 g
CARBOHYDRATE 5 g
FIBER 1 g
SODIUM 3 mg

EXCHANGES Free

2 cups orange juice, chilled
1 cup unsweetened
   pineapple juice, chilled
½ cup rum or unsweetened
   pineapple juice
1 1-liter bottle diet ginger ale, chilled
   Ice cubes*
1 orange, halved and thinly sliced

1 In a large pitcher combine orange juice, pineapple juice, and rum. Slowly pour ginger ale into juice mixture. Serve over ice in chilled glasses. Garnish with orange slices. Makes 12 (about 6-ounce) servings.

*Dress up the punch with citrus ice cubes. To make these decorative cubes, fill the compartments of an ice cube tray with lime, lemon, and/or orange slices (halve or quarter slices to fit). Fill with water. Freeze until firm.

Ginger-Pineapple Punch

START TO FINISH: 10 minutes

NUTRITION FACTS per serving:

CALORIES 56
TOTAL FAT 0 g (0 g sat. fat)
CHOLESTEROL 0 mg
PROTEIN 0 g
CARBOHYDRATE 8 g
FIBER 0 g
SODIUM 29 mg

EXCHANGES 0.5 Other Carbohydrates, 0.5 Fat

1 750-milliliter bottle sweet white wine (such as Pinot Grigio)

¾ cup white grape juice or apple juice

1 1-liter bottle desired flavor low-calorie sparkling water, chilled

   Assorted fresh fruits (such as raspberries, sliced kiwifruit, blueberries, lemon slices, lime slices, halved strawberries, and/or red grapes) (optional)

1 In a large punch bowl combine wine and grape juice. Just before serving, slowly pour in sparkling water. If desired, garnish individual servings with fruit. Makes 10 (6-ounce) servings.

White Wine Spritzer

START TO FINISH: 10 minutes

NUTRITION FACTS per serving:

CALORIES 80
TOTAL FAT 0 g (0 g sat. fat)
CHOLESTEROL 0 mg
PROTEIN 0 g
CARBOHYDRATE 6 g
FIBER 0 g
SODIUM 14 mg

EXCHANGES 0.5 Other Carbohydrates

12 reduced-fat vanilla wafers

1½ 8-ounce packages reduced-fat cream cheese (Neufchâtel), softened

3 ounces white chocolate baking squares (with cocoa butter), melted and cooled

½ cup sugar

¼ cup fat-free milk

1½ teaspoons vanilla

1 egg white, lightly beaten

Chocolate curls, small whole or sliced strawberries, and/or sliced kiwifruit (optional)

White Chocolate Mini Cheesecakes

PREP: 20 minutes   **BAKE:** 20 minutes

COOL: 1 hour 10 minutes   **CHILL:** 3 to 24 hours

OVEN: 350°F

NUTRITION FACTS per serving:

CALORIES 169

TOTAL FAT 10 g (6 g sat. fat)

CHOLESTEROL 25 mg

PROTEIN 4 g

CARBOHYDRATE 17 g

FIBER 0 g

SODIUM 140 mg

EXCHANGES 1 Other Carbohydrates, 1 Medium-Fat Meat, 1 Fat

1 Preheat oven to 350°F. Line twelve 2½-inch muffin cups with foil or paper baking cups. Place one wafer in the bottom of each muffin cup. Set aside.

2 For filling, in a medium bowl beat cream cheese with an electric mixer on medium speed for 30 seconds. Beat in melted white chocolate, sugar, milk, and vanilla until well mixed. Stir in egg white. Spoon filling into prepared muffin cups, filling each about three-quarters full.

3 Bake about 20 minutes or until set. Cool in muffin cups on a wire rack for 10 minutes. (Centers may dip slightly as they cool.) Remove cheesecakes from pans. Cool on a wire rack for 1 hour. Cover and chill for 3 to 24 hours.

4 If desired, garnish with chocolate curls, strawberries, and/or kiwifruit before serving. Makes 12 mini cheesecakes.

How Recipes Are Analyzed

The Better Homes and Gardens® Test Kitchen uses nutrition analysis software to determine the nutritional value of a single serving of a recipe. Here are some factors to keep in mind regarding each analysis:

- Analyses do not include optional ingredients.

- The first serving size listed is analyzed when a range is given. For example, if a recipe makes 4 to 6 servings, the Nutrition Facts are based on 4 servings.

- When ingredient choices (such as butter or margarine) appear in a recipe, the first one mentioned is used for analysis.

- When milk is a recipe ingredient, the analysis has been calculated using fat-free (skim) milk unless otherwise noted.

- The exchanges, listed for every recipe along with the Nutrition Facts, are based on the exchange list developed by the American Dietetic Association and the American Diabetes Association.

Nutrition Notes

Cook's Tips

METRIC INFORMATION

The charts on this page provide a guide for converting measurements from the U.S. customary system, which is used throughout this book, to the metric system.

Product Differences

Most of the ingredients called for in the recipes in this book are available in most countries. However, some are known by different names. Here are some common American ingredients and their possible counterparts:

- Sugar (white) is granulated, fine granulated, or castor sugar.
- Powdered sugar is icing sugar.
- All-purpose flour is enriched, bleached or unbleached white household flour. When self-rising flour is used in place of all-purpose flour in a recipe that calls for leavening, omit the leavening agent (baking soda or baking powder) and salt.
- Light-colored corn syrup is golden syrup.
- Cornstarch is cornflour.
- Baking soda is bicarbonate of soda.
- Vanilla or vanilla extract is vanilla essence.
- Green, red, or yellow sweet peppers are capsicums or bell peppers.
- Golden raisins are sultanas.

Volume and Weight

The United States traditionally uses cup measures for liquid and solid ingredients. The chart below shows the approximate imperial and metric equivalents. If you are accustomed to weighing solid ingredients, the following approximate equivalents will be helpful.

- 1 cup butter, castor sugar, or rice = 8 ounces = ½ pound = 250 grams
- 1 cup flour = 4 ounces = ¼ pound = 125 grams
- 1 cup icing sugar = 5 ounces = 150 grams

Canadian and U.S. volume for a cup measure is 8 fluid ounces (237 ml), but the standard metric equivalent is 250 ml.

1 British imperial cup is 10 fluid ounces.

In Australia, 1 tablespoon equals 20 ml, and there are 4 teaspoons in the Australian tablespoon.

Spoon measures are used for smaller amounts of ingredients. Although the size of the tablespoon varies slightly in different countries, for practical purposes and for recipes in this book, a straight substitution is all that's necessary. Measurements made using cups or spoons always should be level unless stated otherwise.

Common Weight Range Replacements

IMPERIAL / U.S.	METRIC
½ ounce	15 g
1 ounce	25 g or 30 g
4 ounces (¼ pound)	115 g or 125 g
8 ounces (½ pound)	225 g or 250 g
16 ounces (1 pound)	450 g or 500 g
1¼ pounds	625 g
1½ pounds	750 g
2 pounds or 2¼ pounds	1,000 g or 1 Kg

Oven Temperature Equivalents

FAHRENHEIT SETTING	CELSIUS SETTING*	GAS SETTING
300°F	150°C	Gas Mark 2 (very low)
325°F	160°C	Gas Mark 3 (low)
350°F	180°C	Gas Mark 4 (moderate)
375°F	190°C	Gas Mark 5 (moderate)
400°F	200°C	Gas Mark 6 (hot)
425°F	220°C	Gas Mark 7 (hot)
450°F	230°C	Gas Mark 8 (very hot)
475°F	240°C	Gas Mark 9 (very hot)
500°F	260°C	Gas Mark 10 (extremely hot)
Broil	Broil	Grill

*Electric and gas ovens may be calibrated using celsius. However, for an electric oven, increase celsius setting 10 to 20 degrees when cooking above 160°C. For convection or forced air ovens (gas or electric) lower the temperature setting 25°F/10°C when cooking at all heat levels.

Baking Pan Sizes

IMPERIAL / U.S.	METRIC
9×1½-inch round cake pan	22- or 23×4-cm (1.5 L)
9×1½-inch pie plate	22- or 23×4-cm (1 L)
8×8×2-inch square cake pan	20×5-cm (2 L)
9×9×2-inch square cake pan	22- or 23×4.5-cm (2.5 L)
11×7×1½-inch baking pan	28×17×4-cm (2 L)
2-quart rectangular baking pan	30×19×4.5-cm (3 L)
13×9×2-inch baking pan	34×22×4.5-cm (3.5 L)
15×10×1-inch jelly roll pan	40×25×2-cm
9×5×3-inch loaf pan	23×13×8-cm (2 L)
2-quart casserole	2 L

U.S. / Standard Metric Equivalents

⅛ teaspoon = 0.5 ml	
¼ teaspoon = 1 ml	
½ teaspoon = 2 ml	
1 teaspoon = 5 ml	
1 tablespoon = 15 ml	
2 tablespoons = 25 ml	
¼ cup = 2 fluid ounces = 50 ml	
⅓ cup = 3 fluid ounces = 75 ml	
½ cup = 4 fluid ounces = 125 ml	
⅔ cup = 5 fluid ounces = 150 ml	
¾ cup = 6 fluid ounces = 175 ml	
1 cup = 8 fluid ounces = 250 ml	
2 cups = 1 pint = 500 ml	
1 quart = 1 litre	